EXPORTER'S FINANCIAL

AND MARKETING HANDBOOK

EXPORTER'S FINANCIAL

AND MARKETING HANDBOOK

Claude M. Jonnard

NOYES DATA CORPORATION

Park Ridge, New Jersey   London, England

1973

Published in the United States of America by
Noyes Data Corporation
Noyes Building, Park Ridge, New Jersey 07656

To my wife

FOREWORD

The United States' international trade sector, exports and imports, constitutes
one of the major parts of the nation's economy. U.S. exports, in particular,
climbed to over $49 billion in 1972, and are reasonably expected to reach $55
billion this year, 1973. However, the country's export trade has been growing at
a rate lower than that of its imports for almost a decade, creating trade deficits
in 1971 and again in 1972. It is also interesting to note that in the past as well
as in the present, the overwhelming percentage (over 75%) of the country's
trade is conducted by the so-called "Fortune 500" companies, there being
relatively minor participation in international trade by small and medium sized
corporations.

The trend towards a continuing trade deficit now shows promise of being
changed, as a result of a continuing round of dollar devaluations, and as a result
of the U.S. Government's efforts to enlarge the scope of the country's commercial relations with the Soviet Union and with the People's Republic of China.
Indeed, the Government's activities on behalf of the international trading community have been strenuous, to say the least, creating a beach head in a number
of new and promising markets, to be later secured by private U.S. business.

This has all given U.S. Exports a new competitiveness, opening up a myriad of
new opportunities for the American exporter, especially for the smaller, en-
trepreneurially geared company, who, thus far, has been concentrating mainly
on the domestic market.

This book is written specifically to provide the smaller, sales-oriented firm with
an overview of the United States' export trade and with a basic understanding
of the ground rules for engaging in a successful and continuing export sales
enterprise. The book itself does not provide answers for all decision-making in
international business; and many of its parts are destined to become obsolete as

concepts of international commerce change before the onslaught of rapid shifts in the technology of physical distribution, communications and management.

The book is designed to serve principally as a guidance tool for sales- and financially-oriented managers who are also prospective international business-men. Reading this book should enable them to address the proper questions to the appropriate specialists, government and otherwise, in order to resolve their own set of problems, and in order to achieve their own particular sales and profit objectives.

Naturally, no book of this nature can be effectively written without frequent reference to, and considerable assistance from, outside specialists, many of whom are without peers in their knowledgeability of all the finer points of international trade. Consequently, it must be fairly stated at this point that this book does not truly reflect a new body of original thought. This was not its purpose. Its purpose was chiefly to assemble the latest data available relative to the practice of international trade and finance, and to present it in a compre-hensive, yet concise and logical fashion to the business executive.

At the same time, it is also only fair to give credit where credit is due. Hence, a special note of thanks is sincerely addressed to the financial institutions, govern-ment agencies, and specific private corporations, whose generosity with their time and materials, their special expertise, data and other references, was all instrumental in making this book possible.

The individual contributions from these sources are too numerous to document here. Many have already been referred to in the body of the book. It is neverthe-less appropriate to list alphabetically the sources upon which this book relied.

American Chamber of Commerce	Foreign Credit Insurance Assn.
Agency for International Development	International Executive Assn.
Amerford Airfreight Services, Inc.	Morgan Guaranty Trust
Banco do Brazil	National Foreign Trade Council, Inc.
Business International, Inc.	New Jersey Bank
C & J Forwarding, Inc.	Overseas Private Investment Corp.
Chase Manhattan Bank	Sea-Land, Inc.
Chemical Bank, New York	United Nations
Export-Import Bank	U.S. Department of Commerce

CONTENTS

INTRODUCTION

This book is offered to business executives and to students of international trade as both a comprehensive text and a basic methods manual in the fundamentals of exporting and of selling overseas. Its objective is to provide the reader with the necessary background and guidelines for the successful development and effective management of an international sales enterprise with its all its distributive, legal and financial ramifications. The scope of this book therefore runs the gamut from the detailed analysis of a typical export transaction, to the more complex matters dealing with the establishment of overseas distribution channels and manufacturing operations. The book itself is divided into fourteen chapters, the focus in each chapter being upon a particular area of vital concern to the student and to the practitioner of international trade. It starts with a macroeconomic overview of the area of international trade, and ends with a microeconomic, management-oriented perspective of the field.

Chapter 1 presents an overview of the dimensions and direction of world trade. Its purpose is to inform the reader of the tremendous magnitude and the broad and diversified activities which form part of international trade. There are more than three hundred political entities in the world today ranging in size and relative importance from the United States, the U.S.S.R., the People's Republic of China, and the countries of Western Europe, to such romantic areas as Fiji and Pitcairn Island, the latter having a population of about one hundred fifty people. All these countries and/or territories both export and import goods and services in various quantities in order to both survive and to grow. Indeed, for 1973, it is estimated that the exports of all countries may reach almost $400 billion, with the United States still continuing to enjoy the lion's share of world trade of about $55 billion.

Chapter 2 examines the American position as the world's largest economy and leading capital investor as well as the world's leading volume exporter and

1

importer. This section also analyzes the influential and sensitive nature of the United States economy in the area of international business and monetary affairs. Particular attention is paid to the country's paradoxical position of awesome commercial power coupled with extreme vulnerability by virtue of its central position as a global trader, creditor and financier.

Chapter 3 goes into a fairly detailed description of the actual mechanics involved in an export operation. A nation's export-import trade is the normal starting point for all international transactions. Insofar as the United States is concerned, about 25% of all its exports are directed towards meeting the supply requirements of American and American-affiliated companies abroad. About another 25% of U.S. exports are accounted for, directly or indirectly, by the supplying of the nation's vast overseas military establishments, and those of many of its allies. The balance is sold mainly on an open market basis throughout the world, although some exports result as a consequence of U.S.-financed economic assistance programs.

Irrespective of the reasons behind the outward flow of U.S.-made goods to other lands, their physical movement across national boundaries depends upon the effective operation of a universally accepted system of export documentation evidencing the legitimate transfer of title and funds from one party to a specific transaction to another. Goods simply cannot move across national boundaries (smuggling excepted) without accompanying documents, many of which take the form of negotiable instruments, which confirm and evidence shipments and payments. Unless the system runs smoothly, with a minimum of errors and of misunderstandings, the entire export or import transaction might come to grief.

Much of the data and information for this chapter has been obtained and rearranged from materials made publically available to the business community by the U.S. Department of Commerce, the American Chamber of Commerce, Sea-Land Inc., the National Foreign Trade Council, Inc., and banks such as Chase Manhattan, Chemical New York and the Morgan Guaranty Trust.

Chapter 4 is a concise study of the selling terms most commonly used in export sales transactions. Business executives occasionally forget that an impending export sales transaction is in fact a contract between a buyer and seller, no matter what the distances are between the two parties. Unless the terms of sale are spelled out clearly, and are clearly understood by all parties to the transaction, the unencumbered movement of goods from one country to another is rendered difficult. Essentially, selling overseas is really no more complicated than selling domestically. However, a common language has evolved over the generations, along with a complete set of documentation procedures, to help match buyer-seller objectives. Assistance in developing this chapter was received from the New Jersey Bank, the Chase Manhattan Bank, the Foreign Credit Insurance Association, Chemical Bank, New York, and the Morgan Guaranty Trust.

Chapter 5 is a survey of source data, publications and other pertinent bibliographical references with which the reader must become familiar in order to research and evaluate overseas markets from the point of view of their sales potential. The emphasis of this section is upon the use and interpretation of statistical data periodically made available for the benefit of exporters by the U.S. Department of Commerce.

Chapter 6 deals with the subject of export sales financing. The key to successful selling abroad often hinges upon special financing arrangements that the exporter is able to obtain on behalf of his overseas customer. This chapter offers the reader a thorough review of export sales financing programs currently being offered by the United States. Special attention is paid to the functions of the Foreign Credit Insurance Association, the Export-Import Bank, the Overseas Private Investment Corporation, and a relatively new piece of federal legislation commonly known as DISC (Domestic International Sales Corporation). Much of the information in this chapter is available through the individual institutions named above. DISC information is generally available through the U.S. Department of Commerce, the Internal Revenue Service, and through major U.S. banks. Indeed, there is little original material in this chapter. What has nevertheless been accomplished is that all the major sources of export financing and of inevestment, credit and political risk insurance have been compiled, reviewed and explained in one chapter for comparative purposes. This provides the international executive with a source digest, enabling him to consult with specific institutions in terms of his particular needs.

Chapter 7 is actually a continuation of Chapter 6. However, its emphasis is upon several official agencies and federal laws which currently exist to promote U.S. exports and foreign investments through a variety of insurance arrangements and tax incentives. Special attention is paid to the DISC program, which provides tax incentives to exporters, the Western Hemisphere Trading Corporation (WHTC), which has a similar objective, and OPIC (Overseas Private Investment Corporation), which insures the overseas capital assets of U.S. investors.

Chapter 8 focuses upon international agencies which provide programs and incentives to exporters similar to those offered by U.S. organizations. A knowledge of these agencies is important in the sense that overseas funding for U.S. exports may often be available even when U.S. sources are not.

Chapter 9 is an analysis of the steps generally taken by major corporations in developing overseas distributorship agreements. Included in this chapter is a review of several prototype contracts often used by exporters with independent overseas dealers and distributors. Also included in this chapter are selected recommendations and commentaries by Business International, Inc., a research oriented publisher of periodic literature and world renowned specialists in the field of international contracts.

Chapter 10 emphasises the essential nature of licensing agreements to the effective operation of an international business enterprise. It is through licensing agreements that companies who are unprepared to invest relatively large sums of money in direct overseas investments may inexpensively manufacture and market their products abroad. It is also through licensing agreements that transfers of technology are normally effected. Guidelines for the successful establishment of a licensing agreement are included in this chapter along with a sample contract for reference purposes.

Chapter 11 discusses free trade zones. These are physical enclosures within the customs borders of a country into which goods may be brought duty free. Their full potential has never been realized here in the United States despite the fact that about one dozen such zones exist within the country. Not only are free trade zones within the United States available to businesses, but free trade zones throughout the world can also be used by American exporters to engage in the final processing of their goods as close as possible to the point of ultimate distribution.

Chapter 12 surveys the ways and means of developing an effective export oriented pricing system along with a departmental budget apart from domestic operations. This approach enables the export sales department to act as a marketing entity with its own action plan rather than as a mere adjunct of a company's shipping and/or sales departments.

Chapter 13 studies methods of evaluating an importing country's financial viability, i.e., the capacity of its banking institutions to pay for importers' purchases in exporters' currencies. Too often, an importer's own credit rating may be flawless, but his country's foreign exchange reserves may be inadequate. The development of effective criteria to rank and judge countries' financial capacities is critical to minimizing an exporter's own sales collection risk.

Chapter 14 takes a look at the problems and opportunities faced by companies in instituting the appropriate management forms and controls to coordinate what often end up being far-flung international operations. Many U.S. corporations, small and large, have become truly multinational in scope. It is not unusual for even a smaller company, with sales of less than $50 million annually, to be exporting its finished goods to distributors in more than twenty countries at once, and to be producing its products through licensees and/or joint-ventures in another dozen nations. The very spread of these activities creates a need to formulate and implement dynamic and streamlined organizational and communications systems to help coordinate corporate activities and actions throughout the world with overall corporate objectives. This chapter reviews several possible management theories and organizational approaches to improving the effectiveness of multinational businesses in their global enterprises.

THE DIMENSIONS OF WORLD TRADE: AN OVERVIEW

International trade, the exchange of goods and services among countries, is the basis of existence in a civilized state for most nations. Countries like Japan and the United Kingdom, plagued with historical scarcities of natural physical resources within their national borders, are dependent upon their commercial relations with other nations for their prosperity and growth. Smaller and highly industrialized states such as Holland and Belgium tend to develop economies which complement those of other countries, thereby accentuating their dependence upon international trade.

Larger industrial nations like the United States and the U.S.S.R., well-endowed with resources, nevertheless find that their continued growth requires a continuing exchange of goods, raw materials, technology and financial resources with their trading partners.

The importance of countries' external economic (international trade) sectors to the overall viability of their internal economies reaches an even more critical level for the lesser developed nations. These states, faced with shortages of capital, technology and other vital resources, must literally import the very industrial base for their future development. Trade, for the lesser developed countries, has become a conduit for industrialization.

The international trade sector, for many countries, is a large part of their national economies. It is a small part for other national economies, as Figure 1.1 indicates.[1] However, it is incorrect to conclude that a relatively small external sector exercises a correspondingly small influence upon the domestic economy.

An excellent case in point is that of the United States. Both the country's exports and its imports are less than 5 percent of Gross National Product (GNP). The reader will recognize, without becoming involved in a protracted discussion

FIGURE 1.1: 1972 GROSS NATIONAL PRODUCT, EXPORTS AND IMPORTS FOR SELECTED COUNTRIES*

Country	GNP ($ Billion)	Population (millions)	Exports (FOB) ($ Billions)	Imports (CIF) ($ Billions)
Belgium	30.00	10.0	15.0	15.0
Netherlands	45.00	13.0	16.5	16.4
France	200.00	51.5	23.7	24.1
West Germany	220.00	60.0	44.5	38.2
United Kingdom	170.00	56.0	26.0	28.5
United States	1,152.00	210.0	49.6	55.5
Japan	300.00	105.0	28.5	23.6
Brazil	40.00	90.0	4.0	4.0
Chile	9.00	10.0	1.0	1.0
India	60.00	550.0	2.4	2.3

*All figures are estimates based upon annual rates as recorded by the International Monetary Fund.

FIGURE 1.2: WORLD TRADE-DEVELOPED VS. DEVELOPING COUNTRIES ($ BILLIONS)

	Exports FOB					Imports CIF*				
	1938	1948	1968	1971	1972	1938	1948	1968	1971	1972
World**	23.5	57.5	212.8	314.0	350.0	25.4	63.6	225.0	329.5	365.0
Industrial Countries	15.2	36.7	169.7	252.6	285.0	17.9	41.2	179.7	265.4	295.0
L.D.C.s	5.9	17.1	43.1	61.4	65.0	5.8	18.6	45.3	64.1	70.0
Communist Areas and Other Misc. Territories	2.4	3.7	26.0	30.0	39.0	1.7	3.8	25.0	32.0	38.0
World Total**	23.5	57.5	238.8	344.0	389.0	25.4	63.6	250.00	361.5	403.0

*Global CIF Imports will always appear higher than corresponding FOB Exports because they include transport and insurance costs.

**Figures indicate global trade data for 1938 and 1948, and world trade data excluding the Communist areas for 1968 and 1971. "World Total" figures on the bottom row are global figures all the way across. The distinction is made because 1938 and 1948 data was obtained from the 1966 *Yearbook of International Trade Statistics* (United Nations) which includes the Communist countries in the initial data. Data for 1968 and 1971 was obtained from the June, 1972 *International Financial Statistics* (International Monetary Fund) which lists Communist trade in a separate section. Data for 1972 is provisional, based upon annual rates and estimates obtained from the February, 1973 *International Financial Statistics.*

Source: *International Financial Statistics,* Volume XXVI, Number 2, (February, 1973). International Monetary Fund, Washington, D.C.

on the income effects of trade, the intimate relationship that exists between changes in the country's trade and changes in its economy. Indeed, the United States Department of Commerce once estimated that one out of seven jobs in the country is directly or indirectly involved in some phase of international trade, whether it be banking or transportation. If that is correct, and if the country's trade were to collapse tomorrow, 14 percent of the labor force would become unemployed.

This may possibly be an exaggeration. However, the fact remains that a country's so-called "net export" position, or current account balance (the difference between total imports and total exports) is a component part of its GNP. A trade surplus will usually have a positive effect upon GNP; a trade deficit can exercise a negative effect. Changes in "net exports" may therefore mean the difference between a recessionary trend or an expanding economy.

How many countries are engaged in international trade? The International Monetary Fund's International Financial Statistics for February 1973 *lists* 173 distinct political entities. It has been variously estimated, however, that about three hundred political areas exist on earth, all of which are engaged in a degree of trade of one form or another. These range in size from Pitcairn Island with a population of 156 to the People's Republic of China with a population of almost 800 million.

The volume of trade among nations has expanded considerably over the years. In 1948, total world exports were about $57.5 billion. This has risen to about $350 billion in 1972.[2] On the import side, the percentage change is easier to grasp; imports have increased from $63.6 billion in 1948 to $368 billion in 1972, an almost 600% increase in 25 years (Figure 1.2.)

This rapid increase in world trade has not been evenly distributed among all countries, as Figure 1.2 indicates. If one thinks of a country's exports as constituting a percentage share of a global market, several outstanding observations become evident. World exports have been rising rapidly, averaging about 12 percent annually since 1938.

However, exports of the "Industrial Countries" have been rising faster than the world rate, while exports of the "Lesser Developed Countries" (LDCs) have been rising at a rate lagging not only behind the world rate but also behind the export growth rate of the industrialized nations.

Further, it is interesting to note that World War II, the Korean, and Indo-Chinese conflicts have had little overall effect upon the general growth and direction of trade. What seems to have been happening since 1938, and more specifically since 1948, is that the share-of-market of world trade enjoyed by industrial nations has been rising, while that of the LDCs has been declining.

This raises the question: what is the definitional difference between a developed country and an LDC? It is perhaps an arbitrary convenience, but a per capita income of $1,000 is most often used as a dividing line. Using an arbitrary annual per capita income figure as a measure of relative economic position opens up a Pandora's box of conceptual difficulties.

How does one reconcile differences in living styles, living costs, etc.? For example, annual per capita income in the United States is over $4,000; it is approximately $3,000 in Switzerland, a much smaller and heavily specialized economy. Yet even a casual visitor to both countries would concede that there is little or no poverty in Switzerland and that the level of affluence is roughly similar for both countries.

However, a family of four residing in a suburban community resting along some superhighway complex in the United States may require two or three cars and might incur high personal expenditures just for commuting purposes. That same family, living in a pleasant home in the hills overlooking Zurich, will require only one car, and a small one at that, to accommodate the local roads. A second car might easily become a white elephant.

The only position that can be taken is that some countries, in a relative context, are rich, while many, in the same context, are poor. There is no real argument in most instances; it centers rather upon those states in which annual per capita income is close to the $1,000 mark on either the minus or plus side.

Another area of possible error in making share-of-world-trade comparisons between the developed states and the LDCs is that every now and then a few countries are expected to leave the ranks of the LDCs and become so-called industrial nations. This would naturally shift world trade figures, from the LDCs to the "developed" column. Without including the Communist Bloc countries, the February 1973 issue of *International Financial Statistics* includes 26 nations among the industrial and developed countries of the world. However, in the May, 1965 issue of the same publication, 25 countries are listed, the only omission being Malta.[3]

This suggests that in six years, only one new member has joined the ranks of the developed states and that the IMF list of industrial and developed states has remained virtually unchanged. Figure 1.3 provides a country breakdown of the 26 developed nations in question.

This leaves little alternative but to conclude that—barring an increasing number of industrial countries—there has indeed been a genuine shift in the terms of trade away from the developing nations in favor of the world's industrial states.

The communist countries, insofar as figures are officially available, exhibit a slower growth rate in their exports than do the LDCs. From an economic standpoint, this is improbable. It is more probable that these countries' figures are understated (Figure 1.4).

FIGURE 1.3: EXPORTS OF INDUSTRIAL, NON-COMMUNIST AREAS OF THE WORLD*

Country	FOB Exports 1972 ($ Billions)	Country	FOB Exports 1972 ($ Billions)
United States	49.6	Japan	28.5
United Kingdom	26.0	Finland	2.9
Austria	3.8	Greece	0.7
Belgium	15.0	Iceland	0.2
Denmark	4.0	Ireland	1.6
France	23.7	Malta	0.06
Germany	44.5	Portugal	1.1
Italy	17.7	Spain	3.3
Netherlands	16.5	Turkey	0.6
Norway	3.1	Yugoslavia	2.1
Sweden	8.2	Australia	6.5
Switzerland	6.5	New Zealand	1.6
Canada	18.9	South Africa	2.5

*Excluding the Council For Mutual Economic Assistance countries, North Korea, Mainland China, North Viet-Nam and Cuba.

FIGURE 1.4: EXPORTS AND IMPORTS OF COMMUNIST COUNTRIES*

Country	Exports** ($ Billions) 1972	Imports** ($ Billions) 1972
Cuba	1.3	1.5
China, Mainland***	2.0	2.0
Albania***	0.1	0.1
Bulgaria	2.3	2.2
Czechoslovakia	4.8	4.7
Germany (East)	5.5	5.5
Hungary	2.8	3.0
Poland	4.0	4.0
Rumania	2.0	2.0
U.S.S.R.	14.5	13.5
Total	39.3	38.5

*Trade figures for North Viet-Nam, North Korea and Outer Mongolia are too vague to record with any significant level of reliability.

**Estimates only, based upon 1971 data.

***Estimates only, based upon 1963-64 data.

Source: *International Financial Statistics*, Vol. XXVI, No. 2 (February, 1973), International Monetary Fund, Washington, D.C.

FOOTNOTES

[1] Exports are recorded on an FOB port of embarkation basis. Imports are recorded on a CIF port of disembarkation basis. Included on the import cost side are marine and FOB freight and insurance costs.

[2] The figures do not include the trade of the following countries: Cuba, People's Rebublic of China, Albania, Bulgaria, Czechoslovakia, East Germany, Hungary, Poland, Rumania, U.S.S.R., North Korea and North Vietnam.

[3] *International Financial Statistics*, Volume XVIII, Number 5 (May, 1965), International Monetary Fund, Washington D.C.

THE UNITED STATES POSITION

DECLINING BALANCE OF TRADE

The United States balance of trade has gradually changed from a surplus to a deficit position (see Figure 2.1). This change may be correlated with the overall U.S. position in world trade where it is found that the country's share of world exports has also been slipping (see Figure 2.2). There are three broad sets of factors which appear responsible for these trends.

More Trading Nations and Growing Protectionism

The marketing competitiveness of the world's other industrial nations has become keener; there are more countries involved in trade than ever before, and these countries are increasingly expanding their trade as their own economies continue to grow. The heightened competitiveness has affected overseas markets which have traditionally been oriented mainly toward the U.S.

Specifically, the postwar economic recovery of Western Europe and of Japan, while it presented, and continues to present, opportunities for U.S. investments, has created a source of numerous alternatives among all countries, thereby reducing the need to trade mainly with the U.S., especially in the area of finished goods.

Growing protectionism is a function of both economic nationalism (Japan) and economic regionalism (EEC). This has had the unfortunate consequence of dampening the U.S. export drive among industrial nations for a wide range of product lines. Similar protectionist attitudes have also limited the growth of U.S. exports to the LDCs, who are often committed to a policy of promoting the development of import-substituting industries. Consequently, U.S. exports since about 1965 have not grown as fast as those industrial areas such as the EEC and Japan.

FIGURE 2.1: UNITED STATES EXPORTS AND IMPORTS BY AREA
($ BILLIONS)

	Exports						
	1966	1967	1968	1969	1970	1971	1972
All Countries	30.3	31.5	34.4	37.9	43.2	44.1	49.6
Developed Countries	20.0	21.3	23.3	26.4	29.8	30.3	34.2
Lesser Developed Countries	10.1	9.9	10.8	11.2	12.9	13.4	14.5
Communist Areas	0.2	0.2	0.2	0.2	0.3	0.4	0.8
Canada	6.6	7.1	8.0	9.1	9.0	10.3	12.4
Latin America	4.2	4.1	4.3	4.8	5.2	5.6	6.4
Other Western Hemisphere	0.5	0.6	0.7	0.7	0.8	0.8	0.8
Western Europe	9.8	10.0	10.9	12.3	14.4	14.1	15.2
Asia	6.7	7.1	7.5	8.2	10.0	9.8	11.2
Japan	2.3	2.6	2.9	3.4	4.6	4.0	4.9
Other	4.4	4.5	4.6	4.8	5.3	5.8	6.3
Africa	1.3	1.1	1.2	1.3	1.5	1.6	1.5
Australasia	0.8	1.7	1.0	1.0	1.1	1.1	1.0

	Imports						
	1966	1967	1968	1969	1970	1971	1972
All Countries	25.5	26.8	33.1	36.0	42.4	45.6	55.5
Developed Countries	17.5	18.9	34.0	26.4	29.2	33.7	40.8
Lesser Developed Countries	7.7	7.6	8.8	9.3	10.4	11.5	14.3
Communist Areas	0.2	0.2	0.2	0.2	0.2	0.2	0.3
Canada	6.1	7.0	8.9	10.3	11.0	12.7	14.9
Latin America	3.9	3.8	3.9	4.2	4.4	4.8	4.9
Other Western Hemisphere	0.9	1.0	1.0	1.1	1.1	1.1	1.2
Western Europe	7.6	8.0	10.1	10.1	11.1	12.6	15.4
Asia	5.2	5.3	6.9	8.2	9.6	11.7	15.1
Japan	2.9	3.0	4.0	4.8	5.8	7.2	9.0
Other	2.3	2.3	2.9	3.4	3.8	4.5	6.1
Africa	1.0	0.9	1.1	1.0	1.1	1.2	1.5
Australasia	0.5	0.6	0.6	0.8	0.8	0.8	1.1

FIGURE 2.2: VALUE OF UNITED STATES IMPORTS AND EXPORTS
1934-1972

	Exports FOB ($ Billions)	Imports CIF ($ Billions)
1934	2.1	1.7
1939	3.1	2.4
1945	9.8	4.1
1950	10.2	8.9
1960	20.5	15.0
1961	21.0	14.7
1962	21.6	16.4
1963	24.5	17.2
1964	26.6	20.3
1965	27.0	23.1
1966	30.3	25.5
1967	31.5	26.8
1968	34.4	33.1
1969	37.9	36.0
1970	43.2	42.4
1971	44.1	45.6[+]FOB
1972	49.6	55.5[+]FOB

Finally, competition by the industrial nations for the LDC markets has begun to erode the U.S. share of export trade position in areas such as Latin America. In other words, the United States seems to be getting less and less of a declining market.

Unresponsive Export Product Mix Changes and Inelastic Price Structures

U.S. product mix changes and price structures have not been responsive to changes in overseas import demand. There has, for example, been a shift in U.S. exports from low-technology, labor-intensive products to high-technology, capital-intensive products, following trends in domestic economic activity. Figure 2.3, which analyzes the product composition of U.S. exports and imports since 1871 through 1964, indicates that the share of total export product mix occupied by "Semi" and "Finished" manufactured products has historically exhibited the greatest rate of growth, from a combined 19.7% of total U.S. exports in the 1871-1880 period to 72.5% in 1964.

The greater share of the captioned "Finished Manufactures" category is taken by SITC Group 7 (See Figure 2.4), a highly capital-intensive technology dependent product line (Machinery and Transport Equipment). This product group is also the United States' largest total dollar volume exportable, increasing from $9.3 billion in 1965 to $17.8 billion in 1970, a rise of $8.5 billion.

Total U.S. exports rose from $26.0 billion to $49.6 billion between 1965 and 1972, an increase of $23.6 billion; machinery and transport equipment accounted for over 50% of that increase.

The LDC countries do not appear, in terms of their stage of development and in terms of their financial capacities, to be ready to import these types of products in the quantities that would be significant for the United States. The problem is probably twofold. The LDC's economies, on average, and with few notable exceptions, are not developing fast enough to accommodate U.S. export growth requirements. And, whatever import demand there may be among the LDCs is not always backed up by the necessary import capacity, i.e., the capacity of an importing nation to clear bills of exchange and other foreign exchange instruments at maturity.

No longer are the industrial nations easy markets in view of their already competing technologies. The situation, with both the LDC and industrial markets overseas, is aggravated by U.S. rates of inflation which have been spilling over to affect U.S. export prices. While American export product prices and the export prices of most other countries have been rising, U.S. export prices have been rising faster than those of its leading competitors.

High prices, accompanied by relatively hard credit line export financing, have made, and continue to make life difficult for the American exporter whose main objective is to make a profitable sale. The development of credit instruments and institutions (FCIA, Ex-Im Bank, etc.) since the early part of the

FIGURE 2.3: PRODUCT COMPOSITION OF U.S. EXPORTS AND IMPORTS (FOB Basis)

1871 – 1964

(Percent)

Annual Average or Year	Crude Materials		Crude Foodstuffs		Manufactured Foodstuffs		Semi-Manufactures		Finished Manufactures	
	Exports	Imports	Exports	Imports	Exports	Imports	Exports	Imports	Exports	Imports
1871 – 1880	38.6	17.2	19.7	16.0	22.0	20.7	4.6	13.0	15.1	33.0
1921 – 1925	27.5	37.4	9.7	11.1	13.9	13.0	12.5	17.7	36.3	20.9
1936 – 1940	19.0	33.1	3.8	13.1	5.5	14.2	19.3	20.9	52.4	18.7
1951 – 1955	13.0	26.3	7.1	19.5	5.6	10.1	11.6	23.7	62.7	20.4
1956 – 1960	12.9	22.3	7.4	14.1	6.0	10.5	15.0	22.0	58.7	31.1
1964	11.2	18.5	9.8	10.9	6.5	9.7	15.4	21.5	57.1	39.4

FIGURE 2.4: UNITED STATES EXPORTS AND IMPORTS BY MAJOR COMMODITY ($ BILLIONS)

Commodity Group & Commodity	1960 Exports	1960 Imports	1965 Exports	1965 Imports	1970 Exports	1970 Imports	1971 Exports	1971 Imports	1972 Exports	1972 Imports
1. Food and Live Animals	2.6	3.0	4.0	3.4	4.3	3.5	4.3	5.7	5.6	6.5
2. Beverages and Tobacco	0.5	0.4	0.5	0.6	0.7	0.8	0.7	0.8	0.9	1.0
3. Crude Materials, Inedible, Except Fuels	2.8	2.8	2.9	3.1	4.6	3.3	4.3	3.3	5.0	3.8
4. Mineral Fuels	0.8	1.6	0.9	2.2	1.6	3.0	1.4	3.7	1.5	4.7
5. Animal and Vegetable Oils and Fats	0.3	0.1	0.5	0.1	0.5	0.1	0.6	0.1	0.5	0.1
6. Chemicals	1.8	0.8	2.4	0.8	3.8	1.5	3.8	1.6	4.1	2.0
7. Machinery and Transport Equipment	7.0	1.5	10.1	2.9	17.8	11.1	19.4	13.8	21.4	17.4
8. Other Manufactured Goods	3.8	4.6	4.9	7.5	7.6	13.3	7.1	14.8	8.0	18.3
9. Other Transactions	0.7	0.4	1.0	0.7	1.5	1.3	1.5	1.4	1.5	1.5
Total Exports and Imports*	20.4	15.0	27.1	21.4	43.2	42.4	43.1	45.2	48.5	55.3

*Totals differ because of rounding.

Source: Foreign Trade Statistics, FT 410, December, 1970, 1965. 1960, United States Department of Commerce.

nineteen-sixties still lags behind the more eggressive financing programs utilized by Japanese, German, French and Italian competitors as means of promoting export sales.

Accelerating Import Growth

The third factor is the problem of rapidly rising imports into the United States. Part of this is due to the country's propensity to import in relation to its rising national income. Much is also due to growing price differentials between prices of imports and those of domestically produced products. Some of the rise is also certainly due to the prestige image of certain high priced consumer goods.

The main question is this: how severe is the U.S. problem? Or, is there a problem? It seems only natural that as the world progresses, other nations are bound to become as economically active, and perhaps more active, than the United States in world trade. Historically, the United States has sustained trade surpluses. It would seem that a more appropriate objective, in terms of harmonizing world trade movements, would be to maintain overall and continuing trade balances. This may be a necessary direction for all countries in the future (see Figure 2.2).

The slight trade deficit experienced by the United States in 1971 would be unimportant if it could be matched by overall trade balances in the future. However, the trade figures currently show a preliminary $6.0 billion deficit for 1972 and, furthermore, the trade deficit was confined to two areas, Canada and Japan.

Attractive and offsetting surpluses are maintained elsewhere, in Europe, Latin America, Asia and Africa, but these surpluses were literally wiped out during the course of 1972. If the situation with Canada and Japan can be corrected, and if U.S. commercial relations with the U.S.S.R. and the People's Republic of China continue to improve, and if monetary and economic relations with Western Europe can somehow be normalized, the U.S. terms of trade may once again become balanced, or even show a slight surplus. This is all very questionable, however.

The recently eroding trade surplus position of the United States should not disguise the more perplexing and enduring nature of the country's deteriorating balance of payments, and the increasingly sensitive position of the world's international monetary system. Indeed, declining trade balances for the United States may be symptomatic not only of a degree of domestic economic disequilibrium but also of a growing inability of U.S. products to compete on a multinational level.

PROBLEMS OF THE INTERNATIONAL MONETARY SYSTEM

The reader may ask: what is wrong with the monetary system which was organized around the International Monetary Fund (IMF) back in 1944? The answer is that it has been outgrown. Indeed, the success of the system monitored by the IMF seems to have depended upon four conditions. These were, (1) the maintenance of long term, overall trade and payments balances among the participating countries, (2) a well-ordered expansion of world trade and of generalized economic growth holding to proportional relationship changes in economic activity and changes in quantitative monetary resources, (3) the capacities of gold and of the dollar to maintain themselves as cornerstones of the existing monetary structure, and, (4) the maintenance of existing directions of trade, that is, no substantial increase in East-West trade or in trade with the developing nations. All four conditions became altered in time.

Maintaining Overall Trade and Payments Balances

The maintenance of long term, overall trade and payments balances among the IMF member countries is integrally tied to the pivotal position of the United States as a center of economic and financial power and resources in the two decades following 1945.

The country was the principal source of investment capital and of materials for the economic development of much of the world. It had most of the gold, $24 billion out of total recorded gold holdings of $30 billion in 1948;[1]* it supplied the capital to rejuvenate the world's war-devastated economies, about $100 billion between 1946 and 1955, much of which was allocated to Western Europe and Japan.

The nation also became the major supplier of industrial, consumer and agricultural goods, with exports rising annually to over $49 billion in 1972, casting the country in the role of being the world's number one exporter.[2] The United States consequently recorded sizeable annual trade surpluses. However, it recorded continuous balance of payments deficits because inflows generated by exports could never quite compensate for the large capital outflows resulting from the country's net creditor position, foreign investments, and for certain negative current account transactions such as overseas military expenditures and spending by American travelers abroad.[3] (See Figures 2.5, 2.6 and 2.7.)

The Expansion of World Trade and of Economic Growth

The international emphasis, given much support through U.S. foreign policy, upon economic growth through rapid industrialization, created a situation over the years in which all but a small handful of countries came to sustain both trade and payments deficits. Financial and monetary resources were simply not keeping up with increasing demand for more imports and more international investments.

The more affluent economies which were able to generate trade and payments surpluses and/or balances, could do so mainly on a short term basis, and then only at the expense of their neighbors or of the developing nations.[4]

FIGURE 2.5

U.S. BALANCES ON GOODS, SERVICES, AND TRANSFERS

In the third quarter, the deficit for merchandise trade was $1.6 billion (seasonally adjusted), $0.4 billion below the record deficit in the second quarter. The third quarter deficit for goods and services was $0.9 billion, or $0.7 billion less than in the second quarter. According to preliminary data for the fourth quarter, merchandise imports exceeded exports by $1.7 billion, about the same as in the third quarter.

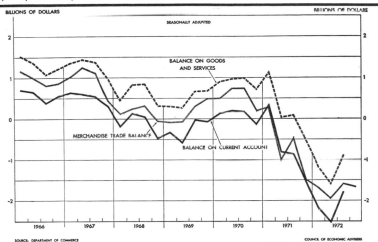

SOURCE: DEPARTMENT OF COMMERCE

COUNCIL OF ECONOMIC ADVISERS

[Millions of dollars]

Period	Merchandise [1][2]			Military transactions			Net investment income		Net travel and transportation expenditures	Other services, net	Balance on goods and services [1][4]	Remittances, pensions, and other unilateral transfers [1]	Balance on current account
	Exports	Imports	Net balance	Direct expenditures	Sales	Net balance	Private [3]	U.S. Government					
1967	30,638	−26,821	3,817	−4,378	1,240	−3,138	5,847	40	−1,763	334	5,136	−3,081	2,055
1968	33,576	−32,964	612	−4,535	1,392	−3,143	6,157	63	−1,565	302	2,425	−2,909	−484
1969	36,417	−35,796	621	−4,856	1,512	−3,344	5,820	155	−1,784	442	1,911	−2,946	−1,035
1970	41,963	−39,799	2,164	−4,852	1,478	−3,374	6,376	−115	−2,061	574	3,563	−3,208	356
1971	42,770	−45,459	−2,689	−4,816	1,922	−2,894	8,952	−957	−2,432	748	727	−3,574	−2,847
1972 [4]	47,391	−54,355	−6,964	−4,716	1,153	−3,563	9,211	−1,803	−2,589	795	−4,913	−3,737	−8,651
Seasonally adjusted													
1971: I	11,017	−10,728	289	−1,175	510	−665	1,899	−101	−498	212	1,136	−791	345
II	10,710	−11,722	−1,012	−1,214	516	−698	2,352	−161	−625	180	36	−846	−810
III	11,479	−11,951	−472	−1,198	474	−724	2,038	−327	−606	182	91	−946	−855
IV	9,564	−11,058	−1,494	−1,230	423	−807	2,663	−368	−703	172	−537	−992	−1,529
1972: I	11,791	−13,478	−1,687	−1,218	334	−884	2,232	−370	−679	200	−1,188	−990	−2,178
II	11,445	−13,393	−1,948	−1,230	281	−958	2,196	−426	−657	192	−1,601	−918	−2,519
III ᵖ	12,307	−13,895	−1,588	−1,080	250	−830	2,480	−556	606	204	−896	−895	−1,791
IV ᵖ	13,185	−14,857	−1,672										

[1] Excludes military grants.
[2] Adjusted from Census data for differences in timing and coverage.
[3] Includes fees and royalties from U.S. direct investments abroad or from foreign direct investments in the United States.
[4] Equal to net exports of goods and services in the national income and product accounts of the United States when converted to an annual rates basis.
ᵖ First 3 quarters on a seasonally adjusted annual rates basis.

Source: Department of Commerce.

FIGURE 2.6

MERCHANDISE EXPORTS AND IMPORTS

In December goods imported into the United States exceeded goods exported abroad by $563 million on a seasonally adjusted basis.

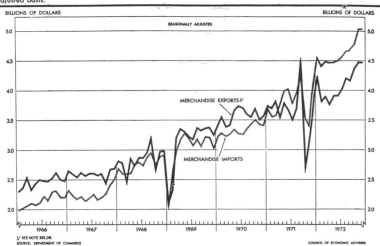

1/ SEE NOTE BELOW.
SOURCE: DEPARTMENT OF COMMERCE
COUNCIL OF ECONOMIC ADVISERS

[Millions of dollars]

Period	Merchandise exports						Merchandise imports						Gross-merchandise trade surplus, seasonally adjusted
	Total (including reexports) [1]		Domestic exports				Total [1]		General imports [3]				
	Seasonally adjusted	Unadjusted	Total [1][2]	Food, beverages, and tobacco	Crude materials and fuels	Manufactured goods	Seasonally adjusted	Unadjusted	Food, beverages, and tobacco	Crude materials and fuels	Manufactured goods	
Monthly average:													
1964	------	2,153	2,123	386	361	1,377	------	1,562	335	419	759	590
1965	------	2,229	2,201	377	356	1,453	------	1,786	334	453	937	444
1966	------	2,458	2,421	432	367	1,602	------	2,135	382	476	1,204	323
1967	------	2,586	2,554	392	394	1,737	------	2,241	392	447	1,313	345
1968	------	2,839	2,802	383	405	1,985	------	2,769	447	503	1,719	70
1969	------	3,111	3,066	370	417	2,232	------	3,004	442	533	1,918	107
1970	------	3,555	3,502	422	558	2,445	------	3,329	519	545	2,159	226
1971	------	3,629	3,576	423	537	2,537	------	3,797	534	606	2,534	−168
1972	------	4,093	4,026	548	591	2,804	------	4,630	614	737	3,146	−537
		Unadjusted						Unadjusted				
1971: Nov	3,160	3,221	3,177	395	471	2,247	3,379	3,522	353	598	2,454	−218
Dec	3,858	4,056	3,999	536	644	2,738	4,128	4,279	606	710	2,822	−270
1972: Jan	4,212	3,807	3,758	506	567	2,593	4,538	4,278	630	702	2,820	−326
Feb	3,803	3,778	3,721	485	527	2,630	4,406	4,180	626	673	2,765	−602
Mar	3,888	4,306	4,247	426	610	3,116	4,475	4,844	554	756	3,401	−587
Apr	3,759	3,885	3,810	396	567	2,753	4,460	4,248	544	659	2,918	−701
May	3,911	4,141	4,075	508	565	2,917	4,466	4,722	604	731	3,254	−554
June	3,905	4,015	3,942	528	557	2,762	4,495	4,766	614	715	3,305	−590
July	4,016	3,599	3,867	496	509	2,540	4,561	4,314	548	712	2,928	−546
Aug	4,192	3,937	3,867	539	548	2,710	4,664	4,727	632	728	3,232	−472
Sept	4,157	3,964	3,894	594	478	2,745	4,671	4,485	628	756	2,969	−514
Oct	4,365	4,443	4,381	637	672	3,009	4,780	5,007	692	775	3,393	−415
Nov	4,469	4,583	4,497	710	760	2,928	5,023	5,190	662	810	3,574	−559
Dec	4,466	4,601	4,528	750	731	2,948	5,029	4,795	639	822	3,190	−563

[1] Total excludes Department of Defense shipments of grant-aid military supplies and equipment under the Military Assistance Program.
[2] Total includes commodities and transactions not classified according to kind.
[3] Total arrivals of imported goods other than intransit shipments.

NOTE.—Data adjusted to include silver ore and bullion reported separately prior to 1969.

Source: Department of Commerce.

FIGURE 2.7

U.S. OVERALL BALANCES ON INTERNATIONAL TRANSACTIONS

The balance on current account and long-term capital was in deficit by $2.2 billion (seasonally adjusted) in the third quarter, compared to a deficit of $1.9 billion in the second quarter. The official reserve transactions balance deteriorated from a deficit of $0.8 billion in the second quarter to a deficit of $4.6 billion in the third quarter. This large increase in the deficit was due to speculative outflows in July.

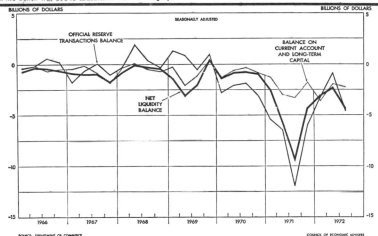

[Millions of dollars]

Period	Long-term capital flows, net — U.S. Government[1]	Private[3]	Balance on current account and long-term capital	Non-liquid short-term private capital flows net[3]	Allocations of special drawing rights	Errors and omissions, net	Net liquidity balance	Liquid private capital flows, net[2]	Official reserve transactions balance	Changes in liabilities to foreign official agencies, net[3]	Changes in U.S. official reserve assets, net[4]	U.S. official reserve assets, net (end of period)
1967	−2,424	−2,912	−3,280	−522		−881	−4,683	1,265	−3,418	3,366	52	14,830
1968	−2,159	1,198	−1,444	230		−399	1,610	3,251	1,641	−761	−880	15,710
1969	−1,926	−50	−3,011	−640		−2,470	−6,122	8,824	2,702	−1,515	−1,187	[5]16,964
1970	−2,018	−1,398	−3,059	−482	867	−1,174	−3,851	−5,988	−9,839	7,362	2,477	14,487
1971	−2,378	−4,079	−9,304	−2,386	717	−11,031	−22,002	−7,763	−29,765	27,417	2,348	[6]12,167
1972[7]	−959	−632	−10,243	−611	710	−2,951	−13,093	1,461	−11,632	11,441	191	13,150
			Seasonally adjusted									Unadjusted
1971: I	−702	−922	−1,279	−534	180	−944	−2,577	−2,848	−5,425	4,743	682	14,342
II	−584	−1,605	−2,999	−315	179	−2,586	−5,721	−745	−6,466	5,807	659	13,504
III	−558	−1,883	−3,296	−883	179	−5,380	−9,380	−2,551	−11,931	10,737	1,194	12,131
IV	−533	330	−1,732	−651	179	−2,122	−4,329	−1,619	−5,948	6,135	−187	[6]12,167
1972: I	−343	1,081	−3,602	−508	178	800	−3,132	−119	−3,251	2,822	429	12,270
II	−95	750	−1,864	592	178	−1,141	−2,235	1,386	−849	1,080	−231	[6]13,339
III[8]	−281	−144	−2,216	−542	177	−1,872	−4,453	−171	−4,624	4,679	−55	13,217

[1] Excludes liabilities to foreign official reserve agencies.
[2] Private foreigners exclude the IMF, but include other international and regional organizations.
[3] Includes liabilities to foreign official agencies reported by U.S. Government and U.S. banks and U.S. liabilities to the IMF arising from reversible gold sales to, and gold deposits with, the United States.
[4] Official reserve assets include gold, special drawing rights, convertible currencies, and the U.S. gold tranche position in the IMF.
[5] Includes gain of $67 million resulting from revaluation of the German mark in October 1969.

[6] Includes $28 million increase in dollar value of foreign currencies revalued to reflect market exchange rates as of Dec. 31, 1971.
[7] First 3 quarters on a seasonally adjusted annual rates basis (except reserve assets, which are for December 31).
[8] Includes increase of $1,016 million resulting from change in par value of the U.S. dollar on May 8.

Sources: Department of Commerce and Treasury Department.

In a theoretical sense, nations entering the "take-off" stage of economic develop-ment described by Rostow and Hirschman[5] seemed to be reacting nicely to pre-dictions of rising marginal propensities to import as national income rose, with all the positive effects being generated by the foreign trade multiplier. However, although the foreign trade multiplier and marginal propensity to import concepts incorporate changes in the money supply and in interest rates within their math-ematical systems, the two latter variables do not appear to have been too widely considered by economic policy planners throughout the world.[6]

The fact that no major group of nations attempted to develop uniform or co-ordinated monetary policies either within or outside of the framework of the IMF until this year (the EEC exchange rate agreement) is probably a major cause of the present chaotic monetary situation.

The United States today is no longer in the central position of economic power that it occupied in 1945. This was to be expected as Europe and Japan recovered, progressed, and now compete with the United States not only for markets but for all the factors of production as well. Essentially, it is impossible at present for any country or group of countries to maintain long term equilibrium posi-tions in their balance of payments, expand their domestic economies and ex-pand their overseas commercial interests, under the relatively restrictive in-fluences of comparatively inelastic international monetary reserves.

The Inadequacies of Gold, Dollars and Foreign Exchange

The growth of world trade is generally associated with the economic growth of nations in the sense that a society's propensity to import increases as its income rises. World trade, specifically world imports, has been rising constantly and evenly since 1950, reflecting fairly constant rates of economic growth for many countries. However, the level of international liquidity has been rising at a more moderate rate and in a more oblique fashion. In 1971 and 1972, for example, a large amount of reserves was hoarded in the form of surpluses by France, Ger-many, Switzerland, and Japan.

Not only has this affected the payments positions of many nations, but it is also limiting their import capacities which are in turn negatively affecting their fu-ture growth potentials. Furthermore, current forms of international liquidity have become unsatisfactory. They presently consist of gold holdings, foreign exchange, reserves with the IMF and Special Drawing Rights (SDRs), all consti-tuting a patchwork of traditional currencies and makeshift arrangements.

Global import capacity, i.e., the import capacity of the 113 member nations of the IMF, had been falling since 1963 before recovering in 1971 and 1972. Un-fortunately, the fruits of that recovery were largely retained in the form of surplus reserves by a small handful of countries.

The concept of import capacity refers to the capacity of a country's banking system to pay for its imports on a contractual due date. Exporters' receivables, on a global average, are turned over about four times annually. This means that importers' banking facilities pay on foreign exchange claims resulting from merchandise transactions within a 90-day period from the date of the claims' presentation. Hence, an average export collection takes about 90 days to be completed. A three months' supply of liquid reserves (a combination of gold, foreign exchange, IMF reserves and SDRs) should, therefore, be sufficient to finance one year's worth of imports, assuming that the country's long term trade position remains in balance.

Or, the import capacity for a nation may be determined by multiplying its total liquidity by a factor of four. In actuality, an individual country's year-end liquidity position should be measured in order to determine its forthcoming year's highest possible level of imports. Figure 2.7 examines the IMF countries' total import capacity relative to CIF[7] imports for the years 1963 through 1972.[8]

Figure 2.7

$BILLIONS

	1963	1964	1965	1966	1967	1968	1969	1970	1971	1972
Total Liquidity	66	69	71	72	74	77	78	92	130	150
Import Capacity		264	276	284	288	296	308	312	368	520
Total Imports		161	175	192	201	225	255	292	329	368
Safety Margin		103	101	82	87	71	53	20	39	152

In 1963, total liquidity stood at $66 billion. Year-end import capacity consequently amounted to $264 billion, which was the import capacity for 1964 imports. Total imports in 1964 were $261 billion, leaving a safety margin of $103 billion. Safety margins dropped annually until 1971 when there was a dramatic reversal which continued through 1972.[9]

This reversal in the trend was never experienced by the United States, whose situation became more and more critical. Its 1970 liquidity position totalled $15 billion,[10] which provided a 1971 import capacity of $60 billion against an import level of $45.6 billion.

U.S. liquidity capacity for 1972 fell to $13.1 billion, allowing a 1972 import capacity of $52.4 billion. Actual imports were $55.6 billion.[11] Present trends show a decline in liquidity this year to $12 billion,[12] which may generate a 1973 import capacity of $48 billion, a drastic drop from 1972. Unless 1973 imports into the U.S. show a decline from 1972 (and this is improbable), the country will have inadequate monetary reserves to finance its trade without substantially altering existing methods for the settling of international obligations.

The other alternative, of course, will be the continued unilateral devaluation of the dollar. Such figures help to explain why the dollar was forced to devalue in December, 1971 and again in February, 1973.

Focusing again upon the global problem of liquidity shortages, we find that total liquidity increased from $50 billion to $120 billion between 1950 and 1972.[13] In that same period, world imports rose from $50 billion to $368 billion, a greater than 700% increase.

Gold and the Dollar: Cornerstones of the Monetary System

The capacities of gold and of the dollar to maintain themselves as cornerstones of the existing monetary structure superintended by the IMF failed because of the very impetus the entire system gave to world economic growth and trade expansion. The system was outgrown.

Under the Gold Exchange Standard, countries could redeem dollars for gold at $35 per ounce since the dollar itself was considered a currency of ultimate redemption. Between 1945 and 1960, dollars which found their way overseas as a result of U.S. direct foreign investments and other transactions usually returned to the United States to pay for exports of American goods and services.

Some unused dollars were redeemed for gold, which contributed to the deficit in the U.S. balance of payments. Dollars remaining overseas, especially in Europe, became known as the "Euro-dollar Market." Sizeable annual trade surpluses for the United States, and high demand for Euro-dollars to finance investments in Europe disguised the nature of this payments deficit problem, assisted also by the fact that the United States held most of the world's recorded gold.

As long as investments in Europe, Japan, and elsewhere in the world rose rapidly, particularly behind the vanguard of American companies, the Euro-dollar and Euro-dollar bond markets exhibited considerable strength. The fact that these dollars could be redeemed at any time for gold at $35 per ounce helped to support those markets, which began to wilt when European and Japanese growth rates began to slacken after 1968.

The decline in U.S. gold holdings began quietly after 1948. The trickle of the late nineteen-forties accelerated in the nineteen-fifties, became a more obvious drain during the first seven years of the nineteen-sixties, and turned into a full-scale erosion thereafter. U.S. gold holdings fell from $24 billion in 1948 to $15 billion in 1960, and to $10.4 billion by August, 1971.[15]

The loss of gold from the United States undermined the Gold Exchange Standard and the dollar as a currency of ultimate redemption. Gold was moving to mainly, Western Europe, but no single or group of nations in Europe or elsewhere was ready or willing to replace the United States as a financial and capital center.

The acute nature of the U.S. payments deficit problem, which continually gnawed at the credibility of gold and the dollar as reliable mediums of international exchange, was hidden further by the multinational practice of signing IOU's on maturing obligations that could not be conveniently liquidated on their due dates.

In other words, the United States did not pay all its monetary debts on demand with gold; it simply allowed, wherever possible, foreign claims on U.S. monetary assets to accumulate. These claims amounted to $30 billion in 1960,[16] and rose to over $65 billion this year, not including $3 to $7 billion in gold bonds which mature shortly. Unless these bonds can be rolled over to some future date, U.S. gold holdings may drop suddenly to between $3 and $7.5 billion, approximately, from current levels.

Aside from the large but specific problems of the United States in losing gold, increases in total gold holdings among the IMF countries have been slight. In 1948, these gold holdings stood at $30 billion; they rose to $41 billion in 1967, and fell back to slightly over $38 billion this year as a result of speculative purchases in the past four years.

Total recorded gold production in 1970 was $1.4 billion, of which $1.1 billion was produced in the Republic of South Africa. To summarize, gold is in short supply; no single country today has a gold stock large enough to back its own money as a currency of ultimate redemption for international transactions.

The movement of gold away from the United States, and its more-or-less even distribution among the world's other industrialized nations, resulting in the virtual elimination of the dollar as an international reserve currency, is indicative of a gradual but momentous shift in the direction of trade in the world. This shift is also responsible for the growing awkwardness of the existing monetary system which has never grown to reflect the needs of the many new states who joined the IMF after its founding.[17]

Changes in the Direction of Trade and Economic Slowdown Abroad

There were, in the fifteen years following 1945, few alternatives to doing business with the United States. Even in 1960, the United States exported $20 billion out of a world total of $100 billion, giving it a share-of-market position of 20%. In 1970, with world exports rising to $280 billion and U.S. exports to $43 billion, the U.S. share-of-market position declined to 14%.

Much of the increase in market shares has been taken by the Europeans, the Japanese, and the Communist nations as well. The expansion of trade with Communist countries in particular is creating additional strains upon the existing monetary system. Most of their currencies are nonconvertible in conventional foreign exchange markets. They must therefore compete along with the rest of the world for convertible currencies and for gold.

Along with the prospects of renewed economic competition with the People's Republic of China, the Soviet Union and other Communist nations, and new competition coming from some of the larger developing states such as India and Brazil, the industrialized countries are also currently faced with uncertain growth patterns as a result of the recent recession coupled with strong inflationary pressures. Among the Common Market countries of Europe, only France is planning a 5% annual rate of real growth for the next five years; and again, it is only a *planned* rate. What happens may be entirely different.

An economic slowdown, or retardation in the processes of economic growth, should generally exercise a leveling effect on imports. Inflation, however, has exactly the opposite effect. Hence, imports into the United States have been rising rapidly since 1965, and especially in 1972 when imports rose $10 billion in one year.

Despite the recession and a stubborn unemployment problem, domestic inflation accelerated the growth of imports into the U.S. There were two main reasons: foreign imports were cheaper as a function of cost-push inflation; foreign imports of a high priced nature were in high demand as a function of so-called demand-pull inflation, i.e., society demanding more and better products at almost any price.

THE CURRENT SITUATION

The quandary facing the United States and the IMF countries is clear. Growth rates for many major economies are slowing down, and inflation is becoming a generalized problem. There is an almost universal increase in demand for more and better goods and services. This is stimulating upward pressure upon import demand throughout the world. At the same time, there exists today a global liquidity crunch.

If the United States economy retrenches and contracts, reduces the level of its spending — at home and abroad — and perhaps further devalues the dollar unilaterally, it is bound to create powerful deflationary pressures overseas, while devaluation may result in inflationary price increases for domestically produced import-substituting goods. If the U.S. economy does nothing, it may completely drain the country's monetary resources, perpetuate the inflationary spiral on a multinational scale, and bring about a financial breakdown. In either case, it is "damned if you do, and damned if you don't".

The objective must be to raise international liquidity levels to enable world trade to expand responsively to meet the requirements of countries' economic development. Currency devaluation can be a useful tool in that respect if the act is tied to a series of related multilateral actions involving broadly-based changes in all major exchange rates.

Currency devaluation generally begets time-lagged inflation upon the country whose currency is being devalued; but that only affects import substituting products, as was pointed out before.[18] Indeed, devaluation is often a remedial consequence of spiraling domestic inflation which has rendered a nation's export product mix too highly priced for overseas markets. This is the situation faced all too often by the developing countries.

In the immediate wake of currency devaluation, a country's products tend to become more internationally competitive. Exports are expanded while imports tend to fall, thereby increasing foreign exchange inflows. This helps to restore exchange rate equilibrium.

When all currencies devalue fairly simultaneously through a prearranged increase in the price of gold, particularly during a time of general economic sluggishness, there is liable to be no inflationary effect at all. This was the experience of 1934 when the price of gold rose from $26 per ounce to $35 per ounce. Although the avowed intent was to raise prices for goods and services back to 1926 levels, those were not reached until 1943.

There was neither a prolonged inflationary nor deflationary effect, and the depression lingered on until the war broke out in 1939. Nevertheless, the increase in gold prices significantly raised liquidity levels to assist the deficit spending plans of governments.

The recent economic slow-down is hardly as drastic as that of the depression. For this reason, an overall but realistic increase in the price of gold, with its corresponding increases in international liquidity, might just help maintain the existing monetary system for a few years longer until new monetary concepts are developed.

If the raising of the price of gold is to exercise any positive influence in restoring the viability of any monetary system, it should be keyed to the creation of a non-national currency whose supply elasticities can expand to meet world import demand.

This would then help resolve two distinct but related issues. It would eliminate the immediate financial plight of the United States by providing the country with the extra "cash," so to speak, with which to liquidate all foreign claims on its monetary assets. This would result from an increase in the price of gold.

The creation of a new, non-national reserve currency would serve to demonitize gold and remove the vulnerability of the dollar, which would no longer be a currency of ultimate redemption. As part of a transitory scheme, gold could be retained as a semi-backing for a non-national money (perhaps an extension of the SDR concept) consisting, hypothetically, of a 20% gold cover requirement.

What could happen is that a country possessing $10 billion in gold could automatically receive $50 billion in SDRs to be used for the purpose of financing its international transactions. The cover requirement can eventually be altered, or even eliminated, just as the 25% gold cover on the dollar was dropped in 1968 by an Act of Congress.

Ideally, there should be an official increase in the price of gold to about $100 per ounce. Then, assuming that U.S. gold bond debts can be rolled over into the future, the U.S. gold stock, worth about $10 billion this year, would become worth almost $30 billion. Without the immediate creation of a new reserve money, U.S. international liquidity would rise from $13 billion to almost $40 billion. This would provide the country with a 1973 import capacity of about $120 billion, it would also give the U.S. adequate reserves to support at least five more consecutive deficit years.

There would be a similar situation among all the IMF countries whose total gold holdings for 1972 were about $38.5 billion, out of a total liquidity position of $150 billion. The value of the gold stock would almost triple to $115 billion, and total liquidity would rise correspondingly to almost $200 billion, generating a 1973-1974 global import capacity of up to $800 billion.

It is apparent that merely raising gold prices presents no long term solution to the problem of the world's liquidity crunch. Neither does it solve the problem of the United States' outsized foreign debt. But it does postpone the crisis for a few years. However, if a new, non-national reserve currency were created as the price of gold increases, and if that new "money" was given a 20% gold cover, a revalued gold stock for the United States of $30 billion would yield $150 billion in fresh, internationally negotiable paper. The United States would be able to liquidate its $65 billion debt almost overnight!

CONCLUSION

A revision of monetary systems may be well and good; but it only attacks the symptoms of a special economic malaise which can be defined roughly as an increasingly uncompetitive position in a global marketplace. This seems to be the affliction striking the United States today. Under any monetary system, a country should somehow strive to achieve a measure of economic equilibrium which, according to Kindleberger, requires *the maintenance of an open economy over a continuing period of time without severe unemployment*. The achievement of this objective should normally be reflected in continuing and overall international payments balances. The U.S. economy, in this restricted sense, is in a position of disequilibrium.

It is probable that the U.S. capital outflows will in time be turned into net inflows. But will they compensate for continuing current account deficits? In all likelihood, the country will have to still try to preserve at least a merchandise trade surplus to balance out all its international transactions. But is this possible, given the high cost problems facing the United States?

Do U.S. exports have a future, if the nation is shifting its economy into a capital-intensive, high technology gear ahead of other countries, as some experts maintain? The key to this answer is one of basic attitude. U.S. exporting, as a business enterprise, has a medieval sales approach. It is product oriented instead of being market oriented. This is simply an anachronistic approach in terms of the contemporary philosophy of organized business.

Big Business, after all, being nothing more than a productive, organizational and financial structure designed to efficiently harness resources for the satisfaction of human needs and wants, poses a very simple question: "What is the Market? We will satisfy it at a price!"

U.S. exporting has never shared this philosophy. Few companies actually maintain separate inventories for their export sales; and export markets are still traditionally regarded as outlets for surplus production. Local quotas are satisfied first; overseas requirements are satisfied last. It is true that many major American corporations are as active with their direct investments overseas as they are in the United States, and even more so. However, this has been at the expense of finished goods and even intermediary goods exports.

Indeed, American industry has historically responded to the erection of overseas import barriers (tariffs, etc.) with the direct investment route as a means of achieving foreign market penetration. This has proven a much easier route to success. There was therefore no need to emphasize a rapidly changing finished goods product line to compensate for shifting trade barriers abroad.

The paradoxical situation is that "Finished Manufactures" have enjoyed the greatest increase in their share of the total U.S. export product mix, from 15.1% in the 1871-1880 period to 57.1% in 1964, one of the last years in which the U.S. enjoyed a very large trade surplus. Finished goods exports rose, therefore, but not fast enough; and they were offset by a severe drop (from 22% to 6.5%) in exports of processed foods, crude foodstuffs and crude materials, (from 19.7% to 9.8% and 38.6% to 11.2% respectively). Semi-manufactured exports rose from 4.6% to 15.4% of the total export product mix between 1881 and 1964. Moreover, one must note that United States "Finished Manufactures" were and still are heavily concentrated in Commodity Group 7, i.e., Machinery and Transport Equipment, which are capital-intensive, technology dependent product lines.

This is in contrast to the practice of many countries, especially among the developing states, who manufacture numerous product lines exclusively for export. A full 50% of U.S. exports exist today only because they serve to meet the raw materials requirements of U.S. affiliated companies overseas and to meet the needs of our global defense system. The other 50% in export sales results from unsolicited orders and sporadic direct sales efforts.

U.S. exports, as a commercial enterprise, has yet to ask the question: "What does Europe want? What does Africa need? We will produce to meet those market demands." The United States remains the world's principal exporter. If the domestic economy requires high technology, capital-intensive products at this particular time, there is still no reason why low technology, labor-intensive product mixes, especially under government subsidies, cannot be produced to compete effectively in export markets.

It would appear that the nation has the diversified resources, the know-how, and a segmented labor force ranging from non-skilled unemployables to Ph. D.-level technicians and managers to operate the economy at different levels at the same time.

The development of a new monetary system alone will not be a cure-all for the economic ills of the United States and of the world. The transition from a labor-intensive, low technology society to a capital-intensive, high technology economy is a growing problem which may eventually engulf all countries; but for the United States, it is now causing certain dislocations. There is some localized un-employment, low productivity in many areas, and a degree of individual and col-lective social malaise as people seek new challenges to replace outworn occupa-tions, and society itself searches for a new manifest destiny to supplant older objectives of community and national effort.

The country is also plagued with inflation. Inflation is perhaps a side effect of these dislocations. Edwin L. Dale may have been correct when he stated, "A bitchy society will be an inflationary society."[19] No monetary system can cure that disease.

FOOTNOTES

1. *International Financial Statistics*, International Monetary Fund, March, 1955.

*It must be noted that the International Monetary Fund, through 1973, continues to report only member countries' financial positions. The statistics do not normally include data from the U.S.S.R., the People's Republic of China and other Communist bloc countries.

2. *International Financial Statistics*, International Monetary Fund, Volume XXIV, No. 9 (Sept., 1971), pp. 36-37. Total world exports were approximately $280 billion. After the United States with $43 billion, came West Germany with $34 billion, then the United Kingdom with $19 billion, followed by France with $18 billion. These rankings have not changed in 1972, and are not expected to change in 1973.

3. For a complete analysis, see *United States Balance of Payments, 1946-1972,* Economic Report of the President, January, 1973, U.S. Government Printing Office, 1973. Pp. 293 through 301.

4. The trade and payments deficits problems of the developing nations seem endemic to their overall problem of economic growth. The more developed Western European economics have historically preserved their surplus positions at the expense of net capital and gold outflows from the United States.

5. See Rostow, W.W., *The Stages of Economic Growth*, Cambridge University Press, London, 1960; and Hirschman, A.O., *The Strategy of Economic Development*, Yale University Press, Inc., Massachusetts, 1958.

6. See also *International Monetary Policy*, 2nd ed.; Scammell, MacMillan, and Co., London, 1961.

7. Ibid., p. 37.

8. Ibid., p. 18.

9. The IMF member countries have been benefitting since 1970 from the injection of Special Drawing Rights, almost $13 billion since 1970. However, the use of SDRs is not as diversified as conventional foreign exchange, gold and IMF reserves.

10. Ibid., p. 18.

11. Ibid., p. 37.

12. Ibid., p. 18. The U.S. began 1971 with a liquidity position of $15 billion.

The U.S. is committed to repaying the IMF $500 million in gold this year, and may lose another $1.5 billion in regular capital and gold outflows to other nations.

13.   See Footnotes 1 and 8.

14.   Ibid., p. 20.

15.   A brief review of America's declining gold position is included in "Foreign Trade + Liquidity + Devaluation," *Business Review*, Fairleigh Dickinson University, Vol. 7, No. 1 (Spring, 1967).

16.   It is obvious why the French wished the United States to agree to tripling the price of gold in 1960. The U.S. gold stock was $17.8 billion in 1960. Tripling the price of gold would have provided the U.S. with $53.4 billion in gold, enough to discharge the U.D. debt and still leave a comfortable reserve. Even England's Sir Roy Harrod agreed with the French suggestion.

17.   The IMF had 30 member countries in 1944. This has risen to 113 members in 1971.

18.   Devaluation tends to encourage exports and to limit imports. The inflationary impact of devaluation is partially dependent upon the reliance of the domestic economy upon the international trade sector.

19.   Edwin L. Dale, Jr., "A Bitchy Society Will Be an Inflationary Society," New York Times Magazine, Sept. 26, 1971, Page 18.

THE MECHANICS OF AN EXPORT OPERATION

BACKGROUND

The basis for all international transactions is the import-export operation. In a sense, the conduct of export order processing and expediting differs little from that of a domestic transaction except that there is greater reliance upon banks, forwarding and customs agents in the transfer of documents evidencing the shipment of goods.

There is therefore greater reliance upon the use of negotiable and financial instruments as collection tools, unless the exporter is shipping abroad on an open account basis. There has also emerged over the generations an almost universally accepted language and code of procedures to make sure that all parties to an international transaction fully understand the essence and substance of their intentions and actions.

Despite the fact that many exporters persist in making open account shipments, either on a freight collect or freight prepaid basis, this is not a recommended practice. It is true that both buyer and seller may be in frequent contact with one another; the fact remains that they are doing business across national borders. This can create difficulties, especially when the importer lives in a soft currency country which imposes restrictions on the convertibility of local currency into dollars for transmittance back to the exporter.

On an open account shipment, the exporter might have to accept payment in the importer's currency, or nothing at all. Operating through a bank, the exporter will at least know that his collection documents will be duly processed by the importing country's central bank and that he will be paid as dollars become available in the importing country's banking system. Thus, the great advantage of utilizing a formal system of export documentation and routing it through a bank lies in a fairly high assurance of payment.

Once the importer accepts the documents from his own correspondent bank, even if the payment terms are for an extended time period, the international banking channels through which the transaction has taken place automatically seeks to make a collection on behalf of the exporter.

This means that if the importer has funds deposited with his bank, his account may be debited to satisfy the amount outstanding owed to the exporter. If the funds on deposit are insufficient, the bank will press the importer for the collection on behalf of the exporter.

Banks dealing in international transactions consequently may have a somewhat exposed position, particularly if they are advancing funds to either the importer, or the exporter. By the same token, the positions of other intermediaries to an import-export transaction are almost equally exposed. Hence, banks, insurers, common carriers, forwarding agents, customs brokers, and even customs officials look to the documentation as prima facie evidence of performance in good faith by both buyer and seller.

The significance of this reliance upon the documentation means that no discrepancies should appear between statements and figures shown on the exporter's invoices and those appearing upon the bills of lading, bank drafts, and all other negotiable and/or financial instruments. Unless all the documents agree with one another, the exporter may not get paid and/or the importer may not receive his goods.

PARTIES TO THE TRANSACTION

Exporter: Insofar as an import-export operation is concerned, and from the point of view of the participating intermediaries and involved government agencies, the exporter is considered to be the "shipper of record" whose name appears on the ocean bill of lading or on the airway bill of lading. He is presumed to be the last party with title to the goods before passage of same to the importer (see Figures 3.1 and 3.2), or to his customers.

Importer: The importer is considered to be the "consignee," as his name appears on the bills of lading. One should bear in mind at this point that an airway bill (airway bill of lading) is not a negotiable instrument in international trade. Therefore, an exporter shipping via air freight on sight draft terms and wanting to make certain that the importer pays for the goods before claiming them at customs, must *consign* the goods to the importer's bank.

Consequently, on an air freight shipment under such conditions, the consignee becomes the importer's bank; the importer becomes the "ultimate consignee." In areas of the world where the airlines provide a COD service, the importer remains the consignee of record.

Forwarding Agent: This company acts on behalf of the exporter in arranging for

FIGURE 3.1

MOORE-McCORMACK LINES, INCORPORATED

American Republics Line — Robin Line

DELIVERING CARRIER — CAR NUMBER - REFERENCE

FORWARDING AGENT - SHIPPER'S REFERENCES: M.P. GOODKIN #35129 — FMC NO.: MOOREMCCORMACK LINES — EXPORT DEC. NO.

FMC No. 1325

C & J FORWARDING INC., 1000 BELLEVILLE TURNPIKE • KEARNY, N.J. 07032 — 8/3/72 — REF # 355

BILL OF LADING

X

SHIPPER: M.P. GOODKIN CO.-140-146 COIT STREET-IRVINGTON, N.J. 07111

CONSIGNED TO ORDER OF: ORDER OF SHIPPER

ADDRESS ARRIVAL NOTICE TO (Without liability to Carrier, see Clause 9)

DAMCO TRADING
P.O. BOX 4550
JOHANNESBURG, SOUTH AFRICA....

ALSO NOTIFY: FREIGHT SERVICES LTD.
DURBAN, SOUTH AFRICA.

SHIP	USA FLAG	PIER	PORT OF LOADING
MORMACCOVE	AM.	23RD ST. BKLYN	NEW YORK

PORT OF DISCHARGE: DURBAN — DESTINATION (If Transshipped) — O / D

PARTICULARS FURNISHED BY SHIPPER OF GOODS

MARKS AND NUMBERS	NO. OF PKGS.	SHIPPERS DESCRIPTION OF PACKAGES AND GOODS	GROSS WEIGHT KILOS	GROSS WEIGHT POUNDS
DAMCO TRADING P.O.BOX 4550 JOHANNESBURG SOUTH AFRICA VIA DURBAN #1/2-2/2	2	"FOR LOADING IN PIER TO PIER CONTAINER" "FRAGILE-SPECIAL STOW" CRATES: ASTRO CAMERAS 2024 220 VOLT -(ENLARGERS & REDUCERS) "FREIGHT PREPAID"	101CFT. "ON BOARD"	800# D 86

License G Dest. (3)
SOUTH AFRICA

Commodity not under validated license control to...
Commodity control list page 84 Dated 6/23/72

FREIGHT TO BE PREPAID IN U.S.A.

Notice: All rates apply from ships tackle at port of loading to end of ships tackle at port of discharge unless otherwise mentioned.

ITEM	WEIGHT (2)	CUBIC FEET (3)	@ RATE	FREIGHT CHARGES	TYPE RATE	TYPE BRKGE	TYPE CARGO	COMMODITY NO.	P.P. or COLL.	COLLECT PORT	ACCOUNT CODE
"U.S. Law prohibits disposition of these commodities to the Soviet block, Communist China, North Korea, Communist controlled areas of Viet Nam and Laos, Macao, Hong Kong, Cuba or Southern Rhodesia except as authorized by the U.S."											
				$							
				$							
				$							
				$							
				$							
				$							
				$							

Freight to be COLLECTED $ — Freight to be PREPAID $

RECEIVED from the shipper herein named, the goods or packages said to contain goods mentioned herein, in apparent good order and condition unless (Terms of this Bill of Lading Continued on Reverse Side Hereof)

In witness whereof, the Carrier by its Agent has signed THREE (3) BILLS OF LADING, all of the same tenor and date, one of which accomplished, the others to stand void.

MOORE-McCORMACK LINES, Incorporated

By ____________ FOR THE MASTER

8 4 72 — MONTH DAY YEAR — DATED AT NEW YORK

B/L NO. 79

FIGURE 3.2

NOT NEGOTIABLE

AMERFORD AIR CARGO

AIR WAYBILL
(AIR CONSIGNMENT NOTE)

ISSUED BY: AMERFORD INTERNATIONAL CORPORATION
218-01 MERRICK BLVD. JAMAICA, N. Y. 11413

AIC- EWR -685 130

AIR WAYBILL NUMBER

CIVIL AERONAUTICS BOARD APPROVED
INTERNATIONAL AIR FREIGHT FORWARDER

DESTINATION (AIRPORT OF)
BRU

CONSIGNED TO	STREET ADDRESS	CITY AND COUNTRY
KODAK 1800 KONINGSLO VILVORDE		BELGIUM

ALSO NOTIFY

NO. OF PACKAGES	METHOD OF PACKING	NATURE AND QUANTITY OF GOODS	MARKS AND NUMBERS	DIMENSIONS OR VOLUME	GROSS WEIGHT (Specify Kilos or Lbs.)
ONE PIECE		DIRECT PROCESOR	AS ADDRESSED		35#
		REF: 35876			
		N.D.R. PER PAR 30.55 F.R.			

These commodities licensed by the United States for ultimate destination BELGIUM   Diversion contrary to United States law prohibited.

SHIPPER'S DECLARED VALUE (Specify Currency)	METHOD OF ROUTING AND CHARGES — Agreed stopping places are those places (other than the places of departure and destination) shown under Air Carriage, and/or those places above in carriers' timetables as scheduled stopping places for the route. SEE CONDITIONS ON REVERSE HEREOF.	SHIPPER MUST INSERT
For Customs	For Carriage		
$234.00	MF		ITEM NUMBER.
			CHARGEABLE TO SELF

AIR CARRIAGE			CHARGEABLE WEIGHT (Specify Kilos or Lbs.)	RATE CLASSI-FICATION	RATES	PREPAID		CHARGEABLE TO CONSIGNEE		
								CUR-RENCY	AMOUNTS IN CURRENCIES AS CHARGED	AMOUNTS IN CURRENCY AT DESTINATION
Departure (Airport of) EWR VIA JFK	(Address of First Carrier)									
1. To BRU	First Carrier				.84			US$	$29.40	
2. To	Carrier									
3. To	Carrier									
4. Valuation Charge From	To									
5. Valuation Charge From	To									
6. INSURANCE: AMOUNT REQUESTED (Specify Currency) $234.00					.385			US$	$ 0.90	
7. At Origin										
8.		AFT						US$	$ 6.15	
9.										
10.		TSC						US$	$ 4.00	
11. In Transit										
12. At Destination										
13.										
14.										
15.										
16. C.O.D. FEE										
17. SHIPPER'S C.O.D.										

If the shipper has requested insurance as provided for on line 6 above, shipment is insured in the amount specified by the shipper (recovery being limited to actual loss) in accordance with Paragraph 8 on the reverse hereof. Insurance is payable to shipper unless another payee is designated in writing by the shipper.

OTHER CHARGES (SPECIFY)

SHIPPER'S C.O.D. IN WORDS

TOTALS $40.45

The shipper certifies that the particulars on the face hereof are correct and agrees to the CONDITIONS ON THE REVERSE HEREOF.

Carrier certifies above described goods were received for carriage SUBJECT TO THE CONDITIONS ON THE REVERSE HEREOF, the goods then being in apparent good order and condition except as noted hereon.

Name of Shipper M.P. GOODKIN CO.,
Address 140-146 COIT STREET
IRVINGTON, N.J.
Signature of Shipper 33-5-2892   V.C.
By Broker/Agent

Executed on 10/24/72 (Date)   At EWR N.J. (Place)
Name and Address of Issuing Carrier's Agent   R. SHRAMEK
Signature of Issuing Carrier or its Agent

PRINTED IN U.S.A.

Copies 1, 2 and 3 of This Air Waybill Are Originals and Have the Same Validity.

AIC- EWR -685 130

5 (Original Invoice)

an ocean or air booking for the exporter's goods. He will also make up and assemble the necessary documentation for submission to the bank in the exporter's name. The forwarding agent, known too as a "freight forwarder," operates
on a fee basis from the exporter and receives an additional percentage of the
freight charges from the common carrier. The fees vary, ranging from $15.00 to
$25.00, plus documentation charges.

Exporters generally estimate forwarding charges on the basis of a total of $50.00
per bill of lading for ocean freight shipments and $25.00 for air freight ship-
ments, particularly on shipments to countries whose laws require an extraordinary amount of documentation, (Figure 3.3). A freight forwarder must be licensed by the Federal Maritime Commission to handle ocean freight, and by the
International Air Transport Association (IATA) to handle air freight.

Consolidation Services: Larger forwarders offer exporters a consolidation service, either containerized or via igloo (air freight container). In this case, the
exporter's goods are traveling on a single bill of lading since they have been
"consolidated" with those of several other exporters on the same vessel. In effect, the exporter has now consigned his goods to the forwarder whose own
name appears on the bill of lading. The consignee becomes the customs broker
on the importing side. Again, if the exporter is shipping via air on a sight draft
basis, and neither the forwarder (customs broker) nor the airline offers a COD
service, the exporter must now instruct the forwarder in writing to further consign the goods to a designated bank upon their arrival.

Customs Broker: Many forwarders act on behalf of importers as well, provided
they possess the necessary government licenses. Their functions are strictly to
clear the goods through customs and eventually have them delivered to the importer's warehouse. Importers may designate in their shipping instructions a
particular customs broker to whom the goods are to first be shipped. The broker
then becomes the consignee or actual importer; the importing buyer now becomes the ultimate consignee.

In all cases where there are double and/or sequential consignees, their names
should appear wherever possible on the documentation, and the exporter must
make it explicitly clear who is liable for payment on the documentation.

Bank: It is recommended that the exporter use the services of a bank having a
foreign or international department. He should also maintain an account at that
bank. Such a bank is bound to have branch banks or correspondent banks in
most trading areas throughout the world.

Correspondent banks maintain reciprocating foreign exchange balances for currency conversion and transmittance purposes. This enables them to credit and
debit the exporter's and importer's accounts respectively.

The Caracas branch of the Chase Manhattan Bank is actually Chase's correspondent bank for import-export transactions for which both seller and buyer decide

FIGURE 3.3

FMC No. 1325

C & J FORWARDING INC.

International Ocean Freight Forwarders

(201) 997-4333

C
&
J

160 IMLAY STREET
BROOKLYN, N.Y. 11231
(212) 852-5566

In making remittance please refer to Our Invoice

M.P. GOODKIN CO.
140-146 COIT STREET
IRVINGTON, NEW JERSEY 07111

358

Date   AUG.11,1972

Our Ref: 355

Your Ref: INV.#35129

Steamer MORMACCOVE	
From NEW YORK	
To DURBAN	
Bill of Lading No. 79	

Description of shipment

2 CRATES:ASTRO CAMERAS-800#
"PIER TO PIER CONTAINER"

TERMS CASH.—THESE ITEMS REPRESENT PRINCIPALLY CASH PAID OUT OR TO BE PAID OUT BY US FOR YOUR ACCOUNT. PROMPT REMITTANCE IN U.S. FUNDS IS THEREFORE RESPECTFULLY REQUESTED.

ENCLOSURES:

_____ ORIGINAL B/L
_8_ COPIES OF B/L
_____ CONSULAR INVOICE
_____ CERTIFICATE OF ORIGIN
_1_ DURN.INSURANCE CERTIFICATE
_2_ COMMERCIAL INVOICE
_____ PACKING LIST
_1_ BANKING, DOCUMENTATION

BILL OF CHARGES	
Inland Freight	
Cartage –PICK UP & UNLOADING	$50.50
Ocean Freight	373.70
Preparation of Consular Docs./Cert. of Origin	10.00
Blanks, etc.	
Consular Fees	
Insurance	60.00
Forwarding Charges & BANKING	20.00
Customs Clearance	
Export Packing	
Whse. Hndl/Storage	
Exchange	
TOTAL	$514.20

SHIPMENTS HANDLED ONLY IN ACCORDANCE WITH TERMS AND CONDITIONS ON REVERSE SIDE, HEREOF.

that this particular bank should be employed. If the importer in Caracas banks at Banco Popular, and the exporter banks at Chase in New York, and both insist on using their respective banks, then Chase, New York, and Banco Popular, Caracas, will act as correspondent banks of one another for this transaction, assuming they already have such a correspondent relationship, or providing that they agree to establish such a relationship. If a correspondent relationship between the two banks is unfeasible at that point in time, either bank will usually locate a third party bank with whom both original banks have an existing correspondent arrangement. In the above example, Chase's Caracas branch, or, Banco Popular's New York branch, could assume a correspondent role; or, either exporter or importer could designate an independent bank with whom they already do business.

Insurer: Either the exporter or the importer must cover the goods with insurance. Coverage is generally on the basis of 110% of the cost, insurance, freight (CIF) value as indicated on the exporter's invoices if the exporter is carrying the insurance charges. The exporter prepays the insurance mainly on CIF shipments. However, it is a good idea for the exporter to maintain a covering policy, known as an "open cargo policy," on *all* his shipments, even if the importer expressly states that he is insuring the goods.

Comprehensive and overall coverage by the exporter will eliminate any possible liability resulting from a general average situation. This is a condition in which the vessel suffers damage and/or is destroyed. The shippers of record become automatically liable for the replacement costs of the damaged parts and/or of the vessel itself, unless it can be shown that the exporter shipped his goods FOB Factory or FAS or FOB Vessel, freight and insurance "collect," with title changing *before* the vessel embarked on its voyage.

Common Carrier: The transportation of goods takes place via truck, air freight, ocean freight, or through any combination of the above. The transportation of goods has become a professional field of its own in the past decade, with complexities created by the advent of more sophisticated modes of physical distribution, eg., containerization, igloo shipments, piggy back shipments, etc. A treatise on the ways and means of international transportation could fill several volumes. The exporter should only be made aware here that the liability of common carriers engaged in international commerce is limited to that of a bailee having physical possession and therefore custody of the goods (see Insurance).

A bill of lading is essentially a contract between the exporter and the common carrier or between the importer and the common carrier, depending upon who has title to the goods along with other factors. It therefore behooves the exporter to read the contractual provisions in the bills of lading and then consult the specialized legal counsel as to his rights and obligations. Such counseling is especially important on container shipments that involve a combination of truck-air or truck-ocean shipments with door-to-door service being provided by the carrier.

INSURANCE

Liability by ocean carriers in international commerce generally revolves around the Carriage of Goods by Sea Act of 1936, other U.S. Statutes, and valid clauses in the carrier's contract of affreightment (Tariff and bill of lading). Marine insurance becomes necessary because of the limits placed on any carrier's liability as regards merchandise damaged or destroyed while in its possession. The governing act of 1936 is reprinted at the end of this chapter for reference purposes.

Practically all letters of credit specify that marine insurance must be obtained and that a certificate of insurance must be furnished along with other required documents before the money can become available to shipper. The obvious exception is Brazil which allows FOB quotations on most transactions with insurance to be carried by the importer.

There are some general terms which are important in marine shipments. "General average" denotes a loss, damage, or expense that is incurred for the *general benefit* of vessel, her freight, money and cargo; a "particular average" is a partial loss or damage *accidentally* sustained by either cargo or vessel.

The effect on the shipper of a general average is that the vessel can expect contributions from other interests such as cargo owners (the exporter) on the vessel, whereas in the case of a particular average, the loss and damage to the cargo or the ship falls on its owner who in turn may collect under his marine insurance, if he has any.

Carriers do not normally provide any automatic insurance coverage to its shippers. They only provide a standard "Carriage of Goods by Sea Act" contract of affreightment. However, carriers offering consolidation and/or containerized services often do offer a group policy to exporters upon request. This benefits the small or occasional exporter who may be unable to afford his own Open Cargo policy.

Group Insurance Coverages

The policy taken by those carriers covers the goods only while they are in the care, custody and control of the carrier and/or its agents or its independent contract pick-up and delivery carriers, except in very special instances subject to advance negotiation.

There are two principal coverages available for general merchandise (not counting War and Strikes, Riots & Civil Commotions Insurance):

(1)   **Marine Risks:** This is to insure the shipper against most of the causes of loss for which the carrier cannot be held liable. Perils insured against are as follows:

        Perils of the Seas

Fire and Explosion
Collision, Stranding and Sinking
Jettisons, Assailing Thieves and Barratry
Latent Defects of the Vessel
Faults or Errors in Navigation and/or Management of the Vessel
General Average and Salvage Charges

Marine Risk insurance protects goods while on shore against the following:

Fire, Lightning, Sprinkler Leakage and Explosion
Hail, Flood, Earthquake and Windstorm
Landslide, Volcanic Eruption and Avalanche
Subsidence of Docks and Structures

Goods are generally insured for their CIF value + 10%. That value must be de-clared by the shipper.

The coverage is against physical loss only, and excludes any kind of "loss of mar-ket" claim or claims caused by delay regardless of what caused the delay. The coverage also excludes War, Strikes, Riots and Civil Commotions losses, although this insurance can be obtained for an additional premium.

In order to get the complete package, the shipper need only request in writing (on the bill of lading or in a letter): "Insure against 'Marine Risks' for $ (+War, S.R. & C.C.)"

(2) **All Risks:** The key clause of this insurance reads: "To cover against all risks of physical loss from any external cause whatsoever..."

Besides "loss of market" or other consequential loss and damage due to delay (regardless of what caused the delay), War and Strikes, Riots & Civil Commotions are also excluded according to the terms of the American Institute of Marine Underwriters Warranties. (Incidentally, these ex-clusions are found in all U.S. and British cargo insurance policies.)

Shipper requests: "Insure against 'All Risks' for $ (+War, S.R. & C.C.)"

The following merchandise is not to be accepted for "All Risks" Insurance, and special contracts must be requested. It is then recommended that the exporter negotiate directly with his insurer.

Aircraft, Boats, Automobiles, and other self-propelled craft and vehicles.
Animals, Birds, Cattle, Livestock and other living creatures.
Candy, Confectionery
Chilled, Frozen or otherwise Refrigerated Cargo. (Subject to special conditions)

China, Glass, Enamelware, Porcelain and similar fragile articles or fixtures.
Dangerous Chemicals
Fresh Fruits, Vegetables and other Perishable Foods. (Unless in refrigerated
containers subject to special conditions)
Gold, Platinum, Silver and other Precious Metals and Bullion.
Grains, Flour and Meal in bags or bulk.
Iron and Steel Angles, Bars, Girders, Pipe, Sheets, Wire, Tinplate and
similar Ferrous Products.
Jewelry, Watches, Furs and Precious Stones — cut and uncut.
Liquid products in glass containers — unboxed.
Money, Notes, Securities, Stock Certificates and other Valuable Papers.
Nuclear Fissionable, Fusionable and otherwise Radioactive Materials.
Paintings, Statues, and other Works of Art.
Refrigerators, Stoves, Washing Machines and other Major Appliances.
Sugar.
Used and/or Reconditioned Machinery, Household and Personal Effects
and Used Goods and/or Merchandise of any kind.

Other specialized insurance coverages are as follows:

Refrigerated Goods: This coverage is against the perils listed in "Marine Risks"
above, but partial losses are payable only in event of sinking, stranding, fire, or
collision. Coverage is also provided against deterioration losses caused by me-
chanical breakdown of the vessel or the refrigeration machinery, provided the
breakdown has lasted for twenty-four hours or more.

Goods which are not in mechanically refrigerated containers may not be insured
against deterioration however caused.

The shipper requests: "Twenty-four hour Reefer Clauses (+War, S.R. & C.C.)"

War and Strikes, Riots and Civil Commotions: This coverage is special. Insurance
companies could be entirely wiped out in event of a war and they protected
themselves by the formation of a separate War Risks Exchange which of course
means that this coverage is, first of all, in standard wording; and secondly, it is
always treated separately.

CARRIAGE OF GOODS BY SEA ACT
[Public—No. 521—74th Congress]
(Approved April 16, 1936, Effective July 15, 1936)

AN ACT

Be it enacted by the Senate and House of Representatives of the United States of America
in Congress assembled, That every bill of lading or similar document of title which is evidence of a contract for the carriage of goods by sea to or from ports of the United States,
in foreign trade, shall have effect subject to the provisions of this Act.

TITLE I

Section 1 When used in this Act—
(a) The term "carrier" includes the owner or the charterer who enters into a contract of
carriage with a shipper.

(b) The term "contract of carriage" applies only to contracts of carriage covered by a bill of lading or any similar document of title, insofar as such document relates to the carriage of goods by sea, including any bill of lading or any similar document as aforesaid issued under or pursuant to a charter party from the moment at which such bill of lading or similar document of title regulates the relations between a carrier and a holder of the same.

(c) The term "goods" includes goods, wares, merchandise, and articles of every kind whatsoever, except live animals and cargo which by the contract of carriage is stated as being carried on deck and is so carried.

(d) The term "ship" means any vessel used for the carriage of goods by sea.

(e) The term "carriage of goods" covers the period from the time when the goods are loaded on to the time when they are discharged from the ship.

RISKS

Sec. 2. Subject to the provisions of Section 6, under every contract of carriage of goods by sea, the carrier in relation to the loading, handling, stowage, carriage, custody, care, and discharge of such goods, shall be subject to the responsibilities and liabilities and entitled to the rights and immunities hereinafter set forth.

RESPONSIBILITIES AND LIABILITIES

Sec. 3. (1) The carrier shall be bound, before and at the beginning of the voyage, to exercise due diligence to—

(a) Make the ship seaworthy;

(b) Properly man, equip, and supply the ship;

(c) Make the holds, refrigerating and cooling chambers, and all other parts of the ship in which goods are carried, fit and safe for their reception, carriage, and preservation.

(2) The carrier shall properly and carefully load, handle, stow, carry, keep, care for, and discharge the goods carried.

(3) After receiving the goods into his charge the carrier, or the master or agent of the carrier, shall, on demand of the shipper, issue to the shipper a bill of lading showing among other things—

(a) The leading marks necessary for identification of the goods as the same are furnished in writing by the shipper before the loading of such goods starts, provided such marks are stamped or otherwise shown clearly upon the goods if uncovered, or on the cases or coverings in which such goods are contained, in such a manner as should ordinarily remain legible until the end of the voyage.

(b) Either the number of packages or pieces, or the quantity or weight, as the case may be, as furnished in writing by the shipper.

(c) The apparent order and condition of the goods: Provided, That no carrier, master, or agent of the carrier, shall be bound to state or show in the bill of lading any marks, number, quanity, or weight which he has reasonable ground for suspecting not accurately to represent the goods actually received, or which he has had no reasonable means of checking.

(4) Such a bill of lading shall be prima facie evidence of the receipt by the carrier of the goods as therein described in accordance with paragraphs (3) (a), (b), and (c), of this section: Provided, That nothing in this Act shall be construed as repealing or limiting the application of any part of the Act, as amended, entitled "An Act relating to bills of lading in interstate and foreign commerce," approved August 29, 1916 (U. S. C., Title 49, Secs. 81–124), commonly known as the "Pomerene Bills of Lading Act."

(5) The shipper shall be deemed to have guaranteed to the carrier the accuracy at the time of shipment of the marks, number, quantity, and weight, as furnished by him; and the shipper shall indemnify the carrier against all loss, damages, and expenses arising or resulting from inaccuracies in such particulars. The right of the carrier to such indemnity shall in no way limit his responsibility and liability under the contract of carriage to any person other than the shipper.

(6) Unless notice of loss or damage and the general nature of such loss or damage be given in writing to the carrier or his agent at the port of discharge before or at the time of the removal of the goods into the custody of the person entitled to delivery thereof under the contract of carriage, such removal shall be prima facie evidence of the delivery by the carrier of the goods as described in the bill of lading. If the loss or damage is not apparent, the notice must be given within three days of the delivery.

Said notice of loss or damage may be endorsed upon the receipt for the goods given by the person taking delivery thereof.

The notice in writing need not be given if the state of the goods has at the time of their receipt been the subject of joint survey or inspection.

In any event the carrier and the ship shall be discharged from all liability in respect of loss or damage unless suit is brought within one year after delivery of the goods or the date when the goods should have been delivered: Provided, That if a notice of loss or damage, either apparent or concealed, is not given as provided for in this section, that fact shall not affect or prejudice the right of the shipper to bring suit within one year after the delivery of the goods or the date when the goods should have been delivered.

In the case of any actual or apprehended loss or damage the carrier and the receiver shall give all reasonable facilities to each other for inspecting and tallying the goods.

(7) After the goods are loaded the bill of lading to be issued by the carrier, master, or agent of the carrier to the shipper shall, if the shipper so demands, be a "shipped" bill of lading: Provided, That if the shipper shall have previously taken up any document of title to such goods, he shall surrender the same as against the issue of the "shipped" bill of lading, but at the option of the carrier such document of title may be noted at the port of shipment by the carrier, master, or agent with the name or names of the ship or ships upon which the goods have been shipped and the date or dates of shipment, and when so noted the same shall for the purpose of this section be deemed to constitute a "shipped" bill of lading.

(8) Any clause, covenant, or agreement in a contract of carriage relieving the carrier or the ship from liability for loss or damage to or in connection with the goods, arising from negligence, fault, or failure in the duties and obligations provided in this section, or lessening such liability otherwise than as provided in this Act, shall be null and void and of no effect. A benefit of insurance in favor of the carrier, or similar clause, shall be deemed to be a clause relieving the carrier from liability.

RIGHTS AND IMMUNITIES

Sec. 4 (1) Neither the carrier nor the ship shall be liable for loss or damage arising or resulting from unseaworthiness unless caused by want of due diligence on the part of the carrier to make the ship seaworthy, and to secure that the ship is properly manned, equipped, and supplied, and to make the holds, refrigerating and cool chambers, and all other parts of the ship in which goods are carried fit and safe for their reception, carriage, and preservation in accordance with the provisions of paragraph (1) of Section 3. Whenever loss or damage has resulted from unseaworthiness, the burden of proving the exercise of due diligence shall be on the carrier or other persons claiming exemption under this section.

(2) Neither the carrier nor the ship shall be responsible for loss or damage arising or resulting from—

(a) Act, neglect, or default of the master, mariner, pilot, or the servants of the carrier in the navigation or in the management of the ship;

(b) Fire, unless caused by the actual fault or privity of the carrier;

(c) Perils, dangers, and accidents of the sea or other navigable waters;

(d) Act of God;

(e) Act of war;

(f) Act of public enemies;

(g) Arrest or restraint of princes, rulers, or people, or seizure under legal process;

(h) Quarantine restrictions;

(i) Act or omission of the shipper or owner of the goods, his agent or representative;

(j) Strikers or lockouts or stoppage or restraint of labor from whatever cause, whether partial or general: Provided, that nothing herein contained shall be construed to relieve a carrier from responsibility for the carrier's own acts;

(k) Riots and civil commotions;

(l) Saving or attempting to save life or property at sea;

(m) Wastage in bulk or weight or any other loss or damage arising from inherent defect, quality, or vice of the goods;

(n) Insufficiency of packing;

(o) Insufficiency or inadequacy of marks;

(p) Latent defects not discoverable by due diligence; and

(q) Any other cause arising without the actual fault and privity of the carrier and without the fault or neglect of the agents or servants of the carrier, but the burden of proof shall be on the person claiming the benefit of the exception to show that neither the actual fault or privity of the carrier nor the fault or neglect of the agents or servants of the carrier contributed to the loss or damage.

(3) The shipper shall not be responsible for loss or damage sustained by the carrier or the ship arising or resulting from any cause without the act, fault, or neglect of the shipper, his agents, or his servants.

(4) Any deviation in saving or attempting to safe life or property at sea, or any reasonable deviation shall not be deemed to be an infringement or breach of this Act or of the contract of carriage, and the carrier shall not be liable for any loss or damage resulting therefrom: Provided, however, That if the deviation is for the purpose of loading or unloading cargo or passengers it shall, prima facie, be regarded as unreasonable.

(5) Neither the carrier nor the ship shall in any event be or become liable for any loss or damage to or in connection with the transportation of goods in an amount exceeding $500 per package lawful money of the United States, or in case of goods not shipped in packages, per customary freight unit, or the equivalent of that sum in other currency, unless the nature and value of such goods have been declared by the shipper before shipment and inserted in the bill of lading. This declaration, if embodied in the bill of lading, shall be prima facie evidence, but shall not be conclusive on the carrier.

By agreement between the carrier, master, or agent of the carrier, and the shipper another maximum amount than that mentioned in this paragraph may be fixed: Provided, That such maximum shall not be less than the figure above named. In no event shall the carrier be liable for more than the amount of damage actually sustained.

Neither the carrier nor the ship shall be responsible in any event for loss or damage to or in connection with the transportation of the goods if the nature or value thereof has been knowingly and fraudulently misstated by the shipper in the bill of lading.

(6) Goods of an inflammable, explosive, or dangerous nature to the shipment whereof the carrier, master or agent of the carrier, has not consented with knowledge of their nature and character, may at any time before discharge be landed at any place or destroyed or rendered innocuous by the carrier without compensation, and the shipper of such goods shall be liable for all damages and expenses directly or indirectly arising out of or resulting from such shipment. If any such goods shipped with such knowledge and consent shall become a danger to the ship or cargo, they may in like manner be landed at any place, or destroyed or rendered innocuous by the carrier without liability on the part of the carrier except to general average, if any.

Surrender of Rights and Immunities and Increase or Responsibilities and Liabilities

Sec. 5. A carrier shall be at liberty to surrender in whole or in part all or any of his rights and immunities or to increase any of his responsibilities and liabilities under this Act, provided such surrender or increase shall be embodied in the bill of lading issued to the shipper.

The provisions of this Act shall not be applicable to charter parties; but if bills of lading are issued in the case of a ship under a charter party, they shall comply with the terms of this Act. Nothing in this Act shall be held to prevent the insertion on a bill of lading of any lawful provision regarding general average.

Special Conditions

Sec. 6. Notwithstanding the provision of the preceding sections, a carrier, master or agent of the carrier, and a shipper shall, in regard to any particular goods be at liberty to enter into any agreement in any terms as to the responsibility and liability of the carrier for such goods, and as to the rights and immunities of the carrier in respect of such goods, or his obligation as to seaworthiness (so far as the stipulation regarding seaworthiness is not contrary to public policy), or the care or diligence of his servants or agents in regard to the loading, handling, stowage, carriage, custody, care, and discharge of the goods carried by sea: Provided, That in this case no bill of lading has been or shall be issued and that the terms agreed shall be embodied in a receipt which shall be a nonnegotiable document and shall be marked as such.

Any agreement so entered into shall have full legal effect: Provided, That this section shall not apply to ordinary commercial shipments made in the ordinary course of trade but only to other shipments where the character or condition of the property to be carried or the circumstances, terms, and conditions under which the carriage is to be performed are such as reasonably to justify a special agreement.

Sec. 7. Nothing contained in this Act shall prevent a carrier or a shipper from entering into any agreement, stipulation, condition, reservation, or exemption as to the responsibility and liability of the carrier or the ship for the loss or damage to or in connection with the custody and care and handling of goods prior to the loading on and subsequent to the discharge from the ship on which the goods are carried by sea.

Sec. 8. The provisions of this Act shall not affect the rights and obligations of the carrier under the provisions of the Shipping Act, 1916, or under the provisions of Sections 4281 to 4289, inclusive, of the Revised Statutes of the United States, or of any amendments thereto; or under the provisions of any other enactment for the time being in force relating to the limitation of the liability of the owners of seagoing vessels.

TITLE II

Section 9. Nothing contained in this Act shall be construed as permitting a common carrier by water to discriminate between competing shippers similarly placed in time and circumstances, either (a) with respect to their right to demand and receive bills of lading subject to the provisions of this Act; or (b) when issuing such bills of lading, either in the surrender of any of the carrier's rights and immunities or in the increase of any of the carrier's responsibilities and liabilities pursuant to Section 5, Title I, of this Act; or (c) in any other way prohibited by the Shipping Act, 1916, as amended.

Section 10. Section 25 of the Interstate Commerce Act is hereby amended by adding the following proviso at the end of paragraph 4 thereof: "Provided, however, That insofar as any bill of lading authorized hereunder relates to the carriage of goods by sea, such bill of lading shall be subject to the provisions of the Carriage of Goods by Sea Act."

Sec. 11. Where under the customs of any trade the weight of any bulk cargo inserted in the bill of lading is a weight ascertained or accepted by a third party other than the carrier or the shipper, and the fact that the weight is so ascertained or accepted is stated in the bill of lading, then, notwithstanding anything in this Act, the bill of lading shall not be deemed to be prima facie evidence against the carrier of the receipt of goods of the weight so inserted in the bill of lading, and the accuracy thereof at the time of shipment shall not be deemed to have been guaranteed by the shipper.

Sec. 12. Nothing in this Act shall be construed as superseding any part of the Act entitled "An Act relating to navigation of vessels, bills of lading, and to certain obligations, duties, and rights in connection with the carriage of property", approved February 13, 1893, or of any other law which would be applicable in the absence of this Act, insofar as they relate to the duties, responsibilities, and liabilities of the ship or carrier prior to the time when the goods are loaded on or after the time they are discharged from the ship.

Sec. 13. This Act shall apply to all contracts for carriage of goods by sea to or from ports of the United States in foreign trade. As used in this Act the term "United States" includes its districts, territories, and possessions: Provided, however, That the Phillipine Legislature may by law exclude its application to transportation to or from ports of the Philippine Islands. The term "foreign trade" means the transportation of goods between the ports of the United States and ports of foreign countries. Nothing in this Act shall be held to apply to contracts for carriage of goods by sea between any port of the United States or its possessions, and any other port of the United States or its possessions: Provided, however, That any bill of lading or similar document of title which is evidence of a contract for the carriage of goods by sea between such ports, containing an express statement that it shall be subject to the provisions of this Act, shall be subjected hereto as fully as if subject hereto by the express provisions of this Act: Provided further, That every bill of lading or similar document of title which is evidence of a contract for the carriage of goods by sea from ports of the United States, in foreign trade, shall contain a statement that it shall have effect subject to the provisions of this Act.

Sec. 14. Upon the certification of the Secretary of Commerce that the foreign commerce of the United States in its competition with that of foreign nations is prejudiced by the provisions, or any of them, of Title I of this Act, or by the laws of any foreign country or countries relating to the carriage of goods by sea, the President of the United States may, from time to time, by proclamation, suspend any or all provisions of Title I of this Act for such periods of time or indefinitely as may be designated in the proclamation. The President may at any time rescind such suspension of Title I hereof, and any provisions thereof which may have been suspended shall thereby be reinstated and again apply to contracts thereafter made for the carriage of goods by sea. Any proclamation of suspension or rescission of any such suspension shall take effect on a date named therein, which date shall be not less than ten days from the issue of the proclamation.

Any contract for the carriage of goods by sea, subject to the provisions of this Act, effective during any period when Title I hereof, or any part thereof, is suspended, shall be subject to all provisions of law now or hereafter applicable to that part of Title I which may have thus been suspended.

Sec. 15. This Act shall take effect ninety days after the date of its approval; but nothing in this Act shall apply during a period not to exceed one year following its approval to any contract for the carriage of goods by sea, made before the date on which this Act is approved, nor to any bill of lading or similar document of title issued, whether before or after such data of approval in pursuance of any such contract as aforesaid.

Sec. 16. This Act may be cited as the "Carriage of Goods by Sea Act."

Approved, April 16, 1936.

EXPORT DOCUMENTATON

The accompanying figures will provide the exporter with an idea of what a complete set of shipping documents executed on letter of credit terms looks like. These sample documents have been reproduced from an actual export shipment, and are further defined at the end of this chapter under "Foreign Trade Terms."

The reader must keep in mind that although the freight forwarder ordinarily "cuts the documentation," as their preparation is called, the obligation is upon the exporter to ensure that the information contained therein is true and correct.

The crucial document for export control purposes, at least in the United States, is the Export Declaration (Figure 3.4), a preprinted, official form in which the exporter describes the goods by generic name and by their appropriate Schedule B number(s), along with their value. The Export Declaration must also indicate whether or not a special export license is required. This document is lodged with U.S. Customs *before* the goods are shipped, and does not become part of the documentation that follows the merchandise to its destination. The reverse side of each Export Declaration contains the text of the U.S. laws and regulations governing the proper execution of the form.

The exact forms of documentation needed to export goods vary with each shipment, and from country to country. Updated information must be provided by the exporter's forwarder.

The routing of the exporter's documentation is an uncomplicated matter, and a time sequence of procedures is indicated below:

1. Exporter completes the commercial invoices.

FIGURE 3.4

Form 7525-V
(Rev. July 1962)
(See Instructions on Reverse Side)

U.S. DEPARTMENT OF COMMERCE
BUREAU OF THE CENSUS—BUREAU OF INTERNATIONAL COMMERCE

SHIPPER'S EXPORT DECLARATION

OF SHIPMENTS FROM THE UNITED STATES

Export Shipments Are Subject To U.S. Customs Inspection

READ CAREFULLY THE INSTRUCTIONS ON BACK TO AVOID DELAY AT SHIPPING POINT

For shipments to foreign countries, the export declaration (*a*) must be presented to and authenticated by the Collector of Customs before the goods are placed on pier or dock or other place of loading for the purpose of exporting by water or air; (*b*) must be presented to and authenticated by the Collector prior to exportation where the goods are exported by other means.

Declarations Should Be Typewritten Or Prepared In Ink

Form approved. Budget Bureau No. 41-R397.5.

CONFIDENTIAL For use solely for official purposes authorized by the Secretary of Commerce. Use for unauthorized purposes is not permitted. (Title 15, Sec. 30.5 (b) C.F.R.; 50 U.S.C. App., 2026c.)

Customs Authentication (For Customs use only.)

FILE NO. (For Customs use only.)

Do Not Use This Area	District	Port	Country (For customs use only)

1. FROM (*U.S. Port of Export*)

2. METHOD OF TRANSPORTATION (*check one*): ☐ Vessel (incl. ferry) ☐ Air ☐ Other (*Specify*) ____

2a. EXPORTING CARRIER (*If vessel, give name of ship, flag and pier number. If air, give name of airline.*)

3. EXPORTER (*Principal or seller—licensee*) ADDRESS (*Number, street, place, state*)

4. AGENT OF EXPORTER (*Forwarding agent*) ADDRESS (*Number, street, place, state*)

5. ULTIMATE CONSIGNEE ADDRESS (*Place, country*)

6. INTERMEDIATE CONSIGNEE ADDRESS (*Place, country*)

7. FOREIGN PORT OF UNLOADING (*For vessel and air shipments only*)

8. PLACE AND COUNTRY OF ULTIMATE DESTINATION (*Not place of transshipment*)

(9) MARKS AND NOS.	(10) NUMBER AND KIND OF PACKAGES, DESCRIPTION OF COMMODITIES, EXPORT LICENSE NUMBER, EXPIRATION DATE (OR GENERAL LICENSE SYMBOL) (Describe commodities in sufficient detail to permit verification of the Schedule B commodity numbers assigned. Do not use general terms. Insert required license information on line below description of each item)	(11) SHIPPING (*Gross*) WEIGHT IN POUNDS [a] (required for vessel and air shipments only)	(12) SPECIFY "D" OR "F" [b]	(13) SCHEDULE B COMMODITY NO.	(14) NET QUANTITY IN SCHEDULE B UNITS (*State unit*)	(15) VALUE AT U. S. PORT OF EXPORT (Selling price or cost if not sold, including inland freight, insurance and other charges to U. S. port of export) (*Nearest whole dollar; omit cents figures*)

16. WAYBILL OR MANIFEST No. (*of Exporting Carrier*)

17. DATE OF EXPORTATION (*Not required for shipments by vessel*)

18. THE UNDERSIGNED HEREBY AUTHORIZES ____ (Name and address—Number, street, place, State)
TO ACT AS FORWARDING AGENT FOR EXPORT CONTROL AND CUSTOMS PURPOSES.

EXPORTER ____ BY (DULY AUTHORIZED OFFICER OR EMPLOYEE) ____

▶ 19. I CERTIFY THAT ALL STATEMENTS MADE AND ALL INFORMATION CONTAINED IN THIS EXPORT DECLARATION ARE TRUE AND CORRECT. I AM AWARE OF THE PENALTIES PROVIDED FOR FALSE REPRESENTATION. (*See Paragraphs I (c), (e), on reverse side.*)

Signature ____ (Duly authorized officer or employee of exporter or named forwarding agent)

For ____ (Name of corporation or firm, and capacity of signer; e.g., secretary, export manager, etc.)

Address ____

▶ Declaration should be made by duly authorized officer or employee of exporter or of forwarding agent named by exporter.

[a] If shipping weight is not available for each Schedule B item listed in column (13) included in one or more packages, insert the approximate gross weight for each Schedule B item. The total of these estimated weights should equal the actual weight of the entire package or packages.

[b] Designate foreign merchandise (reexports) with an "F" and exports of domestic merchandise produced in the United States or changed in condition in the United States with a "D." (*See instructions on reverse side.*)

CARRIERS, FORWARDERS AND EXPORTERS ARE REMINDED THAT IF A DESTINATION CONTROL STATEMENT IS REQUIRED ON A SHIPPER'S EXPORT DECLARATION COVERING A GIVEN SHIPMENT, SUCH STATEMENT MUST ALSO APPEAR ON ALL COPIES OF THE BILL OF LADING AND COMMERCIAL INVOICE. (*See Comprehensive Export Schedule.*)

Do Not Use This Area

2. Exporter completes the Export Declaration.
3. Exporter or freight forwarder makes up the draft (bill of exchange).
4. Exporter mails his invoices, Export Declaration, draft and letter of credit (if this is a letter of credit shipment) to freight forwarder.
5. Freight forwarder assembles the above documentation (except for the Export Declaration) together with the bill of lading and any other required documents.
6. Freight forwarder submits the documentation to the exporter's bank.
7. The exporter's bank forwards the documents to its overseas correspondent bank.
8. The correspondent bank contacts the importer and/or his broker to claim the documents in accordance with the terms of the draft and/or letter of credit.
9. Importer claims the documentation, and pays the amount shown on the draft immediately if it is a sight draft shipment.
10. Importer now goes to the common carrier and exchanges the bill of lading for the merchandise. He may also have to pay the freight bill at that time if it is on a "collect" basis.
11. Importer presents his invoices to customs and pays the import duties (Steps 10 and 11 are reversed in many countries).
12. Importer's local currency account is debited.
13. Importer's bank's dollar account in exporter's bank is debited.
14. Exporter's account is credited for amount shown on his invoice less bank service charges.

It has already been noted that a properly executed Export Declaration is essential for most transactions. The legislative authority providing for export control is based on the "Export Control Act of 1949," which provides for the controls necessary (a) to protect the domestic economy from the excessive drain of scarce materials and to reduce the inflationary impact of abnormal foreign demand, (b) to further the foreign policy of the United States and to aid in fulfilling its international responsibilities and (c) to exercise the necessary vigilance over exports from the standpoint of their significance in the national security.

The controls exercised are regulated by various bureaus of the United States Department of Commerce, such as the Bureau of Census, Bureau of Customs, and the Bureau of International Commerce.

Export Declaration

The most common export control document is the "Shipper's Export Declaration" or "Declaration." This document is otherwise known as Commerce Form 7525-V (Figure 3.4), 7525-V Alternate or the Shipper's Export Declaration for In-Transit Goods, Form 7513. Three copies of the declaration are required by the collector at the port of exit, except in cases of shipments to Canada and shipments between the United States and its territories and possessions for which only two copies are required. Under certain conditions, additional copies of the declaration may be required by the collector or other agencies. The execution of the declaration can only be performed by the shipper, owner or consignor of the merchandise, or by a duly authorized agent.

In view of the critical and legal nature of the Export Declaration, the following points with regard to its proper use must be borne in mind:

1. A "validated license" or a "general license" is required before a product can be exported to any foreign country except Canada.
2. If a "validated license" is required, one must apply to the Office of Export Control, U.S. Department of Commerce, on Form FC-419, "Application for Export License."
3. The Shipper's Export Declaration must be filed with the Collector of Customs or with the Postmaster for all commercial shipments.
4. The Shipper's Export Declaration must indicate the appropriate validated or general license symbol under which the shipment has been authorized.
5. A specified destination must appear on the Export Declaration, bill of lading, and on all commercial invoices.
6. All export control documents must be in agreement with regard to: exporter, commodity, intermediate consignee, ultimate consignee, and country of ultimate destination.
7. No goods must be deposited at any place of loading for export unless the Export Declaration has been authenticated by the collector of customs.
8. Goods must not be exported for re-exportation to a third country without prior approval by the Office of Export Control.

Complete information about U.S. export regulations are contained in the Comprehensive Export Schedule published by the Department of Commerce. The schedule includes, among other things, a listing of commodities called the "Positive List of Commodities," which will generally determine the type of license required for a particular transaction.

Since October 9, 1963, The Foreign Trade Statistics Regulations were amended so that in certain cases declarations are not required for shipments to areas like Puerto Rico. The following are the requirements taken in part from the F.T.S.R. (Title 15, Chapter 30, C.F.R. Section 30.55-H). The reader should consult with his freight forwarder to determine what other areas of the world are in the same category as Puerto Rico.

S 30.55 Miscellaneous Exemptions.
Shipper's Export Declarations are not required for the following shipments:
(H) Shipments (except shipments requiring a validated export license) to Canada, to the United States possessions, and between the United States and Puerto Rico, where the value of the commodities classified under a single Schedule B number and shipped on the same exporting carrier from one exporter to one importer does not exceed $100.

The "Export Dec," as it is often called, is generally completed by the exporter and/or his forwarder. There are instances, however, where the common carrier becomes involved in the preparation of the Export Dec. This is in the case of containerized shipments made on a "through bill of lading" in which the carrier offers a complete door-to-door delivery service which often calls for a combined truck-boat-rail-routing, etc. using the same container to hold the merchandise. There are three ways of handling such a situation.

1. **Containerized Carrier Service Prepares and Authenticates:**

   Where Containerized Carrier Service is to prepare and authenticate the export declaration, the exporter must supply them with all the *correct* information and also submit a "power of attorney" (Figure 3.5) in duplicate. The "power of attorney" assigns the Containerized Carrier Service as the true agent of the exporter for export control and customs purposes. However, it does not appoint the Containerized Carrier Service as the exporter's sole and exclusive forwarding agent for all exportations.

2. **Container Carrier Service Only Authenticates, Shipper (Exporter) Prepares**

   Where the Containerized Carrier Service is to submit the declaration of authentication, a "power of attorney" is not required. A carrier, not otherwise acting as a forwarding agent, may deliver executed declarations without specific authorizations. Since any collector with prior approval may institute and maintain a control of such authentications, it may be necessary to request an identification card from the appropriate collector. This card is known as form #3139 which, filled out, is used for identification by the messenger. In any case, line 18 of the Export Declaration *must* be properly filled out by the exporter whenever he submits an executed declaration for authentication.

3. **Shipper (Exporter) Prepares and Authenticates**

   Where the shipper prepares and authenticates his own declarations, he is to submit a copy of the authenticated declaration, U.S. Department of Commerce Form 7525-V, to the carrier no later than twenty-four hours prior to the sailing or shipping date. Alternate form "7525-V Alternate" has been approved to be used in conjunction with the short form bill of lading. Both forms can be purchased from commercial stationers. At no time should anyone attempt to prepare the declaration without referring to the Department of Commerce's Schedule B which contains all the necessary information regarding classification of goods, licensing, etc.

Freight forwarders today routinely have exporters complete a facsimile of an Export Dec. and then insert all the necessary data in the actual document once they have acquired the exporter's power of attorney (Figure 3.5). There are other export control documents which are important, since errors can lead to costly fines or worse. Before going into them, one should become familiar with

FIGURE 3.5

```
EXPORT CONTROL—Aug. 1948        Form 514—Printed in U.S.A.

        POWER OF ATTORNEY—DESIGNATION OF FORWARDING AGENT

Know all Men by these Presents, That ...........................................................,
                                        (NAME OF EXPORTER)
organized and doing business under the laws of the State of.................................................,

and having an office and place of business at .............................................................,

hereby authorizes .................SEA-LAND SERVICE, INC...................................,
                                        (FORWARDING AGENT)
of ....................................................................................................,

from this day forward to act as its forwarding agent for export control and customs purposes.

        IN WITNESS WHEREOF, the said exporter has caused these presents to be sealed and signed by its...............

....................................................................................................
                (OWNER, PARTNER—OR IF CORP., PRES., VICE-PRES., SEC'Y OR TREAS.)

City of ........................ State of ........................ this ...... day of .................... 19....

                        ....................................................................
                                            (EXPORTER)

(SEAL)              By............................................ Title..................

                                        (over)
```

```
(The following acknowledgment should be taken by the officer of a corporation who executes the designation of forwarding agent)

City.........................., County..........................., State........................., ss:

    On this ...... day of .................., 19...., personally appeared before me ..........................

residing at ............................................... to me known, who, being by me duly sworn, deposes and

says that ...... is the ................ of the ..............................................., the corporation described
in the foregoing instrument; that the seal affixed to said instrument is the corporate seal thereof and was affixed thereto by
authority of the Board of Directors of said company; that he by like authority subscribed the corporate name to said instru-
ment and signed his own name thereto.

                        ..........................................., Notary Public

(The following acknowledgment should be taken where the designation of forwarding agent has been executed by other than
                                a corporation)

City.........................., County..........................., State........................., ss:

    BE IT KNOWN, that on the ........ day of .........................., 19...., personally appeared before me

...................................................., residing at ..............................................,
to me known, who, being by me duly sworn, deposes and says that he is the individual described in, and who executed the

foregoing power of attorney, and acknowledged it to be his free act and deed and that he (and)...................
                                                                                        (is)
...................................................................................................  (are)

the sole and only member(s) trading under the firm name of ......................................................

                        ...........................................
                                    Notary Public
```

-300.4-

the following terms which identify specific control areas.

"In Bond" — Any goods which move "in bond" are under the control and owner-ship of the United States Government and remain so until cleared from customs. Goods to be transported in such a manner should be consigned by shipper, as "In Bond to   " or should note across the body of the bill of lading "In Bond." The various classes of entry involving "in bond" movements are established at the time of importation.

1. Immediate Export Entry or I.E. Entry: Permission is granted for the immediate exportation of the goods to a foreign port from a foreign country without the delay of examination. A major restriction in such movements is that the goods must be exported from the port of entry; i.e., a shipment imported from Japan to New York for consignment to the Virgin Islands would move in this manner.

2. Transportation and Exportation Entry or "T. & E." Entry: This type entry would be taken out whenever an imported shipment is to be re-exported to a foreign destination from a port other than the original port of entry.

3. Immediate Transportation Entry or "I.T." Entry: This allows for customs clearance of goods to be performed at "interior ports of en-try" (San Juan is considered an interior port of entry), rather than at the congested customs house at the sea board.

4. Two other entries, although not too common, are Withdrawal Trans-portation or "W.D.T." Entry and Warehouse Transportation and Ex-portation or "W.T.&E." Both these entries are used in releasing and picking up cargo at "bonded" warehouses.

The following documents are required whenever cargo is moving "in bond" under the entries mentioned in 1, 2, 3, and 4 above.

1. Form 7513, "Shipper's Export Declaration for In-Transit Goods" is required on all shipments which are of foreign origin and are being ex-ported to a foreign destination. (For purposes of export control, the American Virgin Islands are considered a "foreign port.") Additional information besides that outlined on the form may also be required. If there is an intermediate consignee in a foreign destination, he must be shown as such across columns 1-6 below the description of commod-ities. Also, underneath this entry one of the following statements should appear.

     a. "The merchandise described herein is of foreign origin."
     b. "The merchandise described herein is of the growth, production or manufacture of the United States."
     c. "The merchandise described herein is of the growth, production

or manufacture of the United States, but comes within the exception granted by paragraph 371.9 (A-2)."

2. Form 7512 "Transportation Entry and Manifest of Goods Subject to Customs Inspection and Permit" is to be executed by the exporter on all In Bond cargo. This document accompanies the cargo, is receipted by the customs inspector at the pier, and countersigned as received, subject to customs clearance at destination, by a Containerized Carrier Service employee also at the pier. Form 7512, along with a manifest copy of the waybill, is then forwarded to the destination terminal.

    On those consignments moving to Puerto Rico in bond and accompanied by form 7512, *no export declaration* of any type need be prepared; since that port, known as Customs Collector District 49, receives the required statistical data with form 7512.

There are specific commodities for which a validated export license is required. These commodities are designated in a "Commodity Control List." The determination is generally based on the country to which the cargo is destined. The Schedule B Commodity Book does not supply the "Commodity Control List," which can lead to exporters shipping cargo without the required license and the export declaration being rejected. The application for such a license must be made at least two weeks prior to exportation to allow time for processing.

The subject of "drawbacks" is an important one which should not be disregarded. The drawback system was inaugurated by the government to foster and encourage domestic manufacturers to export completed products made up in whole or part of foreign raw materials. Section 313 (a) of the tariff act of 1930 provides for a "drawback" of the duty paid less 1% on all exported merchandise manufactured or produced in the United States with imported materials. If such goods are exported from bonded warehouses in their original form, 100% of duty will be allowed on a drawback. Some of the major imported commodities which are subject to drawbacks are iron and steel, glycerine, tobacco, drugs, medicinal oils, grain and grain products, forest products, sugar, and paper.

The procedure in applying for drawbacks is an involved one. For this reason, experts in this field known as "drawback attorneys" are located in all major ports. These attorneys will perform the necessary functions in securing refunds.

The only obligation a carrier has is to complete the submitted "drawback" by supplying vessel, voyage, sailing date, and waybill number; submitting it on completion to the customs inspector at the U.S. port-of-entry pier.

American Foreign Trade Defintions

The American Foreign Trade Definitions have been developed in the form of a comprehensive statement and list by the United States Chamber of Commerce, the National Council of American Importers, Inc., and the National Foreign

Trade Council, Inc. They form part of the world's contemporary lexicon of international commerce.

It must be noted that there have been numerous changes since the definitions were adopted in 1941. However, the changes take the form of additions resulting from the introduction of the more sophisticated transport forms already discussed. They affect the legal relationship between exporter and common carrier more than they do the buyer-seller contract.

The American Foreign Trade Definitions are being reprinted in their entirety here in view of their importance to the exporter.

Following the American Foreign Trade Definitions is a list of foreign trade terms most commonly used in international trade. This list is prepared and updated periodically by The National Foreign Trade Council and other specialized trade associations.

AMERICAN FOREIGN TRADE DEFINITIONS

Adopted July 30, 1941, by a Joint Committee representing the Chamber of Commerce of the United States of America, the National Council of American Importers, Inc., and the National Foreign Trade Council, Inc.

FOREWORD

Since the issuance of American Foreign Trade Definitions in 1919, many changes in practice have occurred. The 1919 Definitions did much to clarify and simplify foreign trade practice, and received wide recognition and use by buyers and sellers throughout the world. At the Twenty-Seventh National Foreign Trade Convention, 1940, further revision and clarification of these Definitions was urged as necessary to assist the foreign trader in the handling of his transactions.

The following Revised American Foreign Trade Definitions—1941 are recommended for general use by both exporters and importers. These revised definitions have no status at law unless there is specific legislation providing for them, or unless they are confirmed by court decisions. Hence, it is suggested that sellers and buyers agree to their acceptance as part of the contract of sale. These revised definitions will then become legally binding upon all parties.

In view of changes in practice and procedure since 1919, certain new responsibilities for sellers and buyers are included in these revised definitions. Also, in many instances, the old responsibilities are more clearly defined than in the 1919 Definitions, and the changes should be beneficial both to sellers and buyers. Widespread acceptance will lead to a greater standardization of foreign trade procedure, and to the avoidance of much misunderstanding.

Adoption by exporters and importers of these revised terms will impress on all parties concerned their respective responsibilities and rights.

GENERAL NOTES OF CAUTION

1. As foreign trade definitions have been issued by organizations in various parts of the world, and as the courts of countries have interpreted these definitons in different ways, it is important that sellers and buyers agree that their contracts are subject to the Revised American Foreign Trade Definitions—1941 and that the various points listed are accepted by both parties.

2. In addition to the foreign trade terms listed herein, there are terms that are at times used, such as Free Harbor, C.I.F. & C. (Cost, Insurance, Freight, and Commission), C.I.F.C.

& I. (Cost, Insurance, Freight, Commission and Interest), C.I.F. Landed (Cost, Insurance, Freight, Landed), and others. None of these should be used unless there has first been a definite understanding as to the exact meaning thereof. It is unwise to attempt to interpret other terms in the light of the terms given herein. Hence, whenever possible, one of the terms defined herein should be used.

3. It is unwise to use abbreviations in quotations or in contracts which might be subject to misunderstanding.

4. When making quotations, the familiar terms "hundredweight" or "ton" should be avoided. A hundredweight can be 100 pounds of the short ton, or 112 pounds of the long ton. A ton can be a short ton of 2,000 pounds, or a metric ton of 2,204.6 pounds, or a long ton of 2,240 pounds. Hence, the type of hundredweight or ton should be clearly stated in quotations and in sales confirmations. Also, all terms referring to quantity, weight, volume, length, or surface should be clearly defined and agreed upon.

5. If inspection, or certificate of inspection, is required, it should be agreed, in advance, whether the cost thereof is for account of seller or buyer.

6. Unless otherwise agreed upon, all expenses are for the account of seller up to the point at which the buyer must handle the subsequent movement of goods.

7. There are a number of elements in a contract that do not fall within the scope of these foreign trade definitions. Hence, no mention of these is made herein. Seller and buyer should agree to these separately when negotiating contracts. This particularly applies to so-called "customary" practices.

DEFINITIONS OF QUOTATIONS

(I) Ex (Point of Origin)

"Ex Factory", "Ex Mill", "Ex Mine", "Ex Plantation", "Ex Warehouse", etc. (named point of origin)

Under this term, the price quoted applies only at the point of origin, and the seller agrees to place the goods at the disposal of the buyer at the agreed place on the date or within the period fixed.

Under this quotation:

Seller must

(1) bear all costs and risks of the goods until such time as the buyer is obliged to take delivery thereof;

(2) render the buyer, at the buyer's request and expense, assistance in obtaining the documents issued in the country of origin, or of shipment, or of both, which the buyer may require either for purposes of exportation, or of importation at destination.

Buyer must

(1) take delivery of the goods as soon as they have been placed at his disposal at the agreed place on the date or within the period fixed;

(2) pay export taxes, or other fees or charges, if any, levied because of exportation,

(3) bear all costs and risks of the goods from the time when he is obligated to take delivery thereof;

(4) pay all costs and charges incurred in obtaining the documents issued in the country of origin, or of shipment, or of both, which may be required either for purposes of exportation, or of importation at destination.

(II) F.O.B. (Free on Board)

Note: Seller and buyer should consider not only the definitions but also the "Comments on All F.O.B. Terms" given at end of this section, in order to understand fully their respective responsibilities and rights under the several classes of "F.O.B." terms.

(II-A) "F.O.B. (named inland carrier at named inland point of departure)"

Under this term, the price quoted applies only at inland shipping point, and the seller arranges for loading of the goods on, or in, railway cars, trucks, lighters, barges, aircraft, or other conveyance furnished for transportation.

Under this quotation:

Seller must

(1) place goods on, or in, conveyance, or deliver to inland carrier for loading;

(2) provide clean bill of lading or other transportation receipt, freight collect;

(3) be responsible for any loss or damage, or both, until goods have been placed in, or on, conveyance at loading point, and clean bill of lading or other transportation receipt has been furnished by the carrier;

(4) render the buyer, at the buyer's request and expense, assistance in obtaining the documents issued in the country of origin, or of shipment, or of both, which the buyer may require either for purposes of exportation, or of importation at destination.

Buyer must

(1) be responsible for all movement of the goods from inland point of loading, and pay all transportation costs;

(2) pay export taxes, or other fees or charges, if any, levied because of exportation;

(3) be responsible for any loss or damage, or both, incurred after loading at named inland point of departure;

(4) pay all costs and charges incurred in obtaining the documents issued in the country of origin, or of shipment, or of both, which may be required either for purposes of exportation, or of importation at destination.

(II-B) "F.O.B. (named inland carrier at named inland point of departure) Freight Prepaid To (named point of exportation)"

Under this term, the seller quotes a price including transportation charges to the named point of exportation and prepays freight to named point of exportation, without assuming responsibility for the goods after obtaining a clean bill of lading or other transportation receipt at named inland point of departure.

Under this quotation: Seller must

(1) assume the seller's obligations as under II-A, except that under (2) he must provide clean bill of lading or other transportation receipt, freight prepaid to named point of exportation.

Buyer must

(1) assume the same buyer's obligations as under II-A, except that he does not pay freight from loading point to named point of exportation.

(II-C) "F.O.B. (named inland carrier at named inland point of departure) Freight Allowed To (named point)"

Under this term, the seller quotes a price including the transportation charges to the named point, shipping freight collect and deducting the cost of transportation. without assuming responsibility for the goods after obtaining a clean bill of lading or other transportation receipt at named inland point of departure.

Under this quotation:

Seller must

(1) assume the same seller's obligations as under II-A, but deducts from his invoice the transportation cost to named point.

Buyer must

(1) assume the same buyer's obligations as under II-A, including payment of freight from inland loading point to named point, for which seller has made deduction.

(II-D) "F.O.B. (named inland carrier at named point of exportation)"

Under this term, the seller quotes a price including the costs of transportation of the goods to named point of exportation, bearing any loss or damage, or both, incurred up to that point.

Under this quotation:
Seller must
(1) place goods on, or in, conveyance, or deliver to inland carrier for loading;
(2) provide clean bill of lading or other transportation receipt, paying all transportation costs from loading point to named point of exportation;
(3) be responsible for any loss or damage, or both, until goods have arrived in, or on, inland conveyance at the named point of exportation;
(4) render the buyer, at the buyers request and expense, assistance in obtaining the documents issued in the country of origin, or of shipment, or of both, which the buyer may require either for purposes of exportation, or of importation at destination.
Buyer must
(1) be responsible for all movement of the goods from inland conveyance at named point of exportation;
(2) pay export taxes, or other fees or charges, if any, levied because of exportation;
(3) be responsible for any loss or damage, or both, incurred after goods have arrived in, or on, inland conveyance at the named point of exportation;
(4) pay all costs and charges incurred in obtaining the documents issued in the country of origin, or of shipment, or of both, which may be required either for purposes of exportation, or of importation at destination.

(II-E) "F.O.B. Vessel (named port of shipment)"
Under this term, the seller quotes a price covering all expenses up to, and including, delivery of the goods upon the overseas vessel provided by, or for, the buyer at the named port of shipment.
Under this quotation:
Seller must
(1) pay all charges incurred in placing goods actually on board the vessel designated and provided by, or for, the buyer on the date or within the period fixed;
(2) provide clean ship's receipt or on-board bill of lading;
(3) be responsible for any loss or damage, or both, until goods have been placed on board the vessel on the date or within the period fixed;
(4) render the buyer, at the buyer's request and expense, assistance in obtaining the documents issued in the country of origin, or of shipment, or of both, which the buyer may require either for purposes of exportation, or of importation at destination.
Buyer must
(1) give seller adequate notice of name, sailing date, loading berth of, and delivery time to, the vessel;
(2) bear the additional costs incurred and all risks of the goods from the time when the seller has placed them at his disposal if the vessel named by him fails to arrive or to load within the designated time;
(3) handle all subsequent movement of the goods to destination;
    (a) provide and pay for insurance;
    (b) provide and pay for ocean and other transportation;
(4) pay export taxes, or other fees or charges, if any, levied because of exportation;
(5) be responsible for any loss or damage, or both, after goods have been loaded on board the vessel;
(6) pay all costs and charges incurred in obtaining the documents, other than clean ship's receipt or bill of lading, issued in the country of origin, or of shipment or of both, which may be required either for purposes of exportation, or of importation at destination.

(II-F) "F.O.B. (named inland point in country of importation)"
Under this term, the seller quotes a price including the cost of the merchandise and all costs of transportation to the named inland point in the country of importation.
Under this quotation: Seller must
(1) provide and pay for all transportation to the named inland point in the country

of importation;

(2) pay export taxes, or other fees or charges, if any, levied because of exportation;

(3) provide and pay for marine insurance;

(4) provide and pay for war risk insurance, unless otherwise agreed upon between the seller and buyer;

(5) be responsible for any loss or damage, or both, until arrival of goods on conveyance at the named inland point in the country of importation;

(6) pay the costs of certificates of origin, consular invoices, or any other documents issued in the country of origin, or of shipment, or of both, which the buyer may require for the importation of goods into the country of destination and, where necessary, for their passage in transit through another country;

(7) pay all costs of landing, including wharfage, landing charges, and taxes, if any;

(8) pay all costs of customs entry in the country of importation;

(9) pay customs duties and all taxes applicable to imports, if any, in the country of importation.

NOTE: The seller under this quotation must realize that he is accepting important responsibilities, costs, and risks, and should therefore be certain to obtain adequate insurance. On the other hand, the importer or buyer may desire such quotations to relieve him of the risks of the voyage and to assure him of his landed costs at inland point in country of importation. When competition is keen, or the buyer is accustomed to such quotations from other sellers, seller may quote such terms, being careful to protect himself in an appropriate manner.

Buyer must

(1) take prompt delivery of goods from conveyance upon arrival at destination;

(2) bear any costs and be responsible for all loss or damage, or both, after arrival at destination.

COMMENTS ON ALL F.O.B. TERMS

In connection with F.O.B. terms, the following points of caution are recommended:

1. The method of inland transportation, such as trucks, railroad cars, lighters, barges, or aircraft, should be specified.

2. If any switching charges are involved during the inland transportation, it should be agreed, in advance, whether these charges are for account of the seller or the buyer.

3. The term "F.O.B. (named port)", without designating the exact point at which the liability of the seller terminates and the liability of the buyer begins, should be avoided. The use of this term gives rise to disputes as to the liability of the seller or the buyer in the event of loss or damage arising while the goods are in port, and before delivery to or on board the ocean carrier. Misunderstandings may be avoided by naming the specific point of delivery.

4. If lighterage or trucking is required in the transfer of goods from the inland conveyance to ship's side, and there is a cost therefor, it should be understood, in advance, whether this cost is for account of the seller or the buyer.

5. The seller should be certain to notify the buyer of the minimum quantity required to obtain a carload, a truckload, or a barge-load freight rate.

6. Under F.O.B. terms, excepting "F.O.B. (named inland point in country of importation)", the obligation to obtain ocean freight space, and marine and war risk insurance, rests with the buyer. Despite this obligation on the part of the buyer, in many trades the seller obtains the ocean freight space, and marine and war risk insurance, and provides for shipment on behalf of the buyer. Hence, seller and buyer must have an understanding as to whether the buyer will obtain the ocean freight space, and marine and war risk insurance, as is his obligation, or whether the seller agrees to do this for the buyer.

7. For the seller's protection, he should provide in his contract of sale that marine insurance obtained by the buyer include standard warehouse to warehouse coverage.

(III) F.A.S. (Free Along Side)

NOTE: Seller and buyer should consider not only the definitions but also the "Comments" given at the end of this section in order to understand fully their respective responsiblities and rights under "F.A.S." terms.

"F.A.S. VESSEL (named port of shipment)"

Under this term, the seller quotes a price including delivery of the goods along side overseas vessel and within reach of its loading tackle.

Under this quotation:

Seller must

(1) place goods along side vessel or on dock designated and provided by, or for, buyer on the date or within the period fixed; pay any heavy lift charges, where necessary, up to this point;

(2) provide clean dock or ship's receipt;

(3) be responsible for any loss or damage, or both, until goods have been delivered along side the vessel or on the dock;

(4) render the buyer, at the buyer's request and expense, assistance in obtaining the documents issued in the country of origin, or of shipment, or of both, which the buyer may require either for purposes of exportation, or of importation at destination.

Buyer must

(1) give seller adequate notice of name, sailing date, loading berth of, and delivery time to, the vessel;

(2) handle all subsequent movement of the goods from along side the vessel:

(a) arrange and pay for demurrage or storage charges, or both, in warehouse or on wharf, where necessary;

(b) provide any pay for insurance;

(c) provide and pay for ocean and other transportation;

(3) pay export taxes, or other fees or charges, if any, levied because of exportation;

(4) be responsible for any loss or damage, or both, while the goods are on a lighter or other conveyance along side vessel within reach of its loading tackle, or on the dock awaiting loading, or until actually loaded on board the vessel, and subsequent thereto;

(5) pay all costs and charges incurred in obtaining the documents, other than clean dock or ship's receipt, issued in the country of origin, or of shipment, or of both, which may be required either for purposes of exportation, or of importation at destination.

F.A.S. COMMENTS

1. Under F.A.S. terms, the obligation to obtain ocean freight space, and marine and war risk insurance, rests with the buyer. Despite this obligation on the part of the buyer, in many trades the seller obtains ocean freight space, and marine and war risk insurance, and provides for shipment on behalf of the buyer. In others, the buyer notifies the seller to make delivery along side a vessel designated by the buyer and the buyer provides his own marine and war risk insurance. Hence, seller and buyer must have an understanding as to whether the buyer will obtain the ocean freight space, and marine and war risk insurance, as is his obligation, or whether the seller agrees to do this for the buyer.

2. For the seller's protection, he should provide in his contract of sale that marine insurance obtained by the buyer include standard warehouse to warehouse coverage.

(IV) C. & F. (Cost and Freight)

Note: Seller and buyer should consider not only the definitions but also the "C & F Comments" and the "C. & F. and C.I.F. Comments" (see below) in order to understand fully their respective responsibilities and rights under "C.&F." terms.

"C. & F. (named point of destination)"

Under this term, the seller quotes a price including the cost of transportation to the named point of destination.

Under this quotation:

Seller must

(1) provide and pay for transportation to named point of destination;

(2) pay export taxes, or other fees or charges, if any, levied because of exportation:

(3) obtain and dispatch promptly to buyer, or his agent, clean bill of lading to named point of destination;

(4) where received-for-shipment ocean bill of lading may be tendered, be responsible for any loss or damage, or both, until the goods have been delivered into the custody of the ocean carrier;

(5) where on-board ocean bill of lading is required, be responsible for any loss or damage, or both, until the goods have been delivered on board the vessel;

(6) provide, at the buyer's request and expense, certificates of origin, consular invoices, or any other documents issued in the country of origin, or of shipment, or of both, which the buyer may require for importation of goods into country of destination and, where necessary, for their passage in transit through another country.

Buyer must

(1) accept the documents when presented;

(2) receive goods upon arrival, handle and pay for all subsequent movement of the goods, including taking delivery from vessel in accordance with bill of lading clauses and terms; pay all costs of landing, including any duties, taxes, and other expenses at named point of destination;

(3) provide and pay for insurance;

(4) be responsible for loss of or damage to goods, or both, from time and place at which seller's obligations under (4) or (5) above have ceased;

(5) pay the costs of certificates of origin, consular invoices, or any other documents issued in the country of origin, or of shipment, or of both, which may be required for the importation of goods into the country of destination and, where necessary, for their passage in transit through another country.

C. & F. COMMENTS

1. For the seller's protection, he should provide in his contract of sale that marine insurance obtained by the buyer include standard warehouse to warehouse coverage.

2. The comments listed under the following C.I.F. terms in many cases apply to C. & F. terms as well, and should be read and understood by the C. & F. seller and buyer.

(V) C.I.F. (Cost, Insurance, Freight)

NOTE: Seller and buyer should consider not only the definitions but also the "Comments", at the end of this section, in order to understand fully their respective responsibilities and rights under "C.I.F." terms.

"C.I.F. (named point of destination)"

Under this term, the seller quotes a price including the cost of the goods, the marine insurance, and all transportation charges to the named point of destination.

Under this quotation:

Seller must

(1) provide and pay for transportation to named point of destination;

(2) pay export taxes, or other fees or charges, if any, levied because of exportation;

(3) provide and pay for marine insurance;

(4) provide war risk insurance as obtainable in seller's market at time of shipment at buyer's expense, unless seller has agreed that buyer provide for war risk coverage; [See Comment 10(c) below]

(5) obtain and dispatch promptly to buyer, or his agent, clean bill of lading to named point of destination, and also insurance policy or negotiable insurance certificate;

(6) where received-for-shipment ocean bill of lading may be tendered, be responsible for any loss or damage, or both, until the goods have been delivered into the custody of the ocean carrier;

(7) where on-board ocean bill of lading is required, be responsible for any loss or damage, or both, until the goods have been delivered on board the vessel;

(8) provide, at the buyer's request and expense, certificates of origin, consular invoices, or any other documents issued in the country of origin, or of shipment, or both, which the buyer may require for importation of goods into country of destination and, where necessary, for their passage in transit through another country.

Buyer must

(1) accept the documents when presented;

(2) receive the goods upon arrival, handle and pay for all subsequent movement of the goods, including taking delivery from vessel in accordance with bill of lading clauses and terms; pay all costs of landing, including any duties, taxes, and other expenses at named point of destination;

(3) pay for war risk insurance provided by seller;

(4) be responsible for loss of or damage to goods, or both, from time and place at which seller's obligations under (6) or (7) above have ceased;

(5) pay the cost of certificates of origin, consular invoices, or any other documents issued in the country of origin, or of shipment, or both, which may be required for importation of the goods into the country of destination and, where necessary, for their passage in transit through another country.

C.&F. AND C.I.F. COMMENTS

Under C.&F. and C.I.F. contracts there are the following points on which the seller and the buyer should be in complete agreement at the time that the contract is concluded:

1. It should be agreed upon, in advance, who is to pay for miscellaneous expenses, such as weighing or inspection charges.

2. The quantity to be shipped on any one vessel should be agreed upon, in advance, with a view to the buyer's capacity to take delivery upon arrival and discharge of the vessel; within the free time allowed at the port of importation.

3. Although the terms C.&F. and C.I.F. are generally interpreted to provide that charges for consular invoices and certificates of origin are for the account of the buyer, and are charged separately, in many trades these charges are included by the seller in his price. Hence, seller and buyer should agree, in advance, whether these charges are part of the selling price, or will be invoiced separately.

4. The point of final destination should be definitely known in the event the vessel discharges at a port other than the actual destination of the goods.

5. When ocean freight space is difficult to obtain, or forward freight contracts cannot be made at firm rates, it is advisable that sales contracts, as an exception to regular C.&F. or C.I.F. terms, should provide that shipment within the contract period be subject to ocean freight space being available to the seller, and should also provide that changes in the cost of ocean transportation between the time of sale and the time of shipment be for account of the buyer.

6. Normally, the seller is obligated to prepay the ocean freight. In some instances, shipments are made freight collect and the amount of the freight is deducted from the invoice rendered by the seller. It is necessary to be in agreement on this, in advance, in order to avoid misunderstanding which arises from foreign exchange fluctuations which might affect the actual cost of transportation, and from interest charges which might accrue under letter of credit financing. Hence, the seller should always prepay the ocean freight unless he has a specific agreement with the buyer, in advance, that goods can be shipped freight collect.

7. The buyer should recognize that he does not have the right to insist on inspection of goods prior to accepting the documents. The buyer should not refuse to take delivery of goods on account of delay in the receipt of documents, provided the seller has used due diligence in their dispatch through the regular channels.

8. Sellers and buyers are advised against including in a C.I.F. contract any indefinite clause at variance with the obligations of a C.I.F. contract as specified in these Definitions. There have been numerous court decisions in the United States and other countries invalidating C.I.F. contracts because of the inclusion of indefinite clauses.

9. Interest charges should be included in cost computations and should not be charged as a separate item in C.I.F. contracts, unless otherwise agreed upon, in advance, between the seller and buyer; in which case, however, the term C.I.F. and I. (Cost, Insurance, Freight and Interest) should be used.

10. In connection with insurance under C.I.F. sales, it is necessary that seller and buyer be definitely in accord upon the following points:

(a) The character of the marine insurance should be agreed upon in so far as being W.A. (With Average) or F.P.A. (Free of Particular Average), as well as any other special risks that are covered in specific trades, or against which the buyer may wish individual protection. Among the special risks that should be considered and agreed upon between seller and buyer are theft, pilferage, leakage, breakage, sweat, contact with other cargoes, and others peculiar to any particular trade. It is important that contingent or collect freight and customs duty should be insured to cover Particular Average losses, as well as total loss after arrival and entry but before delivery.

(b) The seller is obligated to exercise ordinary care and diligence in selecting an underwriter that is in good financial standing. However, the risk of obtaining settlement of insurance claims rests with the buyer.

(c) War risk insurance under this term is to be obtained by the seller at the expense and risk of the buyer. It is important that the seller be in definite accord with the buyer on this point, particularly as to the cost. It is desirable that the goods be insured against both marine and war risk with the same underwriter, so that there can be no difficulty arising from the determination of the cause of the loss.

(d) Seller should make certain that in his marine or war risk insurance, there be included the standard protection against strikes, riots and civil commotions.

(e) Seller and buyer should be in accord as to the insured valuation, bearing in mind that merchandise contributes in General Average on certain bases of valuation which differ in various trades. It is desirable that a competent insurance broker be consulted, in order that full value be covered and trouble avoided.

(VI) "Ex Dock (named port of importation)"
NOTE: Seller and buyer should consider not only the definitions but also the "Ex Dock Comments" at the end of this section, in order to understand fully their respective responsibilities and rights under "Ex Dock" terms.

Under this term, seller quotes a price including the cost of the goods and all additional costs necessary to place the goods on the dock at the named port of importation, duty paid, if any.

Under this quotation:
Seller must
(1) provide and pay for transportation to named port of importation;
(2) pay export taxes, or other fees or charges, if any, levied because of exportation;
(3) provide and pay for marine insurance;
(4) provide and pay for war risk insurance, unless otherwise agreed upon between the buyer and seller;
(5) be responsible for any loss or damage, or both, until the expiration of the free time allowed on the dock at the named port of importation;
(6) pay the costs of certificates of origin, consular invoices, legalization of bill of lading, or any other documents issued in the country of origin, or of shipment, or of both, which the buyer may require for the importation of goods into the country of destination and, where necessary, for their passage in transit through another country;
(7) pay all costs of landing, including wharfage, landing charges, and taxes, if any;
(8) pay all costs of customs entry in the country of importation;
(9) pay customs duties and all taxes applicable to imports, if any, in the country of importation, unless otherwise agreed upon.
Buyer must
(1) take delivery of the goods on the dock at the named port of importation within the free time allowed;
(2) bear the cost and risk of the goods if delivery is not taken within the free time allowed.

EX DOCK COMMENTS

This term is used principally in United States import trade. It has various modifications, such as "Ex Quay", "Ex Pier", etc. but it is seldom, if ever, used in American export practice. Its use in quotations for export is not recommended.

COMMONLY USED FOREIGN TRADE TERMS

AD VALOREM "According to the value", used for customs duties, fixed as a percentage of value.

ARRIVAL DRAFT A modified sight draft which does not require payment until after arrival of goods at port of destination.

AUTHORITY TO NEGOTIATE Similar to Authority to Purchase, except it is revolving, has no expiration date and usually drafts are in a foreign currency. (Used in Republic of South Africa.)

AUTHORITY TO PAY (Often mistaken for Letter of Credit.) An Authority to Pay is an advice stemming from a buyer, addressed through the buyer's bank to the seller, by way of the correspondent of the buyer's bank in the seller's country, authorizing the correspondent bank to pay the seller's drafts for a stipulated amount. The seller has no recourse against cancellation or modification of the Authority to Pay before the drafts are presented but, once the drafts drawn on the correspondent bank are paid by it, the seller is no longer liable as drawer. Usually not confirmed by the U.S. bank.

AUTHORITY TO PURCHASE (Often mistakenly referred to as a Letter of Credit.) This document while similar to the Authority to Pay differs in that under an Authority to Purchase the drafts are drawn directly on the buyer. They are purchased by the corrrespondent bank with or without recourse against the drawer. Usually not confirmed by the U.S. bank.

BALANCE OF PAYMENTS A statement showing a nation's foreign economic transactions for a given period of time. The main items are imports, exports, insurance, shipping, services, foreign investments, foreign loans, interest and dividends, government transfers and gold shipments.

BALANCE OF TRADE The balance between a country's exports and imports.

BANK DRAFT A check, drawn by a bank on another bank, customarily used where it is necessary for the customer to provide funds which are payable at a bank in some distant location.

BANKERS ACCEPTANCE A time draft of which a bank is drawee and acceptor.

BATTLE ACT Mutual Defense Assistance Control Act of 1951, P.L. 213, 82nd Congress. Under this act, U. S. economic or military assistance to other countries is conditional on their cooperation in selective embargo on exports of strategic goods to the Soviet bloc.

BENEFICIARY The person in whose favor a letter of credit is opened or a draft is drawn.

BILATERAL TRADE Commerce between two countries, usually in accordance with a specific agreement on amounts of commodities to be traded during a defined period. Balances owing to either are settled directly between the two.

BILL OF EXCHANGE (or Draft) May be defined as an unconditional order in writing addressed by one person to another, signed by the person giving it, and requiring the addressee to pay at a fixed or determinable future time a certain sum of money to the order of a specified party.

BILL OF LADING (B/L) 1) A title document issued by a carrier (railroad, steamship, or other common carrier) which 2) serves as a receipt for the goods and 3) is a contract to deliver the goods to a designated person or to his order. The bill of lading describes the conditions under which the goods are accepted by the carrier and details of the nature and quantity of the goods, name of vessel (if shipped by sea), identifying marks and numbers, destination, etc. The person sending the goods is the "shipper" or "consignor", the company or agent transporting the goods is the "carrier", and the person to whom the goods are destined is the "consignee". Bills of lading may be negotiable or non-negotiable.

BRUSSELS NOMENCLATURE A standardized system for classifying commodities for customs purposes developed by the Customs Cooperation Council. The EEC common tariff and the tariffs of other major trading nations, especially in Europe are based on this nomenclature.

CERTIFICATE OF MANUFACTURE A document used in connection with letters of credit wherein drafts are paid or negotiated on presentation of a certificate stating that the goods have been completed and are being held a certificate which has been subject to considerable variation in wording. In order to standardize procedure under certificates of manufacture, as much as possible, the Bankers Association for Foreign Trade, at its 1941 convention, appointed a committee to prepare a "Uniform Certificate of Manufacture". On June 5, 1942, the Association accepted a report of the committee, recommending the promulgation of a concise certificate of manufacture, reading as follows:

(Customer)
        We hereby certify that the attached invoice dated
our No.   covers material which has been manufactured and set apart for
your account and risk at (location).
                                (Manufacturer)
The Committee says in its report: "The Committee does not intend, in promulgating the concise form of certificate, to indicate that it has any objection to the more elaborate certificates currently used by some manufacturers, so long as it is understood that in accepting them their responsibility is no greater than in accepting the concise certificate".

CERTIFICATE OF ORIGIN A document in which the exporter certifies to the place of origin (manufacture) of the merchandise to be exported. Sometimes these certificates must be legalized by the counsul of country of destination, but more often they may be legalized by a commercial organization, such as a Chamber of Commerce, in the country of manufacture. Such information is needed primarily to comply with tariff laws which may extend more favorable treatment to products of certain countries.

CIRCULAR LETTER OF CREDIT See Traveler's Letter of Credit.

CLEAN BILL OF LADING One in which the goods are described as having been received in "apparent good order and condition" and without qualification.

COLONIAL CLAUSE See Interest Bearing Drafts.

CLEAN DRAFT A draft to which no title documents are attached.

CONSULAR INVOICE A commercial invoice that has been "consularized" by means of appropriate notation thereon by the consul of the country of destination. Or, it may be a special form of invoice required by and obtainable from the consul of the importing country to enable customs clearance of the goods and to provide customs officials with information for the assessment of import duties.

CONVERTIBILITY Ability of owners of a currency to exchange it for foreign currencies or gold in the open market. Limited convertibility, frequently referred to as transferability, applies to the changing of one currency into another with government permission. Blocked funds are those denied exchange rights by a government.

COOLEY AMENDMENT See P.L. 480.

COUNTERPART FUNDS Local currencies deposited in a special account by recipient governments substantially equalling grant aid extended by another government. These funds, while remaining the property of the recipient government, can generally only be used by agreement of the donor government.

CUSTOMS UNION An arrangement among two or more countries whereby they eliminate tariffs and other import restrictions on each other's goods and establish a common tariff for the goods of all other countries.

D/A—DOCUMENTS AGAINST ACCEPTANCE Instructions given by an exporter to a bank that the documents attached to a draft for collection are deliverable to the drawee only against his acceptance of the draft.

DATE DRAFT A draft maturing a stipulated number of days after its date, regardless of the time of its acceptance. Unless otherwise agreed upon in the contract of sale, the date of the draft should not be prior to that of the ocean bill of lading or of the corresponding document on shipments by other means.

DEL CREDERE AGENT One who guarantees payments. The sales agent, for a certain percentage additional to his sales commission, will guarantee the payments on shipments made to his customers.

DELIVERY ORDER An order addressed to the holder of goods and issued by anyone who has authority to do so, i.e. one who has the legal right to order delivery of merchandise. It is not considered a good title document.

DEVALUATION Official lowering of the trade value of a country's currency in relation to other currencies by direct government decision to reduce gold content to establish new ratio to another agreed standard, such as United States Dollar.

DISHONOR The refusal of a drawee to accept a draft or to pay it when due.

DOCUMENTARY DRAFT A draft to which documents are attached which ordinarily control title to goods shipped.

DOLLAR AREA The Western Hemisphere generally, United States possessions, and the Philippines comprise the "Dollar area." Although Dollar area currencies tend to be oriented to the United States Dollar, trade and financial relationships are much more loosely knit than in the Sterling area.

DRAFT See Bill of Exchange

DRAWEE The addressee of the draft.

DRAWER The issuer or signer of a draft.

ECS CARNET A document that permits samples and certain other materials to be brought into most European countries with a minimum of customs formalities and without payment of duty. The system was sponsored by the International Chamber of Commerce. Carnets are issued by authorized chambers of commerce who guarantee the payment of customs duties if the products are not re-exported within a specified period of time. ECS is a combined English and French abbreviation for commercial samples.

ESCAPE CLAUSE A provision in U. S. law permitting tariffs on which concessions have been made to be increased if imports increase so as to cause or threaten to cause serious injury to domestic producers. The Tariff Commission makes such recommendations to the President and the final decision rests with him. Article XIX of the General Agreement on Tariffs and Trade contains an escape clause of somewhat similar intent.

EURODOLLARS A claim on the United States, represented by a U.S. dollar deposit in a bank or similar institution abroad, which can be used to finance trade.

EUROPEAN COMMON MARKET (See EEC.)

EXPORT CREDIT INSURANCE A system to underwrite the collection of credits extended by exporters against various contingencies. In some countries only non-commercial risks can be insured. Public or private organizations, or both, may offer export credit insurance in different countries.

EXPORT DECLARATION A document required by the U. S. Government in connection with shipments abroad and used in order to maintain statistics on our exports.

FIRST OF EXCHANGE The original copy of a draft when two or more are drawn.

FOREIGN TRADE ZONE An area where goods may be received and stored without entering a country's customs jurisdiction and hence without payment of duty. It is sometimes called a "free trade zone."

FORWARD (FUTURE) EXCHANGE An exchange contract maturing at a specified future date.

FREE PORT A port, or section thereof, which is a foreign trade zone.

FREE TRADE AREA An arrangement between two or more countries for free trade among themselves while each nation maintains its own independent tariffs toward non-member nations. Not to be confused with "free trade zone", which is synonymous with "foreign trade zone".

HARD CURRENCY The term "hard" is a carry-over from the days when sound money was freely convertible into hard metal, i.e., gold. The term is used today to describe a currency whose value is sound and steady and is generally acceptable at face value internationally.

INDENT MERCHANT One who assembles a number of orders from merchants in his locality, such orders being placed with foreign manufacturers by the indent merchant for his own account. He assume the full credit risk and obtains his commission from those for whom he orders.

INTEREST BEARING DRAFTS Used on either United States Dollar or Pounds Sterling drafts, principally by exporters selling to the Far East and Africa. Such drafts require the drawee to pay interest at the current rate from the date of the draft to the approximate date that remittance is received in New York or other financial center. Other things being equal, exporters can sell these drafts to banks for the face amount without deductions. This clause reads: "With interest added thereto at .....% per annum from date hereof to approximate due date of remittance in .....".

LETTER OF CREDIT (L/C) A formal letter issued by a bank which authorizes the drawing of drafts against the bank up to a fixed limit and under terms specified in the letter. Through the issuance of such letters, a bank pledges its credit on behalf of its customers and thereby facilitates the transaction of business between parties who may not be otherwise acquainted with each other. The drafts may be payable upon presentation to the bank which issued the credit or at some later time, as fixed by the terms of the credit. The letter of credit may be sent directly by the issuing bank or its customer to the beneficiary or the terms of the credit may be transmitted through a correspondent bank. In the latter event the correspondent may add its guarantee (confirmation) to that of the issuing bank, depending on the arrangements made between the seller and the purchaser. When such a guarantee is added, the letter is described as confirmed credit. Letters of credit may be revocable or irrevocable depending on whether the issuing bank reserves the right to cancel the credit prior to its expiration date.

OPEN ACCOUNT (O/A) Open Account, no draft drawn. Transaction payable when specified, i.e. R/M return mail; E.O.M. end of month; 30 days — 30 days from date of invoice; 2/10/60—2% discount for payment in 10 days, net if paid 60 days from date of invoice. If no term is specified O/A usually implies payment by return mail.

ORDER BILL OF LADING Usually, "To Order" Bills of Lading are to the order of the shipper and endorsed in blank, thereby giving the holder of the B/L title to the shipment. They may also be to the order of the consignee or bank financing the transaction. Order Bills of Lading are negotiable (whereas Straight Bills of Lading are not).

PAR VALUE The official value of a nation's currency stated in terms of a quantity of gold or of another currency. Par values of most currencies are established in agreement with the International Monetary Fund.

PERIL POINT Term from the U. S. Trade Agreements Act meaning the point below which a tariff cannot, in the opinion of the Tariff Commission, be lowered without causing or threatening to cause serious injury to the domestic producers of competitive goods.

P.L. 480 The Agricultural Trade Development and Assistance Act of 1954. Under this legislation the President is authorized to assist U. S. agricultural exports in various ways including making sales in the currency of the purchasing country. The Cooley Amendment to this law provides for loans of local currencies generated from the sale of surplus commodities abroad to private American and, under certain conditions, to private foreign enterprises

PRO FORMA INVOICE It is an abbreviated invoice sent in advance of a shipment, usually to enable the buyer to obtain an import permit or an exchange permit or both. The pro forma invoice gives a close approximation of the weights and values of a shipment that is to be made. It is not binding on the exporter until the order is confirmed.

PURCHASING POWER PARITY The relative ability of a unit of currency in one country to purchase goods in that country compared to the ability of a unit of currency in a second country to purchase goods in the second country; the relationship of prices between the two countries.

RECIPROCAL TRADE ACT Common misnomer for Trade Agreements Act (See TA).

SECOND OF EXCHANGE The duplicate copy of a draft, when two or more are drawn.

SIGHT DRAFT (S/D) A draft so drawn as to be payable on presentation to the drawee (or within a brief period thereafter known as days of grace), also referred to as a Demand Draft. Custom, in certain areas, has in effect made an Arrival Draft out of a Sight Draft because buyers often will not pay a Sight Draft until the arrival of the carrying vessel.

SOFT CURRENCY A currency which is not freely convertible into all other currencies, but may be converted into other soft currencies only.

SOFT LOANS Loans with exceptionally lenient terms for repayment such as low interest, extended amortization, or the right to repay in the currency of the borrower.

SPOT EXCHANGE Foreign exchange for immediate delivery by the seller and immediate payment by the buyer.

STALE BILL OF LADING One which has not been presented under a L/C to the issuing bank within a reasonable time after its date, thus precluding its arrival at port of discharge by the time the steamer carrying the related shipment has arrived.

STERLING AREA United Kingdom, Commonwealth Dominions except Canada, British colonies and certain non-British countries with all currencies related to value of Sterling and with monetary reserves chiefly in Sterling.

STRAIGHT BILL OF LADING One in which the goods are consigned directly to a named consignee and not to his order. Delivery can be made only to that person. Such a bill of lading is non-negotiable.

TA or TAA Trade Agreements Act. The basic legislation authorizing the President to negotiate with other nations for reciprocal tariff reductions. First enacted in 1934 and renewed continuously since.

TENOR The term fixed for the payment of a draft.

TERMS OF TRADE The ratio of the prices a country pays for its imports to the prices it receives for its exports.

TIED LOAN Customarily refers to a loan made by a governmental agency which requires the borrower to spend the proceeds in the lender's country.

TIME DRAFT A draft maturing at a certain fixed time after presentation or acceptance. This may be a given number of days after sight (acceptance) or a given number of days after date of draft.

TRAVELER'S LETTER OF CREDIT A letter addressed to all of the issuing bank's correspondents, generally authorizing them to negotiate drafts drawn by the beneficiary named in the credit, upon presentation of proper identification and up to a total limit specified in the credit. Such credits are also known as Circular Letters of Credit because they may be presented for negotiation to a number of banks in the course of use. In addition to the letter of credit itself, the beneficiary is furnished with a separate list of the bank's correspondents and a special form known as a Letter of Indication containing a specimen of the beneficiary's signature, certified by the bank issuing the credit, to serve as a basis of identification for the beneficiary. Payments are endorsed on the reverse side of the letter of credit by the correspondent banks when they negotiate drafts.

TRUST RECEIPT A document signed by a buyer, on the strength of which a bank releases merchandise to him for the purpose of manufacture or sale, but retains title to the goods. The buyer obligates himself to maintain the identity of the goods or the proceeds thereof distinct from the rest of his assets and to hold them subject to repossession by the bank. Trust Receipts are used extensively under letters of credit, so that the buyer may obtain possession of the goods before he pays the issuing bank. They are also used extensively in the Far East, where it is customary to sell on terms of 60 or 90 days, documents against payment. The collecting banks in that area permit buyers of good standing to clear the goods, under a trust receipt contract, before the maturity date of the draft. In some countries, Warrants serve the same purpose.

UNCLEAN BILL OF LADING One in which a notation has been made by the carrier of any defects found in the goods when they are received for transporting. For example, such phrases as "3 hogsheads broken" or "4 sacks torn" may be inserted.

WAREHOUSE RECEIPTS In general a warehouse receipt is a receipt for commodities deposited with a bona fide warehouseman and which identifies the commodities deposited. A warehouse receipt in which it is stated that the commodities referred to thereon will be delivered to the depositor or to any other specified person or company is a non-negotiable warehouse receipt; but a warehouse receipt on which it is stated that the commodities will be delivered to the "bearer" or to the order of any specified person or company is a negotiable warehouse receipt.
Endorsement (without endorsement if issued to the order of "Bearer"), and delivery of a negotiable warehouse receipt serves to transfer the property covered by the Receipt. "There is no difference between a Warehouse Receipt and a Bill of Lading in this respect" (Davis v. Russell, 52 cal., 611). In 1906 the Uniform Warehouse Receipts Act was drafted for the purpose of achieving uniformity among the states in the law relating to the warehouseman

as a bailee for hire. The act since has been adopted by every State in the Union. It has been adopted also by the District of Columbia and Puerto Rico.

WEBB-POMERENE ACT An act which exempts from the antitrust laws associations among business rivals engaged in export trade provided they do not restrain trade within the U. S. or the export trade of any domestic competitor of the association.

WESTERN HEMISPHERE TRADE CORPORATION Any U. S. corporation whose income is subject to a corporate income tax rate presently 14 percentage points lower than the regular tax rate. To qualify, the corporation must meet certain conditions, including that all its income be derived from sales in the Western Hemisphere, that 95% of its gross income be derived from sales in the Western Hemisphere but outside of the U. S. A. and that 90% of its gross income be derived from an active trading business.

Alliance for Progress

A cooperative undertaking based on a "Declaration to the Peoples of America" and "The Charter of Punta del Este", signed by all Member States of the Organization of American States except Cuba, at Punta del Este, Uruguay on August 17, 1961.

The Charter states, "it is the purpose of the Alliance for Progress to enlist the full energies of the peoples and governments of the American republics in a great cooperative effort to accelerate the economic and social development of the participating countries of Latin America." The Declaration asserts; "The United States, for its part, pledges its efforts to supply financial and technical cooperation in order to achieve the aims of the Alliance for Progress. To this end, the United States will provide a major part of the minimum of 20 billion dollars, principally in public funds, which Latin America will require over the next 10 years from all external sources in order to supplement its own efforts." (1)

The Alliance for Progress Information Team has stated: "Under the Alliance, Latin America is to invest at least $80 billion of the minimum $100 billion required for development during the decade. The balance is coming from the U.S., international lending agencies from public and private sources in the capital exporting nations of the Free World." (2)

Balance of Payments

"The U.S. balance of payments is the record of financial transactions which take place between the United States and the rest of the world during a particular period of time. The balance-of-payments statement covers receipts and payments for both private and governmental transactions, whether they are settled in cash or financed by credit. It includes, for example, merchandise trade, tourist expenditures, sales of military equipment, interest and dividends, governmental loans, private investments in factories, transactions in stocks and bonds, and bank credits. It also includes changes in the country's official reserves of gold and foreign currency and in foreign holdings of its currency." (3a)

Balance of Trade

"The relationship between a country's merchandise trade imports and exports. A country's balance of trade is only one aspect of its balance of payments. The United States has had a favorable balance of trade, that is, a surplus of merchandise exports over imports in almost every year since 1874." (3a)

Brussels Tariff Nomenclature

"In many European countries and in a number of countries outside Europe, customs tariff nomenclature is based on the 1955 Tariff Nomenclature (BTN) of the Customs Cooperation Council. This is an internationally agreed nomenclature in which articles are grouped according to the nature of the material of which they are made, as has been traditional in customs nomenclature." (4)

"According to a Nomenclature Committee report made last December in Brussels, 75 countries were operating Brussels-type tariffs and 23 countries were preparing such tariffs as of October 30, 1964. The U.S. does not use the Brussels Tariff Nomenclature. The Brussels Tariff Nomenclature (BTN), officially adopted in 1959, is published in two official languages — English and French — and a Spanish text has been developed by the Spanish-speaking member countries. Countries adhering to the BTN use a common classification for goods going through national customs.

CARIFTA

Caribbean Free Trade Association. Created in 1968 by some of the larger West Indian countries in the Caribbean for the purpose of stimulating greater inter-island commerce and trade and more coordinated economic and industrial development, CARIFTA has since been expanded to include almost all of the English-speaking countries of the Caribbean, including Belize, and was changed into a Common Market in 1973.

Central American Common Market

Established by the General Treaty of Central American Economic Integration effective June 4, 1961. The CACM holds to ten bilateral agreements which exclude a number of commodities of Central American origin from immediate participation in the free arrangement. There are provisions included for a common external tariff. MEMBERS: Guatemala, El Salvador, Honduras, Nicaragua and Costa Rica. (6)

China Trade Act

"The China Trade Act of 1922, as amended, authorizing creation of corporations to engage in business within the China area (now limited to Hong Kong and Taiwan), offers unusual benefits to the prospective investor...Companies chartered under the Act by the U.S. Department of Commerce are entitled to relief, usually full exemption, from Federal income taxation on profits derived from the sale of U.S. goods. Dividends received by stockholders residing in Hong Kong and Taiwan are also exempted from U.S. individual income tax." (7)

COMECON

"COMECON is the Council for Mutual Economic Assistance , an organization established by the USSR and the Eastern European nations in 1949 to promote economic integration of the entire area." (22) Members: USSR, Bulgaria, Czechoslovokia, East Germany, Hungary, Poland, Rumania.

Convention of Paris for the Protection of Industrial Property

"The Paris Convention is the major multilateral agreement in the patent field. (Concluded in 1883, the convention was subsequently revised at Brussels in 1900, at Washington in 1911, at The Hague in 1925, at London in 1934, and at Lisbon in 1958.) Its members constitute a 'Union', generally called the 'Paris Union', for the protection of patents, trademarks, and other forms of industrial property. (These include, under the convention, utility models, industrial designs, trade names, indications of source, and appellations of origin.) Any country may adhere at its request, automatically undertaking all the obligations and receiving all the advantages of the Convention. The Soviet Union is the 68th country to adhere to the convention. Prior to Soviet adherence, the Paris Union had already included all the countries of Eastern Europe except Albania, all the industrialized non-Communist countries, and many developing countries. The United States adhered in 1887... Under the Convention's national treatment' provisions, each member state guarantees to the nationals of each other member state the same treatment it gives its own nationals... According to U.S. Patent Office figures, U.S. nationals are currently filing about 20 percent of all patent applications abroad and foreign nationals are filing about 25 percent of all patent applications in this country. The economic importance foreign patent licensing arrangements can have to a country is indicated by the fact that, according to the U.S. Department of Commerce, such arrangements by U.S. firms brought into the United States in 1964 close to half a billion dollars in royalty payments." (8)

Cooley Loans

"Under Section 104 (e), Title I of Public Law 480, the Agricultural Trade Development and Assistance Act of 1954, up to 25 percent of the foreign currencies received by the U.S. Government in payment for surplus agricultural commodities may be lent to qualified borrowers to develop business and expand trade. These local currency loans, usually referred to as 'Cooley loans', are named after Congressman Harold D. Cooley, who sponsored the amendment to Public Law 480 setting aside some of the proceeds of certain surplus sales for relending to U.S. private business." (9)

Countervailing Duty

"The law relating to countervailing duties is concerned with payments or bestowals of bounties or grants on any articles or merchandise exported to the United States...The act requires that the Secretary of the Treasury shall from time to time ascertain and determine, or estimate, the net amount of each such bounty or grant and shall declare the net amount so determined or estimated....The law states that the amount to be paid shall be an additional duty equal to the net amount of the bounty or grant estimated or ascertained." (10)

Drawback

The term "drawback" is classically used to mean the refunding of import duties paid on imported raw materials when goods containing such materials are exported — "When articles manufactured or produced in the U.S. with the use of imported merchandise (or substituted merchandise of the same kind and quality as the imported merchandise involved) are exported, a refund of 99% of the duties paid on the imported merchandise is allowable as a drawback... A refund of the entire amount of duties paid is allowable when imported goods are exported from a bonded customs warehouse within the warehousing period." (10)

Disc

Domestic International Sales Corporation. Established by Act of Congress in 1972 to provide a tax incentive to companies engaged in export. It allows a tax deferral of up to 50% of corporate pre-tax profits which may become a tax write-off if the funds are spent in export promotion programs. Loans to the parent company are also allowed under certain conditions. Note: a corporation may not be both a DISC and a WHTC.

Duty

"All goods imported into the United States are subject to duty unless specifically exempted therefrom. Customs duties are classified as ad valorem, specific, or compound. An ad valorem rate of duty is a percentage which is applied to the dutiable value of the imported goods. A specific duty is a specified amount per unit of weight, gauge, or other measure of quantity, as 10 cents per pound. A compound duty is one combining specific and ad valorem duties upon a single item of goods, as 10 cents per pound and 35 percent ad valorem." (10)

Edge Act

"Edge Act and Agreement corporation are United States corporations carrying out international banking and financing operations, some of which, notably equity investment abroad, the parent banks themselves are not permitted to undertake under existing laws and regulations. The corporations' actual functions range from acting as holding companies to rendering a wide variety of international banking services; and they include also the financing — through term loans and equity participations — of industrial and financial projects in both developed and underdeveloped countries...In 1916, section 25 of the Federal Reserve Act was amended so that any national bank with a capital and surplus of $1 million or more was authorized to invest, singly or jointly, up to 10 per cent of its capital and surplus in a corporation chartered under Federal or state law to conduct 'international or foreign banking' activities. Each corporation was required to 'enter into an agreement' with the Board of Governors of the Federal Reserve System as to the type of activities it would undertake and the manner in which it would conduct its operations. The wording of this provision gave rise to the name Agreement corporation.

"As an additional inducement to the expansion of the foreign business of the United States, Congress passed a law in December 1919 (sponsored by Senator Walter E. Edge of New Jersey). This act added section 25(a) to the Federal Reserve Act, a section that authorized the Board of Governors to charter corporations 'for the purpose of engaging in international or foreign financial operations...either directly or through the agency, ownership, or control of local institutions in foreign countries'. The stock of these corporations, which have come to be called Edge Act corporations, is also eligible for bank ownership. The corporations must be capitalized at a minimum of $2 million." (27)

Escape Clause

"A provision in existing trade agreement legislation that authorizes the President to take action on the basis of a U.S. Tariff Commission investigation and report when increased imports, due to a trade agreement concession, are causing or threatening serious injury to a domestic industry." (3a)

Euro-dollar

"Euro-dollars are U.S. dollars held on deposit with banks outside the United States and used by them to meet their own temporary needs for additional liquidity or to extend loans to commercial borrowers. The market defies precise statistical measurement....The label 'Euro-dollar' is something of a misnomer. Euro-dollars are not a special kind of dollars but differ from ordinary dollar deposits only in respect to the channels through which they move and in which they can earn higher rates of interest than obtained in the United States." (23)

"Having grown from virtually nothing to more than $10 billion in net assets in the last eight years, the Euro-dollar market is now one of the world's largest markets for short-term funds- mostly dollars...The Euro-dollar market is a market, located principally in Europe, for lending and borrowing the world's most important convertible currencies. The currency mainly dealt in is the dollar, but the market also deals In such major European currencies as the pound sterling, the Swiss franc, the Deutsche mark, the Netherlands guilder, and the French franc. The professional participants in it are commercial banks, but merchant banks, private banks, and some investment banking firms are included...But this description does not touch upon one aspect of the market that gives it its unique character, namely, that the transactions in each currency take place outside the country where that currency originates. The market for Euro-dollars refers to the market in dollars outside the United States, not to the origin or the character of the dollars being dealt in. The Euro-dollar market in, say, London, thus deals overwhelmingly with titles to dollar deposits, i.e., dollars deposited in banks in the United States...

"The process of using Euro-dollars and other currencies begins when some bank in the market collects funds in the form of deposits. The bank uses some of these funds in its own operations, and transfers the balance to another bank in the form of a deposit. This process may be repeated two or more times until all the funds are finally used in either of two ways:

first they are lent to a business enterprise other than a bank to finance commercial or industrial transactions; or second, they are used by banks to improve their reserves or liquidity and thus to contribute to their over-all operations...

"Only a small part of the dollar deposits in the Euro-dollar market at the present time is, therefore, owned by residents of the United States. The overwhelming bulk of these deposits represents dollars already owned by foreigners of purchased by them with other currencies...Commercial banks own a sizable amount of the dollars deposited in the Euro-dollar market. Their funds come from four sources; dollars deposited by their customers; other foreign currencies deposited by their customers and swapped into dollars; domestic currency owned by the bank and swapped into dollars; and dollars borrowed by the bank in the Euro-dollar market and redeposited in other banks at a higher rate of interest or for a more convenient length of time." (24)

European Economic Community (EEC)

"A regional economic grouping of nine European states—France, West Germany, Italy, Belgium, the Netherlands, and Luxembourg. It was established in 1958 by the Treaty of Rome for the purpose of unifying the economies of its member states over a 12 to 15 year period. In addition to the gradual elimination of customs duties and other trade barriers among its members and the establishment of a common outside tariff, the EEC also provides for the free movement of labor and capital, a common agricultural policy, and other integrating measures." (3a) England, Ireland and Denmark were admitted in 1973.

European Free Trade Association (EFTA)

"A regional trade grouping, essentially a free trade area of seven European countries — Austria, Denmark, Norway, Portugal, Sweden, Switzerland, and the United Kingdom. Finland is an associate member. Established in 1960 by the Stockholm Convention, EFTA provides for the gradual elimination of customs duties and other trade barriers among its members. Unlike the EEC, members of EFTA retain their own individual tariffs against outside countries." (3) On December 31, 1966, EFTA made the final reduction on their tariffs on manufactured goods originating in the EFTA countries and trade between them." EFTA is now slowly dissolving into the expanded EEC.

Export Control Act

"No special license is needed to engage in export-import trade. However, the U.S. Government does control exports of U.S. goods to all foreign countries except Canada... The Department of Commerce has established two types of export licenses, validated and general. By far the vast majority of goods can move to free world countries under an appropriate general license. No formal license application is required for a general license as is the case for a validated license... Validated licenses are necessary for certain types of strategic goods, regardless of destination, and for all but certain 'peaceful' items intended for the European Soviet bloc... Under the provisions of the Export Control Act of 1949, as amended, the Congress has charged the Department of Commerce with the responsibility of denying applications for licenses to export any commodity to the bloc if that commodity would make a significant contribution to the military or economic potential of the bloc which would prove detrimental to the national security and welfare of the United States." (11)

Foreign Trade Zone

"A foreign trade zone is an isolated enclosed, and policed area, in or adjacent to a port of entry, operated as a public utility by a public or private corporation, and furnished with facilities for loading, unloading, handling, storing, manipulating, manufacturing, and exhibiting goods and for reshipping them by land, water or air. Foreign and domestic materials, components, and merchandise, unless prohibited by law, may be brought into a zone without being subject to the U.S. customs laws that govern the entry of goods or the payments of duty thereon, and, subject to the Foreign Trade Zones Act, may be: Manufactured, ex-

hibited, packed, stored, destroyed, processed, mixed, marked, consummated, cleaned, pack-
aged, assembled, graded, repacked, sold, manipulated, broken up, labeled." (12)

"Establishment of a zone in Honolulu will result in a total of nine separate zone locations, the largest maximum number ever in operation at one time since the enactment of the
Foreign Trade Zones Act in 1934. There are currently foreign trade zones in New York, New
Orleans, San Francisco, Seattle, Toledo, and Mayaguez, Puerto Rico, as well as two special-
purpose subzones for manufacturing in San Francisco and in Penuelas, Puerto Rico." (13)

Forwarder

"Basically a freight forwarder, as the term suggests, books freight space and sees that
your goods are placed on the boat (or plane) and arrive at their destination. In this connection, he will quote you shipping rates, advise you as to the proper timing of a shipment, prepare any necessary shipping, consular, and other documents, arrange customs clearances, and
advance freight charges and other shipping expenses and consular fees. The services of the
freight forwarder may go far beyond the ones enumerated, depending on your needs. He is
also prepared to handle the inland transportation of your goods both in this country and
abroad, provide (or advise you concerning) packing and marking, arrange for marine insurance and warehousing, and forward banking collection papers. Some will even help you arrange financing, check on potential markets, and assist you in finding agents and customers.
The fees charged are usually on a per-shipment basis. Sometimes, they are based on the value
of the shipment and the services performed and an annual retainer arrangement is not un-
common. Many freight forwarders also act as customhouse brokers." (14)

Free Ports

"More than 100 free ports and trade zones are now in operation in 35 countries, usually
at seaports...for receipt of mass shipments of goods which are then transshipped in small lots
to customers throughout the surrounding area. The United States has six zones, known as
Foreign Trade Zones...Goods from abroad may be brought into these zones and combined
with domestic materials or used in the manufacture of other goods without the payment of
duties unless the combined product is sold in the United States...Goods from abroad may
also be brought into these zones, just as in the free zones of other nations, stored, cleaned,
assembled, exhibited, and repacked there, and then shipped to other countries without payment of U.S. customs duties." (14)

General Agreement on Tariffs and Trade (GATT)

An international trade agreement which was completed on October 30, 1947 and came
into force on January 1, 1948 as a "provisional" or interim understanding by eight trading
nations, including the United States. Today 72 countries are contracting parties to the
GATT. Under the GATT, several rounds of inter-governmental tariff negotiations have taken
place—at Annecy, France, in 1949; at Torquay, England, in 1950-51; The Dillon Round at
Geneva in 1960-61; and the Kennedy Round, at Geneva in 1964-1967. The agreement consists of (1) schedules, or lists of tariff concessions (products for which maximum tariff treatment have been agreed upon); (2) a code of principles and rules governing the import and export trade of contracting parties; (3) a forum for discussion of mutual problems of international trade. (15)

International Centre for Settlement of Investment Disputes

"The International Centre was established as an autonomous international organization
under the Convention on the Settlement of Investment Disputes between States and Nationals of Other States which came into force on October 14, 1966 and has been signed to
date by 49 States...The purpose of the International Centre is to provide facilities to which
Contracting States and foreign investors which are nationals of other Contracting States
have access, on a voluntary basis, for the settlement of investment disputes between them,

in accordance with rules laid down in the Convention. The method of settlement selected might be conciliation or arbitration, or conciliation followed by arbitration, in case the conciliation effort would fail. The initiative for such proceedings could come from a State as well as from an investor. The Centre uses the administrative facilities of the World Bank in Washington." (25)

Latin American Free Trade Association (LAFTA)

Established by the Treaty of Montevideo, signed by seven countries on February 18, 1960 and initially effective on June 1, 1961, the objective is to create a free trade zone by eliminating tariffs among member nations within 12 years, through annual negotiations designed to reduce duties at the average rate of 8% per year. *Members*: Argentina, Brazil, Chile, Mexico, Paraguay, Peru, Uruguay, the original signatories, plus Columbia and Ecuador, which signed the treaty in 1962, Venezuela in 1966, and Bolivia in 1967. (16)

Less Developed Country (LDC)

The "economically less developed countries" have been defined for tax purposes as "All foreign countries (including Trust Territories) in existence on or after the date of this order, other than Australia, Austria, Belgium, Canada, Denmark, Federal Republic of Germany, France, Iran, Iraq, Ireland, Italy, Japan, Kuwait, Kuwait-Saudi Arabia Neutral Zone, Libya, Liechtenstein, Luxembourg, Monaco, Netherlands, New Zealand, Norway, Portugal, San Marino, Saudi Arabia, Spain, Sweden, Switzerland, Union of South Africa, United Kingdom and any foreign country within the Sino-Soviet bloc..." Also excepted are certain overseas territories such as the Bahamas, Bermuda and Hong Kong. In general, therefore, the "less developed" areas of the world would include Turkey, Greece, the Philippines; Latin America except Cuba; Africa except Libya and the Republic of South Africa; and non-communist Asia except Japan and Hong Kong. (17)

Nomenclatura Arancelaria Uniforme Centroamericana (NAUCA)

Tariff classifications as adopted by the Central American Common Market in accordance with the Standard International Trade Classification of the United Nations.

Organization for Economic Cooperation and Development (OECD)

"Established in 1961, the OECD replaced the OEEC (the Organization for European Economic Cooperation). The OECD includes among its 21 members the United States, Canada, and Japan, in addition to 18 Western European countries. Its purpose is to promote cooperation in economic and monetary policies, including coordination of aid to less developed countries of the free world." (3a.)

OPIC

Overseas Private Investment Corporation. Established in 1970 to encourage a greater concentration of U.S. investments in developing countries. OPIC provides a system of insurance to guarantee U.S. overseas investments up to 80% of their value in the event of nationalization through expropriation.

Peril Point

Under the Reciprocal Trade Agreements legislation of prior years, the Peril Point was considered, "A rate of duty below which it is presumed that imports will increase and cause or threaten serious injury to an industry producing like or directly competitive products. Existing trade agreements legislation required, prior to trade agreement negotiations, that such a peril point determination be made by the Tariff Commission on all products upon which tariff concessions are contemplated." (3)

Standard International Trade Classification (SITC)

"Classification published by the United Nations of commodities that are traded internationally. The classification of commodities in U.S. tariff schedules differs from that of the SITC but can be converted into it". (3)

Steamship Freight Conference

"A steamship freight conference is an association of steamship lines serving the same range of ports in world commerce, formed for the purpose of fixing common freight rates and reaching agreements on tariffs and other matters, thus achieving rate stability." (18)

Tariff

"A schedule, system or scheme of duties imposed by a government on goods imported or exported; the rate or rates of duty imposed in a tariff, as the tariff on wool." (3a.)

United Nations Conference on Trade and Development (UNCTAD)

Permanent UN machinery designed to promote international trade and development. Conferences are to be held at intervals of not more than three years; consists also of a Trade and Development Board which is to meet twice a year and a secretariat to service the Conference and the Board. First Conference was held in Spring of 1964; made permanent organ of General Assembly in December 1964.

Warsaw Convention

"Convention for the unification of certain rules relating to international transportation by air," concluded at Warsaw, October 12, 1929. Limited liability of international airlines to $8,300 per passenger death; increased to $75,000 by an agreement in May, 1966. (19)

Webb-Pomerene Export Trade Act of 1918

"Subtitled an Act to Promote Export Trade, provides qualified exemptions for export trade associations from the prohibitions of the Sherman Antitrust Act of 1890 and the Federal Trade Commission and Clayton Acts of 1914...One of the important purposes of the Act was to facilitiate exporting by smaller companies. In general, a Webb-Pomerene association may act as the export sales agent of the members, arrange transportation for the goods of the members, agree upon prices and terms of trade, sale of the members' merchandise in foreign markets. There are at present 33 registered export associations with 320 member companies...Webb-Pomerene associations account for about $1 billion of the U.S. exports annually, or about 4.5% of the total U.S. export volume of $23 billion in 1963." (20)

Western Hemisphere Trade Corporation (WHTC)

"Section 921 of the Internal Revenue Code of 1954 defines a 'Western Hemisphere trade corporation' as a domestic corporation: '...all of whose business (other than incidental purchases) is done in any country or countries in North, Central, or South America, or in the West Indies..If 95 percent or more of the gross income of such domestic corporation...was derived from sources without the United States, and if 90 percent or more of its gross income from such period or such part thereof was derived from the active conduct of a trade or business.' " (26)

FOREIGN TRADE ABBREVIATIONS

AID	Agency for International Development
ASEAN	Association of South East Asian Nations
ASP	American Selling Price
BDSA	Business and Defense Services Administration
BIC	Bureau of International Commerce
BOP	Balance of Payments
BTN	Brussels Tariff Nomenclature
CABEI	Central American Bank for Economic Integration
CACM	Central American Common Market
CARIFTA	Caribbean Free Trade Association
CFC	Controlled Foreign Corporation
CIAP	Interamerican Committee on the Alliance for Progress
CIF	Cost, Insurance, Freight
COCOM	Coordinating Committee of 15 Western Nations for Control of Strategic Materials in East-West Trade
COD	Cash on Delivery
COMECON	Council for Mutual Economic Assistance
CPS	Cost-Price Study
CRU	Composite Reserve Unit
CXT	Common External Tariff
DISC	Domestic International Sales Corporation
ECA	Economic Commission for Africa
ECAFE	Economic Commission for Asia and the Far East
ECLA	Economic Commission for Latin America
ECOSOC	Economic and Social Council
EEC	European Economic Community
EFTA	European Free Trade Association
EURATOM	European Atomic Energy Community
FAO	Food and Agriculture Organization
FAS	Free Along Side
FCIA	Foreign Credit Insurance Association
FOB	Free on Board
GATT	General Agreement on Tariffs and Trade
GNP	Gross National Product
IATA	International Air Transport Association
IBRD	International Bank for Reconstruction and Development (World Bank)
IDA	International Development Association
IDB	Inter-American Development Bank
IFC	International Finance Corporation
IMF	International Monetary Fund
JEA	Joint Export Association
LAFTA	Latin American Free Trade Association
L/C	Letter of Credit
LDC	Less Developed Country
MFN	Most Favored Nation

OAS	Organization of American States
OECD	Organization for Economic Cooperation and Development
OFCS	Office of Foreign Commercial Services
OFS	Office of Field Services
OPIC	Overseas Private Investment Corporation
SDR	Special Drawing Right
SITC	Standard International Trade Classification
TVA	Taxe sur la valeur ajoutee
UNCTAD	United Nations Conference on Trade and Development
UNDP	United Nations Development Program
UNESCO	United Nations Educational, Scientific and Cultural Organization
UNIDO	United Nations Industrial Development Organization
USUN	United States Mission to the United Nations
WHTC	Western Hemisphere Trade Corporation

SOURCES

1. Department of State Publication 7276, reprinted from *Department of State Bulletin* of September 11, 1961.

2. *Alliance for Progress Weekly Newsletter*, Pan American Union, Vol. II, No. 33, August 17, 1964.

3. *ABC's of Foreign Trade*, Department of State Publication 7402, August 1962.

3a. Department of State Publication 7713, Revised October, 1964.

4. *Standard International Trade Classification*, Revised, United Nations, 1961.

5. U.S. Department of Commerce, *International Commerce* magazine, March 29, 1965.

6. U.S. Department of Commerce, *International Commerce* magazine, November 4, 1963 and March 18, 1963.

7. U.S. Department of Commerce, *International Commerce* magazine, May 24, 1965.

8. U.S. Department of State Bulletin, May 17, 1965, "Soviet Adherence to International Patent Convention," by Harold A. Levin.

9. Agency for International Development, "Memorandum to Businessmen — Aids to Business (Overseas Investment)" 1963.

10. U.S. Treasury Department, Bureau of the Customs, *Exporting to the United States*, Revised 1965.

11. U.S. Department of Commerce, *A Summary of U.S. Export Control Regulations*, January 1, 1965 — 58047.

12. 24th Annual Report of the Foreign Trade Zones Board to the Congress of the U.S., June 30, 1962.

13. U.S. Department of Commerce, Press Release G-65-23, dated Feb. 15, 1965.

14. U.S. Department of Commerce, *What You Should Know About Exporting*, August 1964, GPO 0740-213.

15. U.S. Department of State Publication 7235, July 1961, reprinted from *Department of State Bulletin* of June 26 and July 3, 1961. "The General Agreement of Tariffs and Trade; An Article-by-Article Analysis in Layman's Language," by Honore M. Catudal.

16. U.S. Department of Commerce, *International Commerce* magazine, October 21, 1963.

17. Presidential Executive Order 11285, "Designation of Certain Foreign Countries as Economically Less Developed Countries for Purposes of the Interest Equalization Tax," Federal Register, June 11, 1966.

18. New York Port Handbook, 1966, Port Resources Information Committee, Inc.

19. U.S. Department of State Publication 8042, "Treaties in Force," January 1, 1966.

20. U.S. Department of Commerce, *International Commerce* magazine, December 28, 1964.

21. This definition specially compiled from newspapers and other unofficial sources.

22. U.S. Department of Commerce, *International Commerce* magazine, December 5, 1966.

23. First National City Bank, *Monthly Economic Letter*, July, 1966.

24. International Monetary Fund, "Finance and Development," Vol. IV, No. 1, March, 1967.

25. SID Press Release, February 3, 1967.

26. Internal Revenue Bulletin, November 14, 1966 (NFTC M-6661).

27. Federal Reserve Bank of New York, *Monthly Review* magazine, May 1964.

28. National Foreign Trade Council, Inc.

SELLING TERMS

Exporters sell abroad on either of the following terms:

1. Export letters of credit opened by order and for the account of the buyer in favor of the seller.
2. Dollar drafts (or other currency drafts) drawn by the seller on the buyer.

Most import-export transactions occur under either letter of credit or draft terms. Some product sales lend themselves to cash deposits prior to shipment, but these are limited to items which might require a heavy investment by the exporter on behalf of the importer (specialized equipment, etc.), and serve to minimize the exporter's loss in the event of an order cancellation.

Open account terms are still used by exporters with their better customers in hard currency countries (countries with no exchange rate problems), but this approach is not recommended as a matter of rule. Consignment sales are limited to agents and to inter-company branch shipments, and these are virtually in the same class as open account sales.

The major distinction to be made between draft shipments and letter of credit shipments is that in the former case the seller assumes a certain amount of credit risk (the buyer's) plus the risk of sudden and/or unforeseen foreign exchange restrictions until dollars are eventually credited to his account.

These risks are eliminated with letters of credit. The credit of the importer's bank who opens the letter of credit on behalf of the importer replaces the buyer's credit risk. Further, if the L/C is confirmed by the exporter's bank, the exporter is also protected from foreign exchange regulations, fluctuations and other restrictions.

Even without confirmation by the exporter's bank, the fact that the importer's bank has actually opened an L/C in favor of the exporter generally means in many countries that the necessary foreign exchange (dollars if the exporter is in the United States) has been set aside for this particular transaction.

In Brazil, for example, an irrevocable letter of credit opened by the Banco do Brazil in favor of the exporter, coupled with an official Import Certificate, also forwarded directly to the exporter with the L/C, is evidence that the foreign exchange has been designated for the purchase of the exporter's goods.

Prior to opening a letter of credit, the importer will generally request a *proforma invoice* from the exporter. This is the exporter's formal quotation. It spells out in detail exactly what and how much the exporter is offering to sell, the price, all related charges, weights and measures, the proposed manner of shipment, and all other pertinent conditions of sale. It is on the basis of this proforma invoice that the importer will often apply to his bank for the L/C. Summarily, a proforma invoice is a "mirror" of the exporter's final invoice.

THE DOCUMENTARY LETTER OF CREDIT

A letter of credit (L/C) is the written undertaking of a bank, made at the request of a buyer, to honor drafts or other demands for payment upon compliance with the conditions specified in the L/C. The beneficiary of such a L/C is a seller, who is entitled under the terms of the L/C to draw or demand payment.

A letter of credit can be revocable or irrevocable, and irrevocable letters of credit may be confirmed or unconfirmed. A letter of credit which is irrevocable cannot be revoked without the consent of the beneficiary. An irrevocable letter of credit which is issued by a foreign bank may be confirmed by a bank in the seller's country.

Most commercial letters of credit are documentary. This means that payment will be made against the beneficiary's draft, accompanied by documents called for by the letter of credit, such as a commercial invoice, a bill of lading, an insurance certificate, etc. The buyer usually specifies what documentation is required.

Letters of credit may be on a sight or time draft basis. Sight drafts are payable on presentation. Time drafts are payable at some specified future date. The issuing bank accepts the beneficiary's drafts on presentation. This obligates the bank to pay the draft at maturity.

Revocable letters of credit are rarely used in import-export transactions. Consequently, they are not covered here.

Types of Letters of Credit

Confirmed irrevocable letter of credit (Figure 4.1): This type of L/C is issued by

FIGURE 4.1

BANCO DO BRASIL S. A.—mc

Rio de Janeiro(GB), December 20, 1972

CRÉDITO DOCUMENTÁRIO – *DOCUMENTARY CREDIT* IRREVOGÁVEL *IRREVOCABLE*	Crédito número/*Credit number*	
	do banco emitente/*of issuing bank*	do banco avisador/*advising bank*
Banco avisador / *Advising bank*	IC 22-314892	DE-8737

BANCO DO BRASIL S/A New York — U.S.A.	Tomador/*Applicant* COMPANHIA HIDRO ELÉTRICA DO SÃO FRAN CISCO — Rua Visconde de Inhaúma, 134 15° andar — Rio de Janeiro (GB)
Beneficiário / *Beneficiary*	Valor / *Amount*
M. P. Goodkin Company 140 - 145 Coit St., Irvington, N.J. 07111 - U.S.A.	US$2.730,00(two thousand, seven hun- dred and thirty dollars)
	Vencimento / *Expiry*
	Data/*Date* May 26, 1973

Dear Sirs,
We hereby issue in your favour this documentary credit which is available by *payment* against presentation of the following documents: FOB/ves-sel
a) two copy receipt for amount received marked "Drawn under Banco do Brasil S.A. Credit (reference as above)."
b) on board clean Bills of Lading issued to buyers' name (+)   *In case of*
airway transportation, the airbills must evidence the aircraft marks, the departure date and "Goods Shipped" declaration.
c) commercial invoices plus   2   copy(ies) bearing beneficiaries' declaration that the merchandise listed therein is in accordance with respective Import License(s) or Import Permit(s) and respective Amendments or Additives, if any.
d) beneficiaries' statement to the effect that they will or will not avail themselves of the unused balance (if any) and in the latter case, their agreement to its cancellation, quoting the respective amount.

(+)in 3 vias (1 original and 2 copies).
-insurance and freight charges will be paid in cruzeiros in Brazil.
-you may add your confirmation if required by the beneficiaries.
-transportation exclusively on Brazilian flag vessel, including those chartered by Brazilian companies.
"1 CÂMARA FOTOGRÁFICA, MARCA GOODKIN, MODELO VERTICAL 20", as per Im-port Permit n° 01-72/078820.

Each presentation of documents must indicate the credit number of the issuing bank and the credit number of the advising bank.

Despacho/Embarque de *Despatch/Shipment from* any USA port	válido até *expiry date*	Embarques parciais/*Partial shipments*	Transbordos/*Transshipments*
para *to* RECIFE - PE		not allowed	not allowed

Condições especiais:
Special conditions:

Reembolso
Reimbursement   to debit our account (Banco do Brasil S/A-General Manage-ment-Rio de Janeiro) with you.

We hereby engage that payment will be duly made against documents presented in conformity with the terms of this credit. The negotiating bank is hereby authorized to reimburse itself in the above mentioned manner for payments done when the issued documents are received according to the terms of this credit. All documents must be forwarded to us in one single air mail by the negotiating bank. The amount of each utilization must be endorsed on the reverse of this credit by the negotiating bank.	Indicações do banco avisador / *Advising bank's notification* December 27, 1972

Atenciosamente/*Yours truly*,
BANCO DO BRASIL S.A.

Auth. Signature   Auth. Signature
Local, data, nome e assinatura do banco avisador.
Place, date, name and signature of the advising bank.

Mod. 14/567-1

the buyer's bank abroad and must be confirmed by the exporter's bank. The buyer's bank's commitment is irrevocable. However, confirmation by the exporter's bank is wholly discretionary. It must be requested by the exporter. The exporter's bank may or may not accede to the exporter's request.

The confirmed irrevocable L/C gives the seller the greatest protection since it carries the commitment of two banks. The confirming bank (exporter's bank) will pay even if the issuing bank cannot or will not pay for any reason whatsoever. It is used mainly when the exporter has reason to suspect the viability of the importer's financial institutions.

Unconfirmed irrevocable letter of credit: This type of L/C is *not* confirmed by a bank in the United States. It is only the buyer's bank that commits itself irrevocably to pay the seller's drafts. It will usually ask a correspondent bank in the exporter's area to notify him that a L/C has been opened in his favor. The notifying bank is known as the "advising" bank. It may or may not also act as the correspondent bank. If it does, the advising bank may negotiate the seller's drafts. It is, however, under no obligation to honor such drafts. Payment remains the sole responsibility of the issuing bank. Therefore, the value of an unconfirmed irrevocable L/C depends on the credit standing of the foreign issuing bank and on the degree of political risk anticipated.

Most L/Cs are "straight documentary" instruments. This means that the beneficiary negotiates his drafts ultimately with the confirming or advising bank. "Negotiation" credits, when used, allow the beneficiary to negotiate his drafts with outside banks. This becomes important when the currency of final payment is other than the exporter's own national monetary unit.

In the United States, letter of credit "advices" generally state that they are subject to the "Uniform Customs And Practice For Documentary Credits." This has been adopted by the International Chamber of Commerce (1962 Revision), and is reprinted here in its entirety.

UNIFORM CUSTOMS AND PRACTICE FOR COMMERCIAL DOCUMENTARY CREDITS
(1962 REVISION)
THE INTERNATIONAL CHAMBER OF COMMERCE

GENERAL PROVISIONS AND DEFINITIONS

a. These provisions and definitions and the following articles apply to all documentary credits and are binding upon all parties thereto unless otherwise expressly agreed.

b. For the purposes of such provisions, definitions and articles the expressions "documentary credit(s)" used therein mean any arrangement, however named or described, whereby a bank (the issuing bank), acting at the request and in accordance with the instructions of a customer (the applicant for the credit), is to make payment to or to the order of a third party (the beneficiary) or is to pay, accept or negotiate bills of exchange (drafts) drawn by the beneficiary, or authorizes such payments to be made or such drafts to be paid, accepted or negotiated by another bank, against stipulated documents and compliance with stipulated terms and conditions.

c. Credits, by their nature, are separate transactions from the sales or other contracts on which they may be based and banks are in no way concerned with or bound by such contracts.

d. Credit instructions and the credits themselves must be complete and precise and, in order to guard against confusion and misunderstanding, issuing banks should discourage any attempt by the applicant for the credit to include excessive detail.

e. When the bank first entitled to avail itself of an option it enjoys under the following articles does so, its decision shall be binding upon all the parties concerned.

f. A beneficiary can in no case avail himself of the contractual relationships existing between banks or between the applicant for the credit and the issuing bank.

A.—FORM AND NOTIFICATION OF CREDITS

Article 1.—Credits may be either
  a) revocable, or
  b) irrevocable.

All credits, therefore, should clearly indicate whether they are revocable or irrevocable.

In the absence of such indication the credit shall be deemed to be revocable, even though an expiry date is stipulated.

Article 2.—A revocable credit does not constitute a legally binding undertaking between the bank or banks concerned and the beneficiary because such a credit may be modified or cancelled at any moment without notice to the beneficiary.

When, however, a revocable credit has been transmitted to and made available at a branch or other bank, its modification or cancellation shall become effective only upon receipt of notice thereof by such branch or other bank and shall not affect the right of that branch or other bank to be reimbursed for any payment, acceptance or negotiation made by it prior to receipt of such notice.

Article 3.—An irrevocable credit is a definite undertaking on the part of an issuing bank and constitutes the engagement of that bank to the beneficiary or, as the case may be, to the beneficiary and bona fide holders of drafts drawn and/or documents presented thereunder, that the provisions for payment, acceptance or negotiation contained in the credit will be duly fulfilled, provided that all the terms and conditions of the credit are complied with.

An irrevocable credit may be advised to a beneficiary through another bank without engagement on the part of that other bank (the advising bank), but when an issuing bank authorizes another bank to confirm its irrevocable credit and the latter does so, such confirmation constitutes a definite undertaking on the part of the confirming bank either that the provisions for payment or acceptance will be duly fulfilled or, in the case of a credit available by negotiation of drafts, that the confirming bank will negotiate drafts without recourse to drawer.

Such undertaking can neither be modified nor cancelled without the agreement of all concerned.

Article 4.—When an issuing bank instructs a bank by cable, telegram or telex to notify a credit and the original letter of credit itself is to be the operative credit instrument, the issuing bank must send the original letter of credit, and any subsequent amendments thereto, to the beneficiary through the notifying bank.

The issuing bank will be responsible for any consequences arising from its failure to follow this procedure.

Article 5.—When a bank is instructed by cable, telegram or telex to issue, confirm or advise a credit similar in terms to one previously established and which has been the subject of amendments, it shall be understood that the details of the credit being issued, confirmed or advised will be transmitted to the beneficiary excluding the amendments, unless the instructions specify clearly any amendments which are to apply.

Article 6.—If incomplete or unclear instructions are received to issue, confirm or advise a credit, the bank requested to act on such instructions may give preliminary notification of the credit to the beneficiary, for information only and without responsibility; and in that case the credit will be issued, confirmed or advised only when the necessary information has been received.

B.—LIABILITIES AND RESPONSIBILITIES

Article 7.—Banks must examine all documents with reasonable care to ascertain that they appear on their face to be in accordance with the terms and conditions of the credit.

Article 8.—In documentary credit operations all parties concerned deal in documents and not in goods.

Payment, acceptance or negotiation against documents which appear on their face to be in accordance with the terms and conditions of a credit by a bank authorized to do so, binds the party giving the authorization to take up the documents and reimburse the bank which has effected the payment, acceptance or negotiation.

If, upon receipt of the documents, the issuing bank considers that they appear on their face not to be in accordance with the terms and conditions of the credit, that bank must determine, on the basis of the documents alone, whether to claim that payment, acceptance or negotiation was not effected in accordance with the terms and conditions of the credit.

If such claim is to be made, notice to that effect, stating the reasons therefor, must be given by cable or other expeditious means to the bank from which the documents have been received and such notice must state that the documents are being held at the disposal of such bank or are being returned thereto. The issuing bank shall have a reasonable time to examine the documents.

Article 9.—Banks assume no liability or responsibility for the form, sufficiency, accuracy, genuineness, falsification or legal effect of any documents, or for the general and/or particular conditions stipulated in the documents or superimposed thereon; nor do they assume any liability or responsibility for the description, quantity, weight, quality, condition, packing, delivery, value or existence of the goods represented thereby, or for the good faith or acts and/or omissions, solvency, performance or standing of the consignor, the carriers or the insurers of the goods or any other person whomsoever.

Article 10.—Banks assume no liability or responsibility for the consequences arising out of delay and/or loss in transit of any messages, letters or documents, or for delay, mutilation or other errors arising in the transmission of cables, telegrams or telex, or for errors in translation or interpretation of technical terms, and banks reserve the right to transmit credit terms without translating them.

Article 11.—Banks assume no liability or responsibility for consequences arising out of the interruption of their business by strikes, lock-outs, riots, civil commotions, insurrections, wars, Acts of God or any other causes beyond their control. Unless specifically authorized, banks will not effect payment, acceptance or negotiation after expiration under credits expiring during such interruption of business.

Article 12.—Banks utilizing the services of another bank for the purpose of giving effect to the instructions of the applicant for the credit do so for the account and at the risk of the latter.

They assume no liability or responsibility should the instructions they transmit not be carried out, even if they have themselves taken the initiative in the choice of such other bank.

The applicant for the credit shall be bound by and liable to indemnify the banks against all obligations and responsibilities imposed by foreign laws and usages.

C.—DOCUMENTS

Article 13.—All instructions to issue, confirm or advise a credit must state precisely the documents against which payment, acceptance or negotiation is to be made.

Terms such as "first class", "well known", "qualified" and the like shall not be used to describe the issuers of any documents called for under credits and if they are incorporated in the credit terms banks will accept documents as presented without further responsibility on their part.

Documents evidencing Shipment or Despatch (Shipping Documents)

Article 14.—Except as stated in Article 18, the date of the Bill of Lading, or date indicated in the reception stamp or by notation on any other document evidencing shipment or despatch, will be taken in each case to be the date of shipment or despatch of the goods.

Article 15.—If the words "freight paid" or "freight prepaid" appear by stamp or otherwise on documents evidencing shipment or despatch they will be accepted as constituting evidence of the payment of freight.

If the words "freight prepayable" or "freight to be prepaid" or words of similar effect appear by stamp or otherwise on such documents they will not be accepted as constituting evidence of the payment of freight.

Unless otherwise specified in the credit or inconsistent with any of the documents presented under the credit, banks may honour documents stating that freight or transportation charges are payable on delivery.

Article 16.—A clean shipping document is one which bears no superimposed clause or notation which expressly declares a defective condition of the goods and/or the packaging.

Banks will refuse shipping documents bearing such clauses or notations unless the credit expressly states clauses or notations which may be accepted.

Marine Bills of Lading

Article 17.—Unless specifically authorized in the credit, Bills of Lading of the following nature will be rejected:
   a) Bills of Lading issued by forwarding agents.
   b) Bills of Lading which are issued under and are subject to the conditions of a Charter-Party.
   c) Bills of Lading covering shipment by sailing vessels.

However, unless otherwise specified in the credit, Bills of Lading of the following nature will be accepted:
   a) "Port" or "Custody" Bills of Lading for shipments of cotton from the United States of America.

b) "Through" Bills of Lading issued by steamship companies or their agents even though they cover several modes of transport.

Article 18.—Unless otherwise specified in the credit, Bills of Lading must show that the goods are loaded on board.

Loading on board may be evidenced by an on board Bill of Lading or by means of a notation to that effect dated and signed or initialled by the carrier or his agent, and the date of this notation shall be regarded as the date of loading on board and shipment.

Article 19.—Unless transhipment is prohibited by the terms of the credit, Bills of Lading will be accepted which indicate that the goods will be transhipped enroute, provided the entire voyage is covered by one and the same Bill of Lading.

Bills of Lading incorporating printed clauses stating that the carriers have the right to tranship will be accepted notwithstanding the fact that the credit prohibits transhipment.

Article 20.—Banks will refuse a Bill of Lading showing the stowage of goods on deck, unless specifically authorized in the credit.

Article 21.—Banks may require the name of the beneficiary to appear on the Bill of Lading as shipper or endorser, unless the terms of the credit provide otherwise.

Other Shipping Documents, etc.

Article 22.—Banks will consider a Railway or Inland Waterway Bill of Lading or Consignment Note, Counterfoil Waybill, Postal Receipt, Certificate of Mailing, Air Mail Receipt, Air Transportation Waybill, Air Consignment Note or Air Receipt, Trucking Company Bill of Lading or any other similar document as regular when such document bears the reception stamp of the carrier or issuer, or when it bears a signature.

Article 23.—When a credit calls for an attestation or certification of weight in the case of transport other than by sea, banks will accept a weight stamp or any other official indication of weight on the shipping documents unless the credit calls for a separate or independent certificate of weight.

Insurance Documents

Article 24.—Insurance documents must be as specifically described in the credit, and must be issued and/or signed by insurance companies or their agents or by underwriters.

Cover notes issued by brokers will not be accepted, unless specifically authorized in the credit.

Article 25.—Unless otherwise specified in the credit, banks may refuse any insurance documents presented if they bear a date later than the date of shipment as evidenced by the shipping documents.

Article 26.—Unless otherwise specified in the credit, the insurance document must be expressed in the same currency as the credit.

The minimum amount for which insurance must be effected is the CIF value of the goods concerned. However, when the CIF value of the goods cannot be determined from the documents on their face, banks will accept as such minimum amount the amount of the drawing under the credit or the amount of the relative commercial invoice, whichever is the greater.

Article 27.—Credits must expressly state the type of insurance required and, if any, the additional risks which are to be covered. Imprecise terms such as "usual risks" or customary risks" shall not be used.

Failing specific instructions, banks will accept insurance cover as tendered.

Article 28.—When a credit stipulates "insurance against all risks", banks will accept an insurance document which contains any "all risks" notation or clause, and will assume no responsibility if any particular risk is not covered.

Article 29.—Banks may accept an insurance document which indicates that the cover is subject to a franchise, unless it is specifically stated in the credit that the insurance must be issued irrespective of percentage.

Commercial Invoices

Article 30.—Unless otherwise specified in the credit, commercial invoices must be made out in the name of the applicant for the credit.

Unless otherwise specified in the credit, banks may refuse invoices issued for amounts in excess of the amount permitted by the credit.

The description of the goods in the commercial invoice must correspond with the description in the credit. In the remaining documents the goods may be described in general terms.

Other Documents

Article 31.—When other documents are required, such as Warehouse Receipts, Delivery Orders, Consular Invoices, Certificates of Origin, of Weight, of Quality or of Analysis, etc., without further definition, banks may accept such documents as tendered, without responsibility on their part.

D.—MISCELLANEOUS PROVISIONS

Quantity and Amount

Article 32.—The words "about", "circa" or similar expressions are to be construed as allowing a difference not to exceed 10% more or 10% less, applicable, according to their place in the instructions, to the amount of the credit or to the quantity or unit price of the goods.

Unless a credit stipulates that the quantity of the goods specified must not be exceeded or reduced, a tolerance of 3% more or 3% less will be permissible, always provided that the total amount of the drawings does not exceed the amount of the credit. This tolerance does not apply when the credit specifies quantity in terms of packing units or containers or individual items.

Partial Shipments

Article 33.—Partial shipments are allowed, unless the credit specifically states otherwise.

Shipments made on the same ship and for the same voyage, even if the Bills of Lading evidencing shipment "on Board" bear different dates, will not be regarded as partial shipments.

Article 34.—If shipment by instalments within given periods is stipulated and any instalment is not shipped within the period allowed for that instalment, the credit ceases to be available for that or any subsequent instalment, unless otherwise specified in the credit.

Validity and Expiry Date

Article 35.—All irrevocable credits must stipulate an expiry date for presentation of documents for payment, acceptance or negotiation, notwithstanding the indication of a latest date for shipment.

Article 36.—The words "to", "until", "till" and words of similar import applying to the expiry date for presentation of documents for payment, acceptance or negotiation, or to the stipulated latest date for shipment, will be understood to include the date mentioned.

Article 37.—When the stipulated expiry date falls on a day on which banks are closed for reasons other than those mentioned in Article II, the period of validity will be extended until the first following business day.

This does not apply to the date for shipment which, if stipulated, must be respected

Banks paying, accepting or negotiating on such extended expiry date must add to the documents their certification in the following wording:

> "Presented for payment (or acceptance or negotiation as the case may
> be) within the expiry date extended in accordance with Article 37
> of the Uniform Customs."

Article 38.—The validity of a revocable credit, if no date is stipulated, will be considered to have expired six months from the date of the notification sent to the beneficiary by the bank with which the credit is available.

Article 39.—Unless otherwise expressly stated, any extension of the stipulated latest date for shipment shall extend for an equal period the validity of the credit.

When a credit stipulates a latest date for shipment, an extension of the period of validity shall not extend the period permitted for shipment unless otherwise expressly stated.

Shipment, Loading or Despatch

Article 40.—Unless the terms of the credit indicate otherwise, the words "depature", "despatch", "loading" or "sailing" used in stipulating the latest date for shipment of the goods will be understood to be synonymous with "shipment".

Expressions such as "prompt", "immediately", "as soon as possible" and the like should not be used. If they are used, banks will interpret them as a request for shipment within thirty days from the date on the advice of the credit to the beneficiary by the issuing bank or by an advising bank, as the case may be.

Presentation

Article 41.—Documents must be presented within a reasonable time after issuance. Paying, accepting or negotiating banks may refuse documents if, in their judgement, they are presented to them with undue delay.

Article 42.—Banks are under no obligation to accept presentation of documents outside their banking hours.

Date Terms

Article 43.—The terms "first half", "second half" of a month shall be construed respectively as from the 1st to the 15th, and the 16th to the last day of each month, inclusive.

Article 44.—The terms "beginning", "middle" or "end" of a month shall be construed respectively as from the 1st to the 10th, the 11th to the 20th, and the 21st to the last day of each month, inclusive.

Article 45.—When a bank issuing a credit instructs that the credit be confirmed or advised as available "for one month", "for six months" or the like, but does not specify the date from which the time is to run, the confirming or advising bank will confirm or advise the credit as expiring at the end of such indicated period from the date of its confirmation or advice.

E.—TRANSFER

Article 46.—A transferable credit is a credit under which the beneficiary has the right to give instructions to the bank called upon to effect payment or acceptance or to any bank entitled to effect negotiation to make the credit available in whole or in part to one or more third parties (second beneficiaries).

A credit can be transferred only if it is expressly designated as "transferable" by the issuing bank. Terms such as "divisible", "fractionable", "assignable" and "transmissible" add nothing to the meaning of the term "transferable" and shall not be used.

A transferable credit can be transferred once only. Fractions of a transferable credit (not exceeding in the aggregate the amount of the credit) can be transferred separately, provided partial shipments are not prohibited, and the aggregate of such transfers will be considered as constituting only one transfer of the credit. The credit can be transferred only on the terms and conditions specified in the original credit, with the exception of the amount of the credit, of any unit price stated therein, and of the period of validity or period for shipment, any or all of which may be reduced or curtailed. Additionally, the name of the first beneficiary can be substituted for that of the applicant for the credit, but if the name of the applicant for the credit is specifically required by the original credit to appear in any document other than the invoice, such requirement must be fulfilled.

The first beneficiary has the right to substitute his own invoices for those of the second beneficiary, for amounts not in excess of the original amount stipulated in the credit and for the original unit prices stipulated in the credit, and upon such substitution of invoices the first beneficiary can draw under the credit for the difference, if any, between his invoices and the second beneficiary's invoices. When a credit has been transferred and the first beneficiary is to supply his own invoices in exchange for the second beneficiary's invoices but fails to do so on demand, the paying, accepting or negotiating bank has the right to deliver to the issuing bank the documents received under the credit, including the second beneficiary's invoices, without further responsibility to the first beneficiary.

The first beneficiary of a transferable credit can transfer the credit to a second beneficiary in the same country, but if he is to be permitted to transfer the credit to a second beneficiary in another country this must be expressly stated in the credit. The first beneficiary shall have the right to request that payment or negotiation be effected to the second beneficiary at the place to which the credit has been transferred, up to and including the expiry date of the original credit and without prejudice to the first beneficiary's right subsequently to substitute his own invoices for those of the second beneficiary and to claim any difference due to him.

The bank requested to effect the transfer, whether it has confirmed the credit or not, shall be under no obligation to make such transfer except to the extent and in the manner expressly consented to by such bank and until such bank's charges for transfer are paid.

Bank charges entailed by transfers are payable by the first beneficiary unless otherwise specified.

NOTE: In the U.S.A. the Definitions of Export Quotations, which are now in wide use, are known as the "Revised American Foreign Trade Definitions—1941" adopted July 30, 1941.

Adherence of the United States banks, which have subscribed to these regulations is effective July 1, 1963.

Procedures for Shipments Under Confirmed or Unconfirmed Irrevocable Letter of Credit

1. The U.S. exporter in New Jersey and the Brazilian importer in Rio sign a contract, providing for the shipment of equipment valued at U.S. $2,730.00 from New York to Rio under an irrevocable confirmed letter of credit, payable on sight of documentation by the advising bank.

2. The importer asks his bank in Rio, Banco do Brazil:
   a. to open an irrevocable L/C in favor of the exporter for U.S. $2,730.00 worth of equipment, and
   b. to have the credit confirmed by the exporter's bank in New Jersey, New Jersey Bank.

3. New Jersey Bank in New Jersey receives the L/C from Banco do Brazil along with the latter's request to confirm it. New Jersey Bank sends its confirmed L/C to the exporter.

4. The exporter prepares the documents and the draft covering his shipment in accordance with the L/C terms and ships the goods.

5. The exporter presents the documents and his draft to New Jersey Bank, who examines them. If they conform with the L/C terms, it accepts the draft. New Jersey Bank then sends the documents to Bank do Brazil in Rio and returns the accepted draft to the exporter.

6. Banco do Brazil examines the documents and, if in order, sends them on to the importer.

7. The documents give their holder the right to control the goods. Thus the importer can take possession of the goods from the carrier in Rio after the import duties have been paid.

8. In the meantime, immediately after New Jersey Bank accepts the draft, the exporter's account is credited with $2,730.00, less handling charges. New Jersey Bank pays the exporter and debits the amount of U.S. $2,730.00 from the account of Banco do Brazil.

It was pointed out before that confirmed letters of credit are used mainly when conditions urging extreme caution exist. On L/C shipments having other than sight draft terms "payable at sight of documents," confirmation is a good idea as protection against exchange rate fluctuations that may occur in the future but within the life of that particular L/C transaction.

A further advantage of having an L/C confirmed is to enable the exporter to discount the document without recourse to himself at a fairly low interest rate, probably at the bank's own acceptance rate.

Letters of Credits—Comments

Letter of credit terms are used generally when the seller does not normally do business with the buyer in question. A mutual "business at arm's length" attitude may prevail, and both parties may look to the L/C for maximum protection. The exporter must fulfill his obligations as specified in the L/C, originally by the importer, upon which he will get paid. Thus, the importer has a reasonable assurance that he will be paid promptly as prescribed in the L/C.

However, L/Cs cost the importer a financing charge on top of a bank service fee. The exporter is similarly charged a special bank service fee. Finally, it is an accepted practice in countries where there are few or no exchange rate difficulties for business to be conducted on a documentary draft basis. It is less expensive, involves less paper-work, and is overall less complicated than L/C transactions.

The red tape involved for an importer in obtaining an L/C for the account of an exporter is best demonstrated by examining the situation from the point of view of a United States importer. He must first apply to his bank for an L/C (Figure 4.2). The bank then cuts an original L/C in accordance with the importer's instructions (Figure 4.3). This is subsequently forwarded to a correspondent bank overseas (usually the exporter's bank). The exporter's bank forwards the original L/C with a written "Advice" to the exporter (Figure 4.4).

The sample "Advice" shown in Figure 4.4 is actually for U.S. exporters. If the exporter was in Brazil, selling to an American importer, the almost identical "Advice" would be sent to the Brazilian exporter by, say, Banco do Brazil, acting as New Jersey Bank's correspondent.

One of the more significant and perhaps revolutionary developments in the international banking world since 1970 has been a study in cooperation with the International Chamber Of Commerce to help streamline and standardize letter of credit forms and procedures. The International Chamber Of Commerce is currently submitting the text of a brochure describing the proposed changes to the various banking associations of the many countries engaged in world trade. This is the ICC's Brochure No. 268. The English translation is reproduced below.

**PRACTICAL RECOMMENDATIONS
FOR THE USE OF
STANDARD FORMS**

General Observations

This brochure includes the following standard forms:

FIGURE 4.2

258.009-R-5-70   **APPLICATION FOR COMMERCIAL CREDIT**

To NEW JERSEY BANK (NATIONAL ASSOCIATION)   Irrevocable Credit No. ....
          International Department
          Paterson, New Jersey 07505   Date ....

Gentlemen:

The undersigned hereby requests you to establish under his responsibility an irrevocable letter of credit (the "Credit")
                    ☐ cable in full detail
to be advised by   ☐ brief cable full details by mail
                    ☐ air mail

in favor of ....
                              (specify complete name and address of beneficiary)

for account of ....
                                           (name)

available by drafts at ....
                              (specify sight, 30 days sight, etc.)

to the extent of ....
to be drawn on]New Jersey Bank (National Association)/, Paterson, N. J., if Credit is in U. S. Dollars, or on a
correspondent selected by you if Credit is in a foreign currency, for .... per cent
invoice cost, accompanied by the following documents *(indicate by check mark):*
☐ Commercial invoice.
☐ Customs invoice.
☐ Insurance policy/certificate issued by an insurance company in negotiable form covering marine and war risks.
OR
☐ Marine and war risk insurance covered by us.
☐ On board steamer bills of lading made out to order of New Jersey Bank (National Association), Paterson, N. J.
    (L/C ....) marked notify the account party in the Credit.
NOTE: Unless instructed by you to the contrary New Jersey Bank (National Association) may authorize the negotiat
ing/paying bank to send all the documents to it in one airmail.
Other documents and/or additional instructions, if any: ....
....
....
.... purporting to evidence shipment(s) of ....
....
                    (Please specify commodity only, omitting details as to grade, quality, price, etc.)
                                        F. O. B. — C. I. F. — C. & F. . . . .
                                                    (Please indicate which term applies)

from .... to ....
                                                                    (indicate port(s) of destination)
Partial shipments ☐ are ☐ are not permitted.
At your option the sight draft, if required, may be omitted and the Credit be available solely against the documents
specified below.
☐ Bills of lading must show that the merchandise has been loaded on board the steamer named in the bills of lading
    not later than ....
Drafts/documents must be ☐ negotiated ☐ presented to New Jersey Bank (National Association) not later than
    ....

Negotiation charges, if any, are for the account of the beneficiary.
Any goods shipped under this Credit or documents representing the same may be delivered against trust receipt or
otherwise to ....
as agent or Custom House broker of the applicant.
IN CONSIDERATION of your establishment of the Credit substantially as applied for herein, we agree with you that the Terms and
Conditions set forth in the following two pages are hereby made a part of this application and are hereby accepted by us.

                    ....
                                           (Applicant)

                    By ....
                                       (Authorized Signature)

                    ....
                                           (Address)

(If this Application is executed by two or more parties as joint applicants, please also complete the second paragraph of Section 8 of the
Terms and Conditions.)

FIGURE 4.3

1

NEW JERSEY BANK AND TRUST COMPANY
INTERNATIONAL DEPARTMENT
PATERSON, NEW JERSEY   07505, U.S.A.

CABLE ADDRESS: NJBANK

TELEX No. 130432

IRREVOCABLE LETTER OF CREDIT No._____

DATE_____

THIS CREDIT IS ADVISED THROUGH

GENTLEMEN:

WE HEREBY AUTHORIZE YOU TO VALUE ON

FOR ACCOUNT OF

UP TO AN AGGREGATE AMOUNT OF

AVAILABLE BY YOUR DRAFTS AT

FOR

INVOICE COST TO BE ACCOMPANIED BY

BILLS OF LADING MUST BE DATED NOT LATER THAN

DRAFTS MUST BE   NOT LATER THAN

THIS CREDIT IS SUBJECT TO THE UNIFORM CUSTOMS AND PRACTICE FOR DOCUMENTARY CREDITS (1962 REVISION). INTERNATIONAL CHAMBER OF COMMERCE BROCHURE NO. 222. WE HEREBY AGREE WITH THE DRAWERS, ENDORSERS AND BONA FIDE HOLDERS OF THE DRAFTS DRAWN UNDER AND IN COMPLIANCE WITH THE TERMS OF THIS CREDIT THAT THESE DRAFTS WILL BE DULY HONORED BY THE ABOVE DRAWEE.
NEGOTIATING BANK IS TO FORWARD ALL DOCUMENTS IN ONE AIR MAIL.
NEGOTIATING BANK CHARGES, IF ANY, ARE FOR ACCOUNT OF BENEFICIARY. ALL DRAFTS MUST BE MARKED: "DRAWN UNDER NEW JERSEY BANK AND TRUST COMPANY CREDIT NO.

VERY TRULY YOURS,

258.005-R-11-68

Authorized Signature

Authorized Signature

FIGURE 4.4

NEW JERSEY BANK, N.A.
INTERNATIONAL DEPARTMENT
PATERSON, NEW JERSEY   07505, U.S.A.

CABLE ADDRESS: NJBANK

TELEX No. 130432

1

CORRESPONDENT'S IRREVOCABLE LETTER OF CREDIT No............................ DATE...

GENTLEMEN:

WE ARE INSTRUCTED BY

TO ADVISE YOU THAT THEY HAVE OPENED THEIR IRREVOCABLE CREDIT NUMBER   IN YOUR FAVOR FOR ACCOUNT OF

UP TO AN AGGREGATE AMOUNT OF

AVAILABLE BY YOUR DRAFTS ON US AT   TO BE ACCOMPANIED BY THE FOLLOWING DOCUMENTS:

ALL DRAFTS MUST BE MARKED: DRAWN UNDER NEW JERSEY BANK, N.A. ADVICE NO.   EXCEPT SO
FAR AS OTHERWISE EXPRESSLY STATED, THIS CREDIT IS SUBJECT TO THE UNIFORM CUSTOMS AND PRACTICE FOR COMMERCIAL DOCUMENTARY
CREDITS FIXED BY THE INTERNATIONAL CHAMBER OF COMMERCE (1962 REVISION) BROCHURE NO. 222. THE ABOVE MENTIONED CORRESPONDENT
ENGAGES WITH YOU THAT ALL DRAFTS DRAWN UNDER AND IN COMPLIANCE WITH THE TERMS OF THIS CREDIT WILL BE DULY HONORED ON
DELIVERY OF DOCUMENTS AS SPECIFIED IF PRESENTED AT THIS OFFICE ON OR BEFORE   ON WHICH DATE THIS ADVICE
EXPIRES.

THIS LETTER IS SOLELY AN ADVICE OF CREDIT OPENED BY THE ABOVE MENTIONED CORRESPONDENT AND CONVEYS NO ENGAGEMENT BY US.

VERY TRULY YOURS,

....
                    Authorized Signature   Authorized Signature

258.025-R-5/69

Issuing Bank's advice of its irrevocable credit available for negotiation (Forms No. 1).

  Form No. 1A — original for the beneficiary. (See Figure 4.5)
  Form No. 1B — copy for the advising bank.

Issuing Bank's advice of its irrevocable credit available for acceptance (Forms No. 2).

  Form No. 2A — original for the beneficiary.
  Form No. 2B — copy for the advising bank.

Issuing Bank's advice of its irrevocable credit available for payment (Forms No. 3).

  Form No. 3A — original for the beneficiary.
  Form No. 3B — copy for the advising bank.

Issuing Bank's advice of amendment to the credit (Forms No. 4).

  Form No. 4A — original for the beneficiary.
  Form No. 4B — copy for the advising bank.

In addition to the above.

Suggested sequence of text for documentary credit opened by telex or cable (Form No. 5).

Form to be used when the space in Forms Nos. 1, 2 and 3 are insufficient to contain all the required information (Form No. 6).

It is suggested that each of the Forms Nos. 1, 2, 3 and 4 be printed in sets, for example:

Form No. 1A — the original advice for the beneficiary,

Form No. 1B — the copy for the advising bank.

Form No. 1C — the copy for the issuing bank,

Form No. 1D — additional copy(ies) as required, etc.

Forms Nos. 1, 2 and 3 relate to irrevocable credits and no form is included for issuing the comparatively rare "revocable" credit. (See the special chapter on revocable credits, page 28).

It is recommended that the various forms be completed by clear, accurate and complete instructions, avoiding all unnecessary details, particularly concerning the description of goods.

Issuing banks may use different colours for the different groups of forms.

In order to avoid the Banks involved having in each case to examine the printed text of the forms, it is recommended that the phrase "This document conforms with Standard Form No. . . . of the ICC." be inserted in the left hand margin after the words "Except so far as otherwise expressly stated, this documentary credit is subject to the Uniform Customs and Practice for Documentary Credits (1962 Revision) International Chamber of Commerce Brochure No. 222".

It should be remembered that Brochure No. 222 can be obtained:

  — either from the National Committees of the International Chamber of Commerce.

  — or by applying to the Secretary General of the International Chamber of Commerce, 38, Cours Albert-1er, Paris 8e.

Features common to all standard forms

In drawing up the new standard forms, the recommendations of the 5th CIRIB* (commis-

FIGURE 4.5

Banque X / Bank X — Original — 7

Adresse télégraphique / Cable address — *No. de télex* / Telex number — *Lieu d'émission et date* / Place and date of issue

Numéro du crédit / Credit number: *de la banque émettrice* / of issuing bank — *de la banque notificatrice* / of advising bank

CREDIT DOCUMENTAIRE - DOCUMENTARY CREDIT
IRREVOCABLE

Banque notificatrice / Advising bank

Donneur d'ordre / Applicant

Bénéficiaire / Beneficiary

Montant / Amount

Validité / Expiry
Date / Date
à / in — *pour négociation* / for negotiation

M / Dear Sir(s),

Nous émettons en votre faveur ce crédit documentaire / **We hereby issue in your favour this documentary credit**

qui est utilisable par négociation de votre traite à
which is available by negotiation of your draft at

tirée sur
drawn on

et portant la mention: "Tirée en vertu du crédit documentaire No — *de (nom de la banque émettrice)"*
bearing the clause: "Drawn under documentary credit No. — of (name of issuing bank)"

accompagnée des documents suivants:
accompanied by the following documents:

concernant
covering

Expédition/Embarquement de
Despatch / Shipment from
à
to

Expéditions partielles / Partial shipments

Transbordements / Transhipments

Conditions spéciales:
Special conditions:

Nous garantissons aux tireurs et / ou porteurs de bonne foi que les traites émises et négociées en conformité avec les termes de ce crédit seront dûment honorées à présentation et que les traites acceptées conformément aux termes de ce crédit seront dûment honorées à leur échéance.

Le montant de chaque traite doit être inscrit au verso de ce crédit par la banque négociatrice.

We hereby engage with drawers and/or bona fide holders that drafts drawn and negotiated in conformity with the terms of this credit will be duly honoured on presentation and that drafts accepted within the terms of this credit will be duly honoured at maturity.

The amount of each draft must be endorsed on the reverse of this credit by the negotiating bank.

Vos dévoués / **Yours faithfully,**

Nom et signature de la banque émettrice.
Name and signature of the issuing bank.

Indications de la banque notificatrice / Advising bank's notification

Lieu, date, nom et signature de la banque notificatrice.
Place, date, name and signature of the advising bank.

Sauf stipulations particulières expressément définies, ce crédit documentaire est soumis aux "Règles et Usances uniformes relatives aux Crédits Documentaires" (Révision 1962) Chambre de Commerce Internationale (Brochure No. 222).

Except so far as otherwise expressly stated this documentary credit is subject to the "Uniform Customs and Practice for Documentary Credits" (1962 Revision) International Chamber of Commerce (Brochure No. 222).

1 A

sion 14/34) were respected, particularly concerning the format DIN A4 (210 mm x 297 mm), the basic spacing, and the typographical layout.

For purposes of this brochure, the forms have been printed in the two languages generally used for the work of the ICC (French and English). In practice, however, banks are entirely free to select the language(s) to be used; according to the custom of their country, they may choose.

— either their national language, if normally used for dealings with the advising bank and with the beneficiary,

— or two international languages,

— or a single international language if it is understood by all parties to the documentary credit operation.

On each document, the space reserved for the name of the addressee (advising bank or beneficiary as the case may be) is heavily outlined and, in addition, is marked by an oblique arrow. The purpose of these features is to facilitate the despatch of the forms. *For the purpose of the despatch therefore the Advising Bank's copy must be placed uppermost.*

The number 7 printed in the upper right hand corner is intended to facilitate and speed the distribution of mail upon receipt by the Advising Bank (5th CIRIB, 8th item).

If one of the Forms Nos. 1 to 4 is used to confirm a communication already sent by cable or telex, then, to avoid duplication it must be clearly marked "Confirmation of our cable/telex of...".

Special Recommendations

Forms Nos. 1A and 1B - **Issuing Bank's advice of its irrevocable credit available for negotiation.**

It will be noted that these forms require the drawing of a draft as it is the draft which is negotiated and not the documents which accompany it. Unless otherwise stipulated, negotiation in the place specified may be effected by any bank of the beneficiary's choice.

"Amount"

The amount may be indicated:

— either in figures and words,

— or in figures only, if they are perforated or otherwise given with some protective system.

"Expiry"

Type the expiry date in full, example: 30th September, 1970.

Centre section after "We hereby issue... available"

State the draft details.

"Despatch/Shipment from"

In addition to the name of the place/port, the period within which despatch/shipment must be effected may be indicated here.

*CIRIB: International Technical Conference on the Rationalization of Relations between Banks.

Example:

"latest..." or

"during...".

"Partial shipments/Transhipments"

Insert "Permitted" or "Prohibited" as the case may be.

"Special conditions"

This space may be used for additional details not covered elsewhere in the forms such as:

- any instructions for the despatch of documents,

- permitted clauses on Bills of Lading,

- indication, where applicable, that Charter Party Bills of Lading or Forwarding Agents' documents are acceptable,

- indication, where applicable, that the credit is transferable. If transferabel to another country this must be expressly stated,

- under credits available for negotiation of the beneficiary's usance drafts, any indication that the drawee bank is authorized to pay claims for discount charges or difference of exchange between sight and usance negotiation rates, etc.

"Instructions to the advising bank (Issuing Bank's Box Form No. 1B)"

- delete "without adding" or "adding" according to whether the documentary credit has to be confirmed or not.

Box for "Advising Bank's notification"

This space has been left blank to enable the advising bank to:

1) use its own language to notify the beneficiary,

2) indicate that either:

a) the credit is forwarded without its engagement:

Example:

"We hereby advise this credit without any engagement on our part", or

b) the credit is forwarded with the Advising Bank's confirmation:

Example:

"This credit bears our confirmation and we hereby engage to negotiate without recourse, on presentation to us, drafts drawn and presented in conformity with the terms of this credit".

"Multilateral Credits"

It frequently happens that an Issuing Bank is required to establish a credit through and payable in one country overseas, but available for negotiation in another country overseas where the beneficiary resides.

Example:

A South American Bank issues its US-$ credit through and payable with a New York Bank in favour of a beneficiary in France where it is to be available for negotiation.

In such cases, the form is prepared by the Issuing Bank and despatched in original and three copies to the drawee bank designated in the box as Advising Bank, with the addition of the words "through its correspondents in... (insert here the place where the credit is to be available for negotiation)". Upon receipt, the Advising/Drawee bank retains one copy, completes the box in the bottom right hand corner and forwards the original and one copy under covering memorandum to its correspondent in the negotiation centre asking it in turn to pass the original to the beneficiary and retain the copy for its files.

In those cases where the Issuing Bank sends its advise to its own correspondent in the centre of negotiation, a suitably annotated copy must be simultaneously sent direct to the drawee bank for information and necessary action.

Forms Nos. 2A and 2B - **Issuing Bank's advice of its irrevocable credit available for acceptance.**

"Amount"

Same comments as for Forms Nos. 1A and 1B.

"Expiry"

- a) Type the expiry date in full, example: 30th September, 1970.
- b) After the words "at the counters of" indicate the bank upon which drafts are to be drawn.

    Example: "Advising Bank" or "ourselves" (the Issuing Bank).

Center Section after "We issue in your favour this credit..."

State the draft details.

"Despatch/Shipment from"

"Partial shipment/Transhipments"

Same comments as for Forms Nos. 1A and 1B.

"Special conditions"

This space may be used for additional details not covered elsewhere in the forms such as:

- 1) permitted clauses on Bills of Lading,
- 2) indication, where applicable, that Charter Party Bills of Lading or forwarding agents' documents are acceptable,
- 3) indication, where applicable, that the credit is transferable. If transferable to another country this must be expressly stated,
- 4) any indication that the drawee bank is authorized to pay to the beneficiary discount charges, plus bill stamps, if any, etc.

"Instructions to the Advising Bank (Issuing Bank's Box Form No. 2B)"

The Issuing Bank must delete "without adding" or "adding" according to whether the documentary credit has to be confirmed or not.

"Method of Reimbursement when the credit is available at the counters of the Advising Bank (Issuing Bank's Box Form No. 2B)"

The Issuing Bank must give its reimbursement instructions to the Advising Bank at whose counters the credit has been made available by completing the instructions given above to the Advising Bank on Form 2B as follows:

add: "and in reimbursement of its payment(s) at maturity" followed by either:

a) "to debit our account with it", or

b) "to draw on our account with...",

c) "we will provide it (or the bank nominated by it) with the necessary funds at least one day prior to that date".

The reimbursement instructions should *not* appear on Form No. 2A (the original advice for the beneficiary).

The Issuing Bank must also give all instructions for the despatch of documents.

If the space provided is insufficient the "Special Conditions" section should be utilized.

Box for "Advising Bank's notification"

This space has been left blank to enable the advising Bank to:

1) use its own language to notify the beneficiary,

2) indicate that either:

a) the credit is forwarded without its engagement:

Example:
"We hereby advise this credit without any engagement on our part", or

b) the credit is forwarded with the Advising Bank's confirmation:

Example:
"This credit bears our confirmation and we engage that drafts drawn in conformity with the terms of this credit will be duly accepted on presentation and duly honoured at maturity."

Forms Nos. 3A and 3B - **Issuing Bank's advice of its irrevocable credit available for payment.**

"Amount"

Same remarks as for Forms Nos. 1A and 1B.

"Expiry"

a) Type the expiry date in full, example: 30th September, 1970.

b) After the words "at the counters of" indicate the banks at which the documents are payable.

Example: "Advising Bank" or "ourselves" (Issuing Bank).

"Centre Section"

It is the usual practice in certain countries, and particularly in the United Kingdom, to require for the claim of payment, a sight draft drawn on the bank authorized to make the payment.

Therefore, as regards the opening of irrevocable documentary credits available for payment at a bank in these countries, it is recommended to proceed as follows:

— delete "presentation of the following documents",

— type "your sight draft drawn on the Advising Bank, accompanied by the following documents".

"Despatch/Shipment from"

"Partial shipments/Transhipments"

Same remarks as for Forms Nos. 1A and 1B.

"Special Conditions"

Same remarks as for Forms Nos. 1A and 1B.

"Instructions to the Advising Bank (Issuing Bank's Box Form No. 3B)"

The issuing bank must delete "without adding" or "adding" according to whether the documentary credit has to be confirmed or not.

"Method of Reimbursement when the credit is available at the counters of the Advising Bank" (Issuing Bank's Box Form No. 3B)

The Issuing Bank must give its reimbursement instructions to the Advising Bank at whose counters the credit has been made available, by completing the instructions to the Advising Bank on Form No. 3B as follows:

add:

"and in reimbursement of their payments",

followed by:

"to debit our account with them", or

"to draw on our account with...".

Example of the complete phrase:

"The Advising Bank is requested to notify the beneficiary adding their confirmation and in reimbursement of their payments to debit our account with them".

The reimbursement instructions should *not* appear on Form 3A (the original advice for the beneficiary).

The Issuing Bank must also give all instructions for the despatch of docuements.

If the space provided is insufficient, the "Special Conditions" section should be utilized.

Box for "Advising Bank's notification"

This space has been left blank to enable the Advising Bank to:

1) use its own language to notify the beneficiary,

2) indicate that either:

   a) the credit is forwarded without its engagement:

Example:

"We hereby advise this credit without any engagement on our part", or

   b) the credit is forwarded with the Advising Bank's confirmation:

Example:

"This credit bears our confirmation and we engage that documents presented for payment in conformity with the terms of this credit will be duly paid on presentation."

Example:

Forms Nos. 4A and 4B - Issuing Bank's advice of amendment of credit.

Attention is drawn to Art. 39 of "Uniform Customs and Practice for Documentary Credits" (Brochure No. 222) which states:

"Unless otherwise expressly stated, any extension of the stipulated latest date for shipment shall extend for an equal period the validity of the credit.

Where a credit stipulates a latest date for shipment, an extension of the period of validity shall not extend the period permitted for shipment unless otherwise expressly stated."

When a letter of amendment is issued stating that the latest shipment date is extended, the printed clause on the form "All other terms and conditions remain unchanged" has, in the past, given rise to misunderstanding. It is, therefore, strongly recommended that, on all occasions when it is intended that the latest shipment and expiry dates are to be amended, *both amended dates* should be stated on the form.

Example:

"The latest shipment date is extended until..."

"The expiry date is extended until..."

If only the latest shipment date is to be extended then the new shipment date should be stipulated and the amendment should also specify that the expiry date remains unchanged.

Example:

"The latest shipment date is extended until..."

"The expiry date remains unchanged."

Box for "Advising Bank's notification"

This space has been left blank to enable the Advising Bank to use its own language to forward the amendment to the beneficiary.

Example:

"This letter of amendment is forwarded at the request of the Issuing Bank."

Form No. 5 - **Suggested sequence of text for a documentary credit opened by telex or cable.**

— The order of the terms listed closely follows that of the credit forms.

— Banks notifying credits by cable/telex may be guided by the suggested sequence.

Revocable Credits

The Standard Forms comprised in this Brochure, as listed on page 8, are for credits irrevocable by the Issuing Bank. Banks wishing to issue the comparatively rare "revocable" credit have the option either:

— to continue using their "revocable" credit form in current use and to follow the recommendations given in this Brochure, or

— to amend Forms Nos. 1, 2 and 3 in the manner indicated below:

1) Delete the word "irrevocable" in the top part of the Form, and type in the word "revocable".

2) Expiry Box: add the words "unless previously cancelled".

3) Issuing Bank's Box, copy for the beneficiary (Forms Nos. 1A, 2A, 3A): the Issuing Bank's engagement clause appearing on these forms must be deleted and replaced by:

"This credit is revocable and subject to modification or cancellation at any moment, without notice."

4) "Issuing Bank's" Box, copy for the Advising Bank (Forms Nos. 1B, 2B and 3B):

a) — Delete the Bank's engagement clause.

b) — Type in the phrase "This credit is revocable and subject to modification or cancellation at any moment, without notice".

c) — Delete the words "adding/without adding their confirmation" leaving only the words "the Advising Bank is requested to notify the beneficiary".

Furthermore, and to respect the provisions of the 2nd paragraph of Article 2, of the Uniform Customs and Practice for Documentary Credits, it is suggested that the Issuing Bank use an appropriate clause forwards the Advising Bank. The text of this clause would be typed in immediately after the text mentioned hereinabove, sub 4, b.

The following are a few examples of such possible clauses:

Revocable credit available for negotiation

"We engage to honour on presentation drafts drawn and negotiated"
(or)
"to have drafts accepted and honoured at maturity"
(as applicable)

"provided that they have been negotiated by the Advising Bank prior to the receipt by them of notice of modification or cancellation and that drafts and documents comply with the credit terms and amendments thereto received by the Advising Bank up to the time of negotiation."

Revocable credit available for acceptance at the counters of the Advising Bank

"We engage with the Advising Bank that drafts accepted by them will be dully reimbursed by us at maturity provided that they have been accepted prior to receipt by them of notice of modification or cancellation and that drafts and documents comply with the credit terms and amendments thereto received by the Advising Bank up to the time of acceptance."

Revocable credit available for payment at the counters of the Advising Bank

"We engage with the Advising Bank that we will reimburse them immediately for their payments provided that they have been made prior to the receipt by them of notice of modification or cancellation and that documents comply with the credit terms and amendments thereto received by the Advising Bank up to the time of payment.

Should the space provided for in the box not permit the typing of the chosen text in full, use should be made of the additional sheet provided for this purpose (Form No. 6).

5) Advising Bank's Box (Forms Nos. 1A, 2A, 3A): the notification to the beneficiary is to be worded as follows: "We advise you of this revocable credit, without any engagement on our part".

6) Reimbursement instructions from the Issuing Bank to the Advising Bank: for revocable credits opened at the counters of the Advising Bank, please complete the instructions to the Advising Bank following the same procedure as for irrevocable credits.

THE DOCUMENTARY DRAFT

A draft is an unconditional order in writing, signed by the exporter, and addressed to the importer, "ordering him to pay on presentation of the instrument or at some specified future date the amount of the draft."

A draft is a "bill of exchange," in banking terminology. It states to whom payment is to be made and from whom it is to be expected.

The seller's name appears to the right of "to the order of ....;" or, it can be the name of his bank with a notation to credit the proceeds to his account.

The seller signing the draft becomes the "drawer," and the party receiving payment is the "payee"; therefore, both "drawer" and "payee" are usually the same party.

Drafts can be transferred from one party to another by simple endorsement.

The best way to describe a draft is to call it a check made out by the exporter to himself. It becomes "good" once it is "accepted" by the importer's endorsement via signature on the check's reverse side.

Drafts are all "sight drafts" in a generic sense. However, sight drafts are generally understood to be bills of exchange which are payable "at sight" of documents by the importer at his bank. Time drafts are payable at a specified date *after* presentation of the draft and documents by the bank to the importer (buyer) (see Figure 4.6.

Procedures for Use of Documentary Draft

1. A New Jersey exporter and an importer in Rio make a deal for the shipment of parts valued at U.S. $10,000 from New Jersey to Rio on sight draft terms.

2. The exporter prepares the documents covering the shipment, and along with the draft.

3. The exporter presents the shipping documents draft to the exporter's bank, The New Jersey Bank.

4. NJB forwards the documents, the draft, and the exporter's instructions, to Banco do Brazil.

5. BDB notifies the importer in Rio:
   a. that the documents covering a shipment of parts have arrived,
   b. that the shipment is covered by a sight draft, and
   c. that in accordance with the exporter's instructions, the documents will be delivered to the importer on payment of the draft of $10,000 plus charges.

6. The importer visits Banco do Brazil to settle the transaction. Following the exporter's instructions, Banco do Brazil.
   a. collects
      — the equivalent of $10,000 in cruzeiros
      — banking charges, and
      — cable charges for the remittance of the collected funds to New Jersey, and
   b. releases the documents to the importer.

FIGURE 4.6

$ _____   N. J. _____ 19____

At _____ of this First of Exchange (Second unpaid) Pay to the Order of

_____

_____ Dollars

Value Received and charge to the account of

To _____

No. _____   _____   _____

258 002 R 1-70

$ _____   N. J. _____ 19____

At _____ of this Second of Exchange (First unpaid) Pay to the Order of

_____

_____ Dollars

Value Received and charge to the account of

To _____

No. _____   _____   _____

258 002 R 1-70

7. Since documents give their holder the right to control the goods, the importer takes possession of them from the steamship line in Rio.

8. Banco do Brazil remits $10,000 according to the exporter's instructions by cable to New Jersey Bank to be credited to the exporter's account.

Exporters are cautioned not to ship to Brazil unless they have received a copy of an Import Certificate. It is evidence that the Banco do Brazil has the necessary dollar exchange for this transaction.

RESEARCHING EXPORT STATISTICS

There are approximately three hundred distinct political entities in this world which are inhabited by societies of varying degrees of cultural and technological sophistication, and which may all be considered "markets," however limited or specialized. Yet the manufacturing company in the United States wishing to expand abroad, no matter how large and diversified it may be, simply does not have the manpower nor all the product lines with which to effectively and profitably penetrate every single market in the world. Thus it becomes necessary for management to establish a system of market development priorities based upon the relevance of import-export statistics to a company's industry and interests.

From a marketing point of view, this process is often called a "key market identification program," and it proceeds in two parallel paths. The exporter must first establish a statistical frame of reference to determine the relative size of the potential overseas markets, and then he must determine the past and current level of imports for the product(s) in question, beginning with an examination of his own country's exports to the areas involved.

Let us take a case study of toiletries and cosmetics. An exporting company wishes to find out:

1) what the United States is exporting in these product lines;
2) how much is being exported;
3) where it is being exported; and
4) what kind of market potential exists in specific countries.

THE STANDARD INTERNATIONAL TRADE CLASSIFICATION SYSTEM

Most countries throughout the world, including the United States, subscribe to the Standard International Trade Classification System, commonly known as the SITC product coding system. The SITC system is similar in effect to the U.S. Census Bureau's SIC product codes. Every basic product and product group is classified by a numerical three digit prefix which defines the major commodity group. This prefix is followed by a decimal point and a number of numerical digits to the right which identifies the individual product.

All SITC numbers are published in the *United Nations Commodity Indexes*, a two volume series. One volume lists products in alphabetical order with the corresponding SITC number, while the other volume lists the SITC commodity codes in numerical order with their corresponding product or commodity categories. Each volume is a cross-reference of the other.

If, for example, the exporting company wishes to find the SITC number for an after-shaving lotion, the investigator would turn to the page listing lotion (Figure 5.1). The corresponding SITC number shown is 553.0. In the next volume, (Figure 5.2) the researcher would turn to SITC number 553.0, and find the following entry: "Perfumery and Cosmetics, and other Toilet Preparations (except Soaps)."

THE SCHEDULE B COMMODITY CODE SYSTEM (UNITED STATES)

The SITC system is the key to the United States international trade commodity coding system. Every product crossing into the country's external trade sector is classified by a corresponding Schedule B number which is to be found in the Schedule B List portion of the Schedule B book, published periodically by the U.S. Department of Commerce. The Schedule B book actually equates a given SITC number with a more specific Schedule B number.

However, the Schedule B numbers (digits to the right of the decimal) were revised *after* 1964. Consequently, if data prior to 1965 is sought, a conversion table (available in the 1965 Schedule B book) must be used.

The exporter will now be able to locate the following entries:

Commodity Group	1964 and Earlier	1965
Dental Creams	553.87345	553.0025
Face Powder	553.87415	553.0030
Cosmetic Creams	553.87525	553.0035
Rouge, Lipstick and Eye Makeup	553.87575	553.0040
Depilatories and Deodorants	553.87625	553.0045
Hair Preparations	553.87660	553.0020
Cologne, Toilet Water and Perfumes	553.87667	553.0015
Cosmetics and Toilet Preparations	553.87700	553.0050

FIGURE 5.1

LOCKS,ELECTRICALLY OPERATED	698.11
LOCKS, FOR MILITARY FIREARMS	951.03
LOCKS, FOR NON-MILITARY ARMS	894.33
LOCKSMITHS WARES, ANTIQUE	896.06
LOCOMOBILES,STEAM	711.31
LOCOMOTIVE BOILERS	711.1
LOCOMOTIVE ENGINES, STEAM, NOT INCORPORATING BOILERS	711.32
LOCOMOTIVE HEADLIGHT TURBINE SETS, ELECTRIC GENERATORS	722.1
LOCOMOTIVE LANTERNS	812.42
LOCOMOTIVE TENDERS,RAILWAY	731.1
LOCOMOTIVE TENDERS,RAILWAY,MOTOR AXLE	731.1
LOCOMOTIVE TRAVERSERS	719.31
LOCOMOTIVES, ARTICULATED, RAILWAY, STEAM	731.1
LOCOMOTIVES,INDUSTRIAL RAILWAY,ELECTRIC BATTERY OPERATED OR POWERED FROM AN EXTERNAL SOURCE OF ELECTRICITY	731.2
LOCOMOTIVES,INDUSTRIAL RAILWAY,EXCEPT STEAM AND ELECTRIC	731.3
LOCOMOTIVES,INDUSTRIAL RAILWAY,STEAM	731.1
LOCOMOTIVES, MALLET, RAILWAY, STEAM	731.1
LOCOMOTIVES,MINE RAILWAY,EXCEPT STEAM AND ELECTRIC	731.3
LOCOMOTIVES,MINE RAILWAY,STEAM	731.1
LOCOMOTIVES,MINE RAILWAYS,ELECTRIC, BATTERY OPERATED OR POWERED FROM AN EXTERNAL SOURCE OF ELECTRICITY	731.2
LOCOMOTIVES,RACK RAILWAY,STEAM	731.1
LOCOMOTIVES, RAIL, POWERED FROM AN EXTERNAL SOURCE OF ELECTRICITY	731.2
LOCOMOTIVES,RAILWAY,COMPRESSED AIR	731.3
LOCOMOTIVES,RAILWAY,DIESEL	731.3
LOCOMOTIVES,RAILWAY,ELECTRIC RUN BY ACCUMULATORS,BATTERIES	731.2
LOCOMOTIVES,RAILWAY,EXCEPT STEAM AND ELECTRIC	731.3
LOCOMOTIVES,RAILWAY,GAS TURBINE	731.3
LOCOMOTIVES,RAILWAY,INTERNAL COMBUSTION	731.3
LOCOMOTIVES, RAILWAY, PETROL ENGINE	731.3
LOCOMOTIVES,RAILWAY,STEAM	731.1
LOCOMOTIVES, RAILWAY, STEAM, COAL-BURNING	731.1
LOCOMOTIVES, RAILWAY, STEAM, OIL-BURNING	731.1
LOCOMOTIVES, RAILWAY, STEAM, PISTON OR TURBINE DRIVEN	731.1
LOCOMOTIVES, SHUNTING, RAILWAY, STEAM	731.1
LOCOMOTIVES, TRAMWAY, ELECTRIC, BATTERY-POWERED	731.2
LOCOMOTIVES,TRAMWAY,EXCEPT STEAM AND ELECTRIC	731.3
LOCOMOTIVES, TRAMWAY, POWERED FROM AN EXTERNAL SOURCE OF ELECTRICITY	731.2
LOCUST BEAN - SEE ALSO CAROB BEAN	
LOCUST BEAN ENDOSPERM FLOUR	292.91
LOCUST BEAN JUICE,SPIRITS FROM	112.4
LOCUST BEANS,KIBBLED OR GROUND, NOT FURTHER PREPARED	054.89
LOCUST BEANS,WHOLE,FRESH OR DRIED	054.89
LODIGIONO CHEESE	024.0
LOG CHESTS, FLOOR-STANDING	821.09
LOG GRINDING MACHINES FOR PULP MANUFACTURE	718.11
LOG-PARING MACHINES	719.52
LOG-ROLLING TOOLS	695.1
LOGGERHEAD CLAWS	291.14
LOGGERHEAD SHELL AND SCALES, UNWORKED OR SIMPLY PREPARED (NOT CUT TO SHAPE)	291.14
LOGGERHEAD SHELL WASTE	291.14
LOGS,FOR PAPER PULP	242.1
LOGS, FUEL WOOD	241.1
LOGS, SHIPS, AUTOMATIC	861.91
LOGS,TAFFRAIL	861.91
LOGS, VENEER, IN THE ROUGH, CONIFER	242.21
LOGS, VENEER, IN THE ROUGH, NON-CONIFER	242.31
LOGS, VENEER, ROUGHLY SQUARED OR HALF-SQUARED, CONIFER	242.22
LOGS, VENEER, ROUGHLY SQUARED OR HALF-SQUARED, NON-CONIFER	242.32
LOGS, YULE, IMITATION	894.25
LOGWOOD EXTRACT	532.1
LOGWOOD IN POWDER,CHIPS,SHAVINGS	292.1
LOGWOOD LAKE	531.02
LONGERONS,AIRCRAFT HEAVIER THAN AIR	734.92
LONGERONS, LOCOMOTIVE OR ROLLING-STOCK	731.7

LOOFAH	292.99
LOOFAH ARTICLES	899.22
LOOFAH FRICTION GLOVES	899.22
LOOFAH GLOVES	899.22
LOOFAH PADS	899.22
LOOM PICKERS, OF TEXTILE MATERIALS	655.83
LOOM REEDS	717.13
LOOMS, BOX-MOTION, AUTOMATIC	717.12
LOOMS, BRAIDING	717.12
LOOMS, CARPET	717.12
LOOMS, HAND	717.12
LOOMS, HOOK, FOR MAKING TEXTILE TRIMMINGS	717.12
LOOMS, JACQUARD	717.12
LOOMS, PORTABLE	717.12
LOOMS,POWER	717.12
LOOMS, RIBBON (E.G., ZURICH, BAR OR DRUM)	717.12
LOOMS, TAPESTRY	717.12
LOOMS, WARP KNITTING (E.G., RACHEL, MILANESE, LOCKNIT)	717.12
LOOP STITCH EMBROIDERY	654.06
LOOPS, CURTAIN, TEXTILE	656.91
LOOSE-LEAF BINDER FITTINGS,BASE METAL	895.12
LOOSE-LEAF BINDERS, OF PAPER OR PAPERBOARD	642.3
LOPPING SHEARS, TWO-HANDED	695.1
LORAN EQUIPMENT	724.99
LORGNETTE HANDLES	861.21
LORGNETTES,CORRECTIVE OR PROTECTIVE	861.22
LORGNETTES,FRAMES,MOUNTINGS AND PARTS FOR	861.21
LORRIES,BREAKDOWN	732.4
LORRIES, CAMERA MANIPULATING	732.4
LORRIES,CRANE	732.4
LORRIES, DROP-FRAME, HEAVY-DUTY, WITH LOADING RAMPS FOR TRANSPORTING TANKS, LIFTING AND EXCAVATING MACHINERY OR ELECTRICAL TRANSFORMERS	732.3
LORRIES, ELECTRIC, ROAD, FOR TRANSPORT OF GOODS	732.3
LORRIES, FITTED WITH STIRRING DEVICES, FOR TRANSPORTING FRESH CEMENT AND CONCRETE (EXCL. CEMENT MIXERS)	732.3
LORRIES,FLAT-TRUCK	732.3
LORRIES, MOTOR, FITTED WITH ELECTRIC GENERATORS	732.4
LORRIES, MOTOR, FITTED WITH LADDERS OR ELEVATOR PLATFORMS, FOR MAINTAINING OVERHEAD CABLES OR STREET LIGHTING	732.4
LORRIES, MOTOR, FOR TRANSPORT OF GOODS OR MATERIALS	732.3
LORRIES, MOTOR, WITH BUILT-IN CONCRETE MIXERS	732.4
LORRIES, MULTI-FLOORED	732.3
LORRIES, REFRIGERATED OR INSULATED	732.3
LORRIES, ROAD-RAIL	732.3
LORRIES,ROAD - SPRAYING	732.4
LORRIES, SPECIAL PURPOSE (I.E., NOT PRIMARILY FOR TRANSPORT OF GOODS OR PERSONS)	732.4
LORRIES, SPRAYING (WHETHER OR NOT FITTED WITH HEATING EQUIPMENT), FOR SPREADING TAR, GRAVEL OR FOR AGRICULTURAL USE	732.4
LORRIES, STACKING (I.E., WITH A PLATFORM MOVING ON A VERTICAL SUPPORT GENERALLY POWERED BY THE VEHICLE ENGINE)	732.4
LORRIES, STREET CLEANING	732.4
LORRIES,TANK	732.3
LORRIES, TEST, FITTED WITH INSTRUMENTS FOR RECORDING THE TRACTIVE POWER OF MOTOR VEHICLES TOWING THEM	732.4
LORRIES, TIPPING, ROAD MOTOR	732.3
LORRIES WITH AUTOMATIC LOADING OR UNLOADING APPARATUS (EXCL. SPECIAL PURPOSE LORRIES)	732.3
LORRY BODIES OR CABS	732.81
LORRY CHASSIS,WITH ENGINE MOUNTED	732.7
LOTIONS, AFTER-SHAVING	553.0
LOTIONS,COSMETIC	553.0
LOTIONS,PERMANENT WAVING	553.0
LOTIONS,SHAVING	553.0
LOTIONS, TOILET	553.0
LOUDSPEAKERS	724.92
LOUDSPEAKERS, CRYSTAL	724.92
LOUDSPEAKERS, ELECTROSTATIC	724.92
LOUDSPEAKERS, MOVING COIL OR MOVING IRON	724.92
LOUDSPEAKERS, PIEZO-ELECTRIC	724.92

FIGURE 5.2

551.23   553.C

OF THESE SUBSTANCES, WHETHER OR NOT CONTAINING ALCOHOL,
PROVIDED THAT THE MIXTURES RETAIN THE CHARACTER OF RAW
MATERIALS USED IN THE PERFUMERY, FOOD, DRINK OR OTHER
INDUSTRIES. THE HEADING DOES NOT COVER COMPOUND PREPARATIONS
(ALCOHOLIC OR NON-ALCOHOLIC) FOR THE MANUFACTURE OF BEVERAGES.

ALCOHOL MIXED WITH ESSENTIAL OILS
ALCOHOLIC SOLUTIONS OF ODORIFEROUS
  SUBSTANCES
AROMATICS, SYNTHETIC, MIXTURES OF
CONCENTRATES,FLAVOUR,SYNTHETIC
ODORIFEROUS SUBSTANCES (NATURAL OR
  SYNTHETIC) IN ALCOHOLIC SOLUTIONS
OIL,ESSENTIAL,MIXED WITH ALCOHOL
OIL,ESSENTIAL,MIXED WITH ONE ANOTHER

OIL, ESSENTIAL, MIXED WITH RESINOIDS OR
  SYNTHETIC AROMATICS
PERFUME BASES, CONSISTING OF MIXTURES OF
  ESSENTIAL OILS AND FIXATIVES
RESINOIDS,IN ALCOHOLIC SOLUTION FOR PERFUM-
  ERY
RESINOIDS, MIXED WITH ONE ANOTHER, WITH
  ESSENTIAL OILS OR WITH SYNTHETIC AROMATICS

551.24   AQUEOUS DISTILLATES AND SOLUTIONS OF ESSENTIAL OILS   BTN 33.05

THE PRODUCTS OF THIS HEADING REMAIN CLASSIFIED HERE WHEN
INTERMIXED (WITHOUT THE ADDITION OF OTHER MATERIALS) OR WHEN
PUT UP AS PERFUMERY OR MEDICAMENTS.

AQUEOUS SOLUTIONS OF ESSENTIAL OILS
DISTILLATE,AQUEOUS,OF CHERRY-LAUREL
DISTILLATE, AQUEOUS, OF ESSENTIAL OILS
DISTILLATE,AQUEOUS,OF FENNEL
DISTILLATE,AQUEOUS,OF LIME-BLOSSOM
DISTILLATE,AQUEOUS,OF MELISSA

DISTILLATE,AQUEOUS,OF MINT
DISTILLATE,AQUEOUS,OF ORANGE FLOWERS
DISTILLATE,AQUEOUS,OF ROSE
DISTILLATE,AQUEOUS,OF WITCH HAZEL
LIME-BLOSSOM, AQUEOUS DISTILLATE OF
OIL, ESSENTIAL, AQUEOUS DISTILLATES OF

553.0   PERFUMERY AND COSMETICS, DENTIFRICES AND OTHER TOILET   BTN 33.06
    PREPARATIONS (EXCEPT SOAPS)

THIS HEADING COVERS PRODUCTS PREPARED READY FOR USE AS
PERFUMERY, COSMETICS OR TOILET PREPARATIONS WHETHER OR NOT
THEY CONTAIN PHARMACEUTICAL OR DISINFECTANT CONSTITUENTS, OR
ARE HELD OUT AS HAVING CURATIVE OR PROPHYLACTIC VALUE.
PRODUCTS WHICH ARE SUITABLE FOR OTHER USES IN ADDITION TO
THOSE DESCRIBED ABOVE ARE CLASSIFIED IN THE PRESENT HEADING
ONLY WHEN THEY ARE — 1. IN PACKINGS OF A KIND SOLD TO THE
CONSUMER AND PUT UP WITH ANY INDICATION OF PERFUMERY, COSMETIC
OR TOILET USE, WHETHER BY LABEL, LITERATURE OR OTHERWISE, 2.
PUT UP IN A FORM CLEARLY SPECIALIZED TO SUCH USE. THE HEADING
DOES NOT COVER — 1. MEDICINAL PREPARATIONS HAVING A
SUBSIDIARY USE AS PERFUMERY, COSMETICS OR TOILET PREPARATIONS,
2. AQUEOUS DISTILLATES OR AQUEOUS SOLUTIONS OF ESSENTIAL OILS,
EVEN WHEN PUT UP AS PERFUMERY, 3. SOAPS.

ACETONE PUT UP AS NAIL POLISH REMOVER
ALUM PUT UP AS PERFUMERY
ASTRINGENTS,COSMETIC
BRILLIANTINES
CHIROPODY,PREPARATIONS FOR
CLEANERS,DENTURE,OTHER THAN SOAP
COSMETICS,WITH AND WITHOUT ALCOHOL
CREAMS,BEAUTY
CREAMS,CLEANSING,COSMETICS
CREAMS,COLD,COSMETIC
CREAMS, COSMETIC
CREAMS,DENTAL
CREAMS, FACE
CREAMS,HAIR
CREAMS, HAND
CREAMS,MAKE-UP
CREAMS,SHAVING
DENTAL HYGIENE PREPARATIONS
DENTIFRICES

DENTIFRICES,POWDERED CHALK
DEODORISERS,PERSONAL
DEPILATORIES
DRESSINGS,HAIR
DYES,HAIR
EAU DE COLOGNE
FLOCK, TEXTILE, PERFUMED
FOODS,SKIN
FULLERS EARTH, PUT UP FOR COSMETIC OR
  TOILET USE
GLYCEROL,PERFUMED
GLYCEROL WITH ADDED COSMETICS
GREASE PAINT,DRY,PASTE,OR LIQUID
GREASE PAINT,THEATRICAL
INCENSE,PREPARED
JOSS PAPER OR STICKS
LANOLIN, PUT UP AS PERFUMERY
LIPSTICK
LOTIONS, AFTER-SHAVING
             CONTINUED

Whenever an export shipment is prepared, the exporter, or his freight forwarder, must by law enter the correct Schedule B number next to the commodity description on the Export Declaration.

THE FT410

This data manual, published by the U.S. Department of Commerce and prepared by the Bureau of the Census, is the exporter's next point of reference after the appropriate Schedule B number has been located. It provides a monthly tally, on a cumulative basis, of U.S. exports by specific Schedule B number, broken down by country of destination. The annual issue is the December FT410; it usually appears in May of the following year (Figure 5.3).

The FT410 also provides a summary breakdown of U.S. exports by major commodity grouping, an excellent research tool to analyze changes in the country's export mix.

THE FT990

This monthly manual is also published on a cumulative basis, highlighting U.S. exports and imports, by major commodity group and by country of destination (Figure 5.4).

SIGNIFICANCE OF DATA

All data is only as accurate as its original recorders, in this case, the U.S. exporter. The major sources of data are the Export Declaration forms he completes as part of the export documentation process.

If invoice values are understated or overstated, and these inaccuracies are carried over to the Export Declaration, the values shown in the FT's will be distorted.

If the commodity to be exported is misclassified (assigned an erroneous description and Schedule B number), the data will again be distorted in the FT statistics.

For example, a country having a high import duty on cologne may have a lower tariff on alcoholic products which go under the heading "alcohols and polyhydric alcohols, not elsewhere classified," Schedule B number 512.0926. The exporter might handily label his shipment as an alcoholic product, perhaps using the cologne compound's generic title, and show the same information on his invoices and, of course, on the Export Declaration. His customer, the importer, will benefit from a lower landed cost because of the different commodity classification and the correspondingly lower tariff assessment. Consequently, the practice will tend to understate shipments recorded under Schedule B number 553.0015

FIGURE 5.3

Table 2. Schedule B Commodity By Country–Domestic Merchandise

(The figure preceding country designation Canada is the number in the sample for Canada. "SC" at the end of an alphabetic commodity description indicates "Special Category" commodity. See Introduction for coverage, valuation, explanation of Special Category, method of sampling low value shipments, certain types of shipments not classified by commodity, and other definitions and features of the export statistics.)

Country of destination	Current month Net quantity	Current month Value (dollars)	Cumulative, January to date Net quantity	Cumulative, January to date Value (dollars)	Country of destination	Current month Net quantity	Current month Value (dollars)	Cumulative, January to date Net quantity	Cumulative, January to date Value (dollars)
N ANTIL...	-	5 448	-	80 837	PANAMA....	4 552	6 216	24 191	33 920
COLOMB...	-	7 294	-	38 244	BERMUDA...	10 373	12 140	25 549	33 895
VENEZ....	-	2 140	-	52 828	BAHAMAS...	3 754	5 042	36 287	51 189
ECUADOR...	-	507	-	26 215	JAMAICA...	3 896	3 970	60 752	58 199
PERU,....	-	12 607	-	12 607	HAITI....	654	350	68 412	60 747
SWEDEN,...	-	-	-	12 464	TRINID....	1 192	1 116	20 316	19 178
U KING...	-	2 517	-	168 758	N ANTIL...	3 475	5 108	159 213	202 036
FRANCE....	-	7 230	-	118 563	VENEZ.....	5 451	9 181	43 787	59 340
W GERM...	-	1 766	-	36 320	SURINAM...	7 695	9 507	116 872	155 793
ITALY....	-	1 000	-	27 391	ECUADOR...	887	1 686	11 161	18 232
KUWAIT...	-	-	-	39 383	ICELAND...	963	1 220	13 463	16 128
ARABIA...	-	2 200	-	21 203	U KING...	1 274	3 339	50 743	37 273
BAHRAIN...	-	1 236	-	17 967	BELGIUM...	890	1 300	153 066	72 789
CEYLON,...	-	2 772	-	12 038	FRANCE....	1 136	1 340	40 457	17 888
THAILND...	-	1 672	-	15 176	W GERM...	-	-	33 030	17 969
MALAYSA...	-	11 379	-	45 240	ITALY....	-	-	33 401	32 770
SINGAPR...	-	37 152	-	180 841	LEBANON...	4 134	4 058	44 817	41 928
HG KONG...	-	1 389	-	90 208	IRAN......	441	520	14 263	20 909
JAPAN....	-	9 113	-	61 483	KUWAIT....	8 699	8 922	18 890	20 623
NAN IS,...	-	8 097	-	179 044	S ARAB...	1 374	1 868	12 691	16 284
AUSTRAL...	-	486	-	101 626	THAILND...	6 594	11 072	15 343	24 311
REP SAF...	-	-	-	20 283	HG KONG...	28 630	20 072	255 454	170 857
OTH CTY...	-	5 313	-	174 586	JAPAN.....	12 511	0 634	57 428	59 078
TOTAL...	-	175 246	-	2 151 082	T PAC I...	400	566	11 085	12 833
5530020 HAIR PREPARATIONS					REP SAF...	-	-	15 212	18 255
2 CANADA....	-	31 558	-	682 761	OTH CTY...	9 628	10 227	147 438	170 547
MEXICO....	-	27 436	-	299 273	TOTAL...	149 573	150 783	1 762 167	1 664 739
GUATMAL...	-	841	-	23 797	5530030 MOUTH WASHES				
BR HOND...	-	346	-	18 554	1 CANADA....	-	1 160	-	60 992
SALVADR...	-	505	-	21 157	MEXICO....	-	2 960	-	20 624
NICARAG...	-	-	-	14 008	BERMUDA...	-	-	-	12 261
PANAMA....	-	21 629	-	368 436	N ANTIL...	-	622	-	13 873
BERMUDA...	-	5 912	-	122 740	DENMARK...	-	-	-	64 179
BAHAMAS...	-	18 444	-	251 358	FINLAND...	-	-	-	18 333
JAMAICA...	-	3 178	-	76 365	DENMARK...	-	2 745	-	12 985
HAITI....	-	680	-	16 322	NETHLDS...	-	4 970	-	32 412
DOM REP...	-	2 379	-	40 009	SWITZLD...	-	-	-	55 918
LW WW I...	-	2 355	-	29 169	GREECE....	-	1 970	-	30 827
BARBADO...	-	2 561	-	41 430	OTH CTY...	-	9 534	-	198 087
TRINID...	-	13 135	-	141 083	TOTAL...	-	31 601	-	588 491
N ANTI...	-	13 209	-	19 327	5530035 COSMETIC CREAMS, LOTIONS, AND BALMS, NEC				
COLOMB...	-	2 281	-	96 758	5 CANADA....	-	51 435	-	496 216
VENEZ.....	-	5 229	-	28 826	MEXICO....	-	22 628	-	231 530
GUYANA....	-	-	-	42 335	GUATMAL...	-	2 400	-	41 711
SURINAM...	-	4 261	-	13 085	HONDURA...	-	1 972	-	14 130
ECUADOR...	-	850	-	29 074	NICARAG...	-	638	-	16 078
BOLIVIA...	-	-	-	58 148	PANAMA....	-	1 014	-	117 833
ICELAND...	-	-	-	32 743	BERMUDA...	-	3 789	-	64 507
SWEDEN...	-	3 139	-	34 064	BAHAMAS...	-	26 938	-	167 528
FINLAND...	-	764	-	284 046	JAMAICA...	-	3 596	-	55 639
U KING...	-	195 347	-	15 302	HAITI....	-	2 817	-	24 030
IRELAND...	-	-	-	14 947	LW WW I...	-	-	-	40 817
NETHLDS...	-	304	-	23 122	BARBADO...	-	304	-	32 870
BELGIUM...	-	1 480	-	46 540	TRINID...	-	2 800	-	87 903
FRANCE....	-	1 862	-	36 085	N ANTIL...	-	22 234	-	146 832
W GERM...	-	4 747	-	12 611	COLOMB...	-	5 447	-	44 984
SWITZLD...	-	1 216	-	14 151	VENEZ.....	-	2 632	-	42 615
GIBRALT...	-	617	-	65 550	GUYANA....	-	210	-	18 563
ITALY....	-	563	-	15 351	ECUADOR...	-	2 645	-	12 957
RUMANIA...	-	-	-	86 011	PERU.....	-	834	-	16 971
LEBANON...	-	3 587	-	13 000	BOLIVIA...	-	759	-	39 959
JORDAN,...	-	-	-	71 556	SWEDEN...	-	514	-	41 206
KUWAIT...	-	11 337	-	56 616	DENMARK...	-	370	-	13 840
S ARAB...	-	7 000	-	13 940	U KING...	-	38 244	-	189 779
BAHRAIN...	-	2 509	-	180 792	NETHLDS...	-	1 663	-	13 485
THAILND...	-	6 802	-	108 060	BELGIUM...	-	80 067	-	412 101
MALAYSA...	-	2 761	-	332 880	FRANCE....	-	5 247	-	102 684
SINGAPR...	-	14 734	-	42 476	W GERM...	-	2 056	-	130 925
INDNSIA...	-	1 844	-	28 424	SWITZLD...	-	6 865	-	38 233
PHIL R,...	-	3 035	-	816 130	ITALY....	-	14 317	-	186 283
HG KONG...	-	36 792	-	132 830	LEBANON...	-	3 108	-	30 743
JAPAN....	-	3 158	-	28 792	KUWAIT...	-	-	-	16 940
NAN IS...	-	826	-	119 193	THAILND...	-	6 474	-	134 223
AUSTRAL...	-	2 778	-	14 823	MALAYSA...	-	2 793	-	64 675
N ZEAL...	-	-	-	26 602	SINGAPR...	-	8 091	-	90 452
LIBYA....	-	8 686	-	22 252	PHIL R,...	-	240	-	20 722
NIGERIA...	-	-	-	12 006	HG KONG...	-	28 900	-	265 171
ANGOLA,...	-	-	-	15 018	JAPAN.....	-	138 388	-	703 537
I RRFRT...	-	3 443	-	19 691	NAN IS,...	-	1 500	-	24 820
KENYA,...	-	555	-	39 002	AUSTRAL...	-	20 340	-	117 747
REP SAF...	-	1 050	-	155 670	T PAC I...	-	-	-	16 961
OTH CTY...	-	10 562	-	5 103 841	CNRY I....	-	4 756	-	26 755
TOTAL...	-	487 589			NIGERIA...	-	252	-	17 613
5530025 DENTAL CREAMS, TOOTH PASTES, AND DENTAL PREPARATIONS, NEC				1 8	REP SAF...	-	5 876	-	47 944
CANADA....	1 888	9 085	112 727	106 157	OTH CTY...	-	24 794	-	209 931
MEXICO....	20 000	8 872	145 780	83 614	TOTAL...	-	537 810	-	4 599 842
GUATMAL...	3 084	5 372	20 339	31 798					

FIGURE 5.4

Table E-3. **Domestic and Foreign Merchandise–World Area and Country of Destination: 1971 and 1970**

(In millions of dollars. Countries identified with an asterisk (*) exclude information on shipments of Special Category commodities. Such data, if any, are grouped by area, as applicable, and shown at the end of the list of countries for the individual areas affected. Developed countries include Canada, Western Europe, Japan, Australia, New Zealand, and the Republic of South Africa.Developing countries include the rest of the world excluding communist areas in Europe and Asia. The assignment of countries generally follows that made by the United Nations. X–Not aplicable. Z–Less than one-half of rounded unit)

World area and country of destination	1971			1970	
	Current month	Prior month	Cumulative, January to date	Current month	Cumulative, January to date
GRAND TOTAL	4 088.9	3 263.9	44 136.6	3 735.8	43 224.0
SUMMARY TOTALS					
DEVELOPED COUNTRIES	2 830.3	2 342.0	30 347.5	2 506.8	29 877.4
DEVELOPING COUNTRIES.	1 202.9	894.2	13 405.2	1 188.5	12 993.0
COMMUNIST AREAS IN EUROPE AND ASIA.	55.8	27.7	384.0	40.5	353.6
AREAS AND COUNTRIES: INCL. SPECIAL CATEGORY					
WESTERN HEMISPHERE.	1 471.5	1 357.6	16 850.1	1 271.5	15 611.6
CANADA.	876.6	931.9	10 365.7	712.1	9 079.3
20 LATIN AMERICAN REPUBLICS	520.9	372.8	5 667.0	489.8	5 695.2
CENTRAL AMERICAN COMMON MARKET.	31.5	23.3	406.1	33.2	425.2
GUATEMALA	8.3	4.9	95.4	8.8	99.9
EL SALVADOR	4.3	3.3	61.6	4.6	64.5
HONDURAS.	5.8	3.2	83.6	7.5	89.4
NICARAGUA	4.5	3.5	62.8	4.6	76.9
COSTA RICA.	8.7	8.4	102.8	7.7	94.5
LATIN AMERICAN FREE TRADE ASSOCIATION	448.1	326.3	4 851.6	424.4	4 884.6
MEXICO.	150.8	136.1	1 622.1	145.6	1 703.7
COLOMBIA.	29.5	30.2	378.0	35.8	394.8
VENEZUELA	69.3	43.1	787.1	61.3	739.3
ECUADOR	11.0	7.8	134.4	10.5	127.0
PERU.	27.7	14.2	257.5	22.0	214.1
BOLIVIA	4.4	1.7	35.4	3.1	45.7
CHILE	20.5	14.0	223.7	22.7	300.3
BRAZIL.	87.5	60.8	966.3	77.1	840.5
PARAGUAY.	1.8	.9	24.1	2.3	17.8
URUGUAY	1.7	.6	31.9	3.8	40.6
ARGENTINA	43.9	17.0	391.0	40.1	441.0
OTHER LATIN AMERICAN REPUBLICS.	41.2	23.2	409.2	32.2	385.4
PANAMA.	23.3	11.0	208.5	16.9	208.0
CUBA.	(Z)	(Z)	(Z)	(Z)	(Z)
HAITI	3.9	2.4	36.8	3.1	34.1
DOMINICAN REPUBLIC.	14.0	9.8	163.8	12.1	143.3
OTHER WESTERN HEMISPHERE.	74.0	53.0	817.5	69.5	837.1
GREENLAND	(Z)	(Z)	1.8	(Z)	.5
MIQUELON AND ST. PIERRE ISLANDS	(Z)	(Z)	.2	(Z)	.5
BRITISH HONDURAS.	.9	.8	11.1	1.0	10.8
CANAL ZONE.	-	-	-	-	-
BERMUDA	5.7	4.9	90.9	7.8	91.7
BAHAMAS	12.6	12.1	141.3	17.3	173.1
JAMAICA	18.6	13.3	216.2	18.9	218.4
LEEWARD AND WINDWARD ISLANDS.	2.0	1.5	22.9	2.0	32.0
BARBADOS.	1.8	1.4	20.3	1.9	21.8
TRINIDAD AND TOBAGO	12.6	6.4	116.6	5.5	84.3
NETHERLANDS ANTILLES.	13.0	8.7	119.3	10.5	125.6
FRENCH WEST INDIES.	1.1	.8	13.6	1.0	15.1
GUYANA.	2.1	1.4	25.8	1.4	24.8
SURINAM	3.5	1.6	35.6	2.1	35.4
FRENCH GUIANA	.2	(Z)	1.9	.1	3.1
FALKLAND ISLANDS.	-			-	-
WESTERN EUROPE.	1 348.5	961.1	14 190.1	1 241.2	14 463.2
ORGANIZATION FOR ECONOMIC COOPERATION AND DEVELOPMENT.	1 338.8	954.5	13 998.1	1 221.5	14 280.0
EUROPEAN ECONOMIC COMMUNITY	810.7	581.2	8 389.2	736.4	8 422.9
NETHERLANDS	180.2	125.0	1 785.3	139.3	1 651.1
BELGIUM AND LUXEMBOURG.	101.2	79.7	1 077.7	121.4	1 195.0
FRANCE.	125.3	82.8	1 380.2	131.6	1 483.0
WEST GERMANY.	261.4	203.2	2 832.0	222.8	2 740.7
ITALY	142.6	90.5	1 314.0	121.4	1 353.0
EUROPEAN FREE TRADE ASSOCIATION	430.0	297.0	4 260.7	368.3	4 515.4
UNITED KINGDOM.	255.7	153.9	2 374.0	208.8	2 536.3
OTHER EFTA COUNTRIES.	174.3	143.1	1 886.8	159.5	1 979.1
ICELAND	6.6	.6	18.9	.9	12.8
SWEDEN.	47.3	53.9	469.9	35.6	543.2
NORWAY.	12.9	15.5	184.9	15.7	196.1
FINLAND	7.2	6.6	90.5	18.6	98.9
DENMARK	30.1	13.6	252.8	18.4	227.4
AUSTRIA	10.7	6.1	100.6	5.5	74.3
SWITZERLAND	47.0	37.1	626.7	57.2	700.0
PORTUGAL.	12.4	9.7	142.5	7.7	126.4

(Cologne, Toilet Water and Perfumes) and to overstate shipments recorded under Schedule B number 512.0926.

Legally, the exporter should have properly classified the commodity to begin with, and the exporter does run the chance of losing his exporting permit. The probabilities of being caught, however, are remote unless the nature of the commodity itself, and its ultimate destination, is fraught with political implications.

The United Nations Yearbook Of International Trade Statistics, published annually by the U.N., supplies import-export data of all countries by major commodity group. However, most countries publish, under the SITC system, their own specific commodity import-export statistics. Classification of imports by product for every country follow the same coding principle, using SITC numbers which may be obtained from the key contained in the United Nations Commodity Indexes mentioned earlier.

Updated but unrevised information on product imports and exports for each country may be found in the *Commodity Trade Statistics* which run in semi-monthly installments one year behind the current reporting period.

Naturally, all these statistics must be analyzed with the realization that their accuracy depends more or less upon the honesty of individual importers and exporters relative to local customs regulations.

Economic trends and income projections are available through any of the specialized United Nations agency publications. Information supplied by these agencies is generally of the highest accuracy because of the usually high caliber of U.N. staff functionaries. Consequently, there is no problem in assembling data such as wage-price indexes, economic indicators, gross national product, per capita income and disposable personal income projections. The problem is one of meaningful interpretation.

For example, it is widely held, in the area of non-durable consumer goods, that population and per capita income of specific countries compared to U.S. standards would provide some indication of market potential in terms of purchasing power, assuming that maximum standards of marketing performance are achieved in the U.S. at the time of comparison. Therefore, one could state that if U.S. factory sales were $0.60 per capita, with per capita income at $3,600, and if per capita income in the potential market was $1,200 and growing at the rate of 10% per year over the preceeding year, the following formula would be applicable:

$$\text{Sales per capita} = \frac{\text{U.S. Sales Per Capita}}{\text{U.S. Per Capita Income}} \times \text{Per Capita Income of Potential Market}$$

$$S = \frac{\$0.60}{\$3,600} \times 1,200$$

$$S = \$0.20$$

Given a population of 50 million (France), market potential, assuming that similar standards of performance were achieved, could conceivably reach $10 million as against sales in the U.S. of $0.60 x 195 million or $117.0 million.

Of course, this is a static analysis, and companies are vitally interested in the analysis of market potentials for periods of at least five years, depending on their desired pay-out plans and upon the average market life of their product lines. In this case, the formula may be extended as shown below:

$$S^n = \left(\frac{Y}{I} \times I_1\right)\left(1 + r\right)^n \text{ where}$$

S^n = Annual Sales per capita after a specified period of time
n = Time period
Y = U.S. Sales per capita
I = U.S. per capita income
I_1 = Per capita income in the potential market
r = Anticipated rate of increase in per capita income or sales per capita, assuming sales will increase at the same rate as per capita income

For the sake of convenience, the formula may be restated in logarithmic form once $S = \frac{Y}{I} \times I_1$ has been solved. Given $n = 5$ years and $r = 10\%$,

$S^n = 20(1 + r)^n$	$\log 20 = 0.3010$
$\log S^n = \log 20 + 5 \log 11$	$\log 11 = 0.0414$
$\log S^n = 0.3010 + 0.2070 = 0.5080$	$5 \log 11 = 0.2070$
$S^n = \$0.322 =$ per capita sales in five years	

This result may then be multiplied by the estimated population for the fifth year of projection to provide a sales forecast.

However, this analysis is valid only as an operational hypothesis. Other factors must then be considered, such as

1. Competitive conditions and share-of-market ratios
2. Industrial shifts
3. Increasing costs
4. Changing technology
5. Changing cultural patterns
6. Government regulations
7. Problems of economic and political change

Information about these specific areas of inquiry is available through the data sources listed below.

Publication	Publisher	Explanation
Commerce Today	U.S. Dept. of Commerce	Formerly known as *International Commerce*, this biweekly journal lists both investment and export opportunities in its rear section. It also occasionally publishes market studies and fairly accurate political and economic profiles for specific countries.
Overseas Business Reports	U.S. Dept. of Commerce	These reports provide up-dated marketing, economic, political and general commercial information on specific countries. All countries are covered.
Background Country Notes	U.S. Dept. of State	These reports emphasise both general and specific historical and political events and conditions.
U.S. Trade Center Reports, Export Market Guides	U.S. Dept. of Commerce	The various U.S. Trade Centers throughout the world develop these guides for specific industries for which Trade Center Shows are planned.
Bender's Foreign Tax and Trade Briefs	Diamond, New York City	The information in Bender's is similar to that contained in the *Overseas Business Reports*. However, the emphasis is on a country's foreign trade regulations, and on its internal tax structure.
United Nations Economic Survey	United Nations	This annual publication provides macro-economic data and trends throughout the world. It is useful as a source of background information.
United Nations Statistical Annual	United Nations	Published annually, it provides a complete country summary of vital demographic, economic, and social statistics. It includes information such as newsprint consumption, number of motor vehicles, and number of television and radio receivers.
International Financial Statistics	International Monetary Fund	Published monthly, it provides a complete country by country analysis of trade data, balance of payments information, and other pertinent financial and economic data.

EXPORT FINANCING PROGRAMS

BACKGROUND

Export sales financing is crucial to a sustained and successful export program. Prior to 1960, export financing in the United States was largely an entrepreneurial activity with little governmental support. The Export-Import Bank had been extending credits to importers overseas purchasing agricultural and other commodity products from the United States for decades, but its facilities were otherwise limited. The risks of extending longer payment terms to overseas customers was borne mainly by the exporter.

The U.S. government began to take an active part in the financing aspects of American exports in 1960 as part of a broader and continuing export expansion program. The main objective of government supported programs is to minimize the exporter's collection risk when selling abroad in order to encourage him to extend more liberal terms, thereby using credit as a sales leverage tool.

The purpose of this section is to outline in detail the various programs that are available both to exporters and investors.

EXPORT-IMPORT BANK OF THE UNITED STATES

The Export-Import Bank of the United States (Eximbank) is located at 811 Vermont Avenue, N.W., Washington, D.C. 20571. Established in 1934, it is an independent, wholly-owned agency of the United States Government. It operates under the provisions of the Export-Import Bank Act of 1945 as amended. Its purposes are to facilitate and finance the foreign trade of the United States.

Eximbank's loans, made in dollars and repayable in dollars, must be used for purchases of United States goods and services and must have reasonable assurance of repayment. Under its Export Expansion Facility, however, the Bank is authorized to support a limited number of export transactions that may not meet its test of reasonable assurance of repayment but still have sufficient probability of repayment to justify the institution's support in order to foster actively the foreign trade and long-term commercial interests of the United States.

The Bank is directed by statute to supplement and encourage private capital, not compete with it.

In addition to making loans, the Bank issues guarantees covering medium-term export transactions against foreign commercial and political risks, and participates with the Foreign Credit Insurance Association (FCIA) in issuing short-term and medium-term political risk and comprehensive risk insurance policies.

Eximbank has a capital of $1 billion, on which it pays dividends, and may borrow $6 billion from the United States Treasury on a revolving basis, on which it pays interest. In addition, as of June 30, 1969, it had built up from earnings a reserve of about $1.2 billion against possible losses and other contingencies. A major source of its funds in recent years has been the sale of participations in pools of loans, debentures and short-term discount promissory notes.

From its inception through June, 1969, the Bank authorized loans of $22.9 billion, of which more than $15.3 billion were disbursed. In addition more than $8.1 billion of export credit insurance and guarantees had been authorized. Some $7.1 billion of this total of approximately $31 billion expired unused, for various reasons, and $3.3 billion that was committed had not yet been used. Of nearly $20.6 billion that had been used, $13.3 billion was repaid, and $1.2 billion sold, leaving some $6.1 billion outstanding. Some $75 million of loans are uncollectible or of doubtful collectibility, and claims paid under the guarantee and insurance programs totaled about $4.7 million. Thus losses have run at the rate of less than one-half per cent of net authorizations.

Method of Financing

Long-Term Direct Capital Loans: From the beginning the Bank has made what are called "long-term direct capital loans" to public and private entities abroad, the latter being owned by foreign nationals, United States concerns, or, frequently, by both. Although in the past the Bank has financed up to 100 per cent of United States materials and services, it now limits its direct financing to 50 per cent. Under this new arrangement the bank is willing to finance the later installments and to guarantee the early maturities which can be financed by foreign or domestic financial institutions.

Financing for local expenditures must be obtained from other sources. The Bank also demands reasonable equity participation by borrowers, usually about half the total costs of the project. Such loans run from 5 to 20 years or more, with an interest rate on recently authorized loans of 6 per cent per annum.

These loans have ranged in size from a few thousand dollars to as much as $115 million. Their real impact in the United States is on the thousands of sub-contractors who furnish United States goods and services, for whom the Bank finances hundreds of millions of dollars in overseas sales each year through its long-term capital lending program. During the fiscal year 1969 these authorizations amounted to $985 million.

Relending Credits: Eximbank relending credit is a credit made available to financial institutions outside the United States to finance capital goods and related services of United States origin through sub-loans to individual buyers.

Eximbank's relending program is designed to provide financial assistance to buyers—private industrial enterprises, farmers and others—who, because of their size, financial position or inexperience in international trade, cannot get adequate financing elsewhere for their purchases. The sub-loans allow the buyer to deal directly with a bank in his own country and are on terms normal in commercial trade.

Eximbank relending credits usually are established for a specific purpose, such as to provide financing for purchases of products exhibited at a United States Trade Exhibit, or to promote sales of a line of products in an area where normal commercial sources of dollar financing are not readily available to the buyer.

Insurance and Guarantee Program

In the fall of 1961, Eximbank expanded its operations in the short-term and medium-term fields by means of insurance and guarantees. It now offers to United States exporters financial assistance comparable to that available to their counterparts abroad.

Short-Term Insurance (to 180 days)-Foreign Credit Insurance Association (FCIA): FCIA is composed of some 60 of the leading United States casualty marine and property insurance companies. In the short-term field, it issues to exporters (1) comprehensive insurance policies normally covering 90 per cent of credit losses and 95 per cent of political losses, or (2) political-risk-only policies covering 90 per cent of losses.

Credit risks include failure of the importer to pay because of insolvency or protracted default. Political risks include currency inconvertibility, expropriation, cancellation of import license, or other actions taken by foreign governments that prevent payment by the buyer. Premiums are charged according to the economic and political condition of the importing country and the terms of the credit.

Generally speaking, FCIA requires an exporter to insure enough of his eligible short-term sales under this program to provide a reasonable spread of risk. Sales on cash and Letter of Credit terms may be excluded.

Medium-Term (181 days to five years)-FCIA Insurance: This insurance is written on a case-by-case basis. The overseas buyer must make a cash payment of at least 10 per cent of the invoice amount although 20 per cent is preferred and may be required. The remainder is payable in installments and FCIA will insure 90 per cent of this "financed portion" on a comprehensive basis, with the shipper carrying the other 10 per cent at his own risk. In certain higher-risk markets the exporter may be required to carry a larger share of the financed portion.

The same coverage is offered for political risk only, at somewhat lower premium rates. The program also provides for advance commitments and preshipment insurance coverage where they can be justified, and coverage on consignment transactions and sales from consigned or warehoused stocks held abroad.

From July, 1962, through June 30, 1969, FCIA had authorized 5,625 policies for $54.18 million covering comprehensive risk and 464 policies for $53.3 million covering political-risk-only on medium-term export sales. Interest in both types of coverage is increasing.

It should be noted that under both the short-term and medium-term FCIA programs, Eximbank carries 100 per cent of the insured political risk; FCIA carries most of the credit risk. Proceeds both of short-term and medium-term policies are assignable to facilitate borrowing from the customer's commercial bank.

In certain cases, commercial banks may be the named insured both under short and medium term FCIA policies covering exports of U.S. products for one or a number of named suppliers.

Full information on FCIA programs is available from the Foreign Credit Insurance Association, World Trade Center Building, New York, N.Y. 10007, or from local agents, brokers, or banks.

Medium-Term Insurance (181 days to five years)-Eximbank Guarantee Program: Under this program an exporter needing financing may seek a loan from his commercial bank, which in turn may apply for coverage under Eximbank's guarantee program. This requires a cash payment, usually ten per cent, from the overseas buyer. The shipper must carry at least ten per cent of the balance for his own account, and if the commercial bank agrees to finance the remaining portion in full, without recourse on the exporter, Eximbank will guarantee this financing against political loss on all maturities and against credit loss on the later maturities.

This leaves the commercial bank with the credit risk on the early maturities, which are defined as the first eighteen months or the first fifty per cent of the maturities, whichever is shorter. The program also provides for advance commitments and preshipment coverage where they can be justified, and coverage on sales from consigned or warehoused stocks held abroad.

During fiscal 1969, commercial banks received 909 guarantees from Eximbank covering $389.8 million of credit arising from United States exports.

Eximbank's guarantee charges vary by country and term of the loan, but are roughly comparable with those of FCIA.

Guarantees for Foreign Financial Institutions: Eximbank can extend its financial guarantee to cover all, or a portion of the credits issued by foreign financial institutions for the purchase and exportation of United States goods and services.

Foreign financial institutions include branches of U.S. commercial banks and investment banks in other countries; offices overseas of U.S. trading companies and other U.S. financial institutions; foreign commercial, investment and development banks either public or private; and foreign trading companies and other foreign financial institutions.

Under its foreign financial guarantee authority, Eximbank will guarantee repayment by the borrower of principal up to 100 per cent of the credit and interest up to six per cent on outstanding balances. The guarantee will cover commercial risks and/or certain political risks including transfer and convertibility of funds as delineated in the guarantee contract.

Applications for the guarantee may be submitted by the U.S. exporter, his commercial bank, the foreign buyer, or the foreign financial institution. Applications must be accompanied or supplemented by information fully sufficient to enable Eximbank to appraise the quality of the proposed credit and the feasibility, engineering and economics of the proposed project.

As a general rule, the financial guarantee will not be extended to a foreign financial institution of export sales whenever and wherever private U.S. sources of funds are willing and able to finance the transactions on reasonable terms.

Eximbank cannot issue a financial guarantee for loans covering sales of other than U.S. goods and services, or sales of military items to economically less developed countries, or sales of any items to Communist countries (other than Yugoslavia), or to any country in which the government directly furnishes goods or services to a country which is engaged in armed conflict with the United States.

The financial guarantee agreement between Eximbank and the foreign financial institution will refer, of course, to a loan agreement between that institution and its borrower. The borrower who is buying U.S. goods and services may be of the same nationality as the foreign financial institution, or a third country.

The Eximbank program of guaranteeing loans made by foreign financial institutions is merely an extension of the Bank's program of financial guarantees to U.S. commercial banks engaged in financing U.S. exports.

Other Types of Financing

On a case-by-case basis, Eximbank will cover political and credit risks on the sale of technical services abroad by United States firms, including architectural services, design, engineering studies and reports, and economic surveys. Guarantees also are available in connection with United States equipment on lease abroad, on consignment awaiting sales, and on display at trade fairs and similar events, and on equipment being used by contractors in the performance of service abroad.

The Bank also authorizes war risk and expropriation insurance on United States commodities owned by United States citizens and located in friendly foreign countries. This insurance has made possible many shipments of cotton, wheat, barley and tobacco.

Exporters may apply to Eximbank for financial assistance or guarantees on their medium-term transactions if they have been unable to obtain non-recourse financing from their commercial banks or export credit insurance from FCIA.

Eximbank makes emergency foreign trade loans to foreign governments to assure an adequate flow of trade from the United States when temporary dollar shortages threaten to disrupt it.

Eximbank operates a discount facility under which it makes loans to commercial banks against export debt obligations with an original maturity generally of one year or longer, arising from exports made after July 1, 1969. Under this program Eximbank does not normally buy the export obligations; instead, it lends to the commercial bank and gauges the amount, term and interest rate of its loans by amount, term, rate and other characteristics of the export debt obligations held by the borrowing bank.

AGENCY FOR INTERNATIONAL DEVELOPMENT

The Agency for International Development is located at the Department of State, Washington, D.C. 20523. This organization, familiarly known as AID, was created on November 4, 1961, under provisions of the Foreign Assistance Act of 1961, which terminated the International Cooperation Administration and the Development Loan Fund and transferred their functions to the new agency.

The act centralized the administration of most of the Government's foreign economic aid activities in a single agency. Principal features of the Act, as amended, are as follows:

1. Its emphasis on long-term development assistance, within the broader context of economic aid from various free-world sources.

2. Its stress on sound country plans and self-help measures as a pre-

condition for assistance.

3. Gradual shifts from grants to loans, repayable in dollars at low interest rates and with long maturities.

4. Promotion of long-range economic development through increased participation by United States and foreign private enterprise.

5. Government participation in investment surveys undertaken by private enterprise.

6. Broadening of the investment guarantees program.

The Foreign Assistance Act prohibits assistance to countries nationalizing, expropriating or seizing control of United States citizens' property, or repudiating or nullifying contracts and agreements with them.

Financing Activities

Development Loans: The purpose of development loans, under the terms of the Foreign Assistance Act of 1961, is to promote the economic development of less-developed countries and areas, with emphasis on assistance to long-range plans and programs designed to develop economic resources and interest productive capacities.

AID lends dollars to friendly governments and to qualifying private enterprises. These loans are repayable, both principal and interest thereon, in dollars, and must have a reasonable chance of repayment. The availability of funds from other Free World sources at reasonable terms, the debt-bearing capacity of the country or enterprise in question, and other requirements of sound development lending are considered. Proceeds of the loans must be spent for United States goods and services, with few exceptions.

Loan terms are based on the state of economic development in the host country and the nature of the enterprise involved. The longest-term loan at present permits amortization over a 40-year period beginning with a 10-year grace period in which the interest rate is only two per cent per annum, becoming three per cent thereafter. In dollar loans to private enterprises, terms are negotiated to fit the needs of the enterprise.

A procedure also is available whereby a private enterprise borrowing dollars from AID may pay off the loan, under the terms at which it is borrowed, in local currency to the host country, which in turn repays AID in dollars under the longer-term, lower-rate arrangements the country enjoys.

The Foreign Assistance Act defines development projects as undertakings to promote the economic development of the recipient country, and specifies appropriate participation by private enterprise. AID overseas missions work with the countries themselves to decide the relative priorities of the projects.

Cooley Amendment Funds: Under the so-called Cooley Amendment to Title I of the Agricultural Trade Development and Assistance Act (Public Law 480), certain of the foreign currencies received in payment for export sales of agricultural products may be allocated to AID. AID in turn is empowered to lend these funds to United States companies, their branches, subsidiaries or affiliates, for business development or trade expansion in the purchaser country. Host-country firms as well as United States companies may also borrow Cooley funds for both market expansion and consumption of United States agricultural products.

Cooley funds may not be lent for the manufacture abroad of products for export to this country in competition with domestically-made products, and due consideration shall be given to the continued expansion of markets for United States agricultural commodities or the products thereof.

Loans of Cooley funds are made at interest rates comparable to those prevailing in purchaser countries. They carry no maintenance-of-value clauses. AID missions overseas will advise potential borrowers as to the application of the program and will help them appraise the desirability of projects.

Investment Insurance and Guarantees: AID operates three investment guarantee programs: (1) specific risk insurance; (2) extended risk guarantees; (3) extended risk guarantees for housing. Under agreements currently in force with 88 Free World developing countries, covering some or all of the following political risks, the specific risk program protects eligible United States investors in those countries against inconvertibility; expropriation or confiscation; and war, revolution or insurrection.

Eligible investors are United States citizens, corporations, substantially or beneficially owned (more than fifty per cent) by United States citizens, or wholly owned foreign subsidiaries of United States corporations. Investments may take the form of equity and loans, including participations or royalty arrangements. Long-term suppliers' credits may be covered in cases where such arrangements would have a highly favorable effect on economic development.

Insurance for equity investments is for a maximum of 20 years; for loans, for the term of the loan. Rates are as follows:

Inconvertibility: 1/4 per cent of the current amount at risk, plus 1/10 per cent of the standby amount reserved for coverage;

Expropriation: 1/2 per cent of the current amount at risk, plus 1/10 per cent of the standby amount;

War-Revolution-Insurrection: 1/2 per cent of the current amount at risk, plus 1/10 per cent of the standby amount;

Combined Risk (expropriation and war-revolution-insurrection): 7/8 per cent of the current amount at risk, plus 1/10 per cent of the standby amount.

Investment insurance is not available without host-government approval of the project to be covered. The program has a statutory ceiling of $8.5 billion on the specific risk insurance outstanding at any one time. As of March 31, 1969, specific risk guarantees totaling $7.9 billion had been issued, of which approximately $6.7 billion were outstanding.

The extended risk guarantee program permits coverage, up to 75 per cent of an investment, against loss through all risks except the investor's fraud or misconduct. These guarantees emphasize economic development projects that further social progress and development of small, independent business enterprises. The statutory ceiling in this program is $390 million, and guarantees totaling $99.7 million have been authorized. Fees for extended risk guarantees go up to 1 3/4 per cent per annum on the portion of the investment covered by the extended risk guarantees.

The program also permits 100 per cent coverage for loan investments in housing projects (outside Latin America) in which the private investor has appropriate participation. Maximum authority for such housing project guarantees under the Foreign Assistance Act of 1966 is $160-million.

In Latin America, AID is authorized to issue guarantees to eligible United States investors assuring against loss of loan investments made in the following:

1. Pilot or demonstration private housing projects of types similar to those insured by the Department of Housing and Urban Development and suitable for conditions in Latin America.

2. Credit institutions in Latin America, such as savings and loan institutions and other qualified investment enterprises, that are engaged directly or indirectly in financing home mortgages.

3. Housing projects for lower income families and persons, which projects shall be constructed in accordance with maximum unit costs established by the president for families and persons whose incomes meet the limitations prescribed by the president.

4. Housing projects that will promote the development of institutions important to the success of the Alliance for Progress; or

5. Housing projects for which 25 per cent or more of the aggregate of the mortgage financing is made available from sources within Latin America and is not derived from sources outside Latin America, which projects shall, to the greatest extent practicable, have a unit cost of not more than $6,500.

Through implementation of the Housing Investment Guaranty Program, AID has encouraged the growth of institutions concerned with housing. These include savings and loan associations, cooperatives, national home loan banks, building products manufacture and supply industries as well as the construction industry itself. The program also supports, within the limits of available means, provisions of adequate shelter for lower-middle income families throughout the hemisphere.

The 1968 Foreign Assistance Act increased the statutory ceiling on the amount of its investment guarantees issued and outstanding to $550 million. On April 16, 1969, AID announced that applications would be accepted for investment guarantees in Barbados, Argentina, Colombia and Ecuador. Additions of other countries to this list are announced periodically.

Inquiries regarding the Latin American housing investment guarantee program may be made to the Housing and Urban Development Division, Bureau for Latin America, Agency for International Development.

Investment Opportunity Surveys: To encourage private enterprise to make surveys of investment opportunities in less developed friendly countries, AID will repay up to half the cost of a survey to the enterprise that undertakes it and then decides not to invest in the project examined. To obtain such reimbursement, the enterprise must turn over to AID a professionally acceptable technical report on the project.

Information Sources: AID maintains a Businessmen's Information Service to answer general questions and to channel inquiries to pertinent offices of the agency for further information.

A booklet entitled *Aids to Business (Overseas Investment)* is available from the Service. It describes the agency's programs to encourage private investment to developing countries.

AID's Office of Small Business publishes regularly and without charge the details of procurement to be made under AID financing. Suppliers who want to be put on the mailing list for this information should send their requests to the Office of Small Business, Agency for International Development, Washington, D.C. 20523.

COMMODITY CREDIT CORPORATION

The Commodity Credit Corporation, located at Department of Agriculture, Washington, D.C. 20250, is an agency of the Department of Agriculture. It conducts an activity known as the CCC Export Credit Sales Program to promote United States exports of agricultural commodities.

The program is open to export firms of the United States that sell to foreign importers and extend to them the same credit arrangements the CCC grants to the United States exporters. A list of commodities eligible for financing under the program is published each month. As of May, 1969, the following commodities were eligible: cornmeal, grain, sorghums, upland and extra long staple cotton, milled and brown rice, tobacco, cottonseed oil, soybean oil, dairy products, tallow, lard, breeding cattle, rye, raisins.

Export financing is accomplished through purchase of the exporters' accounts receivable. Credit is limited to the value of commodities in the United States (on-board vessel, United States port of export), and may not include marine insurance, ocean freight, and letter of credit charges. It may be used for shipments to any country with which the United States can conduct commercial business, with financing not to exceed 3 years. Exporters should submit applications for credit approvals to: The Assistant Sales Manager (Export Credit), Export Marketing Service, United States Department of Agriculture, Washington, D.C. 20250.

For all transactions an irrevocable letter of credit of the standby type, issued by an acceptable foreign or United States bank, is required. If issued by foreign bank, the instrument must be confirmed at least 10 per cent for commercial risks and fully advised by a United States bank.

Interest rates follow, (as of September, 1969):

On that portion of credits unconfirmed by a United States bank, 7 3/8 per cent per annum:

On credits issued or confirmed by a United States bank, 6 3/8 per cent annum; if the United States bank confirms less than the full amount of the credit, the rate for the unconfirmed portion is 7 3/8 per cent.

Bank letter of credit charges are additional.

Copies of the CCC credit regulations No. GSM-4 and specimen documents containing operating details of the CCC program are available from the Assistant Sales Manager (Export Credit), at the above given address.

FOREIGN CREDIT INSURANCE ASSOCIATION

As indicated previously, the FCIA is an organization of 60 of the nation's leading capital stock and mutual property insurance companies. It was created in 1961 to enable United States exporters to compete on more favorable terms with exporters in other countries and thus effectively contribute to the expansion of U.S. exports.

In cooperation with the Export-Import Bank of the United States FCIA insures exporters against the risk of non-payment by foreign buyers for commercial or political reasons. FCIA insurance also facilitates the financing of term credit sales, thus providing U.S. exporters with support to meet competitive terms of payment offered by other countries.

FCIA Services

FCIA export credit insurance protects the exporter against risks of default by foreign buyers due to commercial or political reasons. Such protection enables the exporter to offer terms competitive with foreign suppliers. It enables exporters to sell in high risk foreign markets. It also assists the exporter in securing financing from the commercial banks and other lending institutions at attractive rates, often on a non-recourse basis.

The small exporter–with annual export sales of under $200,000–and the businessman with no previous exporting experience, can use FCIA in entering new markets through protection of the receivables generated from these overseas sales. He can therefore do more business in proportion to his capital because his risk is minimized. In addition, his bank can extend more liberal financing to the exporter than could otherwise be justified again, because of the insured receivables. In 1972, approximately two-thirds of the policyholders who had their exports supported by FCIA coverage were in the "small business" category.

FCIA insures against both commercial credit and political risks. The member insurance companies cover the normal commercial risks. Eximbank assumes the defined political risks, and also reinsures certain commercial credit risks.

Policies Available: The *Master Comprehensive Policy* provides blanket coverage (normally 90%) for both political and commercial credit risks for all of an exporter's eligible short term credit sales (up to 180 days), as well as for medium term sales (on terms ranging up to five years). A deductible provision for commercial risks is included in the policy. Premium rates vary, and take into account the spread of risks of the exporter's business, his overall export credit experience, the amount of the deductible and the amount of the "discretionary credit limit." Advantages of these policies include simplification or shortening of the reports required under a standard policy.

The Master Comprehensive Policy includes a primary loss deductible. This provides for the insured to retain, for his own account, commercial losses under the policy up to the amount of the deductible. The insured is, however, eligible for repayment for any unrecovered commercial losses to the extent that the sum of such losses exceeds the amount of the deductible. The amount of the minimum deductible in any policy is determined by the Insurers and is based in large part on the discretionary credit limit necessary to cover most of the exporter's foreign buyers.

The deductible feature, similar to that used in automobile and medical insurance, is designed to lower premium rates. By eliminating routine commercial claims which the insured himself is willing and able to bear, it saves money and paper work for him and for the Insurers.

The discretionary credit limit represents a specific dollar amount up to which the insured may extend a line of credit to an eligible buyer without case-by-case prior approval of the Insurers, provided the insured meets the policy conditions governing such limit.

In other words, the higher the deductible limit, the higher the discretionary credit limit under the policy, since this increased deductible lessens the risk of FCIA.

The *Master Political Only Policy* covers an exporter's political risks, and is of special interest for an exporter who ships primarily to his own subsidiaries and affiliates. This recently revised policy offers political coverage of 90% on the exporter's total short and medium term sales. It also provides for a delay in filing transfer risk claims until nine months, rather than six months, after maturity date, with payment three months after filing claim. Such changes in the political risk coverage have permitted a sizable reduction in premium costs, while still providing the exporter with substantial coverage in the event of catastrophic loss because of political reasons.

All Master Policies and standard Short Term Policies have an aggregate limit which represents the maximum liability of the Insurers. This aggregate limit usually corresponds with the insured's maximum outstanding receivables covered under the policy at any one time during the year. This limit may be raised if the insured's exports increase dramatically.

The *Small Business Policy* is available for newcomers in the export trade, and for exporters having a modest sales volume. It is offered to firms whose average annual export volume over the preceding three years did not exceed $200,000. This type of policy covers both commercial credit and political risks. In contrast to other FCIA policies, however, the Small Business Policy may cover only a selected portion of an exporter's foreign accounts sold on terms up to 5 years, depending upon product category. It is intended to serve as an introduction to export credit insurance and as a stimulus to small firms to expand their overseas sales.

The policy may remain in force for a period not to exceed two years, or until the exporter has insured an aggregate contract value of exports of $500,000, whichever comes first. The insured may then convert his policy to a standard form.

The *Short Term Policy* is a blanket type of policy which requires the exporter to insure all or at least a reasonable spread of his eligible short term export credit sales. The *Short Term Comprehensive Policy* covers the commercial credit risks (normally up to 90%) and the political risks (up to 95%) on sales on any type of product (at least 50% of U.S. origin) on terms up to 180 days. U.S. agricultural commodities may also be insured under this policy on payment terms up to one year, with 98% coverage of both commercial and political risks. Under certain conditions, a Short Term Policy may be issued for political risks only (normally up to 90%).

The *Medium Term Policy* is issued on a buyer-by-buyer or a transaction-by-transaction basis, with no requirement that the exporter insure all sales to all buyers. Coverage may be requested for a single sale to a foreign buyer or for repetitive sales to a foreign buyer, or for repetitive sales to a dealer or distributor who may need a line of credit which revolves as installment payments are received. The

Machinery and Equipment, Parts and Accessories
Supported by FCIA Insurance in 1971

	Dollar Volume of Shipments
Construction	$197,276,036
Calculating & Data Processing	122,174,129
Agricultural	116,080,496
Specialized Manufacturing	54,335,592
Textile	47,209,961
Materials Handling & Industrial	33,901,254
Engines, Pumps, Turbines & Compressors	23,675,437
Machinery (Not Elsewhere Described)	23,181,345
Air Conditioning & Refrigeration	19,431,084
Food Processing & Handling	11,778,745
Laundry & Dry Cleaning	9,159,323
Specialized Testing & Servicing	7,969,557
Printing	7,324,186
Oil Field	6,113,814
Lumber Mill	4,180,225
Packaging	3,510,611
Packing	3,133,755
Mining	1,906,760
Plastic Products Manufacturing	1,389,340
Cotton Ginning	1,360,000
Total	$695,091,650

Transportation Equipment, Parts and Accessories
Supported by FCIA Insurance in 1971

	Dollar Volume of Shipments
Motor Vehicles (Cars & Trucks)	$177,447,823
Aircraft	35,539,343
Ocean (Trawlers, Yachts, Boats)	815,295
Other	1,128,050
Total	$214,930,511

Agricultural Commodities Supported by FCIA Insurance in 1971

Product	Dollar Volume of Shipments
Rice	$20,220,990
Soybeans & Peanuts	18,471,000
Grain & Feed	12,924,940
Cotton	4,164,157
Citrus Fruits	4,101,000
Seeds	2,161,257
Tobacco	1,088,238
Other Agricultural Products	4,870,203
Total	$68,001,785

Medium Term Comprehensive Policy covers the commercial credit and political risks (normally up to 90%) on sales of capital or quasi-capital goods (solely of U.S. origin) on terms of up to five years. Livestock, used machinery, and agricultural commodities may also be covered.

A *Medium Term Political Risk Policy* covering an exporter's political risks only (up to 90%) is also available.

The *Combined Short Term-Medium Term Policy* is a policy giving coverage on a dealer-by-dealer basis, and designated specifically to provide protection for U.S. manufacturers of capital and quasi-capital equipment. This policy provides both short and medium term coverage for sales to a specific dealer or distributor under a single policy, subject to one limit of liability.

Special coverages available on certain specified conditions include: Preshipment Coverage, Consignment Coverage, Nonacceptance Coverage and Foreign Currency Sales.

Financing Exports: FCIA does not itself finance exports. But using an FCIA policy as collateral, an exporter can secure financing of his foreign receivables from his commercial bank. Nearly 500 commercial banks are on record as assignees of the proceeds of FCIA policies. When default occurs on the foreign receivable, whether the cause be commercial or political, the assignee bank will ask its insured client to file a claim with FCIA. In return, FCIA will, after verifying the validity of the loss under the terms of the policy, pay the claim by check in joint favor of the insured exporter and the assignee bank.

A special "hold harmless" assignment will be considered for financially capable exporters which affords an unconditional guarantee to the bank, thus permitting financing without recourse. This "hold harmless" assignment is attractive both to banks and to their exporting customers.

FCIA COVERAGE—BY COUNTRY, 1971
(figures in $ thousands—000 omitted)

Country	FCIA Authorizations in 1971	FCIA Insured Shipments during 1971	FCIA Exposure as of 12/31/71
Afghanistan	56.9	56.9	21.0
Algeria	3,071.4	2,083.7	1,268.8
Andorra	*	*	*
Angola	8,172.7	6,046.8	5,407.2
Antigua	192.8	135.1	57.3
Argentina	85,708.8	57,029.3	74,972.6
Australia	53,198.5	36,784.0	21,638.3
Austria	3,745.4	2,818.5	571.6
Azores	*	*	—
Bahamas	6,154.4	4,096.2	2,036.9
Bahrain	438.9	438.9	39.9
Barbados	2,980.2	2,059.2	542.1
Belgium	20,716.7	14,518.2	7,850.8
Bermuda	4,164.9	2,460.4	338.2
Bolivia	11,149.9	7,139.5	9,271.9
Botswana	*	*	—
Brazil	119,039.9	82,992.7	87,707.5
Brunei	3.7	3.7	3.7
Burma, Union of	1,232.4	852.6	684.5
Burundi	5.5	5.5	1.3
Cameroon, Federal Republic of	67.0	67.0	11.7
Canada	97,159.4	67,802.3	42,340.4
Canary Islands	471.7	471.7	150.2
Cape Verde Islands	4.2	4.2	4.2
Central African Republic	10.4	10.4	2.5
Ceylon	125.6	87.7	117.6
Chad	17.1	17.1	—
Chile	15,147.7	6,150.4	7,818.7
Colombia	83,078.8	57,584.3	106,735.8
Comoro Islands	*	*	—
Costa Rica	18,231.2	12,670.9	12,344.9
Cyprus	211.0	211.0	71.8
Dahomey	608.7	608.7	381.3
Denmark	14,511.9	9,986.8	4,179.2

Country	FCIA Authorizations in 1971	FCIA Insured Shipments during 1971	FCIA Exposure as of 12/31/71
Dominican Republic	8,278.3	8,039.9	5,223.1
Ecuador	20,405.3	16,727.8	25,710.4
El Salvador	8,600.1	8,231.3	4,116.1
Ethiopia	5,032.2	5,032.2	1,790.8
Fiji Islands	16.4	16.4	*
Finland	7,331.7	4,915.8	3,688.0
France	94,077.0	64,490.2	23,626.0
French Terr. of Afars & Issas	18.1	18.1	1.0
Gabon	148.3	148.3	90.2
Gambia, The	261.2	261.2	247.1
Germany, Federal Republic of	136,319.8	92,921.8	37,844.5
Ghana	1,011.2	1,011.2	537.4
Gibraltar	37.5	26.0	14.5
Greece	17,506.4	12,313.1	19,141.6
Greenland	*	*	—
Guatemala	30,043.0	23,732.5	15,258.3
Guiana-French	93.8	64.9	12.8
Guinea	211.6	149.1	17.7
Guayana	3,243.1	2,243.8|	2,000.5
Haiti	67.5	46.7	9.7
Honduras	11,088.1	10,240.4	9,139.0
Honduras-British	876.5	604.7	500.0
Hong Kong	16,726.5	11,563.5	4,270.2
Iceland	1,356.1	942.2	244.1
India	4,165.4	2,256.9	1,622.0
Indonesia	3,580.2	3,580.2	100.2
Iran	36,114.2	24,836.6	20,722.4
Ireland	2,970.5	2,101.2	337.2
Israel	11,947.9	8,173.3	5,140.1
Italy	69,879.0	49,014.5	22,920.9
Ivory Coast, Republic of the	3,978.8	2,774.6	433.5
Jamaica	20,570.8	12,240.6	3,961.8
Japan	39,741.5	28,090.3	11,205.3
Jordan	238.9	164.3	855.4
Kenya	1,900.1	1,507.6	673.8
Korea, Republic of	7,947.3	5,493.8	3,607.2

Country	FCIA Authorizations in 1971	FCIA Insured Shipments during 1971	FCIA Exposure as of 12/31/71
Kuwait	18,202.2	14,268.1	15,393.6
Laos	317.5	317.5	—
Lebanon	5,597.8	2,098.8	1,270.7
Lesotho	2.6	2.6	*
Liberia	2,596.5	1,805.2	388.5
Libyan Arab Republic	1,220.3	846.9	4,130.2
Liechtenstein	335.8	233.5	8.0
Luxembourg	729.7	507.4	65.0
Madeira Islands	2.5	2.5	—
Malagasy Republic	2,759.7	2,358.5	765.1
Malawi	45.4	45.4	44.1
Malaysia	1,795.5	1,241.7	811.1
Maldive Islands	1.7	1.7	—
Mali	*	*	—
Malta	619.9	429.8	187.9
Mauritania	5.2	5.2	—
Mauritius	198.2	138.9	146.1
Mexico	174,034.3	116,925.2	101,880.9
Monaco	3.0	3.0	*
Morocco	1,568.2	1,093.3	158.7
Mozambique	1,573.4	1,098.5	1,291.0
Nepal	*	*	—
Netherlands	52,340.7	36,891.5	14,310.6
New Caledonia	136.3	94.2	21.4
New Guinea, East	79.8	79.8	21.4
New Zealand	11,584.8	7,993.9	3,829.0
Nicaragua	13,235.5	9,370.3	7,631.2
Niger	2.3	2.3	1.9
Nigeria	3,675.9	2,404.4	4,683.8
Norway	13,884.0	9,652.0	4,428.8
Oman	760.9	516.7	491.1
Pacific Islands- British	44.8	44.8	158.9
Pacific Islands- French	142.4	122.4	1.8
Pakistan	1,622.5	1,149.6	684.9
Panama	39,886.3	25,560.0	15,375.8
Paraguay	2,980.2	2,096.6	1,635.9
Peru	31,986.5	19,727.1	23,386.7

Country	FCIA Authorizations in 1971	FCIA Insured Shipments during 1971	FCIA Exposure as of 12/31/71
Philippines	29,511.9	20,308.0	15,609.0
Portugal	5,329.5	3,560.9	2,431.4
Portuguese Guinea	71.3	71.3	*
Qatar	326.5	224.7	298.1
Reunion	39.8	39.8	31.3
Rwanda	93.9	93.9	30.0
Ryuku Islands	2,219.0	1,541.3	1,346.7
Sao Tome & Principe	*	*	—
Saudi Arabia	9,292.8	6,352.4	5,632.7
Senegal	476.9	476.9	73.5
Sierra Leone	4.5	4.5	—
Singapore	9,744.2	6,736.5	6,059.8
Somali Republic	239.6	239.6	195.6
South Africa, Republic of	40,431.8	22,144.9	23,760.6
Spain	36,265.2	25,408.6	15,523.7
St. Pierre & Miquelon	7.0	7.0	2.8
Surinam	2,103.7	1,469.3	467.4
Sweden	27,309.9	19,233.4	10,031.0
Switzerland	36,265.2	25,221.7	11,375.7
Tahiti	1,006.2	692.1	178.5
Taiwan	14,676.9	10,146.4	7,573.3
Tanzania	72.2	72.2	273.0
Thailand	14,337.0	9,911.1	6,236.1
Timor	8.4	8.4	—
Togo	970.1	970.1	438.3
Trinidad & Tobago	15,478.3	8,302.1	3,272.6
Trucial States	1,352.7	923.6	286.9
Tunisia	22.0	22.0	5.3
Turkey	131.9	131.9	21.1
Uganda	157.7	157.7	468.0
United Kingdom	105,318.8	73,983.9	23,850.2
Upper Volta	160.5	160.5	131.5
Uruguay	3,856.7	2,863.1	2,034.1
Vatican City	*	*	—
Venezuela	143,661.1	101,794.8	77,142.0
Vietnam, Republic of	6.0	6.0	*

Country	FCIA Authorizations during 1971	FCIA Insured Shipments during 1971	FCIA Exposure as of 12/31/71
Virgin Islands- British	13.1	9.6	4.8
West Indies, British	3,243.1	2,286.9	708.7
West Indies, French	2,279.0	1,593.6	901.5
West Indies, Netherlands	7,295.6	4,870.3	2,223.5
Western Samoa	20.0	20.0	20.0
Yugoslavia	9,105.1	6,332.7	15,910.8
Zaire, Republic of	662.5	662.5	373.7
Zambia	1,256.7	1,256.7	363.3
Total	2,024,300.0	1,398,912.7	1,050,127.8

* = Less than $1,000   — = None

U.S. GOVERNMENT EXPORT EXPANSION PROGRAMS

OVERSEAS PRIVATE INVESTMENT CORPORATION

Introduction

The Overseas Private Investment Corporation (OPIC) is a quasi-governmental institution created in 1970 to encourage U.S. corporations to direct their investments toward the less developed countries. Its objectives are to provide loans for financing overseas capital projects, and insurance to cover up to 80% of the value of those capital investments against a variety of political and economic hazards.

OPIC's facilities have already been both time and stress tested. Nationalization of United States and of other foreign-owned businesses in Chile in 1971 has led to indemnification payments by OPIC to U.S. corporations totaling almost $200 million. It is also interesting to note that OPIC currently insures about $500 million in new investments annually. This represents approximately one-third of the total U.S. investment flow to developing countries.

The creation of OPIC is one of the more significant export and foreign investment encouragement developments of the present decade. Its importance in eventually redirecting the focus of U.S. business away from the world's industrial areas and toward the LDC nations, where the need is greatest, cannot be underestimated.

OPIC programs can help a U.S. bank or financial institution to further develop its financial services for its customers and clients. For instance:

    1. Insurance and guaranties may make it possible to increase its loan and investment resources available for private enterprise projects in less developed countries.

2. Insurance and guaranties may permit more favorable terms on medium and long-term loans to such projects.

3. Insurance and guaranties may assist banks and investment bankers arrange financing for larger projects by organizing consortia of lenders: U.S., foreign and international, public and private.

4. Insurance may make it possible for a bank to extend its facilities by opening new branches in less developed countries.

The following OPIC programs are those of direct interest to financial institutions.

Investment Insurance

OPIC insures medium and long-term loans and equity investments (including capital investments by U.S. commercial banks in their foreign branches) against certain political risks. The insurable risks are: inconvertibility of local currencies into U.S. dollars; loss from expropriation and loss from war, revolution or insurrection.

Inconvertibility: OPIC assures that local currency received by a U.S. financial institution can continue to be convertible indirectly into dollars if at the time the insurance contract is executed there is a means available for converting directly within authorized channels.

Repatriation of dividends and capital on equity investments and principal and interest on loans is covered. Loans may be expressed in dollars or in any other currency convertible at the time of the insurance contract.

The fee payable to OPIC depends on certain elections by the lender/investor but does not exceed 3/10% per annum on the currently insured amount.

Expropriation: The U.S. lender/investor may be insured by OPIC for the loss of the investment through expropriatory actions of the local government. Coverage includes not only direct government seizure of a local private enterprise or its property but also certain types of governmental interference with the lender/investor's fundamental rights in regard to the investment.

Examples are: when the local government prevents repatriation of capital or dividends or payments of principal or interest; when the local government prevents disposition of shares of stock or debt instruments or repatriation of the proceeds of the sale of such securities; or when the local government prevents, for at least a year, the local enterprise from exercising effective control over a substantial portion of its property or from continuing the operation of its business.

The contract of insurance excludes from coverage any expropriation loss which is the result of indirect government action, such as taxation or regulation, unless the action is arbitrary or discriminatory.

OPIC compensation is limited to the amount of coverage in force on the date of the expropriation reduced by any compensation paid by the local government. If the local enterprise is insolvent and its assets are less than its liabilities, compensation for debt securities is limited to the amount the lender would have received if the enterprise had been liquidated and its assets distributed in bankruptcy.

The fee payable to OPIC depends on certain elections by the lender/investor but does not exceed 0.6% per annum on the currently insured amount.

War, Revolution and Insurrection: The U.S. lender/investor may be insured against loss on tangible property of the local enterprise which is caused directly by war, revolution and/or insurrection.

The amount of compensation for loss on a loan or other investment will take into account several factors, including the amount of damage, the original cost of the property adjusted for depreciation, earnings and losses and the lender/investor's proportionate interest in the net worth plus long-term liabilities of the enterprise on the date of the damage.

The fee payable to OPIC depends on certain elections by the lender/investor but does not exceed 0.6% per annum of the currently insured amount.

General Limitations: Coverage on an equity investment is generally for a term of up to 20 years. Loans may be insured for the term of the loan, but the loan must have an average life of at least three years. The lender/investor may terminate any and all coverages on any anniversary date of the insurance contract.

OPIC insurance is available only on new loans/investments and usually does not cover investments which purchase an existing interest in a local enterprise or which refinance existing debt. In addition, a loan or investment made or irrevocably committed prior to applying to OPIC for a Registration Letter is not eligible for insurance.

In providing investment insurance against local political risks, OPIC usually does not make its own evaluation of the commercial soundness of the local private enterprise. OPIC, however, will review the contribution the enterprise will make to local economic and social development and will issue insurance only if potential development benefits are demonstrated. In addition, insurance will not be issued unless OPIC has received the specific approval of the appropriate ministry of the local government. The countries in which insurance is available are listed in Figure 7.1.

The rules which restricted the use of the proceeds of an insured loan or equity investment in an effort to protect U.S. balance of payments were relaxed in 1970. OPIC continues to be concerned, however, with the long- and short-term effects of investments on U.S. balance of payments and, unless justified, insurance will not be available for loans or investments involving substantial procurement in other developed countries.

FIGURE 7.1: OPIC INSURANCE AVAILABLE

Convertibility	Expropriation	War, Revolution and Insurrection
Afghanistan	Afghanistan	Afghanistan (war only)
Antigua	Antigua	Antigua
*Argentina	—	—
Barbados	Barbados	Barbados
Botswana	Botswana	Botswana
Brazil	Brazil	Brazil
British Honduras	British Honduras	British Honduras
Burundi	Burundi	Burundi
Cameroon	Cameroon	Cameroon
Central African Republic	Central African Republic	Central African Republic
Ceylon	Ceylon	Ceylon
Chad	Chad	Chad
China, Republic of	China, Republic of	China, Republic of
Colombia	Colombia	Colombia
Congo (Kinshasa)	Congo (Kinshasa)	Congo (Kinshasa)
Costa Rica	Costa Rica	Costa Rica
*Cyprus	*Cyprus	*Cyprus
Dahomey	Dahomey	Dahomey
Dominica	Dominica	Dominica
Dominican Republic	Dominican Republic	Dominican Republic
Ecuador	Ecuador	Ecuador
El Salvador	El Salvador	—
Ethiopia	Ethiopia	Ethiopia
Gabon	Gabon	Gabon
Gambia	Gambia	Gambia
Ghana	Ghana	Ghana
Greece	Greece	Greece
Grenada	Grenada	Grenada
*Guatemala	*Guatemala	—
Guinea	Guinea	Guinea
Guyana	Guyana	Guyana
Haiti	Haiti	Haiti
Honduras	Honduras	Honduras
India	India	India
Indonesia	Indonesia	Indonesia
Iran	Iran	Iran
Israel	Israel	Israel
Ivory Coast	Ivory Coast	Ivory Coast
Jamaica	Jamaica	Jamaica
Jordan	Jordan	Jordan
Kenya	Kenya	Kenya
Korea	Korea	Korea
Laos	Laos	Laos
Lesotho	Lesotho	Lesotho
Liberia	Liberia	Liberia
Malagasy	Malagasy	Malagasy
Malawi	Malawi	Malawi
Malaysia	Malaysia	Malaysia

FIGURE 7.1: (continued)

Convertibility	Expropriation	War, Revolution and Insurrection
Mali	Mali	Mali
*Malta	*Malta	*Malta
*Mauritania	*Mauritania	*Mauritania
Mauritius	Mauritius	Mauritius
Morocco	Morocco	Morocco
Nepal	Nepal	Nepal
Nicaragua	Nicaragua	Nicaragua
Niger	Niger	Niger
Nigeria	Nigeria	–
Pakistan	Pakistan	Pakistan
Panama	Panama	Panama (war only)
Paraguay	Paraguay	Paraguay
Philippines	Philippines	Philippines
Rwanda	Rwanda	Rwanda
St. Christopher-Nevis-Anguilla	St. Christopher-Nevis-Anguilla	St. Christopher-Nevis-Anguilla
Sta. Lucia	Sta. Lucia	Sta. Lucia
Senegal	Senegal	Senegal
Sierra Leone	Sierra Leone	Sierra Leone
Singapore	Singapore	Singapore
*Somali Rep.	*Somali Rep.	*Somali Rep.
*Sudan	*Sudan	*Sudan
Swaziland	Swaziland	Swaziland
Tanzania (excl. Zanzibar)	Tanzania (excl. Zanzibar)	Tanzania (excl. Zanzibar)
Thailand	Thailand	Thailand
Togo	Togo	Togo
Trinidad-Tobago	Trinidad-Tobago	Trinidad-Tobago
Tunisia	Tunisia	Tunisia
Turkey	Turkey	Turkey
*U.A.R. (Egypt)	*U.A.R. (Egypt)	*U.A.R. (Egypt)
Uganda	Uganda	Uganda
Upper Volta	Upper Volta	Upper Volta
Venezuela	Venezuela	Venezuela
Vietnam	Vietnam	Vietnam
Western Samoa	Western Samoa	Western Samoa
*Yugoslavia	*Yugoslavia	–
Zambia	Zambia	Zambia

*Program currently inoperative.

Investment Guarantees

OPIC guarantees payment on medium and long-term loans to be made to private enterprise borrowers in less developed countries. The guaranty provides that OPIC will pay promptly any defaulted installment of principal or interest on the loan, with interest to the date of payment by OPIC. The guaranty is backed by the full faith and credit of the United States and is issued against a cash reserve at least equal to 25% of the face amount of the guaranty. The guaranty and the guaranteed loan, or promissory notes, are transferable. All claims which have been made under outstanding guaranties have been paid promptly in accordance with the provisions of the guaranty agreement.

The purchase of OPIC guaranteed notes generally constitutes a legal investment for insurance companies, pension funds, savings banks and trusts. In addition, an OPIC guaranteed loan is acceptable collateral at its face value for U.S. Treasury tax and loan accounts.

Terms: The terms of a guaranteed loan are developed for each case through consultation and negotiation among OPIC, the lender and the project borrower or its principal owners. Terms should reflect the project borrower's needs and the risks involved. OPIC uses the following general guidelines:

Amount: usual minimum is $250,000;

Maturity: usually with amortization over a period not shorter than five years and no longer than twenty;

Interest rate: at current U.S. market rates but subject to OPIC approval;

Collateral: determined case-by-case but guaranties of the local government or local bank, or of the project owners, are seldom required;

OPIC fee: minimum of 1 3/4% per annum on the outstanding guaranteed principal amount; payable by the project borrower;

Use of proceeds: for U.S. procurement or for procurement from sources within the less developed countries, including local costs;

Distribution: private placement or public offering, as appropriate.

Debt guaranteed by OPIC may be in the form of a term loan or as promissory notes, bonds or debentures convertible to equity.

Guaranty of equity: OPIC offers guaranties on equity investments. Normally compensation will not exceed 50% of each equity investor's loss in the event the project is unsuccessful and is liquidated. Equity guarantees have been issued to investment companies, such as Edge Act corporations, as well as to industrial firms.

Multi-source Financing: OPIC normally does not guaranty a loan which exceeds 50% of the total project cost. Other unguaranteed debt financing, therefore, frequently is required to complete the project financial plan. OPIC has guaranteed loans to projects where other investment institutions, U.S., local and international, public and private, have also been part of the total financing package. Generally, U.S. commercial banks and investment bankers, with OPIC collaboration, have taken the lead in arranging for this kind of multi-source financing.

General Limitations: The project should be a new venture or an expansion or modernization of an existing enterprise.

As with the investment insurance program an approval from the appropriate ministry of the local government is required as a condition to OPIC's issuing its guaranty. A country list with respect to guaranties is shown in Figure 7.2.

OPIC guaranties are available only for investments in projects which will contribute to the economic and social development of the local country. These can be a wide variety of productive enterprises including manufacturing, processing, storage, agribusiness, utilities, transportation, commercial hotels, tourist facilities and businesses providing services, including financial services.

Loans guaranteed by OPIC are not exempt from the Federal Reserve Board guidelines covering credits to non-U.S. borrowers. Reflecting U.S. Government policy, however, loans made by U.S. non-bank financial institutions have a final maturity of 10 years or more are exempt. In most cases the U.S. Interest Equalization Tax is not applicable.

Nationality of Insured or Guaranteed Lender or Investor: The lender or investor must be a U.S. citizen or a U.S. entity at least 51% U.S. owned. Mutual savings banks and insurance companies and pension funds are eligible if U.S. citizens hold at least 51% of the beneficial interests. A foreign branch of a U.S. bank is eligible, but a foreign affiliate is not unless 100% of its shares are U.S. owned. The affiliate is eligible, however, if no more than 5% of the shares are held by other than the U.S. owners, if this is required by local law.

Inquiries and Applications

General information may be obtained from:

> Information Officer
> Overseas Private Investment Corporation
> Washington, D.C. 20527
> 202-632-1854

Inquiries on investment insurance for a specific proposed investment should be directed to:

> Director for Insurance (Africa, Near East, South Asia, East Asia
> or Latin America)
> Overseas Private Investment Corporation
> Washington, D.C. 20527

FIGURE 7.2: OPIC GUARANTIES AVAILABLE

Antigua
Barbados
Botswana
Brazil
British Honduras
Burundi
Cameroon
Central African Republic
Ceylon
Chad
China, Republic of
Congo (Kinshasa)
Costa Rica
*Cyprus
Dahomey
Dominica
Dominican Republic

Ethiopia
Gabon
Gambia
Ghana
Greece
Grenada
Guinea
Guyana
Haiti
Honduras
India
Indonesia
Iran
Israel
Ivory Coast
Jamaica
Jordon
Kenya
Korea
Laos
Lesotho

Liberia
Malagasy
Malawi
Malaysia
Mali
*Malta
Mauritania
Mauritius
Morocco
Nepal
Nicaragua
Niger
Pakistan
Paraguay
Philippines
Rwanda
St. Christopher-
   Nevis-Anguilla
Sta. Lucia
Senegal
Sierra Leone
Singapore
*Somali Republic
Sudan
Swaziland
Tanzania
   (except Zanzibar)
Thailand
Togo
Trinidad-Tobago
Tunisia
Turkey
*U.A.R. (Egypt)
Uganda
Upper Volta
Venezuela
Vietnam
Western Samoa
Zambia

*Limited Availability

Inquiries on guaranties of a specific proposed loan should be directed to:

> Vice President for Finance
> Overseas Private Investment Corporation
> Washington, D.C. 20527

International agreements covering OPIC Insurance do tend to change. In those countries shown with asterisks the program is inoperative for a variety of reasons. Investors are well advised to check periodically with OPIC to obtain current data.

Investment insurance, against inconvertibility and expropriation only, may be also available for some of the underdeveloped dependencies of France, Netherlands, Portugal and the United Kingdom.

Agreements covering OPIC loan guaranties are similarly under constant review. It may be possible for OPIC to guarantee an investment in a project to be carried out in a country not on any given list, but special arrangements with the government of that country will be necessary. In addition, this list is subject to additions and deletions, as availability is affected by changing economic and political conditions.

In view of the critical importance of OPIC to U.S. investors in helping them shape their overseas investment decisions, the text of Public Law 91-175 is reproduced in this section. This law details with precision the rules and regulations regarding the ways and means for qualifying for OPIC programs.

> Public Law 91-175
> 91st Congress, H. R. 14580
> December 30, 1969

An Act

83 STAT. 805

To promote the foreign policy, security, and general welfare of the United States by assisting peoples of the world to achieve economic development within a framework of democratic economic, social, and political institutions, and for other purposes.

Foreign
Assistance Act
of 1969.

Be it enacted by the Senate and House of Representatives of the United States of America in Congress assembled, That this Act may be cited as the "Foreign Assistance Act of 1969".

PART I—ECONOMIC ASSISTANCE

* * * *

"Title IV—Overseas Private Investment Corporation

"Sec. 231. Creation, Purpose, and Policy.—To mobilize and facilitate the participation of United States private capital and skills in the economic and social progress of less developed friendly countries and areas, thereby complementing the development assistance objectives of the United States, there is hereby created the Overseas Private Investment Corporation (hereinafter called the 'Corporation'), which shall be an agency of the United States under the policy guidance of the Secretary of State.

"In carrying out its purpose, the Corporation, utilizing broad criteria, shall undertake—

"(a) to conduct its financing operations on a self-sustaining basis, taking into account the economic and financial soundness of projects and the availability of financing from other sources on appropriate terms;

83 STAT. 810

"(b) to utilize private credit and investment institutions and the Corporation's guaranty authority as the principal means of mobilizing capital investment funds;

"(c) to broaden private participation and revolve its funds through selling its direct investments to private investors whenever it can appropriately do so on satisfactory terms;

"(d) to conduct its insurance operations with due regard to principles of risk management including, when appropriate, efforts to share its insurance risks;

"(e) to utilize, to the maximum practicable extent consistent with the accomplishment of its purpose, the resources and skills of small business and to provide facilities to encourage its full participation in the programs of the Corporation;

"(f) to encourage and support only those private investments in less developed friendly countries and areas which are sensitive and responsive to the special needs and requirements of their economies, and which contribute to the social and economic development of their people.

"(g) to consider in the conduct of its operations the extent to which less developed country governments are receptive to private enterprise, domestic and foreign, and their willingness and ability to maintain conditions which enable private enterprise to make its full contribution to the development process;

"(h) to foster private initiative and competition and discourage monopolistic practices;

"(i) to further to the greatest degree possible, in a manner consistent with its goals, the balance-of-payments objectives of the United States;

"(j) to conduct its activities in consonance with the activities of the agency primarily responsible for administering part I and the international trade, investment, and financial policies of the United States Government; and

"(k) to advise and assist, within its field of competence, interested agencies of the United States and other organizations, both public and private, national and international, with respect to projects and programs relating to the development of private enterprise in less developed countries and areas.

68 Stat. 832.
22 USC 1750-
1951.

"Sec. 232. Capital of the Corporation.—The President is authorized to pay in as capital of the Corporation, out of dollar receipts made available through the appropriation process from loans made pursuant to this part and from loans made under the Mutual Security Act of 1954, as amended, for the fiscal year 1970 not to exceed $20,000,000 and for the fiscal year 1971 not to exceed $20,000,000. Upon the payment of such capital by the President, the Corporation shall issue an equivalent amount of capital stock to the Secretary of the Treasury.

"Sec. 233. Organization and Management.—(a) Structure of the Corporation.—The Corporation shall have a Board of Directors, a President, and Executive Vice President, and such other officers and staff as the Board of Directors may determine.

"(b) Board of Directors.—All powers of the Corporation shall vest in and be exercised by or under the authority of its Board of Directors ('the Board') which shall consist of eleven Directors, including the Chairman, with six Directors constituting a quorum for the transaction of business. The Administrator of the Agency for International Development shall be the Chairman of the Board, ex officio. Six Directors (other than the President of the Corporation, appointed pursuant to subsection (c) who shall also serve as a Director) shall be appointed by the President of the United States, by and with the advice and consent of the Senate, and shall not be officials or employees of the Government of the United States. At least one of the six Directors appointed under the preceding sentence shall be experienced in small business, one in organized labor, and one in cooperatives. Each such Director shall be appointed for a term of no more than three years. The terms of no more than two such Directors shall expire in any one year. Such Directors shall serve until their successors are appointed and qualified and may be reappointed.

Appointments by President.

83 STAT. 811

Terms of Office

"The other Directors shall be officials of the Government of the United States, designated by and serving at the pleasure of the President of the United States.

"All Directors who are not officers of the Corporation or officials of the Government of the United States shall be compensated at a rate equivalent to that of level IV of the Executive Schedule (5 U.S.C. 5315) when actually engaged in the business of the Corporation and may be paid per diem in lieu of subsistence at the applicable rate prescribed in the standardized Goverment travel regulations, as amended from time to time, while away from their homes or usual places of business.

81 Stat. 638.

"(c) President of the Corporation.—The President of the Corporation shall be appointed by the President of the United States, by and with the advice and consent of the Senate, and shall serve at the pleasure of the President. In making such appointment, the President shall take into account the private business experience of the appointee. The President of the Corporation shall be its Chief Executive Officer and responsible for the operations and management of the Corporation, subject to bylaws and policies established by the Board.

Appointment by President.

"(d) Officers and Staff.—The Executive Vice President of the Corporation shall be appointed by the President of the United States, by and with the advice and consent of the Senate, and shall serve at the pleasure of the President. Other officers, attorneys, employees, and agents shall be selected and appointed by the Corporation, and shall be vested with such powers and duties as the Corporation may determine. Of such persons employed by the Corporation, not to exceed twenty may be appointed, compensated, or removed without regard to the civil service laws and regulations: *Provided*, That under such regulations as the President of the United States may prescribe, officers and employees of the United States Government who are ap-

66 Stat. 662.
31 USC 724.

"(c) Direct Investment.—To make loans in United States dollars repayable in dollars or loans in foreign currencies (including, without regard to section 1415 of the Supplemental Appropriation Act, 1953, such foreign currencies which the Secretary of the Treasury may determine to be excess to the normal requirements of the United States and the Director of the Bureau of the Budget may allocate) to firms privately owned or of mixed private and public ownership upon such terms and conditions as the Corporation may determine. The Corporation may not purchase or invest in any stock in any other corporation, except that it may (1) accept as evidence of indebtedness debt securities convertible to stock, but such debt securities shall not be converted to stock while held by the Corporation, and (2) acquire stock through the enforcement of any lien or pledge or otherwise to satisfy a previously contracted indebtedness which would otherwise be in default, or as the result of any payment under any contract of insurance or guaranty. The Corporation shall dispose of any stock it may so acquire as soon as reasonably feasible under the circumstances then pertaining.

"No loans shall be made under this section to finance operations for mining or other extraction of any deposit of ore, oil, gas, or other mineral.

83 STAT. 813

"(d) Investment Encouragement.—To initiate and support through financial participation, incentive grant, or otherwise, and on such terms and conditions as the Corporation may determine, the identification, assessment, surveying and promotion of private investment opportunities, utilizing wherever feasible and effective the facilities of private organizations or private investors: *Provided however*, That the Corporation shall not finance surveys to ascertain the existence, location, extent or quality, or to determine the feasibility of undertaking operations for mining or other extraction, of any deposit of ore, oil, gas, or other mineral. In carrying out this authority, the Corporation shall coordinate with such investment promotion activities as are carried out by the Department of Commerce.

"(e) Special Activities.—To administer and manage special projects and programs, including programs of financial and advisory support which provide private technical, professional, or managerial assistance in the development of human resources, skills, technology, capital savings and intermediate financial and investment institutions and cooperatives. The funds for these projects and programs may, with the Corporation's concurrence, be transferred to it for such purposes under the authority of section 632(a) or from other sources, public or private.

75 Stat. 453.
22 USC 2392.

"Sec. 235. Issuing Authority, Direct Investment Fund and Reserves.—(a)(1) The maximum contingent liability outstanding at any one time pursuant to insurance issued under section 234(a) shall not exceed $7,500,000,000.

"(2) The maximum contingent liability outstanding at any one time pursuant to guaranties issued under section 234(b) shall not exceed in the aggregate $750,000,000, of which guaranties of credit union investment shall not exceed $1,250,000: *Provided*, That the Corporation shall not make any commitment to issue any guaranty which would result in a fractional reserve less than 25 per centum of the maximum contingent liability then outstanding against guaranties issued or commitments made pursuant to section 234(b) or similar predecessor guaranty authority.

pointed to any of the above positions may be entitled, upon removal from such position, except for cause, to reinstatement to the position occupied at the time of appointment or a position of comparable grade and salary. Such positions shall be in addition to those otherwise authorized by law, including those authorized by section 5108 of title 5 of the United States Code.

80 Stat. 453,
878.

"Sec. 234. Investment Incentive Programs.—The Corporation is hereby authorized to do the following:

"(a) Investment Insurance.—(1) To issue insurance, upon such terms and conditions as the Corporations may determine, to eligible investors assuring protection whole or in part against any or all of the following risks with respect to projects which the Corporation has approved—

"(A) inability to convert into United States dollars other currencies, or credits in such currencies, received as earnings or profits from the approved project, as repayment or return of the investment therein, in whole or in part, or as compensation for the sale or disposition of all or any part thereof;

83 STAT. 812

"(B) loss of investment, in whole or in part, in the approved project due to expropriation or confiscation by action of a foreign government; and

"(C) loss due to war, revolution, or insurrection.

"(2) Recognizing that major private investments in less developed friendly countries or areas are often made by enterprises in which there is multinational participation, including significant United States private participation, the Corporation may make such arrangements with foreign governments (including agencies, instrumentalities, or political subdivisions thereof) or with multilateral organizations for sharing liabilities assumed under investment insurance for such investments and may in connection therewith issue insurance to investors not otherwise eligible hereunder: *Provided, however*, That liabilities assumed by the Corporation under the authority of this subsection shall be consistent with the purposes of this title and that the maximum share of liabilities so assumed shall not exceed the proportionate participation by eligible investors in the total project financing.

"(3) Not more than 10 per centum of the total face amount of investment insurance which the Corporation is authorized to issue under this subsection shall be issued to a single investor.

"(b) Investment Guaranties.—To issue to eligible investors guaranties of loans and other investments made by such investors assuring against loss due to such risks and upon such terms and conditions as the Corporation may determine: *Provided however*, That such guaranties on other than loan investments shall not exceed 75 per centum of such investment: *Provided further*, That except for loan investments for credit unions made by eligible credit unions or credit union associations, the aggregate amount of investment (exclusive of interest and earnings) so guaranteed with respect to any project shall not exceed, at the time of issuance of any such guaranty, 75 per centum of the total investment committed to any such project as determined by the Corporation, which determination shall be conclusive for purposes of the Corporation's authority to issue any such guaranty: *Provided further*, That not more than 10 per centum of the total face amount of investment guaranties which the Corporation is authorized to issue under this subsection shall be issued to a single investor.

61 Stat. 584.
31 USC 849.

"(3) The Congress, in considering the budget programs transmitted by the President for the Corporation, pursuant to section 104 of the Government Corporation Control Act, as amended, may limit the obligations and contingent liabilities to be undertaken under section 234(a) and (b) as well as the use of funds for operating and administrative expenses.

Expiration of
Authority

"(4) The authority of section 234(a) and (b) shall continue until June 30, 1974.

"(b) There shall be established a revolving fund, known as the Direct Investment Fund, to be held by the Corporation. Such fund shall consist initially of amounts made available under section 234(c), shall be charged with realized losses and credited with realized gains and shall be credited with such additional sums as may be transferred to it under the provisions of section 236.

"(c) There shall be established in the Treasury of the United States an insurance and guaranty fund, which shall have separate accounts to be known as the Insurance Reserve and the Guaranty Reserve, which reserves shall be available for discharge of liabilities, as provided in section 235(d), until such time as all

83 STAT. 814

such liabilities have been discharged or have expired or until all such reserves have been expended in accordance with the provisions of this section. Such fund shall be funded by: (1) the funds heretofore available to discharge liabilities under predecessor guaranty authority (including housing guaranty authorities), less both the amount made available for housing guaranty programs pursuant to section 223(b) and the amount made available to the Corporation to section 234(e); and (2) such sums as shall be appropriated pursuant to section 235(f) for such purpose. The allocation of such funds to each such reserve shall be determined by the Board after consultation with the Secretary of the Treasury. Additional amounts may thereafter be transferred to such reserves pursuant to section 236.

"(d) Any payments made to discharge liabilities under investment insurance issued under section 234(a) or under similar predecessor guaranty authority shall be paid first out of the Insurance Reserve, as long as such reserve remains available, and thereafter out of funds made available pursuant to section 235(f). Any payments made to discharge liabilities under guaranties issued under section 234(b) or under similar predecessor guaranty authority shall be paid first out of the Guaranty Reserve as long as such reserve remains available, and thereafter out of funds made available pursuant to section 235(f).

Fees and
revenues.

"(e) There is hereby authorized to be transferred to the Corporation at its call, for the purposes specified in section 236, all fees and other revenues collected under predecessor guaranty authority from December 31, 1968, available as of the date of such transfer.

Appropriation.

"(f) There is hereby authorized to be appropriated to the Corporation, to remain available until expended, such amounts as may be necessary from time to time to replenish or increase the insurance and guaranty fund or to discharge the liabilities under insurance and guaranties issued by the Corporation or issued under predecessor guaranty authority.

"Sec. 236. Income and Revenues.—In order to carry out the purpose of the Corporation, all revenues and income transferred to or earned by the Corporation, from whatever source derived, shall be held by the Corporation and shall be available to carry out its purposes, including without limitation—

"(a) payment of all expenses of the Corporation, including investment promotion expenses;

"(b) transfers and additions to the insurance or guaranty reserves, the Direct Investment Fund established pursuant to section 235, and such other funds or reserves as the Corporation may establish, at such time and in such amounts as the Board may determine: and

"(c) payment of dividends, on capital stock, which shall consist of and be paid from net earnings of the Corporation after payments, transfers, and additions under subsections (a) and (b) hereof.

"Sec. 237. General Provisions Relating to Insurance and Guaranty Programs.—(a) Insurance and guaranties issued under this title shall cover investment made in connection with projects in any less developed friendly country or area with the government of which the President of the United States has agreed to institute a program for insurance or guaranties.

"(b) The Corporation shall determine that suitable arrangements exist for protecting the interest of the Corporation in connection with any insurance or guaranty issued under this title, including arrangements concerning ownership, use, and disposition of the currency, credits, assets, or investments on account of which payment under such insurance or guaranty is to be made, and any right, title, claim, or cause of action existing in connection therewith.

83 STAT. 815

"(c) All guaranties issued prior to July 1, 1956, all guaranties issued under sections 202(b) and 413(b) of the Mutual Security Act of 1954, as amended, all guaranties heretofore issued pursuant to prior guaranty authorities repealed by the Foreign Assistance Act of 1969, and all insurance and guaranties issued pursuant to this title shall constitute obligations, in accordance with the terms of such insurance or guaranties, of the United States of America and the full faith and credit of the United States of America is hereby pledged for the full payment and performance of such obligations.

71 Stat. 357.
22 USC 1872 note.
68 Stat. 846.
22 USC 1933 note.

Insurance fees.

"(d) Fees shall be charged for insurance and guaranty coverage in amounts to be determined by the Corporation. In the event fees to be charged for investment insurance or guaranties are reduced, fees to be paid under existing contracts for the same type of guaranties or insurance and for similar guaranties issued under predecessor guaranty authority may be reduced.

"(e) No insurance or guaranty of any equity investment shall extend beyond twenty years from the date of issuance.

"(f) No insurance or guaranty issued under this title shall exceed the dollar value, as of the date of the investment, of the investment made in the project with the approval of the Corporation plus interest, earnings or profits actually accrued on said investment to the extent provided by such insurance or guaranty.

"(g) No payment may be made under any guaranty issued pursuant to this title for any loss arising out of fraud or misrepresentation for which the party seeking payment is responsible.

"(h) Insurance or guaranties of a loan or equity investment of an eligible investor in a foreign bank, finance company, or other credit institution shall extend only to such loan or equity investment and not to any individual loan or equity investment made by such foreign bank, finance company, or other credit institution.

"(i) Claims arising as a result of insurance or guaranty operations under this title or under predecessor guaranty authority may be settled, and disputes arising as a result thereof may be arbitrated with the consent of the parties, on such terms and conditions as the Corporation may determine. Payment made pursuant to any such settlement, or as a result of an arbitration award, shall be final and conclusive notwithstanding any other provision of law.

Claims
settlement.

"(j) Each guaranty contract executed by such officer or officers as may be designated by the Board shall be conclusively presumed to be issued in compliance with the requirements of this Act.

"(k) In making a determination to issue insurance or a guaranty under this title, the Corporation shall consider the possible adverse effect of the dollar investment under such insurance or guaranty upon the balance of payments of the United States.

"Sec. 238. Definitions.—As used in this title—

"(a) the term 'investment' includes any contribution of funds, commodities, services, patents, processes, or techniques, in the form of (1) a loan or loans to an approved project, (2) the purchase of a share of ownership in any such project, (3) participation in royalties, earnings, or profits of any such project, and (4) the furnishing of commodities or services pursuant to a lease or other contract;

"(b) the term 'expropriation' includes, but is not limited to, any abrogation, repudiation, or impairment by a foreign government of its own contract with an investor with respect to a project, where such abrogation, repudiation, or impairment is not caused by the investor's own fault or misconduct, and materially adversely affects the continued operation of the project;

83 STAT. 816

"(c) the term 'eligible investor' means: (1) United States citizens; (2) corporations, partnerships, or other associations including nonprofit associations, created under the laws of the United States or any State or territory thereof and substantially beneficially owned by United States citizens; and (3) foreign corporations, partnerships, of other associations wholly owned by one or more such United States citizens, corporations, partnerships, or other associations: *Provided, however*, That the eligibility of such foreign corporation shall be determined without regard to any shares, in aggregate less than 5 per centum of the total of issued and subscribed share capital required by law to be held by other than the United States owners: *Provided further*, That in the case of any loan investment a final determination of eligibility may be made at the time the insurance or guaranty is issued; in all other cases, the investor must be eligible at the time a claim arises as well as at the time the insurance or guaranty is issued: and

"(d) the term 'predecessor guaranty authority' means prior guaranty authorities (other than housing guaranty authorities) repealed by the Foreign Assistance Act of 1969, sections

71 Stat. 357.
22 USC 1872
note.
68 Stat. 846.
22 USC 1509
note.
62 Stat. 143;
64 Stat. 198.
22 USC 1933
note.

202(b) and 413(b) of the Mutual Security Act of 1954, as amended, and section 111(b)(3) of the Economic Cooperation Act of 1948, as amended (exclusive of authority relating to informational media guaranties).

"Sec. 239. General Provisions and Powers.—(a) The Corporation shall have its principal office in the District of Columbia and shall be deemed, for purpose of venue in civil actions, to be a resident thereof.

"(b) The President shall transfer to the Corporation, at such time as he may determine, all obligations, assets and related rights and responsibilities arising out of, or related to, predecessor programs and authorities similar to those provided for in section 234 (a), (b), and (d). Until such transfer, the agency heretofore responsible for such predecessor programs shall continue to administer such assets and obligations, and such programs and activities authorized under this title as may be determined by the President.

"(c) The Corporation shall be subject to the applicable provisions of the Government Corporation Control Act, except as otherwise provided in this title.

59 Stat. 597;
61 Stat. 584.
31 USC 841
note.

Corporation
powers.

"(d) To carry out the purpose of this title, the Corporation is authorized to adopt and use a corporate seal, which shall be judicially noticed; to sue and be sued in its corporate name; to adopt, amend, and repeal bylaws governing the conduct of its business and the performance of the powers and duties granted to or imposed upon it by law; to acquire, hold or dispose of, upon such terms and conditions as the Corporation may determine, any property, real, personal, or mixed, tangible or intangible, or any interest therein; to invest funds derived from fees and other revenues in obligations of the United States and to use the proceeds therefrom, including earnings and profits, as it shall deem appropriate; to indemnify directors, officers, employees and agents of the Corporation for liabilities and expenses incurred in connection with their Corporation activities; to require bonds of officers, employees, and agents and pay the premiums therefor; notwithstanding any other provision of law, to represent itself or to contract for representation in all legal and arbitral proceedings; to purchase, discount, rediscount, sell, and negotiate, with or without its endorsement or guaranty, and guarantee notes, participation certificates, and other evidence of indebtedness (provided that the Corporation shall not issue its own securities, except participation certificates for the purpose of carrying out section 231(c)); to make and carry out such contracts and agreements as are necessary and advisable in the conduct of its business; to exercise the priority of the Government of the United States in

83 STAT. 817

collecting debts from bankrupt, insolvent, or decedents' estates; to determine the character of and the necessity for its obligations and expenditures, and the manner in which they shall be incurred, allowed, and paid, subject to provision of law specifically applicable to Government corporations; and to take such actions as may be necessary or appropriate to carry out the powers herein or hereafter specifically conferred upon it.

AID.
Audits and
reviews by
Auditor-
General.

"(e) The Auditor-General of the Agency for International Development (1) shall have the responsibility for planning and directing the execution of audits, reviews, investigations, and inspections of all phases of the Corporation's operations and activities and (2) shall conduct all security activities of the Corporation relating to personnel and the control of classified material. With respect to his responsibilities under this subsection, the Auditor-General shall report to the Board. The agency primarily responsible for administering part I shall be reimbursed by the Corporation for all expenses incurred by the Auditor-General in connection with his responsibilities under this subsection.

Advisory Council.

"(f) In order to further the purposes of the Corporation there shall be established an Advisory Council to be composed of such representatives of the American business community as may be selected by the Chairman of the Board. The President and the Board shall, from time to time, consult with such Council concerning the objectives of the Corporation. Members of the Council shall receive no compensation for their services but shall be entitled to reimbursement in accordance with section 5703 of title 5 of the United States Code for travel and other expenses incurred by them in the performance of their functions under this section.

Ante, p. 190.

"Sec. 240. Agricultural Credit and Self-Help Community Development Projects.—(a) It is the sense of the Congress that in order to stimulate the participation of the private sector in the economic development of less developed countries in Latin America, the authority conferred by this section should be used to establish pilot programs in not more than five Latin American countries to encourage private banks, credit institutions, similar private lending organizations, cooperatives, and private nonprofit development organizations to make loans on reasonable terms to organized groups and individuals residing in a community for the purpose of enabling such groups and individuals to carry out agricultural credit and self-help community development projects for which they are unable to obtain financial assistance on reasonable terms. Agricultural credit and assistance for self-help community development projects should include, but not be limited to, material and such projects as wells, pumps, farm machinery, improved seed, fertilizer, pesticides, vocational training, food industry development, nutrition projects, improved breeding stock for farm animals, sanitation facilities, and looms and other handicraft aids.

"(b) To carry out the purposes of subsection (a), the Corporation is authorized to issue guaranties, on such terms and conditions as it shall determine, to private lending institutions, cooperatives, and private nonprofit development organizations in not more than five Latin American countries assuring against loss of not to exceed 25 per centum of the portfolio of such loans made by any lender to organized groups or individuals residing in a community to enable such groups or individuals to carry out agricultural credit and self-help community development projects for which they are unable to obtain financial assistance on reasonable terms. If no event shall the liability of the United States exceed 75 per centum of any one loan.

83 STAT. 818

"(c) The total face amount of guaranties issued under this section outstanding at any one time shall not exceed $15,000,000. Not more than 10 per centum of such sum shall be provided for any one institution, cooperative, or organization.

"(d) The Inter-American Social Development Institute shall be consulted in developing criteria for making loans eligible for guaranty coverage under this section.

Use of
foreign
currencies.

"(e) The guaranty reserve established under section 235(c) shall be available to make such payments as may be necessary to discharge liabilities under guaranties issued under this section.

"(f) Notwithstanding the limitation contained in subsection (c) of this section, foreign currencies owned by the United States and determined by the Secretary of the Treasury to be excess to the needs of the United States may be utilized to carry out the purposes of this section, including the discharge of liabilities incurred under this subsection. The authority conferred by this subsection shall be in addition to authority conferred by any other provision of law to implement guaranty programs utilizing excess local currency.

Report to
Congress.

Expiration of
authority.

"(g) The Corporation shall, on or before January 15, 1972, make a detailed report to the Congress on the result of the pilot programs established under this section, together with such recommendations as it may deem appropriate.

"(h) The authority of this section shall continue until June 30, 1972.

"Sec. 240A. Reports to the Congress.—(a) After the end of each fiscal year, the Corporation shall submit to the Congress a complete and detailed report of its operations during such fiscal year.

"(b) Not later than March 1, 1974, the Corporation shall submit to the Congress an analysis of the possibilities of transferring all or part of its activities to private United States citizens, corporations, or other associations."

UNITED STATES DEPARTMENT OF COMMERCE

Although the United States Department of Commerce is not engaged directly in foreign trade financing, it conducts a vigorous program of services to businessmen to help increase the sale of American products.

The assistant Secretary of Commerce for Domestic and International Business has major responsibilities in the drive to expand exports of U.S. goods. The operating organizations in the domestic and international business area are the Bureau of International Commerce (BIC), the Business and Defense Services Administration (BDSA), the Office of Foreign Commercial Services (OFCS), and the Office of Field Services (OFS).

To help American businessmen show and sell their products abroad, BIC stages U.S. commercial exhibitions at established international trade fairs and also independent all-U.S. shows, apart from trade fairs, in foreign markets. It maintains U.S. Trade Centers in London, Frankfurt, Milan, Bangkok, Paris, Tokyo and Stockholm as permanent overseas salesrooms. In addition, it assists privately organized mobile trade fairs, in which exhibits of U.S. products are transported to commercial centers overseas, ready for display; it arranges sample displays in several developing countries to help U.S. firms that seek to set up agencies or distributorships there; it assists trade missions, and it provides technical promotional aid to overseas department stores conducting "American Weeks" to promote the sale of American consumer products; it also provides a wide range of commercial and economic information on overseas firms and markets.

Under its new Joint Export Association Program, instituted in 1968, the Department enters into contracts with groups of firms to undertake market development and promotional activities for selected products abroad. The Department will assume up to 50% of the costs of any one project.

BDSA works with domestic industry on export expansion programs, supplies commodity and industry data on potential markets for products and services, and, with BIC, distributes information concerning trade opportunities to businessmen. Thousands of opportunities for direct sales as well as distributorships abroad are announced each year in the weekly news magazine *International Commerce* and in the *Commerce Business Daily*, both available on subscription from the Department of Commerce.

BIC provides a "one-stop investor service" for U.S. firms interested in expanding their overseas activities through licensing and investing arrangements abroad. BIC programs assist American firms in identifying licensees and joint venture partners abroad, in evaluating foreign investment climates, in determining overseas investment and licensing regulations, and in locating domestic and foreign sources of investment capital.

Working with the Agency for International Development, it also locates profitable investment opportunities in developing countries, where licensing of U.S. manufacturing processes, and joint ventures by U.S. and overseas partners may contribute to the creation of a favorable climate for sales and thus indirectly stimulate this country's exports.

The Secretary of Commerce confers the President's export "E" Award upon firms, organizations and individuals contributing significantly to U.S. export expansion.

At the regional level, the Department's forty-two field offices, in cities throughout the country, provide services to businessmen locally. In each field office area, volunteers among business and professional leaders, with guidance from the Department's National Export Expansion Council, operate a Regional Export Expansion Council that conducts regular meetings, seminars and workshops to provide practical instruction and advice for all who are interested in export opportunities.

Detailed information about the Commerce Department's services to businessmen in international trade is available from the Director, Bureau of International Commerce, United States Department of Commerce, Washington, D.C. 20230, or from the field offices.

JOINT EXPORT ASSOCIATIONS

Under the Joint Export Association program announced by President Johnson on January 1, 1968, provision was made for joint Government/industry export undertakings whereby the U.S. Department of Commerce would contract with groups of firms or their representatives to provide financial help for the systematic development of specific export markets over a sustained period. The program was drawn up similar to the one which the Department of Agriculture had been operating successfully for twelve years previously.

The program's concept is good. Unfortunately, it is limited by Congress's budgetary constraints. The JEA assistance is made available on the contract basis. Amounts and terms would vary in relation to the size and character of the project, the product, and the market. Contracts outline the objectives and specify the commitments of both Government and the private participants. There are, since the inception of the program in 1968, about 100 contracts that are still active.

Typical expenditures for trade development activities eligible to be shared under this program include the following:

> Advertising, Publicity
> Participation in trade fairs and other exhibitions
> Market research
> Supplying samples and technical data
> Overseas trade promotional visits
> Preparing the submitting bids (intended to cover specialized equipment
>   and unusual projects, including blueprints, drawings, etc.)
> Training of sales and service personnel
> Product use familiarization programs
> Operation abroad of sales offices, showrooms, warehouses and
>   service centers
> Operation abroad of assembly and packaging facilities for U.S.
>   products

Other promotional techniques may be developed during the course of the program.

The U.S. Department of Commerce may also enter into contracts with trade and industry associations, groups of firms associated expressly for the purpose of export development activities under this program, combination export managers, export intermediaries, and corporations with international sales forces which sell products from unrelated manufacturers (the so-called "piggyback" operation).

The objectives of this program are to cause exporters to expand their operations and to assist nonexporters to enter the field through providing a new technique for export expansion, to assist companies to enter new markets and introduce new products abroad, and to obtain an increased share of existing markets for U.S. suppliers.

The program has a number of short-term and long-term benefits.

Through a share-the-cost program, the government can provide some of the resources for companies to enter new markets. It also increases the exposure by American business of products which require the kind of sustained expense and effort many firms may not be encouraged to undertake on their own, or which they only intend to take several years hence.

The JEA program broadens the base of the exporting community. Long-term contracts would stimulate able and aggressive firms, combination export managers, export intermediaries, groups of firms, and trade associations to invest the time, effort, and money for opening new markets, introducing new products abroad, or obtaining an increased share of the markets for the U.S.

The U.S. Department of Commerce has apparently discussed the potential antitrust aspects of the joint export associations with the Department of Justice which seems to indicate that the program can be carried out effectively without antitrust complications.

DOMESTIC INTERNATIONAL SALES CORPORATION

The Revenue Act of 1971 was designed, in response to the Federal Government's continuing efforts to expand U.S. exports, to create a strong, tax-based incentive to corporations engaged exclusively in international trade. The law provided that exporting corporations—Domestic International Sales Corporations (or DISCs)— are entitled to special tax treatment for taxable years beginning on or after January 1, 1972.

In effect, the DISC legislation allows United States exporters to receive, through the formation and operation of a domestic corporation qualifying as a DISC, preferential tax treatments resulting in a deferment and eventual saving of up to 50% of corporate income taxes. The DISC itself is treated as if it were a foreign-based corporation and not subject to United States Federal income tax. However, the shareholders of the DISC are liable for taxing as having received one half of the DISC's current earnings in the form of dividends, whether or not the earnings have actually been distributed.

The remaining half of the DISC's earnings may be retained by the DISC. It can then be reinvested in the corporation's export business or invested in specified Export-Import Bank debentures. These undistributed earnings can also be tuned into "producer's loans" to related or unrelated U.S. export producers without liability for federal income taxes. In other words, a DISC may finance its own parent company's operations with its tax-deferred earnings.

For example, on a DISC that has $100,000 in export earnings (profit before taxes), $50,000 is automatically treated as a taxable dividend to its shareholders, while the remaining $50,000 may be retained by the DISC on a tax-deferred basis. The only way by which the deferment terminates and a tax is imposed on the shareholders is if these earnings are also distributed as dividends or if the corporation no longer qualifies. There are selected other instances. These are listed in the text of the Revenue Act of 1971.

A DISC can act as either principal or agent, as long as it is engaged in the business of exporting products "manufactured, produced, grown or extracted" in the United States. It can also act as a mercantile exporter, buying and reselling overseas articles produced by related and/or unrelated producers. Its overseas customers can similarly be related or unrelated purchasers. Finally, a DISC may lease or sub-lease such products for use outside of the United States. A DISC may also perform engineering or architectural services for foreign construction projects. In other words, a corporation can qualify as a DISC strictly on the basis of its international licensing and technical service agreements.

As indicated, a DISC may invest its tax-deferred earnings not only in expansion of its export business, but also in certain Export-Import Bank obligations and in "producer's loans" to U.S. exporters. By the use of producer's loans, the DISC may form an economic relationship with its suppliers, sharing in the financing of their facilities, inventory, and research and development.

The DISC legislation contains special rules, designed to provide a simplified allocation method for determining the earnings of a DISC which purchases from, or acts as commission agent for, a related supplier.

A domestic corporation presently engaged almost solely in the export business might well be able to qualify as a DISC. In cases where an export business is conducted in a noncorporate form, by a sole proprietorship or a partnership, it will be necessary to organize a corporation. Since the profits of a DISC are not subject to tax at the DISC level, but only at the shareholder level, the incorporation of a business as a DISC will not result in taxation at two levels.

A corporation engaged in manufacturing or in nonexport sales can organize a DISC for export sales.

It is not the purpose of this chapter to present a complete analysis of DISC. The reader should consult competent professional tax and legal advisors to see exactly how the formation of a DISC may be beneficial. Nor are the extra "profits" to be realized out of a DISC operation extraordinary in the case of the smaller enterprise. An additional tax savings of 10 to 15% may be achieved with the proper planning. DISC will, however, serve the important purpose of helping a company to conserve otherwise taxable earnings in the form of cash for possible reinvestment in export promotion and expansion.

The text of the law governing the formation and operation of a DISC is reproduced at the end of this chapter.

THE WESTERN HEMISPHERE TRADING CORPORATION

Western Hemisphere Trade Corporations (WHTCs) enjoy special tax positions. They are therefore utilized mainly by larger corporations doing a sizeable export business to Latin America. However, the special tax status granted to WHTCs has created a host of sales and legal problems. The reason is that a WHTC must derive at least 95% of its income from *within* the Western hemisphere, but *outside* the United States in order to qualify for tax favors. Puerto Rico, Bermuda and the Falkland Islands are excluded.

General Background

A company qualifies as a WHTC if, over the three year period preceding the close of the taxable year, or since its inception, if that period is shorter, it has derived 90% or more of its gross income from the active conduct of a trade or business, and 95% or more of that income from sources within North, Central, or South America, or in the West Indies, but outside of the United States.

A WHTC must be a U.S. corporation. It may, however, establish overseas branches. It may not establish subsidiaries unless the divided income from them is less than 10% of the total gross income (a higher percentage is considered investment income which violates the "action conduct of a trade or business" concept).

WHTCs are subject to lower tax rates of approximately 34% as compared to the standard corporate rate of 48%. About 15% of dividends paid by a WHTC to a U.S. parent are normally included in the latter's taxable income. The exact tax benefit to a U.S. company depends upon the total income generated through the WHTC. This income is then considered along with the forms of dividend income the U.S. company has received from other sources before preferential tax treatment may be given.

A company usually establishes a WHTC as a separate corporate entity, wholly owned, which has the objective of selling only to Western Hemisphere customers. The parent company and/or suppliers sell to the WHTC which resells the goods overseas. The WHTC is then taxed on its earnings based on the income received from overseas less its cost of purchasing and other expenses.

The difficulties stem from the fact that the "place of sale" must be outside the United States. This means that title must pass outside the United States, and evidence must be available to prove that point. The consensus which has evolved from court decisions is that a CIF shipment effectively establishes such evidence, as long as all the charges are prepaid.

One can make certain that title passes outside the U.S. by selling on a consignment basis. This does not necessarily involve the important distributor to whom the export may prefer selling on draft terms. The exporter has only to consign the goods via the documentation to a bank and/or broker outside the United

States. The exporter simultaneously authorizes the bank or broker to release the goods to the actual importer by executing a delivery order on the common carrier. In effect, the bank and/or broker becomes an import agent, "buying on consignment", although the goods are invoiced directly to the distributor.

In the case that a letter of credit order is necessary, the only solution is to allow the presentation of the exporter's documents to his bank "free of payment." There must also be a corresponding authorization by the exporter to allow the buyer's bank to release the documentation "free of payment." Payment is then made to the exporter upon notification by the buyer's bank that the merchandise has been received.

IV. DISC STATUTE (Title V of Public Law 92—178)

TITLE V—DOMESTIC INTERNATIONAL SALES CORPORATIONS

SEC. 501. DOMESTIC INTERNATIONAL SALES CORPORATIONS.

Subchapter N of chapter 1 (relating to income from sources without the United States) is amended by adding at the end thereof the following new part:

68A Stat. 275;
76 Stat. 1006;
80 Stat. 1565.

"PART IV—DOMESTIC INTERNATIONAL SALES CORPORATIONS

"Subpart A. Treatment of qualifying corporations.
"Subpart B. Treatment of distributions to shareholders.

"Subpart A—Treatment of Qualifying Corporations

"Sec. 991. Taxation of a domestic international sales corporation.
"Sec. 992. Requirements of a domestic international sales corporation.
"Sec. 993. Definitions and special rules.
"Sec. 994. Inter-company pricing rules.

"SEC. 991. TAXATION OF A DOMESTIC INTERNATIONAL SALES CORPORATION.

"For purposes of the taxes imposed by this subtitle upon a DISC (as defined in section 992(a)), a DISC shall not be subject to the taxes imposed by this subtitle except for the tax imposed by chapter 5.

Infra.
68A Stat. 365.
26 USC 1491.

"SEC. 992. REQUIREMENTS OF A DOMESTIC INTERNATIONAL SALES CORPORATION.

"(a) DEFINITION of 'DISC' and 'FORMER DISC'.—

"(1) DISC.—For purposes of this title, the term 'DISC' means, with respect to any taxable year, a corporation which is incorporated under the laws of any State and satisfies the following conditions for the taxable year:

"(A) 95 percent or more of the gross receipts (as defined

Post, p. 538.

in section 993(f)) of such corporation consist of qualified export receipts (as defined in section 993(a)),

"(B) the adjusted basis of the qualified export assets (as defined in section 993(b)) of the corporation at the close of of the taxable year equals or exceeds 95 percent of the sum of the adjusted basis of all assets of the corporation at the close of the taxable year,

"(C) such corporation does not have more than one class of stock and the par or stated value of its outstanding stock is at least $2,500 on each day of the taxable year, and

"(D) the corporation has made an election pursuant to subsection (b) to be treated as a DISC and such election is in effect for the taxable year.

"(2) STATUS AS DISC AFTER HAVING FILED A RETURN AS A DISC.—The Secretary or his delegate shall prescribe regulations setting forth the conditions under and the extent to which a corporation which has filed a return as a DISC for a taxable year shall be treated as a DISC for such taxable year for all purposes of this title, notwithstanding the fact that the corporation has failed to satisfy the conditions of paragraph (1).

"(3) 'FORMER DISC'.—For purposes of this title, the term 'former DISC' means, with respect to any taxable year, a corporation which is not a DISC for such year but was a DISC in a preceding taxable year and at the beginning of the taxable year has undistributed previously taxed income or accumulated DISC income.

"(b) ELECTION.—

"(1) ELECTION.—

"(A) An election by a corporation to be treated as a DISC shall be made by such corporation for a taxable year at any time during the 90-day period immediately preceding the beginning of the taxable year, except that the Secretary or his delegate may give his consent to the making of an election at such other times as he may designate.

"(B) Such election shall be made in such manner as the Secretary or his delegate shall prescribe and shall be valid only if all persons who are shareholders in such corporation on the first day of the first taxable year for which such election is effective consent to such election.

"(2) EFFECT OF ELECTION.—If a corporation makes an election under paragraph (1), then the provisions of this part shall apply to such corporation for the taxable year of the corporation for which made and for all succeeding taxable years and shall apply to each person who at any time is a shareholder of such corporation for all periods on or after the first day of the first taxable year of the corporation for which the election is effective.

"(3) TERMINATION OF ELECTION.—

"(A) REVOCATION.—An election under this subsection made by any corporation may be terminated by revocation of such election for any taxable year of the corporation after the first taxable year of the corporation for which the election is effective. A termination under this paragraph shall be effective with respect to such election—

"(i) for the taxable year in which made, if made at any time during the first 90 days of such taxable year, or

"(ii) for the taxable year following the taxable year in which made, if made after the close of such 90 days, and for all succeeding taxable years of the corporation. Such termination shall be made in such manner as the Secretary or his delegate shall prescribe by regulations.

December 10, 1971   Pub. Law 92-178
85 STAT. 537

"(B) CONTINUED FAILURE TO BE DISC.—If a corporation is not a DISC for each of any 5 consecutive taxable years of the corporation for which an election under this subsection is effective, the election shall be terminated and not be in effect for any taxable year of the corporation after such 5th year.

"(c) DISTRIBUTIONS TO MEET QUALIFICATION REQUIREMENTS.—

"(1) IN GENERAL.—Subject to the conditions provided by paragraph (2), a corporation which for a taxable year does not satisfy a condition specified in paragraph (1)(A) (relating to gross receipts) or (1)(B) (relating to assets) of subsection (a) shall nevertheless be deemed to satisfy such condition for such year if it makes a pro rata distribution of property after the close of the taxable year to its shareholders (designated at the time of such distribution as a distribution to meet qualification requirements) with respect to their stock in an amount which is equal to—

"(A) if the condition of subsection (a)(1)(A) is not satisfied, the portion of such corporation's taxable income attributable to its gross receipts which are not qualified export receipts for such year,

"(B) if the condition of subsection (a)(1)(B) is not satisfied, the fair market value of those assets which are not qualified export assets on the last day of such taxable year, or

"(C) if neither of such conditions is satisfied, the sum of the amounts required by subparagraphs (A) and (B).

"(2) REASONABLE CAUSE FOR FAILURE.—The conditions under paragraph (1) shall be deemed satisfied in the case of a distribution made under such paragraph—

"(A) if the failure to meet the requirements of subsection (a)(1)(A) or (B), and the failure to make such distribution prior to the date on which made, are due to reasonable cause; and

"(B) the corporation pays, within the 30-day period beginning with the day on which such distribution is made, to the Secretary or his delegate, if such corporation makes such distribution after the 15th day of the 9th month after the close of the taxable year, an amount determined by multiplying (i) the amount equal to 4½ percent of such distribution, by (ii) the number of its taxable years which begin after the taxable year with respect to which such distribution is made and before such distribution is made. For purposes of this title, any payment made pursuant to this paragraph shall be treated as interest.

"(3) CERTAIN DISTRIBUTIONS MADE WITHIN 8½ MONTHS AFTER CLOSE OF TAXABLE YEAR DEEMED FOR REASONABLE CAUSE.—A distribution made on or before the 15th day of the 9th month after the close of the taxable year shall be deemed for reasonable cause for purposes of paragraph (2)(A) if—

"(A) at least 70 percent of the gross receipts of such corporation for such taxable year consist of qualified export receipts, and

"(B) the adjusted basis of the qualified export assets held by the corporation on the last day of each month of the taxable year equals or exceeds 70 percent of the sum of the adjusted basis of all assets held by the corporation on such day.

85 STAT. 538

"(d) INELIGIBLE CORPORATIONS.—The following corporations shall not be eligible to be treated as a DISC—

68A Stat. 163.
26 USC 501.

"(1) a corporation exempt from tax by reason of section 501,
"(2) a personal holding company (as defined in section 542),

76 Stat. 977.

"(3) a financial institution to which section 581 or 593 applies,
"(4) an insurance company subject to the tax imposed by

73 Stat. 112.

subchapter L,
"(5) a regulated investment company (as defined in section 851(a)),
"(6) a China Trade Act corporation receiving the special deduction provided in section 941(a), or

72 Stat. 1650.

"(7) an electing small business corporation (as defined in section 1371(b)).

"(e) COORDINATION WITH PERSONAL HOLDING COMPANY PROVISIONS IN CASE OF CERTAIN PRODUCED FILM RENTS.—If—

"(1) a corporation (hereinafter in this subsection referred to as 'subsidiary') was established to take advantage of the provisions of this part, and

"(2) a second corporation (hereinafter in this subsection referred to as 'parent') throughout the taxable year owns directly at least 80 percent of the stock of the subsidiary,

then, for purposes of applying subsection (d)(2) and section 541 (relating to personal holding company tax) to the subsidiary for the

78 Stat. 81.

taxable year, there shall be taken into account under section 543(a)(5) (relating to produced film rents) any interest in a film acquired by the parent and transferred to the subsidiary as if such interest were acquired by the subsidiary at the time it was acquired by the parent.

"SEC. 993. DEFINITIONS.

"(a) QUALIFIED EXPORT RECEIPTS.—

"(1) GENERAL RULE.—For purposes of this part, except as provided by regulations under paragraph (2), the qualified export receipts of a corporation are—

"(A) gross receipts from the sale, exchange, or other disposition of export property,

"(B) gross receipts from the lease or rental of export property, which is used by the lessee of such property outside the United States,

"(C) gross receipts for services which are related and subsidiary to any qualified sale, exchange, lease, rental, or other disposition of export property by such corporation,

"(D) gross receipts from the sale, exchange, or other disposition of qualified export assets (other than export property),

76 Stat. 1006.

"(E) dividends (or amounts includible in gross income under section 951) with respect to stock of a related foreign export corporation (as defined in subsection (e)),

"(F) interest on any obligation which is a qualified export asset,

"(G) gross receipts for engineering or architectural services for construction projects located (or proposed for location) outside the United States, and

"(H) gross receipts for the performance of managerial services in furtherance of the production of other qualified export receipts of a DISC.

"(2) EXCLUDED RECEIPTS.—The Secretary or his delegate may under regulations designate receipts from the sale, exchange, lease, rental, or other disposition of export property, and from services, as not being receipts described in paragraph (1) if he determines

December 10, 1971   Pub. Law 92-178 _{85 STAT. 539}

that such sale, exchange, lease, rental, or other disposition, or
furnishing of services—

"(A) is for ultimate use in the United States;

"(B) is accomplished by a subsidy granted by the United
States or any instrumentality thereof;

"(C) is for use by the United States or any instrumentality
thereof where the use of such export property or services is
required by law or regulation.

For purposes of this part, the term 'qualified export receipts' does "Qualified ex-
not include receipts from a corporation which is a DISC for its port receipts."
taxable year in which the receipts arise and which is a member
of a controlled group (as defined in paragraph (3)) which
includes the recipient corporation.

"(3) DEFINITION OF CONTROLLED GROUP.—For purposes of this
part, the term 'controlled group' has the meaning assigned to such
term by section 1563(a), except that the phrase 'more than 50 78 Stat. 120.
percent' shall be substituted for the phrase 'at least 80 percent' 26 USC 1563.
each place it appears therein, and section 1563(b) shall not apply.

"(b) QUALIFIED EXPORT ASSETS.—For purposes of this part, the
qualified export assets of a corporation are—

"(1) export property (as defined in subsection (c));

"(2) assets used primarily in connection with the sale, lease,
rental, storage, handling, transportation, packaging, assembly,
or servicing of export property, or the performance of engineering
or architectural services described in subparagraph (G) of subsection (a)(1) or managerial services in furtherance of the production of qualified export receipts described in subparagraphs
(A), (B), (C), and (G) of subsection (a)(1);

"(3) accounts receivable and evidences of indebtedness which
arise by reason of transactions of such corporation described in
subparagraph (A), (B), (C), (D), (G), or (H), of subsection
(a)(1);

"(4) money, bank deposits, and other similar temporary
investments, which are reasonably necessary to meet the working
capital requirements of such corporation;

"(5) obligations arising in connection with a producer's loan
(as defined in subsection (d));

"(6) stock or securities of a related foreign export corporation
(as defined in subsection (e));

"(7) obligations issued, guaranteed, or insured, in whole or
in part, by the Export-Import Bank of the United States or the
Foreign Credit Insurance Association in those cases where such
obligations are acquired from such Bank or Association or from
the seller or purchaser of the goods or services with respect to
which such obligations arose;

"(8) obligations issued by a domestic corporation organized
solely for the purpose of financing sales of export property
pursuant to an agreement with the Export-Import Bank of the
United States under which such corporation makes export loans
guaranteed by such bank; and

"(9) amounts (other than reasonable working capital) on
deposit in the United States that are utilized during the period
provided for in, and otherwise in accordance with, regulations
prescribed by the Secretary or his delegate to acquire other
qualified export assets.

"(c) EXPORT PROPERTY. —

"(1) IN GENERAL.—For purposes of this part, the term 'export
property' means property—

"(A) manufactured, produced, grown, or extracted in the
United States by a person other than a DISC,

Pub. Law 92-178   December 10, 1971
85 STAT. 540

"(B) held primarily for sale, lease, or rental, in the ordinary course of trade or business, by, or to, a DISC, for direct use, consumption, or disposition outside the United States, and

"(C) not more than 50 percent of the fair market value of which is attributable to articles imported into the United States.

In applying subparagraph (C), the fair market value of any article imported into the United States shall be its appraised value, as determined by the Secretary or his delegate under section 402 or 402a of the Tariff Act of 1930 (19 U.S.C., sec. 1401a or 1402) in connection with its importation.

46 Stat. 708;
70 Stat. 943.

"(2) EXCLUDED PROPERTY.—For purposes of this part, the term 'export property' does not include—

"(A) property leased or rented by a DISC for use by any member of a controlled group (as defined in subsection (a)(3)) which includes the DISC, or

"(B) patents, inventions, models, designs, formulas, or processes, whether or not patented, copyrights (other than films, tapes, records, or similar reproductions, for commercial or home use), good will, trademarks, trade brands, franchises, or other like property.

"(3) PROPERTY IN SHORT SUPPLY.—If the President determines that the supply of any property described in paragraph (1) is insufficient to meet the requirements of the domestic economy, he may by Executive order designate the property as in short supply. Any property so designated shall be treated as property not described in paragraph (1) during the period beginning with the date specified in the Executive order and ending with the date specified in an Executive order setting forth the President's determination that the property is no longer in short supply.

"(d) PRODUCER'S LOANS.—

"(1) IN GENERAL.—An obligation, subject to the rules provided in paragraphs (2) and (3), shall be treated as arising out of a producer's loan if—

"(A) the loan, when added to the unpaid balance of all other producer's loans made by the DISC, does not exceed the accumulated DISC income at the beginning of the month in which the loan is made;

"(B) the obligation is evidenced by a note (or other evidence of indebtedness) with a stated maturity date not more than 5 years from the date of the loan;

"(C) the loan is made to a person engaged in the United States in the manufacturing, production, growing, or extraction of export property (referred to hereinafter as the 'borrower') ; and

"(D) at the time of such loan it is designated as a producer's loan.

"(2) LIMITATION.—An obligation shall be treated as arising out of a producer's loan only to the extent that such loan, when added to the unpaid balance of all other producer's loans to the borrower outstanding at the time such loan is made, does not exceed an amount determined by multiplying the sum of—

"(A) the amount of the borrower's adjusted basis determined at the beginning of the borrower's taxable year in which the loan is made, in plant, machinery, and equipment, and supporting production facilities in the United States;

"(B) the amount of the borrower's property held primarily for sale, lease, or rental, to customers in the ordinary course

85 STAT. 541

of trade or business, at the beginning of such taxable year; and

"(C) the aggregate amount of the borrower's research and experimental expenditures (within the meaning of section 174) in the United States during all preceding taxable years beginning after December 31, 1971,

68A Stat. 66.
26 USC 174.

by the percentage which the borrower's receipts, during the 3 taxable years immediately preceding the taxable year (but not including any taxable year commencing prior to 1972) in which the loan is made, from the sale, lease, or rental outside the United States of property which would be export property if held by a DISC is of the gross receipts during such 3 taxable years from the sale, lease, or rental of property held by such borrower primarily for sale, lease, or rental to customers in the ordinary course of the trade or business of such borrower.

"(3) INCREASED INVESTMENT REQUIREMENT.—An obligation shall be treated as arising out of a producer's loan in a taxable year only to the extent that such loan, when added to the unpaid balance of all other producer's loans to the borrower made during such taxable year, does not exceed an amount equal to—

"(A) the amount by which the sum of the adjusted basis of assets described in paragraph (2)(A) and (B) on the last day of the taxable year in which the loan is made exceeds the sum of the adjusted basis of such assets on the first day of such taxable year; plus

"(B) the aggregate amount of the borrower's research and experimental expenditures (within the meaning of section 174) in the United States during such taxable year.

"(4) SPECIAL LIMITATION IN THE CASE OF DOMESTIC FILM MAKER.—

"(A) IN GENERAL.—In the case of a borrower who is a domestic film maker and who incurs an obligation to a DISC for the making of a film, and such DISC is engaged in the trade or business of selling, leasing, or renting films which are export property, the limitation described in paragraph (2) may be determined (to the extent provided under regulations prescribed by the Secretary or his delegate) on the basis of—

"(i) the sum of the amounts described in subparagraphs (A), (B), and (C) thereof plus reasonable estimates of all such amounts to be incurred at any time by the borrower with respect to films which are commenced within the taxable year in which the loan is made, and

"(ii) the percentage which, based on the experience of producers of similar films, the annual receipts of such producers from the sale, lease, or rental of such films outside the United States is of the annual gross receipts of such producers from the sale, lease, or rental of such films.

"(B) DOMESTIC FILM MAKER.—For purposes of this paragraph, a borrower is a domestic film maker with respect to a film if—

"(i) such borrower is a United States person within the meaning of section 7701(a)(00), except that with respect to a partnership, all of the partners must be United States persons, and with respect to a corporation, all of its officers and at least a majority of its directors must be United States persons;

76 Stat. 988.

"(ii) such borrower is engaged in the trade or business of making the film with respect to which the loan is made;

"(iii) the studio, if any, used or to be used for the taking of photographs and the recording of sound incorporated into such film is located in the United States;

"(iv) the aggregate playing time of portions of such film photographed outside the United States does not or will not exceed 20 percent of the playing time of such film; and

"(v) not less than 80 percent of the total amount paid or to be paid for services performed in the making of such film is paid or to be paid to persons who are United States persons at the time such services are performed or consists of amounts which are fully taxable by the United States.

"(C) SPECIAL RULES FOR APPLICATION OF SUBPARAGRAPH (B) (v).—For purposes of clause (v) of subparagraph (B)—

"(i) there shall not be taken into account any amount which is contingent upon receipts or profits of the film and which is fully taxable by the United States (within the meaning of clause (ii)); and

"(ii) any amount paid or to be paid to a United States person, to a non-resident alien individual, or to a corporation which furnishes the services of an officer or employee to the borrower with respect to the making of a film, shall be treated as fully taxable by the United States only if the total amount received by such person, individual, officer, or employee for services performed in the making of such film is fully included in gross income for purposes of this chapter.

"(e) RELATED FOREIGN EXPORT CORPORATION.—In determining whether a corporation (hereinafter in this subsection referred to as 'the domestic corporation') is a DISC—

"(1) FOREIGN INTERNATIONAL SALES CORPORATION.—A foreign corporation is a related foreign export corporation if—

"(A) stock possessing more than 50 percent of the total combined voting power of all classes of stock entitled to vote is owned directly by the domestic corporation,

"(B) 95 percent or more of such foreign corporation's gross receipts for its taxable year ending with or within the taxable year of the domestic corporation consists of qualified export receipts described in subparagraphs (A), (B), (C), and (D) of subsection (a)(1) and interest on any obligation described in paragraphs (3) and (4) of subsection (b), and

"(C) the adjusted basis of the qualified export assets (described in paragraphs (1), (2), (3), and (4) of subsection (b)) held by such foreign corporation at the close of such taxable year equals or exceeds 95 percent of the sum of the adjusted basis of all assets held by it at the close of such taxable year.

"(2) REAL PROPERTY HOLDING COMPANY.—A foreign corporation is a related foreign export corporation if—

"(A) stock possessing more than 50 percent of the total combined voting power of all classes of stock entitled to vote is owned directly by the domestic corporation, and

"(B) its exclusive function is to hold real property for the exclusive use (under a lease or otherwise) of the domestic corporation.

"(3) ASSOCIATED FOREIGN CORPORATION.—A foreign corporation is a related foreign export corporation if—

December 10, 1971　　　　　Pub. Law 92-178

85 STAT. 543

"(A) less than 10 percent of the total combined voting power of all classes of stock entitled to vote of such foreign corporation is owned (within the meaning of section 1563 (d) and (e)) by the domestic corporation or by a controlled group of corporations (within the meaning of section 1563) of which the domestic corporation is a member, and

78 Stat. 123.
26 USC 1563.

"(B) the ownership of stock or securities in such foreign corporation by the domestic corporation is determined (under regulations prescribed by the Secretary or his delegate) to be reasonably in furtherance of a transaction or transactions giving rise to qualified export receipts of the domestic corporation.

"(f) Gross Receipts.—For purposes of this part, the term 'gross receipts' means the total receipts from the sale, lease, or rental of property held primarily for sale, lease, or rental in the ordinary course of trade or business, and gross income from all other sources. In the case of commissions on the sale, lease, or rental of property, the amount taken into account for purposes of this part as gross receipts shall be the gross receipts on the sale, lease, or rental of the property on which such commissions arose.

"(g) United States Defined.—For purposes of this part, the term 'United States' includes the Commonwealth of Puerto Rico and the possessions of the United States.

"SEC. 994. INTER-COMPANY PRICING RULES.

"(a) In General.—In the case of a sale of export property to a DISC by a person described in section 482, the taxable income of such DISC and such person shall be based upon a transfer price which would allow such DISC to derive taxable income attributable to such sale (regardless of the sales price actually charged) in an amount which does not exceed the greatest of—

68A Stat. 162.

"(1) 4 percent of the qualified export receipts on the sale of such property by the DISC plus 10 percent of the export promotion expenses of such DISC attributable to such receipts,

"(2) 50 percent of the combined taxable income of such DISC and such person which is attributable to the qualified export receipts on such property derived as the result of a sale by the DISC plus 10 percent of the export promotion expenses of such DISC attributable to such receipts, or

"(3) taxable income based upon the sale price actually charged (but subject to the rules provided in section 482).

"(b) Rules for Commissions, Rentals, and Marginal Costing.— The Secretary or his delegate shall prescribe regulations setting forth—

"(1) rules which are consistent with the rules set forth in subsection (a) for the application of this section in the case of commissions, rentals, and other income, and

"(2) rules for the allocation of expenditures in computing combined taxable income under subsection (a)(2) in those cases where a DISC is seeking to establish or maintain a market for export property.

"(c) Export Promotion Expenses.—For purposes of this section, the term 'export promotion expenses' means those expenses incurred to advance the distribution or sale of export property for use, consumption, or distribution outside of the United States, but does not include income taxes. Such expenses shall also include freight expenses to the extent of 50 percent of the cost of shipping export property aboard airplanes owned and operated by United States persons or ships documented under the laws of the United States in those cases where law or regulations does not require that such property be shipped aboard such airplanes or ships.

85 STAT. 544

"Subpart B—Treatment of Distributions to Shareholders

"Sec. 995. Taxation of DISC income to shareholders.
"Sec. 996. Rules for allocation in the case of distributions and
     losses.
"Sec. 997. Special subchapter C rules.

"SEC. 995. TAXATION OF DISC INCOME TO SHAREHOLDERS.

"(a) GENERAL RULE.—A shareholder of a DISC or former DISC shall be subject to taxation on the earnings and profits of a DISC as provided in this chapter, but subject to the modifications of this subpart.

"(b) DEEMED DISTRIBUTIONS.—

"(1) DISTRIBUTIONS IN QUALIFIED YEARS.—A shareholder of a DISC shall be treated as having received a distribution taxable as a dividend with respect to his stock in an amount which is equal to his pro rata share of the sum (or, if smaller, the earnings and profits for the taxable year) of—

"(A) the gross interest derived during the taxable year from producer's loans,

"(B) the gain recognized by the DISC during the taxable year on the sale or exchange of property, other than property which in the hands of the DISC is a qualified export asset, previously transferred to it in a transaction in which gain was not recognized in whole or in part, but only to the extent that the transferor's gain on the previous transfer was not recognized,

"(C) the gain (other than the gain described in subparagraph (B)) recognized by the DISC during the taxable year on the sale or exchange of property (other than property which in the hands of the DISC is stock in trade or other property described in section 1221(1)) previously transferred to it in a transaction in which gain was not recognized in whole or in part, but only to the extent that the transferor's gain on the previous transfer was not recognized and would have been treated as gain from the sale or exchange of property which is neither a capital asset nor property described in section 1231 if the property had been sold or exchanged rather than transferred to the DISC,

"(D) one-half of the excess of the taxable income of the DISC for the taxable year, before reduction for any distributions during the year, over the sum of the amounts deemed distributed for the taxable year under subparagraphs (A), (B), and (C), and

"(E) the amount of foreign investment attributable to producer's loans (as defined in subsection (d)) of a DISC for the taxable year.

Distributions described in this paragraph shall be deemed to be received on the last day of the taxable year of the DISC in which the gross income (taxable income in the case of subparagraph (D)) was derived. In the case of a distribution described in subparagraph (E), earnings and profits for the taxable year shall include accumulated earnings and profits.

"(2) DISTRIBUTIONS UPON DISQUALIFICATION.—

"(A) A shareholder of a corporation which revoked its election to be treated as a DISC or failed to satisfy the conditions of section 992(a)(1) for a taxable year shall be deemed to have received (at the time specified in subparagraph (B)) a distribution taxable as a dividend equal to his pro rata share of the DISC income of such corporation accumulated during

68A Stat. 321.
26 USC 1221.

68A Stat. 325;
83 Stat. 646.

Ante, p. 535.

December 10, 1971   Pub. Law 92-178

85 STAT. 545

the immediately preceding consecutive taxable years for which the corporation was a DISC.

"(B) Distributions described in subparagraph (A) shall be deemed to be received in equal installments on the last day of each of the 10 taxable years of the corporation following the year of the termination or disqualification described in subparagraph (A) (but in no case over more than the number of immediately preceding consecutive taxable years during which the corporation was a DISC).

"(c) GAIN ON DISPOSITION OF STOCK IN A DISC.—If a shareholder disposes of stock in a DISC or former DISC, any gain recognized on such disposition shall be included in gross income as a dividend to the extent of the accumulated DISC income of such DISC or former DISC which is attributable to such stock and which was accumulated in taxable years of such corporation during the period or periods the stock disposed of was held by such shareholder. If stock of the DISC or former DISC is disposed of in a transaction in which the separate corporate existence of the DISC or former DISC is terminated other than by a mere change in place of organization, however effected, any gain realized on the disposition of such stock in the transaction shall be recognized notwithstanding any other provision of this title to the extent of the accumulated DISC income of such DISC or former DISC which is attributable to such stock and which was accumulated in taxable years of such corporation during the period or periods the stock disposed of was held by the stockholder which disposed of such stock, and such gain shall be included in gross income as a dividend.

"(d) FOREIGN INVESTMENT ATTRIBUTABLE TO DISC EARNINGS.—For the purposes of this part—

"(1) IN GENERAL.—The amount of foreign investment attributable to producer's loans of a DISC for a taxable year shall be the smallest of—

"(A) the net increase in foreign assets by members of the controlled group (as defined in section 993(a)(3)) which includes the DISC, Ante, p. 539.

"(B) the actual foreign investment by domestic members of such group, or

"(C) the amount of outstanding producer's loans by such DISC to members of such controlled group.

"(2) NET INCREASE IN FOREIGN ASSETS.—The term 'net increase in foreign assets' of a controlled group means the excess of—

"(A) the amount incurred by such group to acquire assets (described in section 1231(b)) located outside the United States over,

68A Stat. 325;
83 Stat. 571,
643, 646.
26 USC 1231.

"(B) the sum of—

"(i) the depreciation with respect to assets of such group located outside the United States;

"(ii) the outstanding amount of stock or debt obligations of such group issued after December 31, 1971, to persons other than the United States persons or any member of such group;

"(iii) one-half the earnings and profits of foreign members of such group and foreign branches of domestic members of such group;

"(iv) one-half the royalties and fees paid by foreign members of such group to domestic members of such group; and

"(v) the uncommitted transitional funds of the group as determined under paragraph (4).

Pub. Law 92-178   December 10, 1971
85 STAT. 546

For purposes of this paragraph, assets which are qualified export assets of a DISC (or would be qualified export assets if owned by a DISC) shall not be taken into account. Amounts described in this paragraph (other than in subparagraphs (B)(ii) and (v)) shall be taken into account only to the extent they are attributable to taxable years beginning after December 31, 1971.

"(3) ACTUAL FOREIGN INVESTMENT.—The term 'actual foreign investment' by domestic members of a controlled group means the sum of—

"(A) contributions to capital of foreign members of the group by domestic members of the group after December 31, 1971,

"(B) the outstanding amount of stock or debt obligations of foreign members of such group (other than normal trade indebtedness) issued after December 31, 1971, to domestic members of such group,

"(C) amounts transferred by domestic members of the group after December 31, 1971, to foreign branches of such members, and

"(D) one-half the earnings and profits of foreign members of such group and foreign branches of domestic members of such group for taxable years beginning after December 31, 1971.

"Domestic member." As used in this subsection, the term 'domestic member' means a
Ante, p. 539. domestic corporation which is a member of a controlled group (as
"Foreign member." defined in section 993(a)(3)), and the term 'foreign member' means a foreign corporation which is a member of such a controlled group.

"(4) UNCOMMITTED TRANSITIONAL FUNDS.—The uncommitted transitional funds of the group shall be an amount equal to the sum of—

(A) the excess of—

(i) the amount of stock or debt obligations of domestic members of such group outstanding on December 31, 1971, and issued on or after January 1, 1968, to persons other than United States persons or any members of such group, but only to the extent the taxpayer establishes that such amount constitutes a long-term borrowing for purposes of the foreign direct investment program, over

(ii) the net amount of actual foreign investment by domestic members of such group during the period that such stock or debt obligations have been outstanding; and

"(B) the amount of liquid assets to the extent not included in subparagraph (A) held by foreign members of such group and foreign branches of domestic members of such group on October 31, 1971, in excess of their reasonable working capital needs on such date.

"Liquid assets." For purposes of this paragraph, the term 'liquid assets' means money, bank deposits (not including time deposits), and indebtedness of 2 years or less to maturity on the date of acquisition; and the actual foreign investment shall be determined under paragraph (3) without regard to the date in subparagraph (A) of such paragraph and without regard to subparagraph (D) of such paragraph.

"(5) SPECIAL RULE.—Under regulations prescribed by the Secretary or his delegate the determinations under this subsection shall be made on a cumulative basis with proper adjustments for amounts previously taken into account.

"SEC. 996. RULES FOR ALLOCATION IN THE CASE OF DISTRIBUTIONS AND LOSSES.

"(a) RULES FOR ACTUAL DISTRIBUTIONS AND CERTAIN DEEMED DISTRIBUTIONS.—

"(1) IN GENERAL.—Any actual distribution (other than a distribution described in paragraph (2) or to which section 995(c) applies) to a shareholder by a DISC (or former DISC) which is made out of earnings and profits shall be treated as made—   *Ante*, p. 545.

"(A) first, out of previously taxed income, to the extent thereof,

"(B) second, out of accumulated DISC income, to the extent thereof, and

"(C) finally, out of other earnings and profits.

"(2) QUALIFYING DISTRIBUTIONS.—Any actual distribution made pursuant to section 992(c) (relating to distributions to meet qualification requirements), and any deemed distribution pursuant to section 995(b)(1)(E) (relating to foreign investment attributable to producer's loans), shall be treated as made—   *Ante*, p. 537.

"(A) first, out of accumulated DISC income, to the extent thereof,

"(B) second, out of the earnings and profits described in paragraph (1)(C), to the extent thereof, and

"(C) finally, out of previously taxed income.

"(3) EXCLUSION FROM GROSS INCOME.—Amounts distributed out of previously taxed income shall be excluded by the distributee from gross income except for gains described in subsection (e)(2), and shall reduce the amount of the previously taxed income.

"(b) ORDERING RULES FOR LOSSES.—If for any taxable year a DISC, or a former DISC, incurs a deficit in earnings and profits, such deficit shall be chargeable—

"(1) first, to earnings and profits described in subsection (a)(1)(C), to the extent thereof,

"(2) second, to accumulated DISC income, to the extent thereof, and

"(3) finally, to previously taxed income, except that a deficit in earnings and profits shall not be applied against accumulated DISC income which has been determined is to be deemed distributed to the shareholders (pursuant to section 995(b)(2)(A)) as a result of a revocation of election or other disqualification.

"(c) PRIORITY OF DISTRIBUTIONS.—Any actual distribution made during a taxable year shall be treated as being made subsequent to any deemed distribution made during such year. Any actual distribution made pursuant to section 992(c) (relating to distributions to meet qualification requirements) shall be treated as being made before any other actual distributions during the taxable year.

"(d) SUBSEQUENT EFFECT OF PREVIOUS DISPOSITION OF DISC STOCK.—

"(1) SHAREHOLDER PREVIOUSLY TAXED INCOME ADJUSTMENT.—If—

"(A) gain with respect to a share of stock of a DISC or former DISC is treated under section 995(c) as a dividend or as gain from the sale or exchange of property which is not a capital asset, and

"(B) any person subsequently receives an actual distribution made out of accumulated DISC income, or a deemed distribution made pursuant to section 995(b)(2), with respect to such share,

Pub. Law 92-178   December 10, 1971
85 STAT. 548

such person shall treat such distribution in the same manner as a distribution from previously taxed income to the extent that (i) the gain referred to in subparagraph (A), exceeds (ii) any other amounts with respect to such share which were treated under this paragraph as made from previously taxed income. In applying this paragraph with respect to a share of stock in a DISC or former DISC, gain on the acquisition of such share by the DISC or former DISC or gain on a transaction prior to such acquisition shall not be considered gain referred to in subparagraph (A).

Ante, p. 543.

"(2) CORPORATE ADJUSTMENT UPON REDEMPTION.—If section 995(c) applies to a redemption of stock in a DISC or former DISC, the accumulated DISC income shall be reduced by an amount equal to the gain described in section 995(c) with respect to such stock which is (or has been) treated as gain from the sale or exchange of property which is not a capital asset, except to the extent distributions with respect to such stock have been treated under paragraph (1).

"(e) ADJUSTMENT TO BASIS.—

"(1) ADDITIONS TO BASIS.—Amounts representing deemed distributions as provided in section 995(b) shall increase the basis of the stock with respect to which the distribution is made.

"(2) REDUCTIONS OF BASIS.—The portion of an actual distribution made out of previously taxed income shall reduce the basis of the stock with respect to which it is made, and to the extent that it exceeds the adjusted basis of such stock, shall be treated as gain from the sale or exchange of property. In the case of stock includible in the gross estate of a decedent for which an election

68A Stat. 381;
84 Stat. 1836.
26 USC 2032.

is made under section 2032 (relating to alternate valuation), this paragraph shall not apply to any distribution made after the date of the decedent's death and before the alternate valuation date provided by section 2032.

"(f) DEFINITIONS OF DIVISIONS OF EARNINGS AND PROFITS.—For purposes of this part:

"(1) DISC INCOME.—The earnings and profits derived by a corporation during a taxable year in which such corporation is a DISC, before reduction for any distributions during the year, but reduced by amounts deemed distributed under section 995(b)(1), shall constitute the DISC income for such year. The earnings and profits of a DISC for a taxable year include any amounts includible in such DISC's gross income pursuant to section 951(a) for such year. Accumulated DISC income shall be reduced by deemed distributions under section 995(b)(2).

"(2) PREVIOUSLY TAXED INCOME.—Earnings and profits deemed distributed under section 995(b) for a taxable year shall constitute previously taxed income for such year.

"(3) OTHER EARNINGS AND PROFITS.—The earnings and profits for a taxable year which are described in neither paragraph (1) nor (2) shall constitute the other earnings and profits for such year.

"(g) EFFECTIVELY CONNECTED INCOME.—In the case of a shareholder who is a nonresident alien individual or a foreign corporation, trust, or estate, gains referred to in section 995(c) and all distributions out of accumulated DISC income including deemed distributions shall be treated as gains and distributions which are effectively connected with the conduct of a trade or business conducted through a permanent establishment of such shareholder within the United States.

December 10, 1971   Pub. Law 92-178

85 STAT. 549

"SEC. 997. SPECIAL SUBCHAPTER C RULES.

"For purposes of applying the provisions of subchapter C of chapter 1, any distribution in property to a corporation by a DISC or former DISC which is made out of previously taxed income or accumulated DISC income shall— 68A Stat. 84;
83 Stat. 613.
26 USC 301.

"(1) be treated as a distribution in the same amount as if such distribution of property were made to an individual, and

"(2) have a basis, in the hands of the recipient corporation, equal to the amount determined under paragraph (1)."

SEC. 502. DEDUCTIONS, CREDITS, ETC.

(a) Dividends Received Deduction.—Section 246 (relating to rules applying to deductions for dividends received) is amended by redesignating subsection (d) as subsection (e) and by inserting after subsection (c) the following: 68A Stat. 74;
83 Stat. 625.

"(d) Dividends From a DISC or Former DISC.—No deduction shall be allowed under section 243 in respect of a dividend from a corporation which is a DISC or former DISC (as defined in section 992(a)) to the extent such dividend is paid out of the corporation's accumulated DISC income or previously taxed income, or is a deemed distribution pursuant to section 995(b)(1)." 68A Stat. 73.

Ante, p. 535.

Ante, p. 544.

(b) Foreign Tax Credit.

(1) Section 901(d) (relating to corporations treated as foreign corporations) is amended by adding at the end thereof the following: 68A Stat. 286;
80 Stat. 1569.

"For purposes of this subpart, dividends from a DISC or former DISC (as defined in section 992(a)) shall be treated as dividends from a foreign corporation to the extent such dividends are treated under part I as income from sources without the United States."

(2) The heading of section 904(f) and paragraph (1) of section 904(f) (relating to limitation on foreign tax credit) are amended to read as follows: 76 Stat. 1002.

"(f) Application of Section in Case of Certain Interest Income and Dividends From a DISC or Former DISC.—

"(1) In general.—The provisions of subsections (a), (c), (d), and (e) of this section shall be applied separately with respect to each of the following items of income—

"(A) the interest income described in paragraph (2),

"(B) dividends from a DISC or former DISC (as defined in section 992(a)) to the extent such dividends are treated as income from sources without the United States, and

"(C) income other than the interest income described in paragraph (2) and dividends described in subparagraph (B)."

(3) Section 904(f)(3) (relating to limitation on foreign tax credit) is amended to read as follows:

"(3) Overall limitation not to apply.—The limitation provided by subsection (a)(2) shall not apply with respect to the interest income described in paragraph (2) or to dividends described in paragraph (1)(B). The Secretary or his delegate shall by regulations prescribe the manner of application of subsection (e) with respect to cases in which the limitation provided by subsection (a)(2) applies with respect to income described in paragraph (1)(B) and (C)."

(4) Section 904(f) is amended by adding at the end thereof the following new paragraph:

"(5) DISC dividends aggregated for purposes of per-country limitation.—In the case of a taxpayer who for the taxable year has dividends described in paragraph (1)(B) from more than

85 STAT. 550

one corporation, the limitation provided by subsection (a)(1) shall be applied with respect to the aggregate of such dividends."

68A Stat. 291.
26 USC 922.

(c) WESTERN HEMISPHERE TRADE CORPORATIONS.—Section 922 (relating to special deduction for Western Hemisphere Trade Corporations) is amended by adding at the end thereof the following: "No deduction shall be allowed under this section to a corporation for a taxable year for which it is a DISC or in which it owns at any time

Ante, p. 535.

stock in a DISC or former DISC (as defined in section 992(a))."

(d) INCOME FROM SOURCES WITHIN POSSESSIONS OF THE UNITED STATES.—Section 931(a) (relating to the general rule applicable to income from sources within possessions of the United States) is amended by adding at the end thereof the following: "This section shall not apply in the case of a corporation for a taxable year for which it is a DISC or in which it owns at any time stock in a DISC or former DISC (as defined in section 992(a))."

68A Stat. 370;
74 Stat. 1009.

(e) INCLUDIBLE CORPORATIONS.—Section 1504(b) (relating to definition of "includible corporations") is amended by adding at the end thereof the following new paragraph:

"(7) A DISC or former DISC (as defined in section 992(a))."

(f) BASIS OF DISC STOCK ACQUIRED FROM DECEDENT.—Section 1014 (relating to basis of property acquired from a decedent) is amended by adding at the end thereof the following new subsection:

"(d) SPECIAL RULE WITH RESPECT TO DISC STOCK.—If stock owned by a decedent in a DISC or former DISC (as defined in section 992 (a)) acquires a new basis under subsection (a), such basis (determined before the application of this subsection) shall be reduced by the amount (if any) which would have been included in gross income

Ante, p. 545.

under section 995(c) as a dividend if the decedent had lived and sold the stock at its fair market value on the estate tax valuation date. In computing the gain the decedent would have had if he had lived and sold the stock, his basis shall be determined without regard to the last

Ante, p. 548.

sentence of section 996(e)(2) (relating to reductions of basis of DISC stock). For purposes of this subsection, the estate tax valuation date is the date of the decedent's death or, in the case of an election

84 Stat. 1836.

under section 2032, the applicable valuation date prescribed by that section."

SEC. 503. SOURCE OF INCOME.

74 Stat. 998.

Section 861(a)(2) (relating to dividends) is amended—

(1) by deleting the period at the end of subparagraph (C) and inserting in lieu thereof ", or"; and

(2) by inserting the following new subparagraph (D) immediately after subparagraph (C) as amended:

"(D) from a DISC or former DISC (as defined in section 992(a)) except to the extent attributable (as determined under regulations prescribed by the Secretary or his delegate)

Ante, p. 538.
Ante, p. 544.

to qualified export receipts described in section 993(a)(1) (other than interest and gains described in section 995(b) (1))."

SEC. 504. PROCEDURE AND ADMINISTRATION.

68A Stat. 732;
78 Stat. 843.

(a) RETURNS.—Section 6011 (relating to general requirement of return, statement, or list) is amended by redesignating subsection (e) as subsection (f) and by adding a new subsection (e) which reads as follows:

"(e) RETURNS, ETC., OF DISCS AND FORMER DISCS.—

"(1) RECORDS AND INFORMATION.—A DISC or former DISC shall for the taxable year—

"(A) furnish such information to persons who were shareholders at any time during such taxable year, and to the Secretary or his delegate, and

December 10, 1971   Pub. Law 92-178

85 STAT. 551

"(B) keep such records, as may be required by regulations prescribed by the Secretary or his delegate.

"(2) RETURNS.—A DISC shall file for the taxable year such returns as may be prescribed by the Secretary or his delegate by forms or regulations."

(b) RETURNS OF CORPORATIONS.—Section 6072(b) (relating to returns of corporations) is amended by adding at the end thereof the following: "Returns required for a taxable year by section 6011(e)(2) (relating to returns of a DISC) shall be filed on or before the fifteenth day of the ninth month following the close of the taxable year."   68A Stat. 749.
26 USC 6072.
Ante, p. 550.

(c) CERTAIN INCOME TAX RETURNS OF DISC.—Section 6501(g) (relating to certain income tax returns of corporations) is amended by adding at the end thereof the following new paragraph: 68A Stat. 805;
72 Stat. 1662.

"(3) DISC.—If a corporation determines in good faith that it is a DISC (as defined in section 992(a)) and files a return as such under section 6011(e)(2) and if such corporation is thereafter held to be a corporation which is not a DISC for the taxable year for which the return is filed, such return shall be deemed the return of a corporation which is not a DISC for purposes of this section."   Ante, p. 535.

(d) FAILURE OF DISC TO FILE RETURNS.—Subchapter B of chapter 68 (relating to assessable penalties) is amended by adding at the end thereof the following new section: 68A Stat. 828;
83 Stat. 524.

"SEC. 6686. FAILURE OF DISC TO FILE RETURNS.

"In addition to the penalty imposed by section 7203 (relating to willful failure to file return, supply information, or pay tax) any person required to supply information or to file a return under section 6011(e) who fails to supply such information or file such return at the time prescribed by the Secretary or his delegate, or who files a return which does not show the information required, shall pay a penalty of $100 for each failure to supply information (but the total amount imposed on the delinquent person for all such failures during any calendar year shall not exceed $25,000) or a penalty of $1,000 for each failure to file a return, unless it is shown that such failure is due to reasonable cause."

SEC. 505. EXPORT TRADE CORPORATIONS.

(a) USE OF TERMS.—Except as otherwise expressly provided, whenever in this section a reference is made to a section, chapter, or other provision, the reference shall be considered to be made to a section, chapter, or other provision of the Internal Revenue Code of 1954, and terms used in this section shall have the same meaning as when used in such Code.   68A Stat.3.
26 USC 1 et
seq.

(b) TRANSFER TO A DISC OF ASSETS OF EXPORT TRADE CORPORATION.—

(1) IN GENERAL.—If a corporation (hereinafter in this section called "parent") owns all of the outstanding stock of an export trade corporation (as defined in section 971), and the export trade corporation, during a taxable year beginning before January 1, 1976, transfers property, without receiving consideration, to a DISC (as defined in section 992(a)) all of whose outstanding stock is owned by the parent, and if the amount transferred by the export trade corporation is not less than the amount of its untaxed subpart F income (as defined in paragraph (2) of this subsection) at the time of such transfer, then—   76 Stat. 1029.

(A) notwithstanding section 367 or any other provision of chapter 1, no gain or loss to the export trade corporation, the parent, or the DISC shall be recognized by reason of such transfer;   84 Stat. 2065.

85 STAT. 552

Ante, p. 550.

(B) the earnings and profits of the DISC shall be increased by the amount transferred to it by the export trade corporation and such amount shall be included in accumulated DISC income, and for purposes of section 861(a)(2)(D) shall be considered to be qualified export receipts;

(C) the adjusted basis of the assets transferred to the DISC shall be the same in the hands of the DISC as in the hands of the export trade corporation;

(D) the earnings and profits of the export trade corporation shall be reduced by the amount transferred to the DISC, to the extent thereof, with the reduction being applied first to the untaxed subpart F income and then to the other earnings and profits in the order in which they were most recently accumulated;

(E) the basis of the parent's stock in the export trade corporation shall be decreased by the amount obtained by multiplying its basis in such stock by a fraction the numerator of which is the amount transferred to the DISC and the denominator of which is the aggregate adjusted basis of all the assets of the export trade corporation immediately before such transfer;

(F) the basis of the parent's stock in the DISC shall be increased by the amount of the reduction under subparagraph (E) of its basis in the stock of the export trade corporation;

(G) the property transferred to the DISC shall not be considered to reduce the investments of the export trade corporation in export trade assets for purposes of applying section 970(b); and

76 Stat. 1027.
26 USC 970.
68A Stat. 286.

(H) any foreign income taxes which would have been deemed under section 902 to have been paid by the parent if the transfer had been made to the parent shall be treated as foreign income taxes paid by the DISC.

For purposes of this section, the amount transferred by the export trade corporation to the DISC shall be the aggregate of the adjusted basis of the properties transferred, with proper adjustment for any indebtedness secured by such property or assumed by the DISC in connection with the transfer. For purposes of this section, a foreign corporation which qualified as an export trade corporation for any 3 taxable years beginning before November 1, 1971, shall be treated as an export trade corporation.

(2) DEFINITION OF UNTAXED SUBPART F INCOME.—For purposes of this section, the term "untaxed subpart F income" means with respect to an export trade corporation the amount by which—

26 USC 951,
970.
76 Stat. 1031.

(A) the sum of the amounts by which the subpart F income of such corporation was reduced for the taxable year and all prior taxable years under section 970(a) and the amounts not included in subpart F income (determined without regard to subpart G of subchapter N of chapter 1) for all prior taxable years by reason of the application of section 972, exceeds

76 Stat. 1006.

(B) the sum of the amounts which were included in the gross income of the shareholders of such corporation under section 951(a)(1)(A)(ii) and under the provision of section 970(b) for all prior taxable years,

determined without regard to the transfer of property described in paragraph (1) of this subsection.

(3) SPECIAL CASES.—If the provisions of paragraph (1) of this subsection are not applicable solely because the export trade corporation or the DISC, or both, are not owned in the manner prescribed in such paragraph, the provisions shall nevertheless

December 10, 1971   Pub. Law 92-178

85 STAT. 553

be applicable in such cases to the extent, and in accordance with such rules, as may be prescribed by the Secretary or his delegate.

(4) TREATMENT OF EXPORT TRADE ASSETS.—If the provisions of this subsection are applicable, accounts receivable held by an export trade corporation and transferred to a DISC, to the extent such receivables were export trade assets in the hands of the export trade corporation, shall be treated as qualified export assets for purposes of section 993(b).

(c) LIMITATION OF APPLICATION OF SUBPART G.—Section 971(a) (relating to definition of export trade corporation) is amended by adding at the end thereof the following new paragraph:

Ante, p. 539.
76 Stat. 1029.
26 USC 971.

"(3) LIMITATION.—No controlled foreign corporation may qualify as an export trade corporation for any taxable year beginning after October 31, 1971, unless it qualified as an export trade corporation for any taxable year beginning before such date. If a corporation fails to qualify as an export trade corporation for a period of any 3 consecutive taxable years beginning after such date, it may not qualify as an export trade corporation for any taxable year beginning after such period."

SEC. 506. SUBMISSION OF ANNUAL REPORTS TO CONGRESS.

The Secretary of the Treasury shall, commencing for the calendar year 1972, submit an annual report to the Congress within 15½ months following the close of each calendar year setting forth an analysis of the operation and effect of the provisions of this title.

SEC. 507. GENERAL EFFECTIVE DATE OF TITLE.

Except as provided in section 505 of this title, the amendments made by sections 501 through 504 of this title shall apply with respect to taxable years ending after December 31, 1971, except that a corporation may not be a DISC (as defined in section 992(a) of the Internal Revenue Code of 1954, added by section 501 of this title) for any taxable year beginning before January 1, 1972.

INTERNATIONAL AGENCIES

WORLD BANK

The International Bank for Reconstruction and Development (World Bank) is owned by 110 countries, each subscribing to its capital stock in accordance with that country's own economic strength. The World Bank makes loans to governments, governmental agencies and private enterprises of member countries, mainly for the purpose of helping those countries build the foundations of their economic growth. It has also lent to the International Finance Corporation, an affiliated agency.

The Bank was founded by the Bretton Woods Economic Conference in 1944, began operations in June, 1946, and has almost 700 loans totaling about $20 billion to finance over a thousand projects in more than 100 countries or territories. The first loans, made in 1947, were for European post-war reconstruction.

In 1948 the Bank turned to development lending, and since then an increasing proportion of its funds has been directed to the less-developed areas of the world. Approximately a third of its development loans have been for the production of electric power. Another third has been allocated and spent on transportation and communications development—highways, railways, waterways, air transport and pipelines. In other words, a full two-thirds of World Bank lending has been directed toward what economists call "infra-structure capital projects." The balance of World Bank funding has gone for agriculture, especially irrigation; for industry, especially steel production; for education; for the improvement of water resources; and for general development purposes.

The World Bank lends money when private capital is not available on reasonable terms. If the borrower is not a government, the Bank requires the guarantee of the member government concerned. The Bank never lends the total cost of a project or program. Normally it finances only the foreign exchange costs involved in the purchase of imported goods or services, disbursing the loan over the construction period on presentation of evidence that payments have been made for the agreed purposes of the loan.

The Bank demands efficient procurement of supplies, with competitive bidding on the bulk of the orders which its loan finance. Its funds may be spent in any member country or in Switzerland, which is not a member but has a special arrangement with the Bank.

Total subscribed capital of the World Bank is almost $23 billion of which only the equivalent of about $2.3 billion has been paid in, partly in gold or dollars and partly in local currencies. The rest is subject to call if required to meet the Bank's obligations.

The capital subscribed by the member governments was never intended to finance all the Bank's operations, and the institution itself has been a borrower; it sells its bonds in the capital markets of the world, and has about $3.8 billion outstanding. Although these are for the most part dollar bonds, more than half are held outside the United States.

The loans that the Bank makes are amortized over a period of years determined by the type of project being financed and the debt position of the borrowing country. The Bank's terms also allow a waiting period before the start of repayment of the principal, its length being based on the estimated time required for the project to start earning. The interest rate normally charged on loans presently being made is 7 per cent per annum, charged only from the time of disbursement. A commitment fee of 3/4 per cent per annum is normally charged on the undisbursed portions of loans. Normally the World Bank reviews the interest rate once a year.

Repayments of principal to the Bank and to participants in Bank loans have amounted to more than $3 billion. There have been no losses on loans to date.

The World Bank also enlists the direct participation of private investors in its loans and has sold more than $2 billion of its loans.

Commercial institutions buying participations usually take the early maturities, and they now receive 7 per cent per annum and a commitment commission of 3/4 per cent per annum on the uncalled balances of their participations.

Information can be obtained from World Bank, 1818 H Street, N.W., Washington, D.C. 20433.

INTERNATIONAL DEVELOPMENT ASSOCIATION

The International Development Association (IDA) was established in September,

1960, as a World Bank affiliate "to promote economic development, increase productivity and thus raise standards of living in the less-developed areas of the world." All World Bank members are eligible to join IDA, and 104 countries have done so, contributing more than $1 billion in initial subscriptions.

IDA's resources are entirely separate from those of the World Bank, and from them it makes "development credits" available in the less-developed countries on exceptionally favorable terms. The same public and private entities that may borrow from the World Bank are eligible for IDA assistance. IDA observes the same standard as the Bank in selection of projects, and has similar rules as to disbursement, procurement, competitive bidding, and countries in which its funds may be spent.

The agency started operations in November, 1960, extended the first development credit in May, 1961, and has now extended approximately 140 credits to some 40 countries for a total of about $1.9 billion to finance electric power, road construction, harbor dredging, inland ports, irrigation, drainage and flood protection projects, school construction, small private industry, and water supply.

Because of the easy terms on which it provides finance, IDA relies primarily on the governments of its 20 richest member countries for its resources, and these countries have contributed the bulk of its usable funds. In addition, the World Bank has made transfers to IDA from its net income. IDA is authorized to accept supplementary contributions and is required to maintain a regular review of the adequacy of its resources.

In 1964, formalities were completed for the first general replenishment of IDA funds by about $750 million, and in July, 1969, for a second of about $1.2 billion.

While IDA may vary the terms of its credits at its own discretion, those extended so far were each for 50 years, without interest. Repayment is due in a convertible currency. Amortization is to begin after a 10-year grace period, then 1 per cent of the principal is repayable annually for 10 years and 3 per cent is repayable annually for the last 30 years. A service charge of 3/4 per cent per annum is repayable on amounts withdrawn and outstanding, to meet the agency's administrative costs.

IDA assistance may take the form of agency credits combined with World Bank loans, or agency credits only. In addition to aid to its less-developed members, IDA may extend credits for projects in the dependent and associated territories of member nations that are economically more advanced.

The agency has no separate staff but uses that of the World Bank. Its address is also 1818 H Street, N.W., Washington, D.C. 20433.

INTERNATIONAL FINANCE CORPORATION

The International Finance Corporation (IFC), World Bank affiliate which invests in private industry in developing member countries, has the following principal objectives: (1) provision of equity and loan capital for productive enterprises, in association with private investors and management; (2) encouragement of the development of local capital markets; and (3) stimulation of the international flow of private capital.

The corporation was established in July, 1956, and as of June 30, 1969, its paid-in capital, subscribed by 91 member governments, was $106.54 million, and its reserve against losses was more than $48.6 million.

Authorized to borrow amounts up to a limit of four times its (IFC's) unimpaired subscribed capital and surplus from the World Bank, the corporation invests in a wide variety of industries where private capital is not available on reasonable terms.

Financing and Participations

All IFC's investments are made in association with private business, without the guarantee of any government, and it does not provide more than a portion of the total finance required. IFC expects its financial participation to be substantially less than 50 per cent of the total cost of the project financed.

Financing by IFC is available for foreign exchange and for local currency expenditures. It can be used for fixed assets or for working capital. IFC money is not tied to the purchase of specific equipment or to a specific country.

IFC does not engage in operations that are essentially for purposes of refunding or financing, nor does it finance exports or imports.

IFC's initial commitments normally range from $1 million to $20 million. It also commits funds for promotional purposes, to help bring an enterprise into being. Projects it would seek to promote would be those which have a reasonable prospect of eventual suitability for IFC financing in accordance with established criteria. The corporation has fixed a maximum of $50,000 in promotional costs for a single project.

As of June 30, 1969, IFC had made commitments of 131 private enterprises in 39 countries, for a total investment of $365 million, of which private financial institutions had bought more than a third of their own portfolios, thus freeing more than $123 million of IFC funds for reinvestment.

There are no uniform interest rates for IFC loans; the rate for each is governed by relevant considerations, such as the risks involved and the prospective overall return.

IFC usually charges a commitment fee of 1 per cent on undisbursed portions of its loans.

Information may be obtained from International Finance Corporation, 1818 H Street, N.W., Washington, D.C. 20433.

INTERNATIONAL MONETARY FUND

The International Monetary Fund, also an outgrowth of the Bretton Woods Conference of 1944, is a sister organization of the World Bank. It was formed to promote international monetary cooperation and a balanced growth of world trade. Membership in the Fund is a prerequisite of World Bank membership.

Financial operations of the International Monetary Fund are in the form of drawings and standby credits to member nations. These operations are carried out only with governments and are designed to correct or forestall short-term balance of payment problems. The Fund does not lend for specific projects, but, because it promotes international economic and exchange stability in its member nations, it contributes invaluably to the quality of international investments.

Sixty-seven of the IMF's 113 member countries made drawings in various currencies of sums totaling the equivalent of $17.3 billion between the start of the Fund's exchange transactions in 1947 and the end of February, 1969, by which time $8.62 billion had been repaid. Standby credits totaling $336.2 million were outstanding on that date.

The capital of the Fund comes from gold and currency which the members pay under quotas assigned to them at the time they join. These quotas have later been increased on occasion by general and individual consent. At the end of February, 1969, capital assets totaled $23 billion, including $3.4 billion in gold, $18.7 billion in currencies paid in, $815 million in subscriptions receivable and $52 million in other assets.

In addition, an arrangement completed in 1962 enabled the fund to borrow up to the equivalent of $6 billion under specific terms and conditions from 10 of its industrial member countries. Of this amount, $4.9 billion was available in February, 1969. The arrangement was used to help finance three major British drawings and one French drawing.

Members' drawings from the fund are normally for a term of 3 to 5 years. Standby credits usually are for a one-year term, although some have been renewed or reconstituted on expiration. A number of provisions aimed at stabilizing internal and external financial and monetary positions of a drawing country are normally part of the arangements between the Fund and the member. While there is no provision for direct participation in these credits by commercial banks and other private investors, many governments drawing from the Fund in recent years have negotiated loans concurrently from private sources. Many of these private lenders have predicated their loans on the existence of a satisfactory agreement between the borrowing country and the fund.

In recent years, the Fund has also studied broader questions on the adequacy of international liquidity and its own future role in the functioning of the international payments system. A new IMF facility for the creation of Special Drawing Rights (SDRs) was established in 1970 in order to provide additional international liquidity, when and as the need arises. Participants in the new facility count SDRs in their reserves and transfer them to other participants against convertible currencies in the event of payment difficulties or adverse developments in their reserves. Distribution of the equivalent of $3.5 billion in SDRs was made in 1970, and about $3 billion annually in 1971, 1972, and 1973.

The address of the International Monetary Fund is 19th and H Streets, N.W., Washington, D.C. 20431.

INTER-AMERICAN DEVELOPMENT BANK

The Inter-American Development Bank also administers funds constituted of Canadian, German, Swedish and United Kingdom resources.

The Canadian fund, which now amounts to $50 million (Canadian), is for the financing of economic, technical and educational assistance projects in Latin America. The Bank may lend the resources of this fund for terms up to 50 years, interest-free or with other concessions to which both parties agree. The Bank charges a commission of 1/2 per cent per annum for itself. Up to December 31, 1968, the Bank had made 13 loans amounting to $36.9 million from these resources. Procurement is limited to Canada.

Under an agreement signed in 1961 and supplemented by subsequent protocols, the Federal Republic of Germany has participated with the United States and the Bank in financing a program to rehabilitate Bolivia's national tin mines. As of December 31, 1968, these German funds totaled $8.2 million, lent by IDB for terms up to 10 years at interest rates of 4 per cent per annum.

In December, 1966, IDB entered into an agreement with the government of Sweden to administer a $5 million Swedish Development Fund for Latin America. Loans from this fund are made in dollars at terms and rates the Swedish government applies to its development aid credits, currently 2 per cent per annum and for periods up to 25 years, including grace periods. The Bank also charges a commission of up to 1/2 per cent per annum on amounts committed or outstanding. The loans, which are made in conjunction with ordinary capital resources loans, are united. The entire $5 million has been lent out.

IDB administration of the United Kingdom fund started early in 1966. The fund has resources in Sterling equivalent to $9.9 million which the Bank may lend for terms ranging from 15 to 25 years, with grace periods up to 7 years, at interest rates agreed on case by case. The loans bear appropriate service charges and are repayable in sterling. Procurement is limited to the United Kingdom. As of December 31, 1968, the Bank had authorized three loans totaling $5.8 million.

IDB also has agreements with Canada and the Netherlands, which set aside, respectively, $15 million, (Canadian) and 90 million guilders, ($25 million), for parallel or independent financing operations in cooperation with the Bank.

Fund for Special Operations

From this fund the Bank lends money on terms and conditions adapted to the special circumstances arising in specific countries or in connection with specific projects. These conditions include possible repayment in the currency of the borrower. Starting with $150 million, the Fund's resources now amount to $2.3 billion, of which the United States quota is $1.8 billion. The Fund's scope of operations has also been expanded to include social projects previously financed with the Social Progress Trust Fund. Interest rates, previously 4 to 5 3/4 per cent, thus now start at 2 1/4 per cent per annum for certain social projects. In addition, such loans bear a service charge of 3/4 per cent. Terms generally range from 10 to 30 years, including grace period.

Procurement anywhere in the Free World is permitted with the proceeds of loans from the original resources of the Fund for Special Operations; from the dollar proceeds of the subsequent contributions, procurement is permitted only in the United States, the borrower's country, and anyone of the other IDB member countries. Up to December 31, 1968, IDB had made 197 Fund for Special Operations loans for a total of $1.2 billion, net of cancellations and exchange adjustments.

Social Progress Trust Fund

This is a $525 million fund that the Bank administers under an agreement with the United States. Its purpose is to provide loans for settlement and improved use of land, low-income group housing, water supply and sewage facilities, and advanced education and training. The original loans were made in dollars, repayable generally in the borrower's currency, but IDB now uses some local currency repayments to buy participations in appropriate Fund for Special Operations loans. Interest rates are 1 1/4 per cent per annum for all projects except water supply and sewage facilities, which pay 2 3/4 per cent per annum. There is a service charge of 3/4 per cent per annum, payable in dollars. Terms range up to 30 years, including grace periods.

As of December 31, 1968, the Bank had authorized 116 loans totaling $498.7 million, net of cancellations and exchange adjustments, from this trust fund. United States dollar funds made available under the Social Progress Trust Fund agreement must be spent in the United States or for goods or services of local origin in the borrower's country, unless IDB authorizes procurement in other major countries advantageous to the borrower.

UNITED STATES AND INTERNATIONAL AGENCIES; SUMMARY

United States Agencies

Agency for International Development
(Dollar Loans)

Purpose	To promote economic development of less-developed foreign countries.
Loans	Loans to a country may be for terms up to 40 years, including a 10-year grace period, with interest as low as 1 per cent per annum thereafter. Loans to private enterprise negotiated on basis of enterprise involved.
Guarantees and Insurance	Specific risk and extended risk guarantees available to private investors.
Who Can Borrow	Governments or government entities of less-developed friendly countries, and certain private enterprises. This includes development banks, agricultural banks, housing banks.
Where the Money Must Be Spent	United States, with few exceptions.
Private Participation in Agency Loans	None.
Must Seek Private Capital First	Administrator must take into account whether financing is available from other free-world sources on reasonable terms.
Must Ship Only in United States Vessels	Not less than 50 per cent in U.S. vessels, more if desired; AID will pay freight only on cargo shipped in U.S. vessels.

Export-Import Bank

Purpose	To promote U.S. exports through dollar loans and assistance to exporters by means of financing, guarantees and insurance.
Loans	Lends dollars only. Terms: for agricultural commodities—up to 12 months; for long-term capital loans, 5 to 20 years (interest

	on these loans generally 6 per cent per annum.)
Guarantees and Insurance	Provides medium-term political and credit guarantees to financial institutions in the United States and certain foreign financial institutions. Cooperates with Foreign Credit Insurance Association in providing political and credit insurance for exporters.
Who Can Borrow	United States private enterprises, foreign private enterprises; foreign governments and government agencies.
Where the Money Must Be Spent	United States.
Private Participation in Agency Loans	Eximbank encourages commercial banks and other private financial institutions to participate.
Must Seek Private Capital First	Yes.
Must Ship Only in United States	Yes, unless waived by Maritime Administration. No restriction where assistance is by guarantee or insurance.

Agency for International Development
(Foreign Currency Loans)

Purpose	Business development and trade expansion.
Loans	Lends in local currencies at local interest rates, usually 3 to 10 years, (15 years in exceptional circumstances.) Loans must be acceptable to the foreign country.
Guarantees and Insurance	Not applicable.
Who Can Borrow	U.S. firms and their affiliates, branches, subsidiaries. For overseas market expansion of U.S. agricultural products, firms of the host country also are eligible.
Where the Money Must Be Spent	Within the country in which the funds originate.
Private Participation in Agency Loans	None.

Must Seek Private Capital First	No.
Must Ship Only in United States Vessels	Not applicable.

Commodity Credit Corporation

Purpose	To promote exports of U.S. surplus agricultural commodities.
Loans	Grants credits up to 3 years on applications supported by letters of credit issued, confirmed or advised by U.S. banks.
Guarantees and Insurance	No.
Who Can Borrow	Export firms in the United States.
Where the Money Must Be Spent	United States.
Private Participation in Agency Loans	Not applicable; see LOANS.
Must Seek Private Capital First	See LOANS.
Must Ship Only in United States Vessels	No.

International Agencies

International Development Association

Purpose	Same as World Bank.
Loans	Terms may be varied. To date loans have been for 50 years without interest, with repayment in a convertible currency, after a 10-year grace period. There is a service charge of 3/4 per cent per annum on the outstanding balance.
Guarantees and Insurance	Same as World Bank.
Who Can Borrow	Same as World Bank.
Where the Money Must Be Spent	Same as World Bank.

194 Exporter's Financial and Marketing Handbook

Private Participation in Agency Loans — No.

Must Seek Private Capital First — Yes, and also World Bank.

Must Ship Only in United States Vessels — No.

World Bank

Purpose — To finance projects helping to build the foundations of economic growth in less-developed countries.

Loans — Lends in dollars and other currencies. Terms: 5 to 35 years, depending on project. Current standard rate: 7 per cent per annum. Government guarantees required except on loans to IFC.

Guarantees and Insurance — Has authority to guarantee loans in whole or in part, but does not do so.

Who Can Borrow — Governments of member nations, including territories and political subdivisions; political or private entities; public international or regional organizations.

Where the Money Must Be Spent — Member countries and Switzerland; normally other than the one in which project is located.

Private Participation in Agency — Commercial banks and other financial institutions welcomed.

Must Seek Private Capital First — Yes.

Must Ship Only in United States Vessels — No.

International Finance Corporation

Purpose — To finance only private enterprises contributing to economic development of less-developed member countries.

Loans — Invest in or lends to any enterprise that makes a useful contribution to the economic

	development of a member country. Does not invest in undertakings that are government-owned or government-operated. Can now invest in capital stock.
Guarantees and Insurance	Can underwrite the subscription of capital issues.
Who Can Borrow	Private companies in member countries.
Where the Money Must Be Spent	Member countries and Switzerland.
Private Participation in Agency Loans	Welcomes financial participation by financial institutions or industrial partners in member countries.
Must Seek Private Capital First	Yes.
Must Ship Only in United States Vessels	No.

International Monetary Fund

Purpose	To promote stability of international exchange, and expansion and growth of world trade.
Loans	Credits take the form of foreign exchange transactions (currencies of other member nations advanced in exchange for local currencies) which are to be reversed in a period of 3 to 5 years. Rates are 2 to 5 per cent per annum, plus a service fee.
Guarantees and Insurance	Not applicable.
Who Can Borrow	Governments of member nations.
Where the Money Must Be Spent	No limitations.
Private Participation in Agency Loans	No direct participation, but agreements between Fund and member nations serve to encourage private sources to lend to those countries.
Must Seek Private Capital First	No.

Must Ship Only in United States   Not applicable.
Vessels

Inter-American Development Bank

Purpose	Principally to accelerate the economic development of its Latin American member nations; also finances social development projects.
Loans	Lends in currencies of all member nations. Ordinary loans require repayment in the currency lent, but Special Fund loans may permit repayment in the borrowing nation's own currency. Social Progress Trust Fund loans generally are repayable in local currency.
Guarantees and Insurance	Has authority to guarantee loans but has not yet done so.
Who Can Borrow	Public or private entities in member countries.
Where the Money Must Be Spent	Ordinary capital: worldwide procurement. Special Find and Social Progress Trust Fund: in U.S. or recipient country.
Private Participation in Agency Loans	Encouraged.
Must Seek Private Capital First	Yes, and other public capital.
Must Ship Only in United States Vessels	Ordinary capital: no. Special Fund and Social Progress Trust Fund: yes, unless waived by Maritime Administration.

HOW TO DEVELOP EFFECTIVE DISTRIBUTORSHIP AGREEMENTS

BACKGROUND

This chapter addresses itself to an analysis of the contractual aspects of doing business abroad on either a direct export basis or through a licensing agreement involving a certain amount of local manufacturing. Essentially, the business executive, having determined that there is a market overseas, and knowing that he has the capacity to penetrate that market, must now decide *how* that penetration will occur.

Companies may select any of four different selling formats when exporting or producing their products overseas: an agency agreement, a distributorship, direct selling through manufacturers' representatives, or selling through the manufacturer's own overseas branches or subsidiaries. Larger companies tend to establish their own wholly-owned international sales organizations, relying on other means only in small or marginal markets. Manufacturers' representatives operate mainly in the Caribbean and South Pacific Basin islands with any degree of continuing success. This leaves import agents and import distributors; these are frequently used by small and medium sized exporters as a means of quickly and inexpensively selling their products abroad.

EVALUATING THE COMPETITION

The precise contractual relationship that a company will seek to establish overseas depends partly upon what the competition has already done in the market in question. It will therefore be useful for the company to organize its data in the form of the competitive profile outlined below.

197

Competitive Profile List

Nature of the competition

1. Names of competitive companies.

2. List of competitive products, with prices and price/discount structures.

3. Are competitive products produced locally, or are they imported?

4. What are the import restrictions, if any?

5. Do competitors enjoy special relations with the host government?

6. Are they receiving tax breaks and/or other benefits and incentives?

7. What is the caliber of their management: supervisory, sales, and production; and other employees?

8. What is your analysis of their investment, financial, marketing and sales objectives?

9. What accounting methods are competitors using?

Production Profile

1. What are competitors' production capabilities and capacities?

2. What control do competitors have over their production if they are not operating on a wholly-owned subsidiary basis?

3. What are competitors' sources of raw materials; are they local, or are they imported? From where?

4. What are competitors' labor and production problems, if any?

5. What are competitors' approximate manufacturing costs?

Marketing Profile

1. How do competitors distribute and sell their products?

2. How are competitors' products advertised and promoted?

3. How are after-sales services handled?

4. What are the comparative competitive price/discount structures?

5. What share-of-market does each competitor enjoy?

6. What percentage of the market is supplied by local producers, and what percentage is supplied through imports?

7. How many of those local producers manufacture a product of foreign origin, under license, contract, or a joint-venture arrangement.

The Country Factomatic File

The reader is now ready to establish a complete filing system to classify incoming information on his market(s) for continuing reference purposes. This may seem trite at first, but it is an excellent idea to develop a forward management look at the very outset of doing business abroad and to have all sorts of data available, even of a peripheral nature. The hypothetical filing system shown here was originally developed by Business International. It is of use to both exporters and to companies manufacturing overseas.

> Agriculture - (see Economy)
> Antitrust - (see Rules of Competition)
> Balance of Payments - (see Economic Indicators)
> Capital Sources - (see also Finance). Covers information on institutions that lend and guarantee their terms, and methods of borrowing.
> Cartels - (see Rules of Competition)
> Contract Manufacturing
> Currency - (see Finance)
> Economy - Covers statistics, forecasts, utilities, construction, and transport and communications.
> Exporting - (see also Capital Sources). Covers controls, procedures, incentives, free trade zones, treaties.
> Finance - (see also Investment and Capital Sources). Covers exchange controls and remittances, fiscal policy, etc.
> Government - Covers politics, nationalizations, state industry, aid programs, etc.
> Importing - Covers procedures, regulations, taxes and tariffs.
> Insurance
> International Organizations
> Investment - (see also Finance, Taxes). Covers organization, legal restrictions and incentives.
> Labor
> Licensing
> Management
> Marketing - (see also Rules of Competition). Covers advertising, after-sales servicing, distribution patterns and problems, other regulations, trade fairs, etc.
> Organization
> Patents - (see Licensing)
> Personnel
> Pricing - (see also Taxes)
> Product Sourcing
> Production
> Profitability and Performance
> Research and Development
> Rules of Competition
> Taxes - Covers audits, all types of taxes, intercorporate pricing, etc.

THE EXPORTER'S DECISIONAL MIX

Import restrictions in many markets may be minimal for a wide variety of products. This will provide the businessman with an opportunity to export finished goods directly from his own country to the foreign market in question, assuming he may remain competitive with the added transport and insurance costs, not to mention handling and possibly crating charges at the shipper's end. Furthermore, the exporter will find that he may also be able to sell in high import-duty countries where there is no competitive local production and/or where his ultimate customer is a government agency. Governments always import on a duty-free basis.

The aspect of finding an appropriate distributor or agent to import and sell an exporter's goods in a given market has been covered in an earlier chapter. This part emphasizes the organizational and contractual nature of an emerging exporter-distributor relationship.

There are still some companies who prefer to export and sell their products in overseas markets through import agents rather than through independent distributors. This gives a company the advantage of controlling marketing activities in the agent's area since the exporter retains title to the imported goods until the import agent has actually sold them. If the strict maintenance of a price structure is important to the overall success of a firm's marketing strategy, an agency agreement may be essential. There is also minimization of risk in violating local antitrust and price-fixing laws while controlling the specific operations of an agent selling the exporter's product.

There is also somewhat greater ease in terminating an agency contract in many countries than with a distributor. One must bear in mind that so long as the exporter retains title to his merchandise, and so long as a fiduciary relationship can be shown to exist between exporter and his import agent, the exporter's control, within the framework of their agreement, is fairly complete.

There are problems, however, and the greater marketing and management control that the exporter may achieve will be offset by relatively high administrative costs. In the very first instance, the classical principal-agent relationship which created the fiduciary relationship to begin with does expose the exporter to third-person liability situations in the foreign market. In other words, a plaintiff in the importer's country may bring legal action against either the agent or his principal (the exporter) for an alleged wrong-doing by the agent during the course of his activities on behalf of that principal.

An excellent case in point is the agent's truck making a delivery or service call on behalf of the principle and becoming involved in an accident during the process. The principal might be equally liable if the agent can be shown to be legally at fault.

An import distributor does not expose the exporter to any liability beyond that of the usual product warranties. The distributor, by definition, is an independent company buying and then reselling for its own account. It will assume title to the exporter's goods on or before delivery of those goods to its warehouse. And as a general rule, title will pass by the time the goods clear the import customs line, as was indicated in a previous section. Since title is now vested in the body of the distributor, there is also no further insurance liability upon the exporter, as there might have been with an agency arrangement with the goods being warehoused on the agent's premises. Further, the credit risk on the resale of the goods by the distributor belongs to the distributor and not to the exporter who, under an agency agreement, would sweat until the agent collected from his customer.

The advantages of doing business with an independent distributor may be summarized as follows:

1. As indicated above, the exporter minimizes his own legal liability.

2. The exporter's financial and/or capital investment is limited only to extending a line of credit to the distributor.

3. A distributor, utilizing his own financial resources to run his business, will generally be under greater pressure to sell his products than an agent purchasing on a consignment basis.

There are disadvantages, of course; and these relate mainly to the exporter's lack of marketing and management control. It has already been noted that once title passes from the exporter to the distributor, it is virtually impossible for the former to control the latter's resale prices, even if there are iron-clad clauses to the contrary in the distributorship agreement. However, it is a fairly widespread practice among marketing-oriented exporters to reach an implicit understanding with their distributors as to what resale prices in a given market should be. It should be borne in mind that both exporter and distributor have a vested interest in maximizing sales and profits by being competitive, quality conscious, and service oriented.

This brings up the matter of the basic agreement between the exporter and his overseas distributor. The common practice among smaller manufacturers is simply to provide a potential distributor with a more-or-less casual letter of appointment for specific period of time. Nevertheless, an accepted and widely accepted practice among larger and more marketing oriented companies is to enter into a more formal and mutually binding agreement with a distributor.

ESSENTIAL COMPONENTS OF A DISTRIBUTORSHIP AGREEMENT

Actual contracts vary from country to country in accordance with local customs and laws and also in accordance with the special intent of the participating parties. There are, however, certain key features which have almost universal applicability. Five of the more salient elements are described in detail below with appropriate commentaries.

Parties to the Agreement: It is recommended that when the parties involved are corporations, accurate determination of their financial viability along with an up-dated recording of their actual operating addresses be made, particularly if the distributor is a fairly new corporation. Contracts between private parties (non-incorporated businesses) are not recommended.

Statement that Contract Supercedes All Other Agreements: This is a vague statement that often requires clarification. If the distributor has been in business for some time, he will probably have several on-going contractual commitments. Those commitments should be understood by all parties concerned.

Contract Duration: Trial periods should not be included in a contract which is generally construed as initiating a more lasting relationship. Trial periods should occur before a distributorship agreement is negotiated. The more popular contracts cover annual periods.

Exclusivity: Exporters are always tempted to grant exclusive distributorships on a territorial and product basis. This can result in a weakened marketing position for the exporter in larger markets.

Distributors will always point out that they will be better disposed toward aggressively selling the exporter's product line if they can feel that the exporter will not be selling to anyone else in the same market. There is no evidence to support that contention.

A good distributor will sell a product with or without an exclusive agreement. Indeed, he will sell without a contract, and, quite often, he will seek devious means of obtaining a product line if he feels he can make a decent profit.

Finally, there is more evidence to suggest that distributors who insist on exclusivity are smaller, more marginal entities with only a flimsey footing in their markets. And insofar as smaller markets are concerned, where there are only two or three distributors, exclusive agreements become meaningless.

Cancellation and/or Termination: This is one of the contract's more critical clauses. Business International, in its treatment of the subject, recommends a trial-period clause indicating a time period, e.g., one or two years, automatically renewable, but with a cancellation option that can be exercised by either party (notice in writing), 30 or 60 days prior to the expiration date.[1]

There are some inherent difficulties with this approach. First, it inserts a trial period into a contractual relationship which is unnecessary and tends to confuse the relationship. Second, a specified cancellation option places the burden of uncertainty upon the distributor without the advantage of any contractual redress.

Business International, recognizing the aforementioned problems, suggests a more detailed cancellation clause reproduced on the following page.

1. Termination without notice:
   This agreement will terminate automatically without notice from either party on 1) an attempted assignment of this agreement by distributor without written consent of manufacturer; or 2) an assignment by distributor for the benefit of creditors; or 3) admitted insolvency of distributor; or 4) the institution of voluntary or involuntary proceedings by or against distributor in bankruptcy, or for a receivership, or for the dissolution of distributor (if a corporation or partnership); or 5) the admitted insolvency of any member of distributor (if a partnership); or 6) the death of distributor (if an individual); or 7) the discontinuance of distributor's sales of manufacturers products in the sales area herein referred to or 8) the severance of his connection with distributor by a partner, principal, officer, owner, stockholder, or manager of distributor on whom manufacturer relies to promote its interest; or 9) repeated failure on the part of distributor to pay his bills.
   (Note that most countries would not accept poor sales performance of a distributor as a reason to terminate contract wtihout notice.)

   Distributor will immediately advise the manufacturer in writing of the occurrence of any event specified in this paragraph except No. 6 above, in which case distributor's administrators or executors will immediately advise manufacturer in writing of the death of the distributor.

2. Termination by notice:
   The term of this agreement shall be for a period of one year from the date hereof and shall be thereafter automatically renewed every six months unless one of the parties gives a 60-day written notice before the expiration of the original or extended period not to renew, or unless sooner terminated as provided in Article 1.

3. Neither party will be liable to the other for damages of any kind on account of any termination of this agreement with or without cause, whether damages result from loss through commitments on obligations or leases, from loss of investment, loss of present or prospective profits, or from inability to meet obligations, or from any other cause.

4. Upon termination of this agreement, 1) all indebtedness of distributor to manufacturer will become due and payable, if not already due and payable at the time of such termination; 2) manufacturer shall have the right to repurchase all products, or any portion thereof, then in possession of distributor at prices not in excess of the prices originally paid by distributor; and 3) manufacturer shall have no further responsibility, liability, or obligation to distributor under this agreement, or for unfilled orders even though previously accepted, or for any other reason whatsoever.

The difficulty with such clauses is that their sheer verbosity is often an open invitation to a host of legal squabbles peppered with possible law suits. Essentially, the shorter and simpler the language one can use in a contract, the clearer may be the mutual comprehension of the agreement, and the less chance there will be of misunderstandings.

Business International, in its own analysis of distributorship agreements, divides the other essential elements in a contract between "Manufacturer's Rights" and "Distributor's Limitations and Duties." While complete adherance to the B.I.

format would probably under any contract be too one-sided in favor of the manufacturer-exporter, it nevertheless constitutes an excellent check-list with which to launch negotiations. It is therefore reproduced below.

I   Manufacturer's Rights

1. Arbitration:
   a) if possible in manufacturer's country.
   b) if not, before International Arbitration Association.
   c) define rules to be applied (e.g., in selecting arbitration panel)
   d) make sure award will be binding in distributor's country.

2. Jurisdiction should be that of manufacturer's country (e.g., complete the signing at home).

3. Termination conditions (e.g., manufacturer need not indemnify if contract is cancelled after due notice).

4. Clarification of tax liabilities.

5. Payment and discount terms.

6. Conditions for delivery of goods.

7. Non-liability for late delivery beyond manufacturer's reasonable control.

8. Limitation on manufacturer's responsibility to provide information.

9. Waiver of manufacturer's responsibility to keep lines manufactured outside the U.S. (e.g., by licensees) outside of covered territory.

10. Right to change prices, terms, and conditions at any time.

11. Right of manufacturer or his agent to visit territory and inspect books.

12. Right to repurchase stock.

13. Option to refuse or alter distributor's orders.

14. Training of distributor personnel in U.S. subject to:
    a) practicability.
    b) costs to be paid by the distributor.
    c) waiver of manufacturer's responsibility for U.S. immigration approval.

II Distributor's Limitations and Duties

1. No disclosure of confidential information.

2. Limitation of distributor's right to assign contract.

3. Limitation on distributor's position as legal agent of manufacturer.

4. Penalty clause for late payment.

5. Limitation on right to handle competing lines.

6. Placing responsibility for obtaining customs clearance.

7. Distributor to publicize his designation as authorized representative in defined area.

8. Requirement to remove all signs or evidence identifying him with manufacturer if relationship ends.

9. Acknowledgment by distributor of manufacturer's ownership of trademark, trade names, patents.

10. Information to be supplied by distributor:
    a) sales reports.
    b) names of active prospects.
    c) government regulations dealing with imports.
    d) competitive products and competitors' activities.
    e) price at which goods are sold.
    f) complete data on other lines carried on request.

11. Information to be supplied by distributor on purchasers.

12. Accounting methods to be used by distributor.

13. Requirement to display products appropriately.

14. Duties concerning advertising and promotion.

15. Limitation on distributor's right to grant unapproved warranties, make excessive claims.

16. Clarification of responsibility arising from claims and warranties.

17. Responsibility of distributor to provide repair and other services.

18. Responsibility to maintain suitable place of business.

19. Responsibility to supply all prospective Customers.

20. Requirement that certain sales approaches and literature be approved by manufacturer.

21. Prohibition of manufacture or alteration of products.

22. Requirement to maintain adequate stock, spare parts.

23. Requirement that inventory be surrendered in event of a dispute which is pending in court.

THE EXPORT DISTRIBUTORSHIP CONTRACT

There are two contractual formats that are recommended by the author and which are frequently used today in the development and implementation of distributorship agreements. Prototypes of both contracts are included in this section.

Export Contract No. 1 covers a situation in which the exporter achieves a greater degree of marketing control in the distributor's area. Summarily, the exporter sells to the distributor at "cost-plus" (assume cost plus 5%) under agreed payment terms, and then receives a "royalty" on the distributor's marked-up resale price. This approach is useful in high-import duty countries because it lowers the base upon which the tariff may be assessed. In this connection, one must note that not all customs collection offices may agree to this practice, especially if they have access to the actual market prices.

Further, the "royalty" is really more in the form of a fee periodically paid by the distributor in consideration for the exporter's marketing, sales and technical advisory services. It is not a true royalty, and the exporter may be faced with remittance difficulties, particularly in soft-currency markets, unless it can be proven to the satisfaction of the central bank authorities that services have actually been performed by the exporter. However, arrangements under Contract No. I have been found successful in Panama, Central America, selected countries in the Caribbean, Asia and Western Europe. It is naturally suggested that the exporter solicit a legal opinion to evaluate the practicalities of implementing such a contractual arrangement under local law.

Export Contract No. 2 is a conventional and straightforward agreement. Although it minimizes the exporter's marketing control to a certain extent, it also minimizes his liability. It serves the main purpose of establishing the ground rules for an on-going exporter-distributor commercial relationship. The legitimacy of the document is generally unquestioned in most overseas markets.

The question now arises: just how good are formal distributorship contracts? The answer is that they are only as good as the intent of the parties to engage in a mutually profitable commercial relationship, respecting one another's committed positions and other related obligations. Very few businessmen enter into a transaction with the objective of "buying" a lawsuit. From that point of view, a written contract may be unnecessary.

However, if the exporter suddenly finds himself doing business in a growing number of overseas markets at once, he will find that it is indeed in his best interests to formalize the relationship with his foreign distributors in order to preserve a written record of the understandings that the parties have reached and are operating under. Consequently, one might state that a distributorship contract will not prevent a lawsuit; it simply will not invite one.

EXPORT CONTRACT #1

THIS AGREEMENT made this   day of
Nineteen Hundred and Sixty   between:

THE XYZ COMPANY, a corporation organized
and existing under the laws of the State of New
Jersey, United States of America, and domiciled
in Wayne Township, New Jersey, party of the
first part, hereinafter referred to as XYZ.

and

WITNESSETH:

That for and in consideration of the mutual promises and undertakings hereinafter contained, the parties hereto do agree as follows:
1. **Appointment:** XYZ hereby constitutes and appoints its exclusive selling representative in the   hereinafter termed the "TERRITORY", for its various products (hereinafter termed "XYZ PRODUCTS").
DISTRIBUTOR is authorized for the term of this agreement to purchase XYZ PRODUCTS from XYZ in Wayne, New Jersey, and to distribute and to sell the said products

out   under the conditions that all advertising and publicity undertaken by DISTRIBUTOR, that all methods of distribution, merchandising and sales, will be
subject to the prior approval of XYZ. DISTRIBUTOR, therefore, agrees to work in accordance with the requirements of XYZ with regard to the production and use of all advertising
material, with regard to the formulation and implementation of advertising policies, programs and campaigns, and in establishing the following approved sales procedures.

    2. **Definitions:** For purposes of this agreement, the following words shall have the
definitions given below.

    A. **Sales Period:** A period of one month beginning on the first day of the month
terminating on the last day of the month.

    B. **Gross Sales:** Are these sales of XYZ PRODUCTS purchased from XYZ by DIS-
TRIBUTOR and then resold to the trade throughout the TERRITORY and involved at the
DISTRIBUTOR'S current wholesale price before deducting any cash discount to the retailers
or others or any discount on the value of XYZ PRODUCTS or products of any other description granted to anyone as a bonus, free merchandise or for any other reason. For purposes of this agreement, DISTRIBUTOR wholesale prices for XYZ PRODUCTS will be listed
in a schedule to be composed by DISTRIBUTOR with the ratification of XYZ, and shall become part of this contract. Any proposed future changes in DISTRIBUTOR'S wholesale
price structure for XYZ PRODUCTS shall be promptly reported to XYZ for written approval before said changes are made and incorporated into this contract.

    C. **XYZ PRODUCTS:** Are those products sold by XYZ to DISTRIBUTOR for resale
throughout the TERRITORY in accordance with this agreement. XYZ PRODUCTS are listed
in Schedule "A" attached to and made part of this agreement. Additions to Schedule "A"
may be made from time to time by means of notification by XYZ to the DISTRIBUTOR.

    D. **Annual Period:** For purposes of this agreement, "Annual Period" is understood
to cover the period from December 1 through November 30, which corresponds to XYZ's
fiscal year. However, this "Annual Period" is construed to apply strictly to all aspects of
marketing, including planning, advertising, sales, the establishment of the advertising budget,
sales reports, advertising expenditure reports, and the remittance of all monies due by the
DISTRIBUTOR to XYZ.

    3. **Term of Agreement:** The duration of this contract will be for the period of one
(1) year from this date, and will be considered automatically renewed unless notification of
termination is given in accordance with the terms of the following paragraph.

    4. **Termination:** Either party may terminate this agreement by giving the other
party thirty (30) days written notice of termination. Any such notice shall be deemed to
have been given and to be effective when mailed by registered airmail, postage prepaid,
addressed to the other party at the address as set forth above, or at such other address as it
may designate in writing.

    5. **Competitive Products:** DISTRIBUTOR shall not, during the continuance of this
agreement, without XYZ's written consent, handle or have any interest in any similar or
competing line of products provided that nothing herein shall prevent DISTRIBUTOR from
continuing to handle any products it is already handling at the date of this agreement.

    6. **Reports:** DISTRIBUTOR shall report gross sales to XYZ in detail as rapidly as
possible and not later than the fifteeneth (15) day following the close of each monthly sales
period. DISTRIBUTOR shall also simultaneously make a report on his inventory position
and on his advertising expenditures for that same sales period

    A. **Sales:** For the purpose of evaluating performance, this report is to show the
balance in dozens of finished goods at the end of the month, all sales invoiced in dozens
multiplied by DISTRIBUTOR's selling price in the month, identified by each product and
each product totaled individually, prepared on a comparative basis using a sales reporting
form supplied by XYZ.

    A complete set of two (2) copies of each invoice substantiating the sale to the cus-
tomer will be kept by the DISTRIBUTOR at the disposal of XYZ. These invoices are to
show full details of quantities and price, trade discounts if allowed, cash discount if allowed,
all terms of payment granted, and the full name and address of the customer. Invoices will
be held for one year after the closing of the Distributor's fiscal year.

    B. **Advertising Expenditures:** This report will show all credits accrued during each
sales period, as well as all advertising and promotional expenditures of any nature whatsoever by both product and media, supported by vouchers.

7. **Prices:** Prices and terms of sale shall be established by the DISTRIBUTOR in agreement with XYZ, and in no case shall such prices be modified without the written consent of XYZ. Said prices shall be subject to all the applicable laws and regulations and shall be stated in local currency. The extension of credit to customers shall be decided by the DISTRIBUTOR. who shall bear the credit risk.

8. **Sales by XYZ to the DISTRIBUTOR:** The sale of XYZ PRODUCTS by XYZ to the DISTRIBUTOR shall be made at XYZ's published cost plus 10%. This (cost plus 10%) shall constitute XYZ's selling prices to DISTRIBUTOR and are included in this contract. XYZ shall make all revisions in its cost plus prices as it may deem necessary from time to time, and will advise DISTRIBUTOR of all changes made by publishing revised cost plus price lists whenever necessary which shall automatically become part of this contract.

9. **Payments by DISTRIBUTOR to XYZ:** All shipments shall be made by XYZ to DISTRIBUTOR on an open account basis, and payment by DISTRIBUTOR for finished goods purchased shall be made on the basis of 35% of DISTRIBUTOR's gross sales to the trade of XYZ PRODUCTS calculated under a method of accounting which will clearly distinguish the sale of XYZ PRODUCTS to customers where other products are also handled by DISTRIBUTOR. This payment of 35% by DISTRIBUTOR to XYZ shall include 20% of DISTRIBUTOR's gross sales to cover all services rendered XYZ, such as the right to distribute and to sell XYZ PRODUCTS, administrative assistance, sales and advertising assistance.

The balance, consisting of 15% of gross sales, shall constitute the advertising budget which shall be held by XYZ for the account of DISTRIBUTOR and shall be remitted to DISTRIBUTOR or to DISTRIBUTOR'S duly appointed advertising agents, against the presentation of vouchers or invoices for advertising expenditures incurred on programs and campaigns previously approved by XYZ.

Such payments will be made to the person, corporation or firm and in currency indicated by XYZ as long as there is no legal impediment. Payment shall be made within thirty (30) days after the close of each monthly sales period.

10. **Interpretation:** This agreement shall be construed in accordance with the laws of the State of New Jersey, United States of America.

11. **Assignment:** This agreement shall not be assignable by either party subscribing hereto.

IN WITNESS WHEREOF, the parties hereto have caused these presents to be duly executed, the day and year first above written.

EXPORT CONTRACT #2

THIS AGREEMENT made this   day of
Nineteen Hundred and Sixty   between:

THE XYZ COMPANY, a corporation organized and existing under the laws of the State of New Jersey, United States of America, and domiciled in Wayne Township, New Jersey

and

WITNESSETH:

That for and in consideration of the mutual promises and undertakings hereinafter contained, the parties hereto do agree as follows:

1. **Appointment:** "XYZ" hereby constitutes and appoints "DISTRIBUTOR" its exclusive selling agent (hereinafter termed the "Products").

2. **Term:** The term of this agreement shall be for one year from date made.

3. **Sales promotion advertising:** "DISTRIBUTOR" agrees to use its best efforts to increase sales of the "XYZ PRODUCTS" throughout the "Territory." All advertising is to be authorized in advance and directed by "XYZ".

4. **Local Stocks:** "DISTRIBUTOR" shall purchase from "XYZ" and "XYZ" shall sell such products to "DISTRIBUTOR" at "XYZ's" standard F.A.S. prices as established from time to time. Delivery and terms of payment shall be as mutually agreed. (Or, the terms, F.O.B. Vessel or C.I.F. Port of Destination may be substituted).

5. **Reports:** "DISTRIBUTOR" shall furnish "XYZ" with all reports necessary to keep "XYZ" informed of the market and competitive conditions and the progress of "DISTRIBUTOR" in promoting the sales of the "Products".

6. **Monthly Sales Reports:** This report will be furnished to "XYZ" showing the monthly ex-stock sales of all "Products" in units. This report will also show the stock on hand.

7. **Compensation:** "XYZ" shall pay "DISTRIBUTOR" a commission of ten per cent (10%) of the F.A.S. price of imported products purchased by "DISTRIBUTOR" from "XYZ" (Or, if no commission is involved, DISTRIBUTOR shall sell XYZ products at a wholesale price no greater than 20% over his landed cost.)

8. **Competitive Products:** "DISTRIBUTOR" shall not, during the continuance of this agreement, without "XYZ" written consent, handle or have any interest in any similar or competing line of products, provided that nothing herein shall prevent "DISTRIBUTOR" from continuing to handle any products it handles at the date of this agreement.

9. **Re-Sale Prices:** Prices and terms of re-sale shall be fixed by "XYZ" and "DISTRIBUTOR" and in no case shall such prices be modified without the written consent of "XYZ". Said re-sale prices will be subject to all the applicable laws and regulations and shall be stated in local currencies. The extension of credit to customers shall be decided by "DISTRIBUTOR", who shall bear the credit risk.

10. **Contracts and Obligations:** "DISTRIBUTOR" shall make no contracts and shall incur no obligations for or in "XYZ's" name unless specifically authorized in advance, in writing, by "XYZ".

11. **Termination:** Either party may terminate this agreement by giving the other party thirty days (30) written notice of termination. Any such notice shall be deemed to be given and to be effective when mailed by registered airmail, postage prepaid, addressed to the other party at its address set forth above, or at such other address as it may designate in writing.

12. **Construction:** This agreement shall be construed in accordance with the laws of the State of New Jersey.

13. **Assignment:** This agreement shall be binding upon and shall enure to the benefit of "XYZ", its successors or assigns, and "DISTRIBUTOR", its successors and assigns, except that "DISTRIBUTOR" may not assign this agreement without the written consent of "XYZ".

IN WITNESS WHEREOF, the parties hereto have caused this instrument to be executed in duplicate as of the day first above written:

FOOTNOTE

[1]*Setting Up a World Wide Distributor Network.*   Business International, New York, 1964.

INTERNATIONAL LICENSING

BACKGROUND

A manufacturer's export business usually evolves from a straight export operation into a more complex form of international business enterprise via the licensing route. This enables him to feel his way into an overseas market without
requiring a necessarily large capital investment. It also provides him with a relatively quick and easy way to remain in, or to enter, a foreign market once it has
been determined that the direct export of finished goods is no longer feasible.
Even large corporations still enter into direct licensing agreements in many countries as a means of minimizing their risks while still maximizing their market exposure by placing their know-how and technology to work.

The benefit of a licensing arrangement to the foreign licensee is four-fold. He may
now be able to operate his existing production, marketing and sales facilities at
capacity, producing and selling new products under license. He will be expanding
his product line, and he will be acquiring new know-how and technology from
the licensor. Finally, if the licensor is carrying a well-known branded product,
the licensee will profit from the established market position of the licensor so
long as he can provide the production and sales.

It may therefore be said that a licensing agreement is a marriage of convenience.
It is the conditional grant by a manufacturer to another producer (the licensee),
of the limited right to manufacture and market the manufacturer's (licensor's)
enumerated products in a designated territory for a specified period of time, in
return for which the licensee normally pays the licensor a royalty which is usually based upon a percentage of the licensee's FOB factory sales.

LICENSING AGREEMENTS

The following is a checklist of items that are normally found in licensing agreements:

I.   Definitions

    A. Product

    B. Territory
      1. manufacturing
      2. sales (optional)

    C. Parties (subsidiary)

    D. Fees and down payments
      1. conversion rate
      2. convertibility guaranties
      3. royalty base - per cent of:
        a. licensee's total production, including products other than licensor's, or
        b. production of licensor's models and comparable models, or
        c. production of licensor's models only
      4. equity interest or right to acquire stock (optional)
      5. right to buy per cent of production
      6. requirement of volume in given period, or yearly minimum payment

    E. Confidential disclosures

    F. Export rights

    G. Transfer of title
      1. foreign base company

    H. Foreign taxes
      1. who pays

    I. Arbitration

    J. Place of jurisdiction

    K. Right of termination plus reopening clause

    L. Term of agreement
      1. corresponding to years of production regardless of time lapse between signing of agreement and when licensee picks up model
      2. where patent licensee, tied to life of patent
      3. automatic renewal clause, with minimum advance notice

    M. Accounting provisions

    N. Option to buy

O. Management participation

P. Licensor's capital investment (if any)

Q. Schedule of payments and form of invoice
   1. penalty clause for late payment

R. Weights and measures system to be used

II.   Grants

A. Patents (plus "identifiable information")
   1. acknowledgement of validity
   2. reversion of rights or title in case of expropriation, bankruptcy, etc.
   3. protection, including cost of infringement, prosecution
   4. cross licensing, including improvements
   5. exclusivity
   6. immunities outside country of manufacture
   7. acquired patents (right to them by acquisition)

B. Trademarks
   1. acknowledgement of validity, especially where they cannot be registered
   2. reversion in case of expropriation, bankruptcy, etc.
   3. protection, including cost of infringement, prosecution
   4. quality and advertising control
   5. trademark registration, user agreement

C. Right to services (and charges for them)
   1. training
   2. access to plants
   3. know-how
   4. term of services
   5. technical material
   6. exchange of commercial information
   7. purchase of equipment, sales of components
      a. price of components, equipment
   8. start-up supervision

III. Requirements

A. Host government approval of agreement and remittances
   1. non-validity of agreement until received

B. Non-competitive clause

C. Retention of sales rights

D. Recognition of pre-existing exclusive licensees

E. Right to license components

F. Interchangeability of parts among licensees

G. Right to audit

H. Exact reproduction of trademark (no adulteration)

I. Caveat regarding laws of country of licensor
   1. "total agreement subject to any laws, regulations or restrictions of (country)"

Patents and Trademarks

The largest part of a royalty is generally considered to be paid in return for the use of the trademarks, patents and copyrights and for a territorial franchise. However, no sooner does the dollar exchange position of a country deteriorate (to the point where exchange controls are introduced) than royalty agreements and the percentage royalty rate paid come under close scrutiny by the Central Banks and other governmental authorities concerned with the outflow of foreign exchange. Further experience shows that certain markets have a tendency not to offer the licensor what he considers effective protection against patent process and/or design infringement.

There are several possibilities of avoiding that danger:

1. The trademark agreement is written in such a way that it will include detailed know-how provisions as outlined above. In other words, the contractual arrangement may be made to partly, or even wholly reflect a payment arrangement for technical services provided by the U.S. licensor. Such a construction may have the effect of placing the question of payments by the licensee into a fact pattern of *payment for tangible services rendered*, leaving it outside the intangible zone of licensor-licensee relations of which foreign courts sometimes take a dim view.

2. The trademark agreement between licensor & licensee takes the form of a very simple private contract and a separate agreement is drawn up, outlining in great detail the know-how, services, and assistance provided by the licensor to the licensee. The obvious implication is that the licensee is indeed fortunate since he is being provided with a finished product or products and/or with know-how which took the licensor years to develop. In most cases the licensee in a foreign country could never have developed this know-how by himself, either due to lack of financial resources or manpower or because he would have been reluctant to engage in an extended research and development program with lengthy trial and costly error along the road. This argument, of course, must be most carefully and diplomatically handled, especially since the technology of many countries in certain fields is equal to U.S. know-how. In the case of Japan, companies are usually requested to outline exactly what the technical services shall consist of, to justify a royalty rate, generally a percentage of net factory sales.

This type of arrangement is also desirable where patents, trademarks and copyrights do not receive the same legal protection that is available here in the U.S.A.

Services Which Companies Can Offer

The following are the major areas in which companies can itemize their expertise for which services are offered without being open to serious question by the investigating authorities.

Production:

Assist in plant layout and organization for increased production efficiency, assist in calculation of labor cost comparisons, labor and time standards and controls;

Assist in process design, layout and installation supervision;

Assist in preliminary planning for production phases of plant expansion or modification;

Make available, as requested from time to time, engineers and/or technicians for the purpose of assisting with manufacturing problems;

Supply technical information, descriptive materials, formulations, manufacturing procedures and product specifications;

Assist in translating unit sales forecasts into production schedules, on which to base raw- and packaging-material requirements, and assist in materials management and procurement.

Sales and Sales Education:

Provide advice, assistance and instruction on sales problems and techniques by appropriate means both from U.S. headquarters and through a licensor-paid regional manager located in the area;

Assist in the drafting and preparation of market surveys;

Furnish information on competitive products with regard to prices and discount structures in the U.S. and in other markets that might be pertinent to improving sales performance in the licensee's area;

Assist in the selection of sales personnel and the expansion of the sales force and development of a competent management and marketing organization;

Supply sales educational material for sales conferences or for salesmen's use when calling on the trade;

Furnish trade journal reprints and abstracts for sales promotion;

Provide visual aid, such as slides, charts and other materials for promotional and/or instructional purposes;

Furnish films, sound tape recordings and conference material for salesmen's training and for sales aids.

Financial:

Assist in the development and implementation of effective policies of financial management;

Assist in preparation of monthly reports in accordance to established policies and procedures;

Assist in the design and installation of product cost systems;

Assist in the preparation of annual financial budgets and monthly operating budgets;

Assist in the development of sound pricing practices based upon marketing requirements and information.

Legal:

Assist in general legal and corporate matters;

Assure trademark, patent, health and other registrations and handle all matters relating to such registrations;

Assist in such areas such as product liability insurance and general liability and loss coverage;

Provide liaison between U.S. and foreign governments for the purpose of obtaining visas, permits, and transfers of personnel.

Advertising:

Supply domestic advertising materials, copy, artwork and layouts for use by the licensee;

Supply literature, direct mail pieces and other advertisements, films, or finished printed material;

Provide mailing services from the U.S. to prospective customers;

Give assistance on all matters pertaining to advertising and sales promotion.

Personnel:

>Assist and advise on wage and salary administration;

>Assist in establishing personnel policies and procedures;

>Assist in training programs either locally or through courses conducted at U.S. corporate headquarters for the benefit of personnel from overseas locations.

Engineering:

>Provide technical and engineering information from U.S. corporate head-quarters or from outside sources for the benefit of overseas associates in improving operations;

>Supply data on product research and development, and on manufacturing specifications;

>Assist in obtaining supplies and production materials in the U.S. or else-where to supplement local resources;

>Procurement assistance in obtaining machinery, parts and other supplies;

>Offer items that are new or of special interest to overseas affiliates;

>Supply quality control laboratory data and systems information when required.

THE LICENSING CONTRACT

Actual licensing contracts must be modified to meet the specific requirements of the parties and the legal requirements of the host country. Certain countries, like Brazil, limit the amount of royalty that can be remitted back to the licensor. Other countries, like Argentina, impose a high one-time sales tax at the first point of sale. What happens there is that the licensee takes the form of a contract manu-facturer who then sells his output to an independent distributor of his recom-mendation or of the licensor's selection in order to reduce the base upon which the tax is imposed. The royalty is therefore small, and the licensor must somehow arrange to take a share in the distributor's marked-up price. Fortunately, this is a common practice in these countries, and a mutual accord among all parties in-volved is not difficult to achieve.

Similarly, technology-oriented products having little or no brand identification expose the licensor to possible contractual breach by the licensee involving pre-mature termination of the agreement and theft of the licensor's know-how and technology. Here, the licensor may protect himself by under-playing the royalty part of the agreement while binding the licensee to a separate, yet concurrent technical service contract in which the licensor can seek the recovery of what both parties feel is a legitimate consideration via a technical service fee, payable in installments. Thus, while the licensing agreement may fall, and may even prove unenforceable, the technical service contract might still stand as a binding agreement, the proof being that the licensee did receive enough assistance to produce the product.

The contract below is a recommended format for a branded consumer product. Many of its parts, however, are valid for all products.

Licensing Contract #1
Branded Consumer Goods

THE XYZ COMPANY

WAYNE, NEW JERSEY

THIS AGREEMENT made this   day of
Nineteen Hundred and Sixty-Four between:

XYZ, a corporation organized and existing
under the laws of the State of New Jersey,
United States of America, domiciled in
Wayne, Passaic County, New Jersey, party
of this first part, hereinafter referred to as
"XYZ.

and

WITNESSETH:

That for and in consideration of the mutual promises and undertakings hereinafter contained, the parties hereto do agree as follows.

1. **Appointment:** XYZ hereby constitutes and appoints
           its exclusive distributor in the Republic of Colombia. DISTRIBUTOR is authorized for the term of this agreement to manufacture, distribute, and sell XYZ products in the Republic of Colombia under the conditions that all publicity carried out by DISTRIBUTOR will be subject to the approval of XYZ, and that all product standards and methods of sale will be subject to the approval of XYZ. DISTRIBUTOR, therefore agrees to work in accordance with the requirements of XYZ with regard to advertising material, in maintaining product standards and in establishing and following approved sales procedures.

2. **Definitions:** For purposes of this agreement, the following words shall have the definitions given below.

A. **Sales Period:** A period of one month beginning on the first day of the month and terminating the last day of the month.

B. **Gross Sales:** Are those sales of Distributor's manufactured products invoiced at the lowest current wholesale price before deducting any cash discount to the retailers or others or any discount on the value of XYZ products or products of any other description granted to anyone as a bonus, free merchandise or for any one reason.

C. **Distributor's Manufactured Products:** Are those products manufactured by the DISTRIBUTOR in accordance with this agreement. Distributor's Manufactured Products are listed in Schedule "A" attached to and made part of this agreement. Additions to Schedule "A" may be made from time to time by means of notification by XYZ to the DISTRIBU-TOR.

D. **Annual Period:** For the purpose of this agreement the term "Annual Period" is understood to cover the period from December 1st through November 30th.

3. **Products Included:** The DISTRIBUTOR is hereby licensed to manufacture, distribute and sell Distributor's Manufactured Products.

4. **Territory:** XYZ hereby authorizes DISTRIBUTOR to manufacture, sell and distribute Distributor's Manufactured Products throughout the Republic of Colombia and to the best of its ability prevent their exportation from the Republic of Colombia unless specifically requested to do so by XYZ.

5. **Term of Agreement:** The duration of this agreement will be for a period of ten (10) years from this date, but the agreement may be cancelled if either party notifies the other in writing, by registered mail, at least ninety (90) days in advance.

XYZ will consider as sufficient reason for cancellation of this contract the failure of DISTRIBUTOR to aggressively exercise the concessions and privileges granted hereby, failure to maintain product standards, failure to follow approved sales procedures or failure to increase the yearly sales volume in dozens by at least ten (10) per cent of such other amount as agreed by XYZ and the DISTRIBUTOR as the quota for the annual period, unless XYZ is satisfied that the adverse economic conditions of the country or "force majeure" justifies failure of agreement. Additions of new Distributor's Manufactured Products to Schedule "A" are excluded from all sales increase requirements until the second year.

6. **Trademarks:** DISTRIBUTOR is hereby authorized for the duration of this agreement to use all patents or trademarks which are the property of XYZ, as well as licenses of the Department of Health for XYZ products, whether they be registered in the name of XYZ or any other person or entity. However, DISTRIBUTOR will not acquire any right whatsoever with regard to such licenses, patents and trademarks and will not take advantage of the use granted in this agreement to claim any right against the total exclusive right of XYZ or the grantee. The use of the licenses, trademarks and patents will inure exclusively to the benefit of the registrant or his assignees.

7. **Purchase of Materials:** DISTRIBUTOR shall buy all raw materials, material for the promotion of sales, packaging materials, and other items required for the manufacture, sale and distribution of Distributor's Manufactured Product from XYZ or from other persons and firms approved by XYZ, and the materials so purchased shall require prior approval by XYZ.

8. **Competitive Products:** DISTRIBUTOR shall not, during the continuance of this agreement, without XYZ'S written consent, handle or have any interest in any similar or competing line of products provided that nothing herein shall prevent DISTRIBUTOR from continuing to handle any products it handles at the date of this agreement.

9. **Quality Control Standards:** XYZ shall supply DISTRIBUTOR from time to time information necessary for the maintaining of the quality of the product as required by XYZ; and DISTRIBUTOR at all times shall work in accordance with said standards of manufacture and packaging of XYZ products.

10. **Reports:** The DISTRIBUTOR shall report gross sales to XYZ in detail as rapidly as possible and not later than the fifteenth (15) day following the close of each sales period, and not later than the twentieth (20) day on raw materials and advertising expenditures and accruals as follows:

A. **Raw Materials:** For purposes of indicating that adequate supplies are on hand for anticipated sales, this report is to include the quantity of raw materials and packaging materials received from XYZ or purchased elsewhere during the preceding month, the quantities of raw and packaging materials withdrawn for purposes of manufacture, and the balance of all materials on hand the last day of the month.

B. **Sales:** For the purpose of evaluating performance, this report is to show the balance in dozens multiplied by the lowest wholesale billing price in the month, identified by each product and each product totaled individually, prepared on a comparative basis using a sales reporting form supplied by XYZ.

A complete set of two (2) copies of each invoice substantiating the sale to the customer will be kept by the DISTRIBUTOR at the disposal of XYZ. These invoices are to show full details of quantities and price, trade discounts if allowed, cash discount if allowed, all terms of payment granted, and the full name and address of the customer. Invoices will be held for one year after the closing of the Distributor's fiscal year.

C. **Advertising Expenditures:** This report will show all credits accrued during each sales period. Also, all promotional expenditures of any nature whatsoever are to be listed by both product and media, supported by vouchers.

D. **Costs:** For the purpose of cost analysis and to assist in the determination of establishing satisfactory prices, a cost-price report will be submitted for each product and size by the DISTRIBUTOR to XYZ prior to the beginning of each annual period. The cost-price report will show in full detail the manufacturing cost, the price structure, and the cost structure, for each product by size, on a per-dozen basis, using a form supplied by XYZ.

11. **Prices:** Prices and terms of sale shall be fixed by XYZ in agreement with the DISTRIBUTOR and in no case shall such prices be modified without the written consent of XYZ. Said prices will be subject to all the applicable laws and regulations and shall be stated in local currency. The extension of credit to customers shall be decided by the DISTRIBUTOR, who shall bear the credit risk.

12. **Inspection:** XYZ shall have the unlimited right to inspect the facilities and manufacturing procedures of DISTRIBUTOR and to examine the books and files of DISTRIBUTOR, insofar as they apply to XYZ products.

13. **Advertising:** An amount equal to fifteen per cent (15%) of gross sales of Distributor's Manufactured Products effected by the DISTRIBUTOR shall be used by DISTRIBUTOR to advertise XYZ products.

All such advertising must be placed through an advertising agency approved by XYZ and shall be subject to the previous approval of XYZ with regard to content, media and other characteristics.

14. **Payment:** In consideration of the license hereby granted the DISTRIBUTOR shall pay to XYZ an amount equal to fifteen per cent (15%) of gross sales of Distributor's Manufactured Products calculated under a method of accounting which will clearly distinguish the sale of XYZ products to customer where other products are also handled by DISTRIBUTOR.

This payment shall cover all services rendered by XYZ such as the right to manufacture and sell XYZ products, the use of trademarks and formulas, plus such services rendered by XYZ as administrative assistance, sales and advertising assistance, manufacturing supervision, technical and laboratory assistance, reimbursement for expenses of occasional coverage of the country by an XYZ representative in order to get first-hand information relative to economic conditions and activities of competitors, and franchise payment for these various privileges and services.

Such payments shall be made to the person, corporation or firm and in currency indicated by XYZ as long as there is not legal impediment. Otherwise the DISTRIBUTOR shall pay in Colombian currency, to any account in Colombia indicated by XYZ. Payments shall be made within thirty (30) days after the close of each sales period.

The DISTRIBUTOR shall reimburse XYZ for losses incurred by XYZ because of delayed payment for services under conditions of local currency devaluation unless XYZ is satisfied that the adverse economic conditions of the country or "force majeure" justifies failure of agreement.

15. **Charges:** Expenses incurred, if any, by DISTRIBUTOR on behalf of XYZ are deductible from gross payment provided the charges are approved in advance by XYZ. The charges must be supported by vouchers and the vouchers approved by XYZ. Approved charges shall be deducted from the gross payment due for the month charges are incurred.

16. **Audit:** XYZ shall have the right, through their officials, employees, or accountants chosen by them, to examine the books and files of DISTRIBUTOR to verify the accuracy of its reports. It is understood that should this examination indicate that manufacturing costs as submitted are subject to correction, then XYZ and DISTRIBUTOR shall mutually agree upon suitable changes of the wholesale and retail prices of the said products and/or the percentage to be spent on advertising and/or the amount of payment for services to XYZ.

17. **Taxes:** DISTRIBUTOR shall pay all collectable taxes to any government authority on the manufacture and sale of Distributor's Manufactured Products and for all acts completed in accordance with this agreement, with the sole exception that XYZ shall be responsible for taxes on income received by them in accordance with this agreement.

18. **Insurance:** XYZ shall provide fire insurance coverage for equipment and machinery and any other material owned by XYZ in the possession of the DISTRIBUTOR. XYZ shall cover its interest in terms of general liability and product liability.

19. **Termination:** Upon cancellation becoming effective, the right of DISTRIBUTOR to manufacture, distribute and sell XYZ products shall terminate.

In the event there are raw materials remaining in the possession of the DISTRIBUTOR at the effective date of termination and materials have been obtained by DISTRIBUTOR for the manufacture, sale, and distribution of XYZ products, XYZ shall purchase such materials if the materials are in accord with current XYZ specifications and if their future use by XYZ will be legally authorized and agreed to by DISTRIBUTOR under such rights as he may have under local health permits.

On the effective date of the termination XYZ, if it so desires, shall have the right to purchase from DISTRIBUTOR in accordance with this agreement, and DISTRIBUTOR shall sell to XYZ, at cost price to DISTRIBUTOR, all XYZ finished products in the possession of the DISTRIBUTOR. Cost price is defined as the manufacturing cost of the distributor as submittted to XYZ in DISTRIBUTOR'S Cost-Price Report in accordance with Paragraph 10D. above.

In the event of cancellation or termination, the DISTRIBUTOR reserves the right to sell or not to sell to XYZ the machinery that was purchased with the approval of XYZ expressly for the production of XYZ products by the DISTRIBUTOR. XYZ agrees to purchase said machinery at cost to DISTRIBUTOR less an annual depreciation of ten per cent (10%).

20. **Interpretation:** This agreement shall be construed in accordance with the laws of the State of New Jersey, United States of America.

21. **Bankruptcy:** In the event of either party committing any act of bankruptcy or going into compulsory liquidation, the other party may terminate this agreement forthwith but without prejudice to any accrued rights.

22. **Assignment:** This agreement shall not be assignable by either party subscribing hereto.

IN WITNESS WHEREOF, the parties hereto have caused these presents to be duly executed, the day and year first above written.

THE XYZ COMPANY

Witness

                      By:

    (Name)

    (Occupation)

Witness

                      By:

    (Name)

    (Occupation)

THE LEGALITY OF "EXCLUSIVITY"

Exclusive territorial grants, along with restrictive covenants on prices, are subject to increasing scrutiny by governments all over the world. A distributor is naturally interested in some sort of territorial protection, while a manufacturer wishes to limit competition as much as possible.

Many countries have legislated against exclusive territory agreements in distributorship contracts. Such arrangements are held to be possible only through the grant of a franchise in which there is actually a consignment "sale" to an agent. In other words, the theory is that a manufacturer may issue a franchise through an agent so long as he (the manufacturer) retains title to the goods until they are sold to the agent's customer.

The Sherman, Clayton, and Robinson-Patman Acts have been incorporated to a certain extent into Articles 85 and 86 of the Treaty of Rome which is the governing body of law for the now expanded European Common Market. Many other countries outside the Common Market have incorporated similar laws into their own legal systems. It should therefore be reasonably expected that exclusive distributorship agreements will one day pass into business history.

In the meantime, the manufacturer may avoid burdensome future problems by consulting with legal experts on the following points.

1. What are the special statutes that govern distributorship contracts?
2. How does Country "X" differentiate between an agent and distributor?
3. How much notice must be given prior to termination of an agreement without incurring any liability?
4. How must such notice be conveyed?
5. Under what conditions may the distributor claim indemnity after cancellation or termination of a contract by the manufacturer?
6. Can a distributor legally sell competitive products regardless of a restricting clause in the contract?
7. What are the laws governing unilateral cancellation of contract?
8. How is compensation calculated, if at all?
9. Are distributors entitled to a lien on manufacturers' goods?
10. When is title of goods transferred?
11. Does Country "X" recognize arbitration provisions?
12. What "force majeure" provisions are enforceable?

THE INTERESTS OF THE DISTRIBUTOR

A licensee and an import distributor are by nature distributorship organizations. When a manufacturer negotiates a licensing agreement, he is also negotiating a distribution contract. He should therefore appreciate fully the objectives of his counterpart in entering into a more or less binding arrangement. It is therefore appropriate at this point to list the various special interests that the distributor and/or the licensee have and which they would like to see incorporated in a contract.

1. Manufacturer to provide sales and technical training.
2. Rapid delivery of materials and supplies by manufacturer.
3. Availability of parts and service by manufacturer when necessary.
4. Effective implementation of manufacturer's warranties.
5. Manufacturer to replace defective products at his own cost.
6. Advertising and merchandising support, or an advertising allowance.
7. Special discounts and deals.
8. Favorable credit terms.
9. Commissions on "house" accounts.
10. Commissions on direct sales by manufacturer in distributor's area.
11. Minimum visits by manufacturer to create good will and to provide services when and where needed.
12. Manufacturer to keep other sales outlets from selling in distributor's territory.
13. Guarantee or security that line will not be taken away once the territory becomes established.
14. Freedom to handle other lines.

It is clear that not all conditions can be met by all manufacturers. However, it is also clear that if a mutually rewarding relationship is ever to develop, all parties to these distributorship agreements will have to negotiate and then operate with a "live and let live" spirit.

FREE TRADE ZONES

INTRODUCTION

Practitioners of international business have long been familiar with the concept of free trade zones, which have existed since the dawn of commercial history. Their full potential, however, for the U.S. importer bringing goods into the country, or for the American exporter and/or manufacturer seeking entree to overseas markets, still remains to be realized.

Briefly, a *free* or *foreign trade zone* in the U.S., and in other countries, is understood to be an enclosed geographic area considered by law to be *outside* the customs region of a country, although income produced by commercial endeavors undertaken in such zones is normally taxable by the surrounding political jurisdiction.

The official United States Department of Commerce definition is as follows:

> A free trade zone or foreign trade zone is an enclosed and policed area in a seaport, airport, or some other inland point where goods of foreign origin may be brought in for re-export by land, water or air without the payment of customs duty. Usually these zones allow foreign traders to store, exhibit, sample, blend, mix, sort, repack, and manufacture various commodities within the zone area.

This means that merchandise entering directly into a free zone from other countries may exempt from all import duties, during which time such merchandise may be manipulated, processed and/or manufactured into other products, or simply warehoused, before final disposition outside the zone, whereupon appropriate import duties are then levied and paid.

There are several variants to the free trade zone concept throughout the world. They are of limited interest to the manufacturer and/or processor of goods; nevertheless, they do provide duty-free areas for warehousing and even for merchandising purposes. These variations are summarized below.

A *free port* is an area, generally encompassing a port and its surrounding locality, into which goods may enter duty-free or subject only to minimal revenue tariffs (with the exception, perhaps, of a limited number of items) whether these goods are for re-export or for local consumption. Free port privileges, it should be noted, may not be confined to the immediate port area, but may be extended by law to a considerable surrounding area. In the case of French Somaliland, for example, the free port privileges are not limited to the port of Djibouti but extend to the colony as a whole. In the case where the free port is merely a delimited area of a country, goods leaving this area to pass into national customs territory are subject to customs duties.

An *entrepot* (sometimes called a transit zone) is a port of entry in a coastal country established for the convenience of a neighboring country lacking adequate port facilities. The entrepot is administered so that the customs of the coastal country do not interfere with the transit of goods to the neighboring country.

A *free perimeter* is similar to a free port but is generally confined to a remote or underdeveloped region in a country.

ADVANTAGE OF A FREE ZONE LOCATED IN THE U.S.

Fruit Importer Saves on Inventories and Import Duties

An importer of bulk semi-dried fruit normally paid import duties on a weight basis at New York, the port of entry, before the goods were shipped to his Ohio facilities for curing, drying and warehousing prior to sale. Relocation of his processing facilities to the free zone in Staten Island produced the following benefits:

1. Payment of import duties could be deferred until after the curing and drying process.

2. There was a 30% reduction in dutiable weight after processing. This resulted in a substantial saving on import duty charges.

3. Warehousing costs were competitive with the Ohio facilities.

4. There was only a slight savings in processing costs.

5. There was a substantial savings in inland freight costs. The importer no longer had to transport his goods to Ohio before booking orders. He could now ship directly to his customers from finished goods inventories warehoused in the free zone.

U.S. Manufacturers Employing Foreign-made Components

Manufacturers using foreign-made components in their domestically produced goods are also in a position to take advantage of free trade zones, although the comparative cost of utilizing these facilities along with relocation costs must be weighed against a product's existing cost structure. It becomes attractive to use a free zone if the manufacturer enjoys a relatively large export business. He can eliminate the confusion and red tape which is involved in processing in bond shipments of components or in applying for duty drawbacks (at a cost of almost 5% of levied import duties, including brokerage charges) by simply locating his entire manufacturing operation in a free zone having the necessary facilities. Unfortunately, facilities in free zones in the U.S. are frequently inadequate.

A Foreign Import Becomes "Made in U.S.A."

There is another distinct advantage to the use of free zones. Imported components are sometimes used in a manufacturing process whose end-product has a high content of domestic parts. This final product may legally qualify for a "Made in U.S.A." label. There is a clear administrative advantage to locating such enterprises in a free trade zone, especially if the "Made in U.S.A." product is to be shortly exported.

ADVANTAGES OF FREE TRADE ZONES LOCATED IN OTHER COUN-TRIES

Most major markets have free trade zones. Their location and facilities are discussed under "Customs Areas of the World" at the end of this chapter. An alphabetical listing of Free Trade Zones, Free Ports, Entrepots, and Free Perimeter is also included.

The tax havens or holidays offered by free trade zones in Europe are extremely attractive. More elaborate processing and/or manufacturing establishments placed in European zones are also a means, quite often, of by-passing EEC or EFTA bloc tariff barriers.

An interesting question at this point is whether a processing or manufacturing operation established by a U.S. company in a free zone in Western Europe would in fact fall within the purview of the Executive Order restraining new American investments in that part of the world. This question is presently being put to the Commerce Department in Washington.

This may require a redefinition of what is called a "foreign investment" and "foreign country" as it relates to (1) free zones which are not legally considered to lie within a country's customs area, and (2) balance of payments concepts as they concern the statistical treatment of capital outflows.

The Panama Free Trade Zone at Colon

The best known success story is Panama's free trade zone at Colon. About $600 million in merchandise was warehoused, processed, manufactured and then trans-shipped or re-exported through the Colon zone in 1972. Fifteen percent of this total passed into Panama itself.

Most raw materials, components and finished goods arrive in Colon by steamer and then depart again in altered form by air for other points in Latin America. The zone now serves over 400 companies, including about 300 U.S. firms.

Some Recently Established Free Trade Zones

Exporters and potential exporters can familiarize themselves with free trade zones and other customs-privileged facilities located near their overseas markets by obtaining a U.S. Department of Commerce publication entitled "Free Trade Zones and Related Facilities Abroad." This booklet discusses free trade zones outside the United States, the economic factors influencing their use, and current trends in their operation and mangement. It further provides detailed descriptions of the zones in operation.

Since the 1970 publication of the booklet, several new free trade zones have already appeared. Further, an additional number of zones are now in various stages of planning or development by governments and private organizations throughout the world.

Four zones of particular interest to businessmen are: La Romana, Masan, Lappeeranta, and Mauritius. These zones have all become operational since publication of "Free Trade Zones and Related Facilities Abroad."

Industrial Free Zone, La Romana, Dominican Republic: The city of La Romana is situated on the southern coast of the Dominican Republic. It has a population of about 37,000 with its own airport and port facilities. The Romana Free Zone was established in 1969 by a 30-year contract between the Dominican Government and Gulf & Western American Corporation empowering the latter to manage and operate the Romana Free Zone. Operadora Zona Franca, a subsidiary of Gulf & Western, operates and administers the zone.

Companies in the La Romana Zone may import free of duty and excise taxes, from all sources, most materials that may be necessary for the installation of their facilities and the production of goods. Companies chartered outside the Dominican Republic receive complete exemption on all taxes, including corporate, profit, dividend, production or sales, patent and municipal.

Dominican customs service is available within the zone. Material consigned to the zone is inspected at the plant, meaning that a shipment arriving in another port of entry in the Dominican Republic may go in bond to the zone without being opened for inspection until it reaches its destination.

All goods and products exported or re-exported to foreign countries are shipped free of duties or excise taxes. Goods shipped into the Dominican Republic which are not manufactured elsewhere in the country receive special customs treatment, paying only 90 percent of the normal duty.

Paved asphalt roads connect La Romana with the principal cities of the island. The port, located a short distance from the zone, has a 700-foot wharf capable of serving ships of up to 15,000 tons deadweight and a draft of about 32 feet. The airport has a 6000-foot asphalt paved runway permitting piston-engine commercial aircraft and small jets to land and takeoff with ease. Customs and immigration clearance for incoming and outgoing international flights is available, as well as refueling services.

Additional information may be obtained from La Romana Industrial Free Zone, P.O. Box 135, La Romana, Dominican Republic.

Free Export Zone, Masan, Korea: The city of Masan, located on the southern coast of Korea 45 miles east of Pusan, has a population of about 225,000.

The Masan Free Export Zone was established in January 1970 by the Korean Government. Masan is essentially a "limited" free trade zone. Free trade zone privileges (i.e., duty free raw material and equipment imports) are limited to industrial concerns and associated service enterprises which produce, process or assemble goods solely for the export market. The zone's purpose is to attract new investment by highly technical and labor-intensive export industries. It is not intended to facilitate the importation of goods into the domestic Korean market or to be used for the warehousing of goods intended for third-country markets.

Enterprises eligible to operate within the zone are those engaged in the production, processing or assembly of goods for export. They must be either wholly foreign-owned enterprises or joint ventures between foreign and Korean investors in which foreign equity interest represents over 50 percent of paid-up capital. Occupants of the zone must have definite prospects for export, a high ratio of foreign exchange earnings, advanced manufacturing techniques and labor-intensive production. Related service operations such as warehousing, banking, transportation, stevedoring and packing are provided at support facilities within the zone. Occupants of the zone may either purchase or lease land from the administering authority.

Foreign firms operating in the zone will be exempted in full from the payment of income, corporation, property, and property acquisition taxes, as well as taxes imposed on dividends or surplus funds accruing from the principal owned by foreign investors, for five years from the start of business operations. A 50 percent reduction of such taxes will also be granted for the following three years. Income and corporation taxes on profits from exports will, in general, be reduced by 50 percent after completion of the tax-free periods. In addition, business and commodity taxes will not be imposed on the export activities of occupant-enterprises nor will customs duties be imposed on raw materials and equipment required for export production. Foreigners will also be exempt from the payment of personal income taxes.

The port of Masan is capable of handling vessels up to 20,000 tons at two berths, and domestic airline service connects Masan with the international airport at Pusan.

Additional information may be obtained from the Office of the Masan Free Export Zone Administration, Room 803, Ssangyong Building, 24, 2-ka, Chu-dong, Chung-ky, Seoul, Korea.

Free Trade Zone, Lappeenranta, Finland: Lappeenrannan Vapaavarasto Oy, a private company owned by the city of Lappeenranta, opened Finland's fourth free trade zone in November 1971. Lappeenranta is located in eastern Finland near the border with the Soviet Union. It is not as conveniently located as Finland's other free trade zones at Helsinki, Turku and Hanko for use by United States exporters to that country, but it is nevertheless useful to firms engaged in trade with the Soviet Union.

This new free trade zone covers an area of approximately 17 acres with cold storage facilities of 8,000 square meters. It is served by a rail line which is the same gauge as that in the Soviet Union.

Goods may be brought into the Lappeenranta Free Trade Zone without customs clearance and can there be repacked, divided, assorted, blended, mixed and otherwise handled as if they were outside the customs area of Finland. Industrial activities, however, may not be carried on in the free trade zone without special permission from the government. Goods brought from outside Finland into the free trade zone must be cleared through customs only when taken from this area for sale in Finland. The importer is not obliged to have goods cleared when they cross the Finnish border into the country in direct transit to the free trade zone.

Additional information may be obtained from the Managing Director, Lappeenrannan Vapaavarasto Oy, Valtakatu 37 B, 53100 Lappeenranta 10, Finland.

Export Processing Zone, Mauritius: Mauritius is an island of 720 square miles in the southwest Indian Ocean. It is about 500 miles east of Madagascar and 1,250 miles off the African coast. The island has a population of over 800,000 of which about 140,000 live in Port Louis, the capital and largest city.

The government of Mauritius is establishing a number of export processing zones throughout the country. The first export processing zone has been opened in the large industrial estate of Plaine Lauzun at Port Louis. Additional export processing zones are being developed at La Cure and Les Salines near Port Louis, at Curepipe in the Central Plateau, at Beau Bassin, and near Plaisance Airport. All categories of goods may be brought in except alcohol and tobacco.

The island has a good road system, about 80 percent of which is paved. Port Louis can accommodate vessels with a draft of up to 29 feet. An international airport is located at Plaisance in the eastern part of the island.

Additional information may be obtained from the Secretary for Industrial Development, Ministry of Commerce and Industry, 4th Floor, Anglo-Mauritius House, Port Louis, Mauritius.

Zones Still in Planning Stages

A number of free trade zones and related facilities have been authorized by various governments within the past two years. However, these are not yet fully operational.

In Malaysia an industrial estate of 220 acres adjacent to the airport at Bayan Lapas on Penang Island has been set aside as a free trade zone. Completion is scheduled for 1974.

Development has also begun on the 175-acre Mariveles Foreign Trade Zone being established at Mariveles, Bataan, in the Philippines. Completion of the Batan installation is expected in 1975.

Work has also just begun on the Industrial Park free zone located near the airport at Port-au-Prince, Haiti. This is to be completed in 1974.

Business Company SRL, a Paraguayan firm, is the sole concessionaire for a 25-acre free zone that Paraguay is establishing at Puerto Presidente Stroessner on the Parana River.

Colombia is presently establishing two additional free trade zones, one at the Pacific coast port of Buenaventura and the other inland at Palmaseca International Airport near Cali.

More detailed information on free trade zones throughout the world is to be found in two U.S. Department of Commerce publications. One, which relates to such zones in the U.S. only, is the "Annual Report of the Foreign-Trade Zones Board of the United States." The 33rd Annual Report is currently available. The other, mentioned earlier in this chapter, and relating only to zones overseas, is entitled, "Free Trade Zones and Related Facilities Abroad." Both may be obtained from the Superintendent of Documents, U.S. Government Printing Office, Washington, D.C., 20402.

SUMMARY

Free trade zones, free ports and other similar customs-privileged facilities in foreign countries afford important advantages to United States exporters, in an increasingly competitive era.

They provide exporters a base at the doorstep of their foreign customers from which export goods may be processed, sold, distributed and serviced. Export firms using free trade zones abroad often find many advantages, including tax relief or exemption, inexpensive land and plant or warehouse facilities, access to raw materials in neighboring countries which may be imported free of duty for use in production for re-export, and nearby markets for finished goods. Efficient use of free trade zones can bring about savings for the United States exporter, especially in transportation costs.

Indicated in the following pages is a list of free trade zones, free ports, entrepots, free perimeters and other related facilities. Also included is a sampling of seven major free trade and free port areas which may be of interest to international traders. The last part of this chapter is a reproduction of *Customs Areas of The World*, a 1970 United Nations Statistical Paper. This will be of importance to businesses seeking to establish manufacturing facilities in tax and/or duty free areas.

FREE TRADE ZONES

AUSTRIA:	Graz, Linz, Solbad Hall (Tyrol), and Vienna.
BAHAMAS:	Freeport (Grand Bahama Island).
BERMUDA:	Freeport (Ireland Island).
BRAZIL:	Manaus.
CAMBODIA:	Sihanoukville. (Not in operation).
CHILE:	Africa and Punta Arenas.
COLOMBIA:	Barranquilla.
DENMARK:	Copenhagen.
DOMINICAN REPUBLIC:	Puerto Plata (Not yet in operation).
FINLAND:	Hanko, Turku, Helsinki
FED. REPUBLIC OF GERMANY:	Bremen, Bremerhaven, Cuxhaven, Emden, Hamburg, and Kiel.
GREECE:	Piraeus and Salonika (Thessaloniki).
INDIA:	Kandla.

IRELAND:	Shannon Free Airport.
ITALY:	(In Italy, Free Trade Zones are known as "Free Points") Naples, Torre Annunziata, Trieste, and Venice. Authorized, but not yet in operation: Brindisi, Genoa, and Messina.
LEBANON:	Beirut, Beirut International Airport, and Tripoli.
LIBERIA:	Monrovia.
LIBYA:	Tripoli.
MEXICO:	Coastzacoalcos (also known as Puerto Mexico) and Salina Cruz; Topolobampo (authorized, but not yet in operation).
MOROCCO:	Tangier.
NETHERLANDS ANTILLES:	Orangestad (Aruba) and Willemstad (Curacao).
OKINAWA:	Naha.
PANAMA:	Colon and Tocumen International Airport.
SPAIN:	Barcelona, Cadiz, and Vigo.
SWEDEN:	Goteborg, Malmo, and Stockholm.
SWITZERLAND:	Aarau, Basel-Dreispitz, Basel-Rheinhafen, Basel-CFF, Chiasso-Stazione P.V., Geneva, Geneva-Aerodrome de Cointrin, Geneva-Cornavin, Lausanne, St. Gallen, St. Margrethen, Zurich-Albisrieden, Zurich-Aerodrome.
SYRIA:	Damascus
TURKEY:	Iskenderun. (Not in operation).
UNITED ARAB REPUBLIC:	Alexandria, Port Said, and Port Tewfick (city of Suez).
UNITED STATES:	(In the United States, Free Trade Zones are known as Foreign Trade Zones.) Mayaguez (Puerto Rico), New Orleans, New York, San Francisco, Seattle, and Toledo.

URUGUAY: Colonia and Nuevo Palmira.

FREE PORTS

ADEN.

CANARY ISLANDS   All the islands of this group are Free Ports. The
(SPAIN):   principal ports serving the Canary Islands are:
                       Arrecife, La Orotava, Las Palmas, Puerto de Cab-
                       ras, San Sebastian de la Gomera, Santa Cruz de la
                       Palma, Santa Cruz de Tenerife, Sardina de Galder,
                       and Valverde.

COLOMBIA: Providencia Island and San Andres Island.

FRENCH SOMALILAND.

FRENCH WEST   St. Barthelemy (served by the Port of Gustavia)
INDIES: and St. Martin (served by the Port of Marigot).

GIBRALTAR.

HONG KONG.

KUWAIT.

FEDERATION OF   Penang, Labuan and Singapore. (NOTE: Agree-
MALAYSIA: ment has been reached with Singapore and is being
                       sought with Penang by the central government to
                       end their free port status and incorporate them in
                       the Malaysian customs area; to preserve their entre-
                       pot trade, however, Singapore and Penang will
                       each establish a free trade zone in the ports of
                       Singapore and Georgetown (Penang).

NETHERLAND   Saba, St. Eustatius, and St. Martin
ANTILLES:

SPAIN: Ceuta and Melilla. (These enclaves on the North
                       African coast are administered as a part of metro-
                       politan Spain.)

IRAN: Siri, Shaikh Shuaib, Kish, Farur, and Hendorabi.

ENTREPOTS

ADEN:	(For Yemen).
ANGOLA:	Lobito for the Congo (Leopoldville).
ARGENTINA:	Barrangueras and Formosa (for Bolivia). Buenos Aires and Rosario (for Bolivia and Paraguay). Concordia (for Uruguay). Concordia and Monte Caseros (for Brazil and Paraguay). Empedrado and Paso de Los Libres (for Brazil). Mendoza, San Juan, Salta and Jujuy (for Bolivia and Chile).
BAHREIN:	(For neighboring Persian Gulf Countries).
BRAZIL:	Belem (for Peru and Bolivia). Corumba (for Bolivia). Manaus (for Ecuador). Paranagua (for Paraguay). Port Velho (for Bolivia). Santos (for Bolivia and Paraguay).
CHILE:	Antofagasta and Africa (for Bolivia).
FRENCH SOMALILAND:	Djibouti (for Ethiopia).
GREECE:	Salonika (for Yugoslavia).
IRAN:	Bandar Shahpour, Khorramshahr, and Meshed (for Afghanistan).
IRAQ:	Goods in transit through Iraq are exempt from customs duties.
ITALY:	Trieste (for Austria, Czechoslovakia, and Hungary).
JORDAN:	Goods in transit to or from Lebanon, Saudi Arabia, and Syria are exempt from Jordanian customs duties.
KUWAIT:	(For neighboring countries).
LEBANON:	Beirut (for neighboring countries).
LIBERIA:	Monrovia (for Guinea).
LIBYA:	Tripoli — authorized but not yet in operation (for West and Central Africa).

MOZAMBIQUE: Beira [for Rhodesia, the Congo (Katanga), and
                             Malawi] . Lourenco Marques (for Rhodesia,
                             Swaziland, and South Africa).

NORWAY: Trondheim (for Sweden).

PAKISTAN: Karachi (for Afghanistan).

PARAGUAY: Concepcion (for Brazil), Asuncion (for the
                             reception, storage, and distribution of goods of
                             Spanish origin destined to be exported to Paraguay
                             and other countries - not yet in operation).

PERU: Matarani and Mollendo (for Bolivia).

SAUDI ARABIA: Jidda and Dammam (for neighboring countries).

SYRIA: Latakia (for neighboring countries).

YUGOSLAVIA: Rijeka and Koper (for Austria, Czechoslovakia,
                             and Hungary).

NOTE: Transit trade of each other's goods among Lebanon, Jordan, Saudi
        Arabia, and Syria is governed by an agreement of December, 1959,
        which provides for the duty-free transit of such goods among these
        countries.

FREE PERIMETERS

ARGENTINA: Tierra del Fuego.

CHILE: The Provinces of Aysen, Chiloe, and Magallanes;
                             Arica.

INDONESIA: Riouw Archipelago.

MEXICO: All of Baja California; northwestern area of the
                             State of Sonora, including San Luis Rio Colorado
                             and Sonoyta; Nogales and Agua Prieta, in the
                             State of Sonora; Chetumal, Cozumel, Xcalak, and
                             Islande Mujeres, in the Territory of Quintana Roo.

PROPOSED FREE TRADE ZONES

(The following facilities are under consideration; however, there are no indications as yet that they will be established.)

BOLIVIA:	Cobija.
BRAZIL:	Rio de Janeiro.
REPUBLIC OF CHINA:	Kaohsiung.
GHANA:	Tema.
GUATEMALA:	Matias de Galvez.
IVORY COAST:	Abidjan.
NEW ZEALAND:	Auckland.
PAKISTAN:	Karachi.
SAUDI ARABIA:	Jidda and/or Dammam.
SYRIA:	Tartous.
TUNISIA:	Cap Bon.
YUGOSLAVIA:	Rijeka and Koper.

OTHER RELATED FACILITIES

BELGIUM: Antwerp and Ghent (Bonded Warehouses). Unlimited storage of imports in bonded warehouses, duty-free storage of imports destined for re-exportation, and the Authorization of certain manipulation of goods in storage enable these ports to be likened to free trade zones.

Brussels National Airport ("Free Area"). Sabena operates a warehouse in the free area in which goods may be stored duty-free for 6 months; goods may be re-exported or, upon payment of customs duties, be brought into Belgian customs territory.

DOMINICAN REPUBLIC: Santo Domingo (Free Port Retail Stores). The only operation authorized is retail sales under Customs supervision to tourists and diplomatic personnel with free entry privileges.

ICELAND: Reykjavik (Bonded Warehouse).
                            Keflavik International Airport (Duty-free Store).

                            Reykjavik has a bonded warehouse which provides
                            storage and re-packing facilities but none for manu-
                            facturing. Imported goods are landed free from
                            customs fees and duties; these changes are paid
                            only at the time of removal from the warehouse
                            for domestic distribution.

                            Keflavik International Airport has a duty-free store
                            selling only to transient international travelers.

ITALY: Leghorn and Palermo (Free Depots). In Italy, a
                            free depot is a facility that provides a limited free
                            storage area in a port. Manipulation of goods is
                            generally not permitted.

NETHERLANDS: Rotterdam and Amsterdam.
                            Rotterdam has no free trade zone but its liberal
                            customs practices give it many of the advantages
                            of a free trade zone. Customs regulations are mini-
                            mal. Storage of goods in transit and goods cleared
                            for importation in special customs house sheds is
                            virtually unlimited; manipulation, and to a limited
                            degree manufacturing, are permitted in bonded
                            warehouses; and dutiable goods can be readily
                            moved in a specified time and route from one
                            part of the port to another.

                            Amsterdam offers the same privileges as Rotter-
                            dam, but on a lesser scale.

NORWAY: Kristiansand, Oslo, and Trondheim (Free Ware-
                            houses). In Norway free warehouses offer most
                            of the facilities of free trade zones.

PORTUGAL: Lisbon (Bonded Depots).
                            Bonded warehouses in Lisbon provide open and
                            covered storage space where goods of foreign
                            origin may be stored duty-free for two years.

SPAIN: Aguilas, Algeciras, Alicante, Almeria, Aviles,
                            Bilbao, Cartagena, Castellon, El Ferrol del Caudillo,
                            Gijon, Mahon, Palamos, Palma de Majorca, Pasajes,
                            Ribadeo, San Sebastian, Santander, Tarragona,
                            Villagercia, and Vinaroz (Free Depots).

In Spain a free depot offers privileges similar to but not as extensive as those provided by a free trade zone.

La Coruna, Huelva, Sevilla, Malaga, and Valencia (Commercial Depots).

In Spain a commercial depot is similar to a free depot but does not offer quite as extensive privileges.

CUSTOMS AREAS OF THE WORLD

(The customs area coincides with the geographical area unless otherwise stated. Mention is made of the existence or absence of customs free areas whenever information is available.)

NAME OF AREA	COMMENTS
ADEN	Part of Southern Yemen (which see).
AFGHANISTAN	The customs area corresponds to the administrative territory; each province has its associated customs house and the customs boundaries are designated administratively, different from the geographic boundaries.
	There are no free areas.
ALGERIA	From 1960 to 1962 the departments of Sahara were excluded from the customs area.
	There are no free areas.
ALHUCEMAS	Part of the customs area of Spain (which see).
AMERICAN SAMOA	The customs area includes Tutuila, Aunu'u, the Manu'a group, and Swains Island.
	There are no free areas.
ANDORRA	
ANGOLA	Includes Cabinda.
	There are no free areas.
ANTIGUA	There are no free areas.
	(See Leeward Islands)

ARGENTINA

There are no free areas.

Goods entering Tierra del Fuego for consumption are duty-free.

ARUBA

Part of the customs area of Netherlands Antilles (which see).

AUSTRALIA

The customs area comprises the States of New South Wales (including Australian Capital Territory), Victoria, Queensland, South Australia, Western Australia and Tasmania, and the North Territory. The State of New South Wales includes Lord Howe Island; the State of Tasmania includes Macquarie Island and the Northern Territory includes Ashmore and Cartier Islands.

There are no free areas.

Non-contiguous territories and mandated areas are treated as foreign countries.

Customs control is not maintained in the Antarctic Territory claimed by Australia.

AUSTRIA

The customs area differs from the geographic area to the extent that there are two customs exclaves:
(1) Mittelberg im Kleinen Walsertal in Vorarlberg
(2) Jungholz in Tyrol

There are free areas at Linz, at Graz and at Solbad Hall (Innsbruck, Tyrol), and at Vienna. Foreign consumer and capital goods intended for use in the free areas are subject to duty. Goods manufactured in the free areas incorporating materials of foreign origin are subject, upon import into the rest of the customs area, only to duty rates applicable to the foreign components in the form in which they entered the free areas. At present the movements of goods into and out of the free areas are not recorded.

BAHAMAS

There is a free port at Grand Bahama.

BAHRAIN

BARBADOS

There are no free areas.

BASUTOLAND

Beginning 4 October 1966, named Lesotho (which see).

BECHUANALAND	Beginning 30 September 1966, named Botswana (which see).
BELGIUM-LUXEMBOURG (ECONOMIC UNION OF)	Belgium and Luxembourg form an economic union and the customs area includes both countries.
	There are no free areas in the Economic Union. Belgium, Luxembourg and the Netherlands form a customs union called Benelux (which see). In the statistics of the Economic Union of Belgium and Luxembourg trade with the Netherlands is considered external trade.
BENELUX	Customs Union of Belgium, Luxembourg and the Netherlands. Trade statistics of the Customs Union, excluding the intertrade of the Benelux countries, are published in the *Quarterly Bulletin of Statistics* by the Secretariat of the Benelux. The separately published statistics of Belgium-Luxembourg, however, show trade with the Netherlands as foreign trade and those of the Netherlands show trade with Belgium-Luxembourg as foreign trade.
	There are no free areas in the Customs Union.
BERMUDA	There are no free areas.
BOLIVIA	There are no free areas.
BOTSWANA	Prior to 30 September 1966, known as Bechuanaland. Botswana is included in the customs area of South Africa.
BRAZIL	The port of Manaus is a free area.
BRITISH ANTARCTIC TERRITORY	The customs area comprises that part of the Falkland Islands (Malvinas) dependencies lying south of latitude 60° south and between 20° and 80° of west longitude (i.e., the South Shetland Islands, South Orkney Islands and Graham Land).
	There are no free areas.
BRITISH GUIANA	Beginning 26 May 1966, named Guyana (which see).
BRITISH HONDURAS	There are no free areas.

BRITISH INDIAN OCEAN TERRITORY	The customs area comprises the Chagos Archipelago (formerly a dependency of Mauritius and of which Diego Gracia is the principal island), Aldabra, Farquhar and Des Roches (the latter three formerly dependencies of the Seychelles). There are no free areas.
BRITISH SOLOMON ISLANDS	There are no free areas.
BRITISH VIRGIN ISLANDS	There are no free areas. (See Leeward Islands)
BRUNEI	There are no free areas.
BULGARIA	There are no free areas.
BURMA	There are no free areas.
BURUNDI	Prior to 1 January 1964 Burundi and Rwanda formed a customs union. There are no free areas.
CAMBODIA	
CAMEROON	There are no free areas. Beginning 1966, Cameroon joined the Customs and Economic Union of Central Africa.
CANADA	There are no free areas.
CANARY ISLANDS	Part of the customs area of Spain (which see).
CANTON AND ENDERBURY ISLANDS	Part of the Gilbert and Ellice Islands customs area (which see).
CAPE VERDE ISLANDS	The customs area comprises all the islands of the Cape Verde Archipelago. There are no free areas.
CAYMAN ISLANDS	There are no free areas.
CENTRAL AFRICA, CUSTOMS AND ECONOMIC UNION OF	The following five countries form the Customs and Economic Union of Central Africa: Cameroon, Central African Republic, Chad, Congo (Braaza-ville) and Gabon.

CENTRAL AFRICAN REPUBLIC	There are no free areas.
	The Central African Republic is a member of the Customs and Economic Union of Central Africa.
CEUTA	Part of the customs area of Spain (which see).
CEYLON	There are no free areas.
CHAD	There are no free areas.
	Chad is a member of the Customs and Economic Union of Central Africa.
CHAFARINAS	Part of the customs area of Spain (which see).
CHANNEL ISLANDS	Consists of the Bailiwick of Jersey and the Bailiwick of Guernsey, each of which has its own Customs Administration. (See United Kingdom).
CHILE	There are areas in the Department of Arica and in the Provinces of Chiloe, Aysen and Magallanes in which some merchandise is exempt from certain duties and imposts.
CHINA (TAIWAN)	There are no free areas.
CHRISTMAS ISLANDS (AUST.)	There are no free areas.
COCOS (KEELING) ISLANDS	There are no free areas.
COLOMBIA	There is a free area in Barranquilla.
	Goods for local consumption that enter through the free port of Leticia (Comisaria del Amazonas) and the free port of San Andres and Providencia are duty-free and exempt from other taxes.
COMORO ISLANDS	There are no free areas.
CONGO (BRAZZAVILLE)	There are no free areas.
	Congo (Brazzaville) is a member of the Customs and Economic Union of Central Africa.
CONGO (DEMOCRATIC REPUBLIC OF)	Prior to 1 August 1964, known as Congo (Leopoldville). Since 1962, the customs area coincides with the geographic territory. Prior to 1962, the

CONGO (DEMOCRATIC REPUBLIC) (continued)	customs area excluded Katanga. There are no free areas.
COOK ISLANDS	Customs area comprises the islands : Rarotonga, Mangaia, Atiu, Mauke (or Parry), Aitutaki, Mitiaro, Manuae (or Hervey), Takutea, Penrhyn (or Tonga-reva), Manihiki, Pukapuka (or Danger), Rakahanga, Palmerston, Suwarrow, Nassau, but excludes Niue Island. There are no free areas.
COSTA RICA	There are no free areas.
CUBA	The United States naval base adjacent to the town of Caimanera is excluded from the customs area. There are no free areas.
CURACAO	Part of the customs area of the Netherlands Antilles (which see).
CYPRUS	There are no free areas.
CZECHOSLOVAKIA	There are no free areas.
DAHOMEY	There are a number of free areas in Dahomey— e.g. in the port of Cotonou. Dahomey is a member of the West African Customs Union.
DENMARK	Customs area excludes the Faeroe Islands and Greenland. There is a free area in the port of Copenhagen. The free area is, for statistical purposes, considered as inland (i.e., as part of the customs area). Movements of goods between the free area and the rest of the customs area are not recorded.
DOMINICA	There are no free areas. (See Windward Islands).
DOMINICAN REPUBLIC	There is a free area on the grounds of the international exhibition known as the Free Area of the Centro de Los Heroes. Goods destined for this area are delivered to customs bonded warehouses from which they are moved duty-free by their respective consignees.

DOMINICAN REPUBLIC (continued)	Imports destined for this area are included in the regular import statistics.
EAST AFRICA	Comprises Kenya, that part of Tanzania formerly known as Tanganyika, and Uganda.
ECUADOR	There are no customs controls in the Oriente region. Fishing activities and exports of the Colon Archipelago (or Galapagos Islands) are supervised by the Customs and Maritime Authorities of Ecuador.
EL SALVADOR	There are no free areas.
EQUATORIAL GUINEA	The customs area comprises the Provinces of Fernando Poo (comprising Fernando Poo Island, Annobon Island and adjacent islands) and Rio Muni (comprising Rio Muni, Corsico Islands, Elobey Grande, Elobey Chico and adjacent islands). There are no free areas.
ETHIOPIA	There are no free areas.
FAEROE ISLANDS	There are no free areas.
FALKLAND ISLANDS (Malvinas)	The Falkland Islands (Malvinas) constitute a free area except for matches, tobacco, spirits and some import controls, (i.e., licenses required for importation of certain goods).
FIJI	There are no free areas.
FINLAND	In 1965 a free area was established in the port of Hanko.
FRANCE	The customs area of France includes continental France, Corsica, the other French coastal islands, the principality of Monaco, and the overseas departments of Guadeloupe, Guiana, Martinique and Reunion. There are no free areas. Certain regions of Gex and Upper Savoy are called "free zones" because entries from abroad and shipments abroad are exempt from customs duties although they are subject to certain other taxes

FRANCE (continued)   normally levied on goods imported into the rest of
                            the customs area. Movements of goods in these
                            regions are also subject to import and export con-
                            trols. The movement of goods between the rest of
                            the customs area and the free zones is treated as
                            special trade.

                            For statistical purposes the overseas departments
                            (Guadeloupe, Guiana, Martinique and Reunion)
                            are considered as territories separate from France.

FRENCH GUIANA   Part of the customs area of France, but for statisti-
                           cal purposes it is considered as a separate territory.

                           There are no free areas.

FRENCH POLYNESIA   The customs area includes the Society Archipelago
                           (of which Tahiti is the most important island),
                           Marquezas Islands, Austral Islands, the Tuamotu
                           group and the Gambier group.

                           There are no free areas.

FRENCH SOMALILAND   Beginning 3 July 1967, named the French Terri-
                           tory of the Afars and the Issas (which see).

FRENCH SOUTHERN   Comprises the islands of Saint Paul and Nouvelle
AND ANTARCTIC   Amsterdam, the Kerguelen and Crozet Archipela-
TERRITORIES   gos, and Terre Adelie.

                           There are no free areas.

FRENCH TERRITORY   Prior to 3 July 1967, known as French Somali-
OF THE AFARS AND   land.
THE ISSAS
                           This territory is a free area.

                           Merchandise which enters the territory and is des-
                           tined for local consumption is subject to taxes.

GABON   There are no free areas. Gabon is a member of the
                           Customs and Economic Union of Central Africa.

GAMBIA   There are no free areas.

GERMANY, EASTERN*   There are no free areas.

*(The customs area is that controlled by the authorities of the Democratic Republic of Germany which compiles the data on international trade of this customs area.)

GERMANY, FEDERAL   Since 6 July 1959, the Saar is a part of the cus-
REPUBLIC OF   toms area of Germany.

The external trade statistics of the Federal Republic of Germany refer to movements of goods into and out of the German Federal Republic and Berlin-West. Separate figures are not available for the trade of West Berlin. Customs enclaves are the Austrian communities of Jungholz and Mittelberg. Busingen is an exclave surrounded by the territory of Switzerland.

There are free areas in the ports of Hamburg, Bremen, Bremerhaven, Cuxhaven, Emden and Xiel. In both the general and special trade statistics, the trade of the free areas is treated in the same way as the rest of entrepot trade. Separate data on the movements of goods to or from the free areas are not available.

The trade with Eastern Germany is excluded from international trade statistics.

GHANA   There are no free areas.

GIBRALTAR   Gibraltar is a free area, but a small number of goods are subject to duty when entered for local consumption.

GILBERT AND ELLICE   Includes Canton and Enderbury Islands.
ISLANDS
                      There are no free areas.

GREECE	The customs area includes the Greek islands. The Free Yugoslavian Zone at Salonika is a customs exclave of Greece.
	There are free areas at Piraeus and at Salonika.
GREENLAND	There are no free areas.
GRENADA	There are no free areas. (See Windward Islands).
GUADELOUPE	Part of the customs area of France, but for statistical purposes it is considered as a separate territory. The territory of Guadeloupe includes the islands of Desirade, Les Saintes, Marie Galante, St. Barthelemy and St. Martin (French part).
	There are no customs services on St. Barthelemy and St. Martin (French part) which are, in fact, free areas.
	The movement of merchandise between the rest of the customs territory and the free areas is treated as special trade. Separate foreign trade statistics for St. Barthelemy and St. Martin (French part) are not recorded.
GUAM	There are no free areas.
GUATEMALA	There are no free areas.
GUIANA	(See French Guiana; Guyana; Surinam).
GUINEA	There are no free areas.
GUYANA	Prior to 26 May 1966, known as British Guiana.
	There are no free areas.
HAITI	There are no free areas.
HOLY SEE	This is a customs area separate from that of Italy (which see).
	There are no free areas.
HONDURAS	There are no free areas.
HONG KONG	Hong Kong is a free area, except for intoxicating liquors, tobacco and manufactures thereof, table waters and hydrocarbon oils. There are also some import controls.

HUNGARY	There is a free area at the Danube port of Csepel. Goods traffic from other parts of the country to the free area and from the free area to other parts of the country is treated as foreign trade.
ICELAND	There are no free areas.
IFNI	Part of the customs area of Morocco.
INDIA	The Laccadive, Minicoy and Amindivi Islands are within the customs area of India but the trade of these islands is exlcuded from the foreign trade statistics of India. The area of Jammu and Kashmir, the status of which has not yet been determined, is administered as part of the customs area of India.
	There are no free areas.
INDONESIA	Comprises Java and Madura, Sumatra, Kalimantan (Borneo), Sulawesi and Maluku (Celebes and the Moluccas), Nusa Tenggara (the Lesser Sunda Islands) and West Irian.
	The Riouw Archipelago is a free area. The trade of the free area is not included in the statistics, however exports of tin ore, tin and bauxite produced in the free area and exported directly are included in the national export statistics.
IRAN	There are no free areas.
IRAQ	There are no free areas.
IRELAND	There is a "free area" at Shannon Airport which includes the Shannon Industrial Estate. Trade between the free area and the rest of the State is included in the trade statistics as foreign trade. Trade between the free area and other countries is not recorded in the official trade statistics. Certain data regarding this trade are, however, collected by means of a special inquiry. While the general trade system is in operation, insofar as movement into and out of customs bonded warehouses is concerned, the treatment of the free area at Shannon is in accordance with the special trade system.
ISLE OF MAN	Part of the customs area of the United Kingdom.

ISRAEL   There are no free areas.

ITALY   The customs territory comprises the area within
                       the land and sea frontiers except the Vatican City
                       State and the Communes of Livigno and Campione.
                       Italy maintains a customs union with the Republic
                       of San Marino. The Italian trade statistics, however,
                       include the trade of the Vatican City.

                       There are free areas in the ports of Venice, Naples
                       and Trieste. There are free areas of minor impor-
                       tance known as "depositi franchi" in a number of
                       Italian ports. Movements of goods between the
                       customs area and the free areas are treated as
                       special trade.

                       For the purpose of analysis of trade by country of
                       origin or destination, domestic goods or goods
                       which have been cleared for home use which enter
                       the free areas are recorded as being exported to
                       'places and warehouses in the free areas', which for
                       statistical purposes are considered as a foreign
                       country. Imports from the free areas, on the other
                       hand, are recorded according to the country of
                       origin of the goods; if the country of origin can-
                       not be determined, they are considered as coming
                       from 'an unknown country.' Goods which enter
                       the free areas and are re-exported are included in
                       the indirect transit statistics.

                       Data on exports abroad of wine, spirits and ver-
                       mouth from the "Cantine vigilate," situated in the
                       free areas, are published separately.

IVORY COAST   There are no free areas.

                       Ivory Coast is a member of the West African
                       Customs Union.

JAMAICA   The customs area consists of the Island of Jamaica.

                       There are no free areas.

JAPAN   The customs area comprises Honshu, Shikoku,
                       Kyushu, Hokkaido and the islands belonging to
                       those areas. It also includes: (1) Nanposhoto
                       Archipelago (including Ogasawara-gunto (Bonin
                       Islands), Nishinoshima Island (Rosario Island) and
                       Kazan Retto Islands (Volcano Islands)) located
                       south of Sofu-iwa and (2) Okino-torishima Island
                       (Parece Vela) and Minami-torishima Island (Marcus

JAPAN (continued)	Island). It excludes: (1) the Islands of Yuo-torishima and Iheya-jima, and Nansei-shoto Archipelago (Ryukyu Islands) (including Daito-shoto Archipelago) located south of latitude 27° north and (2) Habomai-gunto Archipelago, and the Islands of Shikotan-to, Kunashiri-to and Etorofu-to.

There are no free areas. |
JORDAN	There are no free areas.
KENYA	There are no free areas.
KOREA, Republic of	There are no free areas.
KUWAIT	The customs area excludes the Neutral Zone.
LAOS	There are no free areas.
LEBANON	The ports of Beirut and Tripoli each contain a free area.
LEEWARD ISLANDS	In the Leeward Islands there are four customs areas: (1) Antigua, (2) Montserrat, (3) St. Kitts-Nevis-Anguilla, (4) British Virgin Islands.

There are no free areas. |
| LESOTHO | Prior to 4 October 1966, known as Basutoland. Lesotho is included in the customs area of South Africa.

There are no free areas. |
LIBERIA	A free area exists in the port of Monrovia. Movements of goods between the rest of the customs area and the free area are treated as special trade. Separate data are not available.
LIBYA	There are no free areas.
LIECHTENSTEIN	(See Switzerland).
LUXEMBOURG	(See Belgium-Luxembourg Economic Union).
MACAU	Macau, which includes the islands of Taipa and Coloane, is a free area.

MADAGASCAR   There are no free areas.

MALAWI   Prior to 6 July 1964, known as Nyasaland.

                      There are no free areas.

MALAYSIA   Comprises three separate customs areas: West
                      Malaysia, Sabah and Sarawak.

MALAYSIA, EAST   As of 5 August 1966, designation used for the two
                      states of Malaysia located on the island of Borneo.
                      (See Sabah and Sarawak).

MALAYSIA, WEST   Prior to 16 September 1963, known as the Federa-
                      tion of Malaya. Between 16 September 1963 and
                      5 August 1966, known as Malaya.

                      Penang is a free area, Duties are, however, levied on
                      intoxicating liquors, tobacco, motor and aviation
                      spirit when entered for local consumption, and on
                      the import of certain other commodities which
                      compete with goods produced in Penang. Separate
                      data for the free area are published.

MALDIVES   Previously known as Maldive Islands.

                      There are no free areas.

MALI   There are no free areas.

                      Mali has control over a number of warehouses,
                      known as "free ports", in the ports of Dakar and
                      Abidjan for the storage of goods in direct transit
                      from or to foreign countries.

                      Mali is a member of the West African Customs
                      Union.

MALTA   The customs area includes Gozo and Comino.

                      There are no free areas.

MARTINIQUE   Part of the customs area of France, but for statis-
                      tical purposes it is considered as a separate terri-
                      tory.

                      There are no free areas.

MAURITANIA   The customs area comprises the geographical area
                      except for a free area which exists in the northern
                      part of the country — the entire area to the north
                      of the parallel passing one kilometer to the south

MAURITANIA (continued)   of Bir-Moghrein.

Mauritania is a member of the West African Customs Union. It also forms a customs union with Senegal.

MAURITIUS   The customs area consists of Mauritius, the island of Rodrigues and Six Islands, Peros Banhos, Solomon Islands, Agalega, St. Brandon group, Trois Freres.

There are no free areas.

MELILLA   Part of the customs area of Spain (which see).

MEXICO   The customs area of Mexico comprises the continental part of the country, including the peninsulas of Yucatan and Baja California. It also includes the islands of Cozumel, Cedros, Balandra and Los Angeles but excludes the Marias Islands, the Revillagigedo Islands and Tiburones Islands.

Under the Mexican customs system there are so-called free areas (zonas libres), free districts (perimetros libres) and free ports (puertos libres), which conform to the definition of a free area.

The free area includes all of the peninsula of Baja California and part of the State of Sonora. Foreign goods may be imported for consumption, use or transformation provided that they are not prohibited goods and provided that similar goods are not produced within the area. Goods produced, manufactured or transformed within the area are exempt from export taxes.

Free districts are located at Nogales and Agua Prieta in the State of Sonora and at Cozumeland Ciudad Chetumal in the Territory of Quintana Roo. The customs privileges in the free districts are similar to those in the free area, the difference lies in the extent of the territory in which they are applicable. In the case of the free districts they are applicable only in the urban area of the town or city concerned. These areas are unlikely to have natural resources that can be developed and the customs privileges are generally used to obtain supplies of consumer goods.

Free ports are situated in Salina Cruz, Oaxaca; Coatzacoalcos, Vera Cruz; and Topolobampo,

MEXICO (continued)	Sinaloa. The free ports are considered as territory outside customs control in which loading, unloading, storage, packing, processing, refining or mixing operations may take place without the intervention of the customs authorities.

Import statistics relating to the free areas, districts and ports are compiled separately but are included in the national trade statistics. Exports from the free areas, districts and ports are included in the trade statistics and are not published separately. |
| MIDWAY ISLAND | (See Pacific Islands under U.S. Administration). |
| MONACO | Part of the customs area of France (which see). |
| MONTSERRAT | There are no free areas.

(See Leeward Islands). |
| MOROCCO | The customs area coincides with the geographic area except for Ceuta and Melilla which are under Spanish sovereignty.

A free area was established in Tangiers on 1 January 1962. |
| MOZAMBIQUE | There are no free areas. |
| NAMIBIA | Prior to 12 June 1968, known as South West Africa.

Namibia is included in the customs area of South Africa (which see). |
| NAURU | There are no free areas. |
| NETHERLANDS | Belgium, Luxembourg and the Netherlands form a customs union called "Benelux" (which see). However, the statistics of the Netherlands show trade with Belgium-Luxembourg as foreign trade.

There are no free areas. There are shops at the airport in Amsterdam which have the administrative status of a customs bonded warehouse. Spirits, champagne, tobacco manufactures and chocolate and, except to residents of the Netherlands, photographic and optical articles, films, watches and perfumery may be sold duty-free to travellers leaving the Netherlands by air for destinations outside Europe. Goods imported into these shops |

NETHERLANDS
(continued)

from abroad are recorded by the Netherlands as "special imports". Purchases of these goods by air travellers and movements of goods to these shops from the rest of the customs area are not statistically recorded.

NETHERLANDS ANTILLES

The customs area comprises the islands of Aruba, Bonaire and Curacao.

A free area comprises the islands of Saba, St. Eustatius and St. Martin (Netherlands part). There is also an area, locally called "free zone", in the port of Willemstad, Curacao, which differs from the free area in that a simple customs declaration must be made for merchandise entering the "free zone" and that there is a rough control.

Early in 1969 a "free zone" will be installed in the port of Oranjestad, Aruba, similar to the one in Willemstad, Curacao.

NEUTRAL ZONE

This is a separate customs area under the joint control of Kuwait and Saudi Arabia.

NEW CALENDONIA

The customs area includes the Loyalty Islands, the Huon Islands and the Chesterfield Islands. Wallis and Futuna Islands are not included in the customs area, but the trade statistics of these islands are included with those of New Caledonia.

There are no free areas.

NEW GUINEA (TRUST TERRITORY)

The customs area comprises Northeastern New Guinea, the Bismarck Archipelago (New Britain, New Ireland and the Admiralty Islands) and a portion of the Solomon Islands (including Bougainville and Buka).

There are no free areas.

NEW HEBRIDES

There are no free areas.

NEW ZEALAND

The customs area comprises North Island, South Island and outlying islands including Stewart Island, Chatham Islands and minor islands (e.g., Kermadec Islands and Campbell Island) but excludes Cook Islands, the Tokelau (or Union) Islands and Niue Island. Trade with the Cook Islands, Niue Island and the Tokelau Islands is excluded from the foreign trade statistics of New Zealand.

NEW ZEALAND (continued)	The value of the movement of goods to and from the Cook Islands, Niue Island and the Tokelau Islands is separately compiled from New Zealand customs entries. There are no free areas.
NICARAGUA	There are no free areas.
NIGER	There are no free areas. Niger is a member of the West African Customs Union.
NIGERIA	There are no free areas.
NIUE ISLAND	There are no free areas.
NORFOLK ISLAND	There are no free areas.
NORTH BORNEO	Beginning 16 September 1963, named Sabah (which see).
NORWAY	There are no free areas. Customs control is not maintained on Svalbard and Jan Mayen Islands.
PACIFIC ISLANDS (TRUST TERRITORY)	Comprises the Caroline, Marshall and Marianas Islands (except Guam), and extends from 1° to 20° north latitude and from 130° to 172° east longitude. There are no free areas.
PACIFIC ISLANDS UNDER U.S. ADMINISTRATION	The customs area consists of Midway Island, Wake Island, and the Ryukyu Islands (including Daito Islands) south of 29° north latitude. There is a free area at Naha, Okinawa.
PAKISTAN	There are no free areas.
PANAMA	The customs area excludes the Panama Canal Zone. There is a free area in the city of Colon. Data on the movement of goods into and out of the free area and customs bonded warehouses are published separately.

PANAMA CANAL ZONE   The cities of Balboa and Cristobal are within the
                     geographical area of the Canal Zone; these ports
                     handle foreign trade of both the Republic of
                     Panama and the Canal Zone.

PAPUA   The customs area comprises, in addition to south-
                     eastern New Guinea, the following groups of is-
                     lands: D'Entrecasteaux, Louisiade, Trobriand and
                     Woodlark.

                     There are no free area.

PARAGUAY

PENON DE VELEZ   Part of the customs area of Spain (which see).
DE LA GOMERA

PERU   There are no free areas.

PHILIPPINES   There are no free areas.

PITCAIRN ISLAND   There are no free areas.

POLAND   There are no free areas.

PORTUGAL   The customs area includes in addition to continen-
                     tal Portugal the archipelago of Madeira and the
                     Azores.

                     There are no free areas.

PORTUGUESE GUINEA   The customs area consists of the entire continental
                     territory of Portuguese Guinea and the small ad-
                     jacent islands, the most important of which are the
                     islands of Bissau, Bolama, Bubaque, Orango, Rosa,
                     Formosa, Uno, Caraxe, Carabela and Pichiche
                     (Bi jagos Archipelago).

                     There are no free areas.

PORTUGUESE INDIA   Now part of the customs area of India.

PORTUGUESE TIMOR   The customs area comprises the eastern part of the
                     island of Timor and the territory of Ocusse-Ambe-
                     no, the island of Atauro and the islet of Jaco.

                     There is a "free area" at Baucau airport, where
                     there is a tax-free store selling tax- and duty-free
                     merchandise to passengers travelling abroad.

PUERTO RICO	Included in the customs area of the United States (which see).
QATAR	There are no free areas.
REUNION	Part of the customs area of France, but for statistical purposes it is considered as a separate territory.
	There are no free areas.
ROMANIA	There are no free areas.
RWANDA	Prior to 1 January 1964 Rwanda and Burundi formed a customs union.
	There are no free areas.
RYUKYU ISLANDS	(See Pacific Islands under U.S. Administration.)
SABAH	Prior to 16 September 1963, known as North Borneo.
	There is a free area in Labuan. Duties are, however, levied on intoxicating liquors, tobacco and petroleum products when entered for local consumption. Matches are also dutiable.
ST. HELENA	The customs area includes Ascension Island, Tristan da Cunha and other smaller islands.
	There are no free areas.
ST. KITTS-NEVIS-ANGUILLA	There are no free areas. (See Leeward Islands).
ST. LUCIA	There are no free areas. (See Windward Islands).
ST. PIERRE AND MIQUELON	There are no free areas.
ST. VINCENT	There are no free areas. (See Windward Islands).
SAN MARINO	San Marino forms a customs union with Italy (which see).
SAO TOME AND PRINCIPE	There are no free areas.
SARAWAK	There are no free areas.

SAUDI ARABIA	The Neutral Zone is not part of the customs area of Saudi Arabia. There are no free areas.
SENEGAL	Senegal is a member of the West African Customs Union. It also forms a customs union with Mauritania.
SEYCHELLES	The customs area consists of Seychelles and its Dependencies, the principal ones of which are Mahe, Praslin, Silhouette, La Digue, Curieuse and Felicite. The are no free areas.
SIERRA LEONE	There are no free areas.
SINGAPORE	Singapore is basically a free area, but revenue duties are imposed on intoxicating liquors, tobacco and petroleum when entered for local consumption. Protective duties are also levied on a number of other items. Originally revenue duties were imposed on 51 items covering intoxicating liquors, tobacco and petroleum. Since 1965 some protective duties were imposed on an additional number of items and by 1 March 1968 the list of commodity items for which duties are collected had been extended to 239 items making a total of 290 items in all.
SOMALIA	There are no free areas.
SOUTH AFRICA	Customs area includes Lesotho, Botswana, Swaziland and Namibia. There are no free areas.
SOUTH WEST AFRICA	Beginning 12 June 1968, named Namibia (which see).
SOUTHERN RHODESIA	There are no free areas.
SOUTHERN YEMEN	Prior to 30 November 1967, known as Aden and the Protectorate of South Arabia. Aden is a free area. Duties are levied on tobacco and its manufactures, intoxicating liquors, motor spirit and aerated waters when entered for local consumption.

SPAIN

The customs area consists of the Spanish mainland, the Balearic Islands, the Canary Islands, the territories of Ceuta and Melilla, with their dependencies of Alhucemas, Chafarinas and Penon de Velex de la Gomera.

There are free areas in Barcelona, Cadiz and Vigo. The Canary Islands, the territories of Ceuta and Melilla and their dependencies of Alhucemas, Chafarinas and Penon de Velez de la Gomera also correspond to the concept of a "free area", but are really "free territories", in that goods are exempt from export and import duties throughout their geographical area, with the exception of certain small non-customs taxes.

Movements of goods between the rest of the customs area and the free areas are included in the regular statistics of special trade. Data on goods moving to or from the free area from or to foreign countries are published separately by customs tariff divisions with a summary by tariff sections; however, movements of goods from abroad into customs bonded warehouses are not recorded. Data on the quantity and value of goods imported or exported by the Canary Islands, the territories of Ceuta and Melilla and their dependencies are published by country of origin and country of real destination by customs tariff items.

SPANISH EQUATORIAL REGION

Now Equatorial Guinea (which see).

SPANISH NORTH AFRICA

Comprises Ceuta and Melilla with their dependencies of Alhucemas, Chafarinas and Penon de Velez de la Gomera. Part of the customs area of Spain (which see).

SPANISH SAHARA

There are no free areas.

SUDAN

There are no free areas.

SURINAM

There are no free areas.

SWAZILAND

Is included in the customs area of South Africa (which see).

SWEDEN

There are free areas in the ports of Stockholm, Goteborg (or Gothenburg) and Malmo.

SWEDEN (continued)	The movement of goods from the free areas to the rest of the customs area is recorded as imports at the time of movement. Goods from the rest of the customs area to the free areas are recorded as exports when shipped from the free areas to foreign countries. The movement of goods abroad from the free areas (i.e., direct re-exports) is, however, not recorded.
SWITZERLAND	The customs area does not correspond to the geographical area owing to the fact that the Principality of Liechtenstein constitutes a customs enclave of Switzerland. The German district of Busingen and the Italian Commune of Campione are also Swiss customs enclaves. The Swiss valleys of Samnaun and Sampuoir are customs exclaves.
	There are no free areas.
SYRIA	There is a free area at Damascus.
	Separate data are not available on the movement of merchandise into and out of the free area except for goods sent into the rest of the customs area. Commodities re-exported from the free area to foreign countries are recorded in the indirect transit statistics.
TANZANIA, UNITED REPUBLIC OF	Comprises Tanganyika and Zanzibar (including Pemba).
THAILAND	There are no free areas.
TOGO	A free area is located in Togo port.
TOKELAU ISLANDS	The customs area of the Tokelau (or Union) Islands comprises the atolls of Atafu, Nukunono and Fakaofu.
	There are no free areas.
TONGA	There are no free areas.
TRINIDAD AND TOBAGO	There are no free areas.
TRUCIAL OMAN	There are no free areas.
TUNISIA	The customs area includes, in addition to the mainland, the Tunisian islands.

TUNISIA (continued)	There are no free areas.
TURKEY	There are two free areas in Istanbul and one in Iskenderun. One of the free areas in Istanbul is limited to the trade of Oriental rugs.
TURKS AND CAICOS ISLANDS	There are no free areas.
UGANDA	There are no free areas.
UNION ISLANDS	(See Tokelau Islands).
UNION OF SOVIET SOCIALIST REPUBLICS	There are no free areas.
UNITED ARAB REPUBLIC	There are free areas in Alexandria, Port Said, Suez and in the interior of the country.
	Activities in the free areas include construction and assembly of private cars, lorries, tractors, planes and ships, and repairs. Any industry can be established in the free areas provided they do not compete with similar local industries. All kinds of equipment and machinery imported for construction in a free area are exempted from customs duties and taxes. Customs duties and taxes are charged on goods released from a free area for local consumption as if they were imported from abroad and in accordance with their state after manufacture even if they contain raw material of local origin. Export customs duties and taxes are charged on goods and local materials entering a free area.
UNITED KINGDOM	The customs area comprises Great Britain, Northern Ireland and the Isle of Man, but excludes the Channel Islands.
	There are no free areas.
	Beginning 1959, external trade statistics refer to the customs area and the Channel Islands.
UNITED STATES	The customs area includes Puerto Rico. Alaska and Hawaii are included prior as well as subsequent to Statehood.
	There are free areas known as foreign trade zones in New York, New Orleans, San Francisco, Seattle,

UNITED STATES
(continued)

Toledo, Honolulu and Mayaguez and Penuelas
(Puerto Rico). The free areas conform to the general definition except in regard to exports which
may not be sent to all foreign destinations without being subject to export controls.

Data on domestic and foreign merchandise entered into the free areas are recorded not at the time
of admission but at the time the merchandise is
shipped from the free areas except that:

(1) Foreign merchandise for which privilege
has been requested of paying duty within
two years at rates in effect at time of arrival
in zone is recorded in imports at time of
request, and in re-exports if exported from
free area;

(2) Domestic merchandise (including foreign
goods cleared for domestic consumption or
for movement under customs supervision)
entered into the zone for eventual return
to the rest of the customs area after storage
or processing, is not recorded at all.

Movements, via the free areas, of foreign goods
into the rest of the customs area and of domestic
goods to foreign countries are included in the
regular import and export statistics. Foreign goods
re-exported directly to foreign countries from
the free areas are included in the in-transit statistics.

In addition to the inclusions in the trade statistics
described above, separate data by value and quantity on the total movements of goods into and out
of the free areas are published annually by the
Foreign-Trade Zones Board in the "Annual Report
of the Foreign-Trade Zones Board to the Congress
of the United States".

UNITED STATES
VIRGIN ISLANDS

There are no free areas.

UPPER VOLTA

Upper Volta is a member of the West African
Customs Union.

There are no free areas.

URUGUAY

The ports of Colonia and Nueva Palmir are free
areas.

VATICAN CITY STATE	(See Holy See).
VENEZUELA	A free area exists at Estado Nueva Esparta on Margarita Island.
VIET-NAM, REPUBLIC OF	There are no free areas.
WAKE ISLAND	(See Pacific Islands under U.S. Administration).
WALLIS AND FUTUNA ISLANDS	There are no free areas. The trade statistics of these islands are included with those of New Caledonia.
WEST AFRICA, CUSTOMS UNION OF	The following seven West African Republics form a customs union: Dahomey, Ivory Coast, Mali, Mauritania, Niger, Senegal, Upper Volta.
WESTERN SAMOA	There are no free areas.
WEST IRIAN	Prior to 1 October 1962, known as Netherlands New Guinea. From 1 October 1962 to 30 April 1963, known as West New Guinea (West Irian). Part of the customs area of Indonesia (which see).
WINDWARD ISLANDS	The Windward Islands comprise four separate customs territories, namely Dominica, Grenada, St. Lucia and St. Vincent.
YEMEN	There are no free areas.
YUGOSLAVIA	The customs area includes, as an enclave, the Yugoslavian free trade zone in the port of Salonika in Greece. There also exist free areas in the ports of Beograd (Danube), Koper, Novi Sad (Danube), Rijeka and Split.
ZAMBIA	Prior to 24 October 1964, known as Northern Rhodesia. There are no free areas.
ZANZIBAR AND PEMBA	Part of the customs area of the United Republic of Tanzania (which see).

LOCATION, FACILITIES AND SERVICES OF A SELECTED SAMPLING OF SEVEN FREE ZONES AND FREE PORT AREAS

	Antwerp, Belgium	Bermuda	Willemstad, Curacao	Grand Bahama Free Port	Colon Free Zone, Panama	Mayaguez, Puerto Rico	Shannon International Airport
Geographical Location	Central north coast of Europe	Atlantic island, off US east coast	South American north coast, off Venezuela	Bahama Islands, Florida east coast	Crossroads of Atlantic-Pacific in Central America	Central Caribbean Sea	Limerick, Ireland
Principal area served	Western Europe to Iron Curtain and Italian border	US east coast, Canada Caribbean area	Northern South America, Central America, and Caribbean region	Caribbean Island, US east coast, Central America, some South America	Northern and Western regions of South America, Caribbean, Central America, Mexico, Far East	Caribbean Islands, US east coast, Central America	Western Europe Scandinavia Africa
Year founded	1946	1950	1956	1955	1948	1960	1958
Land area	12,000 acres	100 acres	20 acres	100 acres	100 acres (45 being added)	35 acres	300 acres
A-Transshipping and warehousing	A	A	A	A	A	A	A
B-Assembling and processing	B	B	B	B	B	B	B
C-Manufacturing	C	C	C	C	C	C	C
Principal Transportation service	Sea, air, rail and truck	Sea and air	Sea and air	Sea and air	Sea, air, rail and truck	Sea and air	Sea and air

LOCATION, FACILITIES AND SERVICES OF A SELECTED SAMPLING OF SEVEN FREE ZONES AND FREE PORT AREAS
(Continued)

	Antwerp, Belgium	Bermuda	Willemstad, Curacao	Grand Bahama Free Port	Colon Free Zone, Panama	Mayaguez, Puerto Rico	Shannon International Airport
Nearest port	On site	11 miles (30 minutes)	On site	On site	1,800 yards (5 minutes)	4.5 miles (15 minutes)	10 miles (30 minutes)
Nearest airport	40 miles (75 minutes)	15 miles (1 hour)	8 miles (20 minutes)	10 miles (25 minutes)	50 miles (75 minutes)	3.5 miles	On site
Nearest railroad	On site	None	None	None	On site for transisthmian service	None	On site
Controlling Agency	City of Antwerp Port Administration	Bermuda Crown Lands Corp.	Bureau of Economic Affairs	Grand Bahama Port Authority (pvt. corp.)	Colon Free Zone Authority (govt.)	Puerto Rico Industrial Development Co.	(Govt.) Shannon Free Airport Development Co.
Government Warehousing	No	Yes	No	Yes	Yes	No	No
Leased Warehousing	Yes	Yes	Yes	Yes	Yes	Yes	Yes
Commercial Warehousing	Yes	No	Yes	Yes	Yes	No	Possible
User-owned Facilities	Yes	No (Crown Lands Corp. will alter buildings to specif.)	Yes	Yes	Yes	Yes	Yes

LOCATION, FACILITIES AND SERVICES OF A SELECTED SAMPLING OF SEVEN FREE ZONES AND FREE PORT AREAS
(Continued)

	Antwerp, Belgium	Bermuda	Willemstad, Curacao	Grand Bahama Free Port	Colon Free Zone, Panama	Mayaguez, Puerto Rico	Shannon International Airport
Incentives							
Fiscal	Yes	Yes	Yes	No taxes	Yes	Yes	Yes
Investment*	Yes	Yes	Negotiable	Negotiable	Yes	Yes	Yes
Industrial†	Yes	Yes	Negotiable	Negotiable	Yes	Yes	Yes
Foreign base corporations	Yes	Yes	Yes	Yes	Yes	Yes	Yes

*Investment incentives take various forms, not all of which are common to all free trade areas. They include repatriation of capital, tax relief, government grants against capital outlay, etc.

†The same applies to industrial incentives. In some cases, laws relating to locally owned industry may apply to manufacturing within the free trade zone — or they may not. Tax exemptions may also apply to certain industrial activity — noncompetitive within the country, for instance.

EXPORT PRICING AND PROFIT/LOSS MANAGEMENT

BACKGROUND

The profitable operation of an export sales function implies that export sales earnings are to be measured apart from those of the domestic sales department and even apart from those of the international division which may be concerned with all overseas activities. Therefore, it is usually recommended both for operational and analytical purposes that the export organization be placed on its own profit/loss (P/L) budget.

This enables the export sales department to act as a marketing entity with its own self-contained plan of action rather than as a mere adjunct of the shipping and/or sales section. "Export Sales," as the department is often called, can now have its area of geographic jurisdiction; it can develop its own marketing plans and strategies; it can consequently develop and assume its own sales forecast and income statement or profit/loss responsibility.

The task of formulating a budget is facilitated by the fact that each product sold for export has already been costed out on a per unit of production basis. The information should be available through periodically updated cost-price studies (CPS's).

Each CPS, therefore, can form the basis of an "Export Sales" cost per unit of product analysis.

The additional sales generated through exports do not usually alter to any great extent the domestic sales forecast and cost/sales ratio unless the export sector begins to contribute more than 10% of total factory sales. In any case, one can expect manufacturing costs (fixed and variable) to remain relatively stable per unit of production once the export sales forecast is integrated with the corporate

266

sales projection. Any significant deviation of actual sales performance from the established target will naturally change the cost picture. This is the reason why companies periodically "recost" their products during the course of the marketing year.

COST PER UNIT OF PRODUCTION ANALYSIS

Figure 12.1 is an example of a typical CPS form for an over-the-counter product. The gross operating margin in this instance is 40% of sales. However, Export Sales gross operating margin may be somewhat different, even assuming no change in net factory billing prices between exports and domestic sales. This will be because departmental costs (the general and administrative expenses) will be different for exports than for domestic sales.

A totaling of all product CPS's will provide the overall product cost mix for domestic operations from which the export sales manager can now determine his own product cost mix and estimate the percentage contribution *his* sales will make to *total* corporate sales for these given products.

For example, assume that the company manufactures and sells three products, A, B, and C with net factory (FOB) selling prices as shown below. Product A's sales forecast is $900,000; product B's forecast is $1.8 million and its total operating cost is $0.72 per unit; product C's forecast is $2.7 million and its total operating cost is also $0.72 per unit. The factory billing price in all three cases is shown below:

Product	$/Unit	$ Sales	Unit* Sales	Op. Cost/Unit*	Tot. Op. Cost
A	1.00	$ 900,000	900,000	$0.60	$ 540,000
B	1.20	$1,800,000	1,500,000	$0.72	$1,080,000
C	1.20	$2,700,000	2,250,000	$0.72	$1,620,000
Total		$5,400,000			$3,240,000

*Unit here refers to a package of a dozen.

The percentage of total operating costs to domestic sales is about 60%. This could remain the same with the export department, *if* manufacturing and other costs were to remain proportional to sales as planned production increases to meet the requirements of the export sector. Consequently, a forecast increase of 10% over domestic projections would generate $540,000 in additional sales and might generate $324,000 in additional costs. Conversely, the percentage contribution of the export sector to total corporate sales for these products would be 9.04%.

However, situations are rarely so simple. Some costs remain fixed while others are indeed quite variable. Increasing production to create special inventories for

FIGURE 12.1: COST PRICE STUDY FORM — DOMESTIC OPERATIONS

PRODUCT A

	%
Manufacturing Cost	
Ingredient material	10.4
Packaging material	19.7
Direct labor	1.3
Mfg. overhead	1.3
Subtotal	32.7
Cost of shipper	0.7
Distribution expense	4.2
Plant general services, research & depreciation	5.9
Total	43.5
Administrative	3.7
Marketing except advertising and promotion	9.4
Returns and allowances discounts	3.4
Subtotal	16.5
Total operating cost	60.0
Gross operating margin	40.0
Billing price	100.0

export can have the effect of reducing total costs if the plant's fixed cost areas are not being fully utilized, or it might actually raise the total costs if the plant is currently operating at capacity and new capitalization is required to meet increased sales activity.

The thorny question of departmental cost allocation must also be raised. The perceptive export manager, with his own P/L responsibility, can insist that the accounting department allocate any potential cost savings to his sector. He may temporarily succeed because by the time companies do agree to establish separate P/L areas for international operations, their computers and/or accounting procedures are still programmed to handle input data solely on the basis of domestic operations.

A special export P/L with its own income and balance sheet statements, could create a certain amount of havoc unless the company's financial manager decided henceforth to treat the export sector as a permanent part of the enterprise's sales and marketing structure and to develop a true cost allocation system based upon product performance anywhere in the world.

Another source of difficulty is the possible lack of relevance which certain domestic cost factors have in the export sector and the need to include other costs that do not normally occur domestically. Two problem areas are advertising, and research and development. The latter is often not allocated to export. This explains the frequent higher profitability that the foreign department shows over the domestic.

The development costs of many products have simply been absorbed internally *before* those products have begun to be sold overseas. The same is true, to a lesser extent, with advertising expenditures. A company's export sector, (indeed, its entire international operation) may receive unintentional "spin-off" benefits from the domestic campaign without having to pay a penny. This ranges all the way from know-how to point-of-purchase materials and completed story boards for commercials; and sometimes the commercials themselves.

THE EXPORT PROFIT/LOSS STATEMENT

An OTC goods company will often quote a *delivered* price to its customers. This shows up as a *distribution expense* on line #8 of Figure 12.1. This same company, if situated near a port city, could consider waiving this expense item in the export sector. Hence, a special export CPS form for Product A could be created as in Figure 12.2. Further administrative, departmental, selling and marketing expenses may be entirely different in Exports. There might even be some fresh costs such as the need for export packaging or crating along with maritime transport and insurance expense if the company has a policy of quoting C&F or CIF destination.

Figure 12.3 casts for consideration an Export Profit/Loss pro forma statement

FIGURE 12.2: EXPORT COST PRICE STUDY FORM, PRODUCT XYZ

Total Cost of Sales 49.3%
Expenses (less advertising) 6.5%
Full Available (Gross operating profits) 44.2%

FIGURE 12.3: GENERAL EXPORT PROFIT AND LOSS ESTIMATE

Gross Sales	%
Returns & Allowances	—
Discounts	
Net Sales (CIF to Destination)	100
Cost of Sales	
Mfg. Cost	39.3
Shipping	10.0
Total Cost Sales	49.3
Gross Operating Margin	50.7
Expenses	
Corporate Assessments	0.5
Depreciation	
General Administration	
Advertising & Promotion	20.0
Selling Commissions	2.0
Regional Administration	2.0
Divisional Administration	2.0
Total Expenses	26.5
Pre-Tax Profit/ (Loss)	24.2

that attempts to resolve this difficulty. The cost of sales is shown at 49.3%. This includes the products' manufacturing costs (taken from Figure 12.1, and assuming the percentages shown hold true for all the company's products) at 32.7%, shipper cost at 0.7% and line 9 at 5.9% (note that line #8, distribution expense, has been omitted), for a sub-total of 39.3% of sales. Historical analysis and current international transport costs surveys will provide an estimate of average percentage shipping expenses to sales, assuming the policy is to quote CIF. It has been shown here at 10% of sales for a total cost of sales of 49.3%.

Expenses as shown include three items: corporate assessments, depreciation and general administration, which are usually costs allocated by the comptroller based upon Export Sales usage of corporate facilities. The advertising and promotion item is a flexible entry; its extent or even existence depending upon the products' need for such expenditures.

Selling commissions are shown to be a relatively low percentage of sales because quotations are normally made on a net basis except when dealing through certain brokers and/or manufacturers' representatives. Regional administrative expenses relate generally to travel and entertainment abroad while divisional administrative expenses cover the costs of operating the export department.

It is important to note that the resulting pro forma income statement or budget estimate is only a mirror of domestic selling prices from which point the domestic sales for forecast has been derived. The assumption is that the overseas forecast for finished goods also stems from estimated unit sales at prevailing domestic prices. Unfortunately, that which is a competitive price level in the home market may be under-or over-priced in any number of overseas markets.

EXPORT PRICING

The next objective, therefore, is to find the desired price to the end-user, or consumer, in each overseas market where the product is to be sold, and then work the price through existing overseas trade discount structures, through the landing costs (import duties, etc.) and international transport charges back to the exporters' FOB vessel selling price.

The exporter may find that he must eventually reduce his selling price in order to remain competitive, or that in fact he may be able to raise his prices. In any case, he will usually have to consider altering his dollar sales forecast, which naturally means altering the pro forma income statement.

The retailer or dealer discount will vary by product line and type of outlet, and the same rules which obtain in the United States are applicable among many overseas markets. Drug traders generally purchase at *list less a third* (33 1/3%), while food trades usually buy at *list less a quarter* (25%), "list" being the price to the consumer or end-user. Assuming that the overall retail discount in any one particular market is list less 33%, the markup then becomes the wholesale price plus 50%.

Many import distributors of non-durable consumer goods insist on a 15% mark-up over their landed cost, and agree to absorb the actual landing costs outside of import duties in their mark-up. This means that what the importer refers to as the "landed cost" is really the CIF-duty-paid price which he must pay to legally gain possession of the merchandise. Reciprocally a 15% mark-up for a distributor provides him with a 13% discount on the retail, discounted price. (Price-discount structures are calculated in reverse, starting with the list price.)

A brief market survey consisting of several store checks on a random sample basis will indicate what the retail price of a produce should be in order to be competitive. Working back from the retail price, a discount structure may easily be fashioned as follows:

Retail	Importer (Wholesaler)	CIF-Duty Paid
List less 33%	less 13% off 33%	Landed cost

The U.S. local currency (LC) exchange ratio should be reconciled at this point. This can be done without difficulty within the framework of the import price structure as recommended below (assume U.S. $1.00 = 2.00 LC):

Retail price unit (LC)	Retail price per dozen* (LC)	Retail Discount (33 1/3% LC)	Wholesale Discount (13% LC)	Landed Cost
5.00	60.00	40.00	5.20**	34.80 ($17.80/ doz.)

*It is assumed that the selling price is on a per dozen basis.
**This is the reciprocal of 15%.

Or, working forward from the landed cost:

Landed Cost U.S.$	LC	Wholesale Mark-up (15%)	Retail Mark-up (33 1/3%)	Retail Price per dozen	Retail Price per unit (LC)
$17.40	34.80	5.20	40.00	60.00	5.00

This landed cost, given the above prevailing price-discount structure in the foreign market, is the one both importer and exporter must aim to achieve if the product is to be competitive.

If there are no import duties, the U.S. CIF price will equal the landed cost. If import duties are a factor—and they would be in the vast majority of overseas markets—the CIF price will then have to be worked back further.

The following is an example:

1. Import duty = 25% on the CIF price

2. Working back from the landed cost, the desired CIF price should be the landed cost less 20% or, expressing this reciprocally, CIF plus 25% equals the landed cost.

3. Landed cost less 20% = CIF price
$17.40 − $3.48 = $13.92

4. Or, CIF plus 25% = Landed cost
$13.92 + $3.48 = $17.40

In this particular instance, if a competitive product has an end-user price of 5.00 LC, and all the above factors exist, the exporter must price his product to reach a CIF figure not exceeding $13.92/dozen, or $1.16/unit. Import duties, mark-ups and discounts may be expected to remain relatively constant at least over a period of one year. Transport costs also tend to remain constant within predictable time periods. It then becomes feasible to draw a direct mathematical relationship between the end-user unit price in local currency and the exporter's CIF price in U.S. dollars. The preceding example indicates that given a tariff of 25% on the CIF price, a commodity quotation of CIF $13.92 U.S. should retail at 5.00 LC per unit. A constant, k, may then be derived by dividing 5.00 by 13.92; the quotient 0.36 is the constant.

Hence, the desirable and competitive CIF price per dozen for the above given market may be found by dividing the unit retail price by the constant, k, which in this instance is 0.36.

It now becomes possible to engage in a complete survey of end-user prices for all products in a given market having specified distribution channels with a common price discount structure and import duty cost, and divide the end-user price by the constant as previously derived, to speedily develop a competitive CIF price list to see if it is competitive by multiplying all CIF prices by k.

The desired CIF price, however, is shown on a per dozen basis. The CIF price per unit in the above case would be $1.16. Assuming that the product in reference was Product A (Figure 12.1), the exporter could actually consider increasing his price from $1.00/unit, assuming there were no legal obstacles.

Variations in company policy will cause conceptual variations as to what is or what is not to be included in the export budget. The objectives of effecting pricing remain nevertheless the same, i.e., to find the desirable end-user price in the local market, to place all intermediary cost/price factors into fixed mathematical relations to one another, and to compute the numerical constant for the forecast period that will relate the local price that must be met with the exporter's own selling price.

HOW TO MINIMIZE EXPORT SALES COLLECTION RISKS

BACKGROUND

The decision by the exporter in favor of specific payment terms to his overseas customers is influenced by company policy, by the customer's credit rating, and by the financial, economic and political conditions that exist in the importing customer's country. Company policy is basically directed by corporate objectives. These may relate to achieving optimum turnover of inventories and receiveables as well as to the broader aims of the corporate whole. This has already been discussed elsewhere, along with the methodology for determining an overseas customer's credit rating.

The evaluation of an importing country's financial viability, i.e., the capacity of its banking institutions to pay for importers' purchases in exporters' currencies, is the subject matter of this chapter.

THE CONCEPT OF IMPORT CAPACITY

It is often a fact of life that although an importer's own credit rating is impeccable, the financial resources of his country may be inadequate to discharge his foreign obligations fully and on time. This form of incapacity has today become a major source of inconvenience to both exporters and importers. It has been noted in previous chapters that an importer's bank requires foreign exchange (foreign currencies) in order to discharge the importer's obligation.

In other words, the importer's bank must possess reserves in the exporter's currency into which the importer's local money may be converted at the prevailing rate of exchange; or the importer's bank must at least possess monetary assets which may ultimately be converted into the exporter's currency and credited to the exporter's bank and finally to the exporter's account.

It does not always follow that because import demand is high, as a consequence of income changes and/or as a result of implementing economic development projects requiring large scale imports of capital products, import capacity will also be high. The reader has already observed the liquidity problem that exists in the world today.

To make a long story short, the developing nations (or "soft currency" countries, as they are often called) are no longer alone in suffering short term or long term crises. It must be recalled that the United Kingdom, followed by more than twenty other countries (some of them industrialized), were forced to devalue their currencies by a range of 14% to 20%, between November 18th, 1967, and the following spring. Although the pound sterling rise in value followed the floating of the dollar in August, 1971, it again devalued in the summer of 1972.

Changes in a country's level of international liquidity is of critical significance in anticipating not only fluctuations in its exchange rate, but also changes in its capacity to pay for imports. The concept of import capacity expresses the capacity, therefore, of an importing country's banking system to liquidate bills of exchange (exporters' drafts drawn on importers' banks) on or before the contractual due date. Its primary assumption is a correlation between a nation's international liquidity and its import financing capabilities. This seems to be supported by empirical evidence in Figure 13.1.

In quantitative terms, import capacity may be defined as a country's year end liquidity position multiplied by a factor of four to reflect average global collection rates which approximate ninety days per bill of exchange. This means that, on the average, exporters shipping overseas finally receive payment for their goods about ninety days from the bill of lading date, which should conform to the date on the exporter's invoices, and which should also conform to the date on his draft.

If this is true, a country's banking system needs only three months' "cash," so to speak, with which to finance one year of imports. Or, one may now determine a given country's 1973 import capacity by taking its end-year 1972 liquidity position and multiplying it by the factor of four. The resultant answer would indicate the maximum level of imports an entire country could tolerate (its import capacity) without harboring any significant exchange rate and/or balance of payments disequilibrium.

A country whose projected imports are higher than its import capacity is liable to experience financial difficulties during the period in question. It may have to face the prospects of currency devaluation, and it may have to impose exchange control regulations which ration the availability for foreign exchange to importers. Any exporter wants to be made aware of these developments before they happen.

A country whose projected imports are much lower than its import capacity will probably experience disequilibrium in its exchange rate and/or balance of pay-

FIGURE 13.1: IMPORT CAPACITY FOR SELECTED COUNTRIES (MILLIONS OF U.S. DOLLARS)

Country	Dec. 1969 Liquidity	1970 Imp. Capacity	1970 Imports	Dec. 1970 Liquidity	1971 Imp. Capacity	1971 Imports	Dec. 1971 Liquidity	1972 Imp. Capacity	1972 Imports (est.)
World	78,205	312,820	293,900	92,525	370,100	347,000	117,380	469,520	420,000
United States	16,964	67,856	42,469	14,487	57,948	48,475	12,130	48,520	56,556
United Kingdom	2,527	10,108	21,724	2,827	11,308	24,000	6,583	26,332	28,328
France	3,833	15,332	19,114	4,960	19,840	21,323	8,235	32,940	26,396
Germany	7,129	28,516	29,814	13,610	54,440	34,322	18,382	73,528	38,284
Italy	5,045	20,180	14,970	5,352	21,408	15,960	6,787	27,148	18,000
Japan	3,654	14,616	18,896	4,840	19,360	19,727	15,360	61,440	21,688
Argentina	538	2,152	1,695	673	2,692	1,796	290	1,160	2,000
Chile	344	1,332	931	388	1,552	1,000	221	884	1,000
Brazil	656	2,624	2,849	1,187	4,748	3,370	1,746	6,984	4,000
Denmark	446	1,784	4,406	484	1,936	4,613	728	2,912	5,000

ments manifesting itself in the form of surplus liquidity. It might have to up-value its currency, a boon to exporters of the area, but of negative value to importers from that country.

A country's international liquidity position is used synonymously with its international reserves. These reserves consist of foreign exchange (a country's holdings of other countries' currencies), gold, reserves with the International Monetary Fund, and SDR's (Special Drawing Rights). Changes in a country's trade will affect changes in its liquidity.

However, there are other variables which will affect the measure of import capacity; e.g., changing payment terms reflecting changes in lines of credit, perhaps as a result of changes in public policy which provide more or less government support to exporters, changes in borrowing and/or lending mechanisms and techniques, etc. Nevertheless, these seem to be short-term variables which do not upset the overall and longer-term relationship between a country's international liquidity and its import financing capabilities.

These short-term variables are quite well summarized in the Balance of Payments equation worked out by the economist, Kindleberger (1):

$$X - M - LTC - STC_p = O = STC_o + G$$

$X - M$ = Current Account Balance (includes merchandise trade balance)
LTC = Long Term Capital Transactions
STC_p = Private Short Term Capital Transactions
STC_o = Official Short Term Capital Transactions
G = Gold Movements

The equation is divided between "autonomous" movements on the left side and "compensatory" movements on the right side. The autonomous movements occur without any avowed objective of restoring equilibrium in the balance of payments. Indeed, if the national economy itself is in equilibrium relative to its multi-national setting, then the balance of payments equation will be satisfied without having any compensatory movements take place. Consequently, compensatory movements are defined as induced capital and/or gold transfers destined to restore equilibrium from a disequilibrium position caused by uneven autonomous flows, e.g., an excess of imports over exports. But these compensatory movements (gold transfers and transfers of short term capital, namely convertible foreign exchange among central banking systems) are all short term in their duration and effects.

Where does one find the data to develop an Import Capacity Chart? The data is published monthly by the International Monetary Fund in a publication called, *International Financial Statistics*. The appropriate pages have been reproduced at the end of this chapter.

The significance of the measure of import capacity to the exporter lies in its use as one of several management tools to assist him in deciding lines of credit to overseas customers which will minimize the risks of bad debts and of overdue collections.

MULTI-BANK COLLECTION HISTORY

Another valuable management tool is the collection history on overseas drafts that is published by some major banks for the exclusive use of their clients. The Chase Manhattan Bank publishes such a guide under the title *Guide For Exporters*, which may be purchased at a $60.00 annual fee. This guide is also commonly available at any business library.

These bank guides to their own overseas collection histories suffer from the singularity of their experiences. All banks do not operate in all countries, and there is a variation in collection experience from bank to bank in given countries. For example, exporters may generally expect faster collections on documents routed through an English or Canadian bank on shipments to Trinidad & Tobago than if those same documents were routed through an American bank.

FOREIGN CREDIT INSURANCE ASSOCIATION RECORDS

The operation of this organization has been discussed in another chapter. What remains to be stated is that companies whose foreign receivables are insured or insurable by FCIA will automatically receive periodic reports from FCIA ranking individual countries by both credit and political risk.

AN EXPORT SALES RISK EVALUATION CHART

What follows is a recommended format for exporters to follow in systematically developing a sales risk evaluation chart based on the inputs discussed earlier in this section. It should be stated, however, that such a chart is not a panacea for all decision-making in establishing export sales credit terms. The exporter is advised to contact his bank periodically to continually check upon the changing financial situation in specific countries.

Explanation of Classifications and Codes

Country Designations: One hundred and five countries are included in this sample survey. They are separated into industrial and developing nations before being further divided into their geographical areas. The country listings (26 industrial nations and 79 developing states) were obtained from the International Monetary Fund's *International Financial Statistics* (Volume XXV, No. 6, June, 1972).

Collection History, 1971 Summary and First Half 1972 Summary: This is a composite perspective of multi-bank collection experiences for documentary sight and time drafts. The exporter is urged to rely on reports from a variety of banking sources in developing this part of the chart for greater accuracy and reliability.

At this writing, it was found both convenient and appropriate to contrast the year-end 1971 collection summary with the experience of the first half of 1972. The reader is nevertheless cautioned again against rash judgments in settling upon a particular line of credit or payment terms. There are few bad debts in export transactions dealing with documentary sight and time drafts. However, delayed payments stemming from a variety of reasons, ranging from the vagaries of human nature to central bank exchange rate difficulties and other economic and political factors, are to be expected.

The data presented covers *paid collections* only. The Sight Draft letter codes indicate the percentage of collections completed within four weeks of the *dating* of the drafts. The Time Draft letter codes indicate the percentage of collections completed within four weeks of the *maturity date* shown on those drafts. The letter coding system was simply and quite arbitrarily developed by the author. More sophisticated, computerized coding, together with instant feedback systems are also available.

Code	Percentage Collected Within Four Weeks
A	80% +
B	60 to 79%
C	40 to 59%
D	39% −

Risk Coverage For First Half 1972: The exporter is already aware that many foreign receivables can be insured and even discounted without recourse to the exporter by banks who have themselves purchased a comprehensive FCIA policy. This enables these banks to offer 180 day (maximum) credit and political risk insurance on their customers' export receivables. Moreover, these same banks will often discount those receivables, providing the exporter with almost "instant cash," on a *no recourse* basis.

It may further be noted that the discounting bank will also frequently discount the foreign receivable, if it is of "A" grade, at 100% of its value, again on a *no recourse* basis.

The Foreign Credit Insurance Association establishes it own criteria for the definition of "A," "B," "C," and "D" grade categories to which specific countries are assigned. This has been discussed in detail in an earlier chapter. The reader is simply reminded that these grades relate to rankings by economic, monetary and political risk factors. The proposed codes shown on the following page for the Risk Evaluation Chart have been selected on the basis of one particular bank's manner of insurance coverage to their customers, under that bank's own FCIA policy. Slight variations in rankings may occur from bank to bank.

Code	Percentage of Foreign Invoice to Be Discounted Without Recourse to Seller on Max. 180 Day Terms.
A	100%
B	90%
C	65%
D	45%
Dx	Subject To Negotiation

Recommended Payment Terms For Second Half 1972: This is the last column that the exporter may wish to include in his Risk Evaluation Chart. Thus far, the proposed chart makes no mention of a country's import capacity. This can be developed in the same chart by inserting another column before the "Recommended Payment Terms", showing a nation's liquidity margin, i.e., the difference between its import capacity and actual and/or projected imports.

A proposed coding system for the chart's last column is shown below.

Code	Explanation
A	Open Account
B	Time Draft
C	Sight Draft
D	Irrevocable Letter-of-Credit
Dx	Irrevocable Confirmed Letter-of-Credit

The final product is an Export Sales Risk Evaluation Chart such as the one produced on the next few pages. The value of the chart lies in its being continually reviewed and updated, preferably on a monthly basis.

REFERENCE

(1) Kindleberger, C. P. in *International Economics*, 4th ed., Richard D. Irwin, Inc., Homewood, Ill., 1968, Chapter 24, Page 463.

FIGURE 13.2: EXPORT SALES RISK EVALUATION CHART

1	2	3	4	5	6	7
			1st Half 1972			
Country	Collection Sight Drafts 1971 Summary	History Time Drafts	Collection Sight Drafts First Half 1972 Summary [Only changes from 1971 are indicated]	History Time Drafts	Risk Coverage 1972 [Brackets indicate changes from 1st Quarter, 1972]	Payment Terms 1972
Industrial Countries						
Australia	B	A			A	A
Austria	B	B			B	A
Belgium	B	C			B	B
Canada	A	B			A	A
Denmark	A	A	B	B	B[C]	B[C]
Finland	B	A	C	B	C	B
France	B	C			B	B
Germany W.	C	C			A	B
Greece	D	C			C	C
Iceland	B	A	D	A	B	A
Ireland	B	B	C	C	C	C
Italy	B	B			B	B
Japan	C	A			A	A
Netherlands	B	B			B	B
New Zealand	B	A	C	A	B	B

FIGURE 13.2: (continued)

1 Country	2 Collection Sight Drafts	3 History Time Drafts	4 Collection Sight Drafts	5 History Time Drafts	6 Risk Coverage 1972	7 Payment Terms 1972
Norway	B	Nil			B	C
Portugal	C	A	D	A	C	B
Spain	C	A	D	B	C	B
Sweden	A	A	B	A	B	A[B]
Switzerland	B	C	A	C	A	B
South Africa	B	B	C	B	C	B
United States	C	B	C	C		
United Kingdom	B	C	C	C	B	B
Turkey	LC	Nil			C	D
Yugoslavia	LC	Nil			D	D
Israel	C	B	C	D	B[C]	C
Developing Countries						
South America						
Argentina	C	B	D	C	D[x]	D[x]
Bolivia	C	C	D	C	D	D
Brazil	D	B	C	C	C	C
Chile	D	D			Dx	Dx
Colombia	D	D			D	D
Ecuador	D	C	D	C	C	C
Fr. Guiana	B	B	C	C	C	C
Guyana	C	Nil	D	Nil	C	C

FIGURE 13.2: (continued)

1 Country	2 Collection Sight Drafts	3 History Time Drafts	4 Collection Sight Drafts	5 History Time Drafts	6 Risk Coverage 1972	7 Payment Terms 1972
Paraguay	LC	Nil			D	D
Peru	C	D			C	C
Surinam	C	D			C	D
Uruguay	LC	Nil			D	D
Venezuela	C	C			A	B
Central America						
Costa Rica	D	D			C	D
El Salvador	D	D			C	D
Guatemala	C	B	C	C	C	C
Honduras, Br.	C	C			C	C
Honduras	C	C	LC	Nil	C	C
Mexico	C	D	C	C	C	C
Nicaragua	D	A	C	A	C	C
Panama	B	B	C	C	B[C]	C
Caribbean						
Bahamas	C	Nil			C	C
Barbados	B	B			A	B
Bermuda	A	B	B	C	B	B
Cuba	Nil	Nil				
Dominican Rep.	LC	Nil			D	Dx

FIGURE 13.2: (continued)

1 Country	2 Collection Sight Drafts	3 History Time Drafts	4 Collection Sight Drafts	5 History Time Drafts	6 Risk Coverage 1972	7 Payment Terms 1972
Haiti	D	C			Dx	Dx
Jamaica	C	A	C	B	B	A
Martinique	Nil	Nil			C	C
Netherlands Ant.	C	D	C	C	C	C
Trinidad	C	B	C	C	C	B
Middle East						
Bahrain	D	Nil			D	D
Cyprus	D	Nil	D	C	D	D
Egypt	LC	Nil			Dx	Dx
Iran	D	B			C	C
Iraq	LC	Nil	LC	LC	B	D
Jordan	Nil	Nil			D	D
Kuwait	C				A	C
Lebanon	C	B	C	C	C	C
S. Arabia	D	B			B	B
Syria	LC	Nil			Dx	Dx
Asia						
Afghanistan	LC	Nil	D	Nil	D	Dx
Burma	LC	Nil			Dx	Dx
Bangladesh	LC	Nil			D[C]	Dx

FIGURE 13.2: (continued)

1 Country	2 Collection Sight Drafts	3 History Time Drafts	4 Collection Sight Drafts	5 History Time Drafts	6 Risk Coverage 1972	7 Payment Terms 1972
Cambodia	LC	Nil			Dx[C]	Dx
China, Rep. [Taiwan]	LC	Nil			Dx	D
Ceylon	LC	Nil			Dx	D
Hong Kong	C	C	C		B[C]	C
India	D	Nil		B	C	C
Indonesia	LC	Nil			D[C]	D[C]
Laos	LC	Nil			Dx	Dx
Korea, S.			B	Nil	[C]	[C]
Malaysia			D	C	[C]	[C]
Pakistan, W.			C	Nil	[C]	[D]
Philippines			_C	Nil	[D]	[C]
Singapore	B	D	C	D	C	C
Thailand			LC	Nil	[C]	[C]
Vietnam, S.	LC	Nil	LC	Nil	D	D
Africa						
Algeria	LC	Nil			D	D
Angola	LC	Nil			D	D
Cameroons	Nil	Nil			D	D
Congo, Rep. [Zaire, Rep.]	LC	Nil			D	D
Ethiopia	LC	Nil			Dx	Dx
Ghana	LC	Nil			Dx	Dx

FIGURE 13.2: (continued)

1 Country	2 Collection Sight Drafts	3 History Time Drafts	4 Collection Sight Drafts	5 History Time Drafts	6 Risk Coverage 1972	7 Payment Terms 1972
Ivory Coast	Nil	Nil	D	Nil	D	D
Libya	D	D			Dx	Dx
Kenya	D	B	C	C	C	C
Malawi	D	A	D	D	B	B
Morocco	LC	Nil			D	D
Mozambique	D	Nil			D	D
Nigeria	D	Nil			D	D
Sudan	LC	Nil			D	Dx
Tunisia			Nil	Nil	[D]	[D]
Uganda	C	Nil	D		C	C
Zambia	A	A	D	Nil	B	B
Tanzania	LC	Nil			C	D
Liberia			C	A	[C]	[C]
S.W. Africa			Nil	A	[C]	[C]

Code	Explanation
A	Open Account
B	Time Draft
C	Sight Draft

Code	Explanation
D	Irrevocable Letter of Credit
Dx	Irrevocable Confirmed Letter of Credit
LC	Letter of Credit

THE GLOBAL MANAGEMENT CONCEPT

BACKGROUND

The trend today is toward corporate activities of increasing magnitude at the International level. Many corporate giants sell more overseas and generate greater earnings outside the country than within the United States. This is also becoming true for the larger European and Asian corporate entities.

Much has been written on the problems and opportunities that corporate bigness creates on a multinational level. Two of the more prominent writers on this subject are J.J. Sewan Schreiber *(The American Challenge)* and Peter Drucker *(The Age of Discontinuity)*. This section seeks only to survey observations on the trend toward bigness from the point of view of developing effective management controls over all aspects of globally flung corporate activities.

THE GLOBAL BUSINESS PERSONALITY

Who is "Our Man in Bogota"? Does he represent the same company image as do his associates in Bangkok or in Boston?

The reader will recall the various bank advertisements which used to portray the local man on the job, usually standing in a red-dotted circle. He is a market man and a corporate symbol — the company man who is ready to give needed service to the local customer whether it is at the Place Vendome in Paris, or the Strand in London, or the Berliner Alle in Dusseldorf. For the most part, he is a new man on the scene since 1950, or even later. It is important to understand fully exactly what he represents.

Except for a relatively small group of U.S. companies whose foreign growth began at the turn of the century, the great overseas expansion of U.S. business has occurred since World War II. The old export manager type who ran the global business from a back room in an ivory tower in Pittsburgh, Dayton, Toledo or elsewhere has been replaced by a whole bevy of men on the spot and a staff of globe-trotting executives from the home office.

With the advent of the international company with subsidiaries abroad, business has become complicated and big. Not only has the sales firing line been pushed out beyong the borders of the U.S., but also the production line has gone along with it, posing intricate problems for the company who must establish itself as a local citizen in a foreign land.

Because of this, corporate activities ranging from public relations and marketing to research and development and financial planning in the modern supersensitive world, require the closest type of coordination and control from headquarters. Today, effective management forms must be instituted internationally at the start rather than later in the game.

"Our man in Bogota," therefore, is both a baron — that is, the company's local governor or regent — and a high-powered, specialized coordinator functioning between corporate headquarters and field operations and making sure that what goes on in the field fits within corporate objectives.

The important word in the catch phrase "our man in Bogota" is "our," for this man is not just a salesman, an agent, or an administrative representative, he is the company itself and everything it stands for — its relationships with the local government, the local national employees, the banking and financial circles, the local stockholders and the communities in which his company is established. Thus, whatever he says and does become the responsibility of the company.

In the old days of the satrap or local governor, successes and mistakes were relatively isolated, and it took a long time to find out about them. Their ripple effect was slow. Parenthetically, some major disaster in the field of diplomacy could lose an entire province, and it would take months before the new governor and his conquering legion might be dispatched to rectify matters.

Today, such things can be acted upon swiftly. Thus, time and distance now work both to a company's advantage and disadvantage. Costly marketing or communications errors are likely to be magnified quickly because of modern communications; they can also be more easily identified and corrected. Similarly, successes can be merchandised to the company's benefit everywhere, provided internal communications are good.

The company's problem is to establish a methodology and flexible organization for this. The control issue of responsibility in an era in which time and distance have been telescoped must first be clearly defined.

First, there are many companies, including the relatively sophisticated ones, which have come to rely too heavily on the supposed security of time and distance. They tend to feel that mistakes can be quickly rectified or assume that adequate safeguards are operating *within* the company's communications system to prevent costly errors — sins either of omission or commission. The cable and the telephone have made them smug and complacement about their ability to communicate.

Second, for some companies decentralization or over-centralization at the opposite extreme has become a fetish, almost an article of fatih ; there is many a management which confuses the problems of centralization with those of coordination and control. Briefly examining the usual history of companies which formerly only were exporters, we see that in their period of rapid international growth there is a tendency to decentralize many functions closely allied to communications — such as sales and advertising — along with production and administrative management.

While in recent years the more sophisticated and experienced international companies have found it necessary to provide an increasing amount of control and coordination, both by area and from corporate headquarters at home, the tendency among relative newcomers often is to leave the local team of experts too much alone.

Decentralization in sales, marketing and advertising — all requiring external communications — means a "Let George (or Alfonso or Guido or Heinz) do it." This can work moderately well in the sales area, but it can be disastrous in others. But there are certain U.S. techniques, tried and tested, which can be easily adapted to the field, if the know-how is there. It often takes firm direction and education from home base to get the necessary action in the field.

The responsibility of field sales management abroad is mainly to yield a healthy harvest of sales and profits for the company back home, but top management has other responsibilities as well.

The measurement of healthiness overseas is not solely in short-term profitability. The U.S. company abroad is a foreigner and is thus susceptible to all of the pressures of competition which it has at home, plus the political pressures of the country from both the right and left, and from the almost natural antiforeign animus. The company may have made its original investment in a climate relatively as friendly as that which it found at home. Although still highly profitable, it may now exist in a precariously hostile atmosphere which eventually will have an impact on profits, if not upon the original investment itself.

Thus, the local manager finds that he has an added long-term responsibility which he is not able to shoulder by himself; and he must draw strength from the total company at home and abroad. Some managers are slow to see this long-term responsibility. Others have lived too long in the old era of peace and calm to change their attitudes about headquarters at home or about the impact of events on their operations, not only from within their own country, but also from without. There are always the old refrain, "What does headquarters know, anyway?"

"L'etat c'est moi" was the attitude of many of these old timers. If trouble arose they could take care of it because they knew this minister or that one. But headquarters knew better and insisted on instituting program controls and coordination.

The almost tragic consequences of complete decentralization, with corporate headquarters looking only to "bottom line" performance on subsidiaries' income statements, can be seen from the example below.

A few years ago, a corporate subsidiary company in Scandinavia had made a sale in Finland, but the deal had fallen through because of financing complications. The prospective Finnish customer then made a wild statement that the company had called the deal off because it considered Finland to be an Iron Curtain country, which was pure nonsense. The local Scandinavian subsidiary treated this strictly as a sales department problem; but, in fact, the company's corporate policy had been questioned.

Moreover, at that very time the company was exhibiting another line of goods at a trade fair in an Iron Curtain country, with the approval of the U.S. Department of Commerce. The Finnish charge required much more than a local answer, especially since the story was picked up by the UPI and was reprinted in at least a few West German newspapers where the company also had developing markets for many product lines.

Fortunately, everything quieted down and turned out all right; but corporate headquarters did not learn of the event until one month afterwards — and not from the Scandinavian subsidiary either. The fetish for decentralization in this case caused a subsidiary to assume the handling of a corporate policy matter; untold complications might have resulted from this lapse.

It is clearly the responsibility of "the man from Bogota" to project the best image of his company in the local ambiance. It is clearly his responsibility to emphasize the qualities of his company which headquarters have determined to be the strongest everywhere in the world. It is clearly the responsibility of headquarters to see that *"their* man in Bogota" puts the best company foot forward.

One must start with the fact — it's more than an assumption — that *the corporate whole is greater than the sum of its parts.* The reason is simple. Behind the company's local name, local personnel and local operations stands the strength of the company around the world, its reputation for fine products, its ability to pioneer through its big investment in research, its total engineering capability in all of its plants, its history and tradition, and the soundness of its financial structure.

While there are mutations of this locally from country to country, these strengths tend to bring each local subsidiary through in periods of adversity and enhance its growth in good times.

The true role of international headquarters is to exploit these corporate strengths everywhere in the world within the framework of carefully laid down overall policy, through a flexible organization which will allow maximum freedom of action and initiative consistent with the policy. To implement this successfully requires control and coordination but not necessarily a high degree of centralization. It does necessitate good internal communications and constant evaluation of local activities in terms of total corporate welfare.

In order to set this up properly, the first step for any multi-national company is to define clearly the basic objectives of the corporation, together with basic operating concepts and policies. This should be done at the beginning, for each new foreign enterprise, rather than later on. Too many companies "have grown like Topsy" overseas.

Ultimately this requires the establishment of an administrative layer to bring order out of chaos, along with the promulgation of policy directives and such. This is hard to do because the local people feel at this late date that some liberties are being taken away from them. A re-education job is then necessary; and that can be expensive and traumatic.

The benefits of coordination and control are extremely evident in the area of financial management. John Webb, a USM Corporation vice-president, uses the following illustration. (34)

A Danish subsidiary "had excess cash which it lent to another Danish subsidiary that was receiving goods from the Swedish subsidiary. The Danish company prepaid its account with the Swedish subsidiary, and this money financed the movement of Swedish products into the Finnish subsidiary.

"What did this maneuver accomplish?

"If Finland had been required to pay for the goods, it would have had to borrow at 15%, the going Finnish rate. If the Swedish subsidiary had financed the sale, it would have had to borrow at about 9%, but cash in Denmark was worth only 5 or 6%. Moreover, Danish currency was weak in relation to Swedish; by speeding up payments to Sweden, we not only obtained cheaper credit, we hedged our position in Danish kroner as well."

Even these relatively simple financial manipulations would be impossible without a strong measure of central control and coordination.

In the field of communications and finance marketing, corporations are dealing with ideas, attitudes and problems which, like the techniques used to solve them, have no national boundaries and frequently require a common approach. It remains for the company itself, either unilaterally or with the help of outside counsel, to give some "codification" to these on an international basis. Thus, there must be an international organization which will harness all of these different elements and give them some uniformity, direction, efficiency and effectiveness.

"Our man in Bogota" now turns out to be almost the same man as "our" man in Paris or Stockholm or anywhere else because he is *"our"* man and *he is* the Company. In this world of modern communications which knows no national frontiers the company cannot present a totally different image from one country to the next. The corporate image should be approximately the same everywhere, and hopefully the corporate reputation will be also.

What a corporation does wrong in one country will quickly become known elsewhere. Its local successes should be used to advantage in all markets everywhere. It may operate differently in each country, it may sell and market differently, it can produce differently and even bank differently, but it cannot relate differently, because in the final analysis, it is the *whole* company that is being assessed.

FORMS OF INTERNATIONAL BUSINESS ORGANIZATION

Introduction

The method of operation of the international company taxes the ingenuity of the corporate manager. He must forge new ways of organizing against a background of changing technologies, markets, financial problems, and tariff and other governmental policies. Hence the methods and operations are in flux, and do not lend themselves to easy generalizations or to the status of eternal or even long-time truths.

Corporate Organizational Formats

In his book *International Management*, R.D. Robinson (32) outlines four types of international firms. Type A is a "domestic" firm with its various divisions, some or all of which have foreign markets. One problem with this structure is that the foreign market potential from the point of view of each division may be seen as relatively small, in which event no one in the firm develops sufficient interest to examine the potential of various foreign markets and to combine corporate resources.

Type B is the "foreign oriented" firm. It differs from type A only in that a foreign department has been established to help concentrate marketing to the various foreign markets. Type C is the "international" firm. In this organizational arrangement, there is an international division and one or more domestic divisions. It differs from type B in that the foreign department, which was a staff agency operating from corporation headquarters, now tries to become an independent division parallel to the various domestic divisions. This very frequently causes difficulties.

> Type C is probably an unstable setup, for rarely would an international division have the expert staff, including production specialists, to exist autonomously. Generally, it finds itself required to call on both corporate headquarters and the operating divisions for assistance, which assistance may

or may not be readily forthcoming — particularly from the operating divisions which historically may have been domestically oriented. (32)

The International Chamber of Commerce (20) quotes the work of Harvard University's Professor Fouracre in this regard:

> ...as the international division grows, the anxiety of domestic executives over the size of the overseas component tends to topple it. Quantitatively, the examination of some 24 U.S. companies ...indicates that the international division is slated for break-up into other product divisions when it becomes between 80% and 120% of the size of the largest domestic division.

Type D, in Robinson's description, is the "multinational" firm. This organization has a corporate headquarters with various regional headquarters below it. Thus, for example, Region A "North American Operating Divisions," Region B, "Latin American Operating Divisions" and Region C, "European Operating Divisions." The regional setup of Type D tends to eliminate both the frictions and the isolation of the international element inherent in Type C.

Often the path from A to D type organizations is followed chronologically. As a company grows more and more committed to overseas markets, its structure becomes more complex and sophisticated. (11)

Handling the Problem of Corporate Diversification

The Type D form of organization is sufficiently sophisitcated to handle problems requiring maximum corporate flexibility in dealing with overseas situations such as the sudden possible need to change the equity distribution of a subsidiary. It also enables area specialization on a product line basis using a modified grid analysis approach. "When a low product diversity company with area diversion, starts to diversify its foreign operation, or when the products diversions grow to outsize proportions, the company turns to a grid system: both products and areas abroad. Although this type of organization is difficult to reduce to easily describable relationships, some of the most successful international companies, including Phillips and Procter and Gamble seem to favor it." (20)

THE GRID ORGANIZATION PATTERN

Products: Area:	Stove	Refrigerator	Washers	Dryers
Europe	×	×	×	×
North America	×	×	×	×
Latin America	×	×	×	×

[Based on a concept described in (20), p. 74)

Martyn (27) gives a summary of some actual organizations:

> Companies with large and widespread foreign interests, like Colgate, IBM, and Unilever, have problems owing to too many lines of operational authority. Colgate formed regional groups with assistant vice-presidents for Australasia, Europe, and Latin America. Procter and Gamble followed this example in 1962. Unilever uses its twin company in the Netherlands as a decentralized management for Continental Europe, and its United Africa subsidiary for central Africa and the Near East. For the remainder of its foreign operations it uses an overseas committee composed of several members with operational authority, supplemented by staff services that provide advice to subsidiary company managers on production, finance, marketing, and legal matters. Standard Oil of New Jersey has a new top management structure that includes an executive committee like Unilever's special committee and directors with area responsibilities like Unilever's contact directors. Standard Oil of New Jersey is also forming submanagements for regional groupings of national companies, with their own staffs of special advisors.

Operations Within the Multinational Corporation

The tasks of controlling and managing overseas operations in terms of establishing contractual relationships remain about the same under any organizational framework. The multinational avenue simply creates greater overall coordination and control. Four basic types of alternatives are open: wholly-owned subsidiary, licensing agreement, contract manufacturing, and joint venture.

A. Wholly-owned subsidiary: This operational format is preferred by most large companies who wish maximum control over their overseas destinies. They form a corporation in the particular area of operation whose stock they own outright. As a general rule, a company becomes a subsidiary once more than 75% of its stock is owned by a so-called parent company.

B. The Licensing Agreement: The firm which does not want to get involved in a particular national market first hand, may arrange with an indigenous firm to become a licensee with rights to sell the product on a royalty basis. In exchange, the licensee gets the technical know-how (in 98% of licenses), production techniques (in 91% of the licenses) and any special marketing and promotional instructions (in about 50% of licenses) (23). Usually a license is granted for a limited time.

C. Contract Manufacturing: In this arrangement, the company decides to have its product manufactured in-place in the foreign country but it does not wish to build its own facilities. It therefore lets contracts to local producers usually on a cost-plus basis.

D. Joint Venture: Under this arrangement, the U.S. based firm and the foreign firm combine to capitalize a new, third firm in the foreign nation. This arrangement provides control through ownership but the management is done completely within the new firm. (Although, of course, the managers may simply be on leave from their U.S. based parent company. The problem of maintaining a balance of power between the partners is crucial.) As a measure of protection, the new firm is often granted a limited term license to sell the U.S. product so that a pullout can be made in the future.

In summary, the move to international business is usually accompanied by a reorganization in patterns such as those described in Types A-D. The process gets increasingly complex as the firm moves more and more into the foreign market. Some companies sidestep this process by various legal arrangements with foreign companies. This latter move should be explored carefully however.

> Earlier licensing agreements or exclusive distribution rights can cripple moves overseas. One manufacturer of marine equipment is doing fairly well in Europe, but is encountering tough competition from a German company, which was "educated" with patent exchanges and a licensing agreement several years ago. Many companies that would now like to move abroad are locked out of certain countries by exclusive licensing agreements that seemed wise, low-risk, profitable decisions just a few years ago. (11)

Management Control in International Business

The famed mathematician and founder of cybernetics, Norbert Wiener, defined control as the "sending of messages which effectively change the behavior of the recipient." (26) A more specific definition for our purposes is offered by Robinson: (32) "Control may be defined as the relationships and devices designed to assure that strategy or policy decisions are made by designated authority and that tactical or operating decisions conform to the selected strategies."

The most prevalent problem in management control is how much control should be centralized in the company head and how much should be decentralized to the various operating levels. This problem is greatly accentuated when the operating levels are separated from the head by great geographic, cultural, national, and environmental distances. In the international firm, the control problem can be restated as a tension between slow or garbled communication and the need to respond rapidly and efficiently to local situations.

> The international corporation has become possible because communication technology has expanded the scope of administrative control. The company once confined to a local or regional market now finds its purview extended, with reasonable facility, 3,000 miles east, or west, or in any direction. But the markets the company enters are still in many ways diverse. The problem then is to strike a balance between fragmentation to fit the diversity among markets and nations, and unification to benefit from the potential of the global business system. (20)

James Fayerweather tries to set forth this principal in a conceptual framework when he states: "Unless the parent company can make contributions to the local organization which permit it to function in a manner superior to an independent local national unit, the international business will not be competitive and therefore will not survive. (15)

At this point, it is not clear which tendency, centralization or decentralization, is going to characterize international management control in the future. Centralization seems to predominate in manufacturing because of the reliance of one part of the company for components or research findings from another part, the need for common standards of production, quality control and accounting.

Many divisions don't make a complete anything; they fit in an international system. Similarly, in corporate financial management, a survey taken by I.W. Meister of the National Industrial Conference Board in 1970 indicated that "more than half of the companies cooperating in this study (a total of 202) rely on the corporate financial unit to perform essentially all aspects of the international financial function.(28)

> (On the other hand) the oil industry, first of the genre of international corporations, and still the greatest single source of international investment, shows the opposite trend, i.e. to decentralization. To illustrate briefly, the total employment in Standard Oil New York headquarters—including secretaries and clerks—has been reduced to approximately 1,000 persons out of the company's total employment of some 140,000 throughout the world. Similarly Shell has consistently reduced its headquarters staff. Many of the decisions made at the center have been decentralized with the consequence that the number of central personnel, including directors, has been reduced while those in the individual companies operating outside headquarters has tended to increase.
>
> A similar case may be made for a number of consumer-oriented products, e.g. tobacco, where international investment is heavy and the role of the central authority light—restricted largely to advice.(20)

A guiding principle seems to be: "centralize responsibility for strategic planning and control; decentralize responsibility for local planning and operations.(5)

The Communications Problem

It has often been suggested that the crucial problem in international management control is communication. If there were no gaps in communication between the local office and headquarters, the problem of centralization and decentralization would be simple indeed.

Fayerweather(15) states that there are four kinds of communication gaps: cultural, national, environmental and geographical. (While these problems are found in a domestic firm also, they are more critical when they occur in the international firm.)

A. Cultural: "The difficulty encountered in communications between people from groups which differ in values, social mores, and other aspects of interpersonal attitudes and relationships" is the cultural gap. For example, two French managers may have quite different personalities, but from long conditioning by their cultures they will have acquired sufficient common patterns of communications so that they can communicate with reasonable effectiveness. But these common patterns might not be present between a Frenchman and an American, for instance.

B. National: "Most people in an organization will fairly clearly identify themselves with a single nation which commands their nationalistic and patriotic loyalties. For example, Indian executives who are sympathetic with typical national attitudes are likely to disagree with their U.S. management associates in the degree to which they should press against their government for scarce foreign exchange for repatriation of profits or departure from prevailing policies on acceptance of Indian capital in joint ventures."

C. Environmental: This pertains to the problem of individuals in one location attempting to make decisions which are sound for other locations. Most frequently this is the problem of the man in the home office with responsibility for decisions affecting field operations. The gap "involves the acquisition of adequate information about a foreign environment. Even when substantial information has been gathered, however, there remains a psychological difficulty for the individual attempting to project his thinking into a foreign situation while being immediately surrounded by his local culture which is typically his natural environment to which he is most fully adjusted."

D. Geographical: This is the gap caused by distance. It causes both a time lag and a lag in the consistent flow of information. While it may be possible for radio messages to travel around the world in milliseconds, that is not of much practical value since only a small portion of a company's internal communication can be put in the form of radio messages. The large bulk of meaningful communication is still done in face to face conversation or written memos. Thus, the geographical gap, while it is diminishing significantly, is still formidable.

The Rating Scale Problem to Determine the Level of Overseas Involvement

In summary, international management control is primarily concerned with the proper balance between centralization and decentralization. This decision is in turn affected by the type of industry and various communication gaps. In practice, however, management must look to certain key indicators to first determine exactly how deeply they should become involved in any of their overseas operations.

> Possible measures of overseas management performance include (1) degree of conformance to decisions by higher authority, (2) local profit, (3) contribution to consolidated profit, (4) rate of return on investment, (5) dollar flows, (6) local currency flows, (7) physical volume of products sold, (8) efficiency (that is, cost or input output ratios), (9) market share, and (10) sales profit (net sales revenue less selling cost). (32)

Farmer(12) points out that perhaps the most frequently used indicator is simply profit. However, Christopher Tugendhat has developed a specimen rating table that is reproduced on the next page (40). Some companies use such rating systems in determining the depth of their involvement in specific countries. Such a ranking device offers the obvious advantage of establishing ground rules or criteria for considering specific markets for investment or exports or for other forms of activity. Its great disadvantage, pointed out by Tugendhat, is that it sets absolute standards which are never really absolute.

Corporate rating scale for determining
a country's investment climate

	Number of points	
Item	Individual subcategory	Range for category
Capital repatriation:		0-12
No restrictions	12	
Restrictions based only on time	8	
Restrictions on capital	6	
Restrictions on capital and income	4	
Heavy restrictions	2	
No repatriation possible	0	
Foreign ownership allowed:		0-12
100% allowed and welcomed	12	
100% allowed, not welcomed	10	
Majority allowed	8	
50% maximum	6	
Minority only	4	
Less than 30%	2	
No foreign ownership allowed	0	
Discrimination and controls, foreign versus domestic businesses:		0-12
Foreign treated same as local	12	
Minor restrictions on foreigners, no controls	10	
No restrictions on foreigners, some controls	8	
Restrictions and controls on foreigners	6	
Some restrictions and heavy controls on foreigners	4	
Severe restrictions and controls on foreigners	2	
Foreigners not allowed to invest	0	
Currency stability:		4.20
Freely convertible	20	
Less than 10% open/black market differential	18	
10% to 40% open/black market differential	14	
40% to 100% open/black market differential	8	
Over 100% open/black market differential	4	

| | Number of Points | |
Item	Individual subcategory	Range for category
Political stability:		0-12
Stable long term	12	
Stable, but dependent on key person	10	
Internal factions, but government in control	8	
Strong external and/or internal pressures that affect policies	4	
Possibility of coup (external and internal) or other radical change	2	
Instability, real possibility of coup or change	0	
Willingness to grant tariff protection:		2-8
Extensive protection granted	8	
Considerable protection granted, especially to new major industries	6	
Some protection granted, mainly to new industries	4	
Little or no protection granted	2	
Availability of local capital:		0-10
Developed capital market; open stock exchange	10	
Some local capital available: speculative stock market	8	
Limited capital market; some outside funds (IBRD,AID) available	6	
Capital scarce, short term	4	
Rigid controls over capital	2	
Active capital flight unchecked	0	
Annual inflation for last 5 years:		2-14
Less than 1%	14	
1%-3%	12	
3%-7%	10	
7%-10%	8	
10%-15%	6	
15%-35%	4	
Over 35%	2	
Total		8-100

Source: Harvard Business Review: September-October 1969

BIBLIOGRAPHY

1. Blough, Roy. *International Business: Environment and Adaptation*. McGraw-Hill Book Company, New York. 1966.
2. Brannen, Ted R. and Frank X. Hodgson. *Overseas Management*. McGraw-Hill Book Company, New York. 1965.
3. Brooke, Michael Z. *The Strategy of Multinational Enterprise*. American Elsevier, New York. 1970.
4. Bryson, George D. *American Management Abroad*. Harper and Row Publishers, Inc., New York. 1961.
5. Clee, Gilbert H. and Alfred di Scipio. "Creating a World Enterprise". *Harvard Business Review*. November-December, 1959. P. 77-89.
6. Clee, Gilbert H. and Wilbur M. Sachtjen. "Organizing a Worldwide Business". *Harvard Business Review*. November-December, 1964. P. 55-67.
7. Coyle, John J. and Edward J. Mock. *Readings in International Business*. International Textbook Company, Scranton, Pa. 1965.
8. Crosswell, Carol McCormick. *International Business Techniques*. Oceana Publications Inc., Dobbs Ferry, N.Y. 1963.
9. Davis, Stanley M. *Comparative Management*. Prentice-Hall, Englewood Cliffs, N.J. 1971.
10. Drucker, P.F., *The Age of Discontinuity*. Harper and Row, Publishers, New York, 1968.
11. Ewing, John S. and Frank Meissner. *International Business Management-Readings and Cases*. Wadsworth Publishing Co., Belmont, Cal. 1964.
12. Farmer, Richard N. and Barry M. Richman. *International Business: An Operational Theory*. Richard D. Irwin, Inc., Homewood, Ill. 1966.
13. Fayerweather, John. *The Executive Overseas*. Syracuse University Press, Syracuse, N.Y. 1959.
14. Fayerweather, John. *Facts and Fallacies of International Business*. Holt, Rinehart and Winston, Inc., New York. 1962.
15. Fayerweather, John. *International Business Management: A Conceptual Framework*. McGraw-Hill Book Company, New York. 1968.
16. Fayerweather, John. *International Marketing*. Prentice-Hall, Englewood Cliffs, N.J. 1965.
17. Fayerweather, John. Management of International Operations, *Texts and Cases*. McGraw-Hill, New York. 1960.
18. Friedman, W.G. and George Kalmanoff. *Joint International Business Ventures*. Columbia University Press, New York, 1961.
19. Garbutt, Douglass. "International Management". *The Accountant*. September 17, 1970. P. 377.
20. *The International Corporation*. 22nd. Congress of the International Chamber of Commerce. 1969.
21. *International Management Association Report #1*. American Management Association, New York. 1957.
22. Kramer, Roland L. *International Marketing*. South-Western Publishing Co., Cincinnati, Ohio. 1970.
23. Lovell, E.B. *Appraising the Foreign Licensing Performance*. Business Policy Study #128, National Industrial Conference Board Inc., New York. 1969.

24. Lovell, E.B. *The Changing Role of the International Executive*. National Industrial Conference Board, Inc. New York. 1966.

25. Madeheim, H., E.M. Mazze and C.S. Stein. *International Business Articles and Essays*. Holt, Rinehart and Winston, Inc. 1963.

26. Malcolm, Donald G. and Alan J. Rowe. *Management Control Systems*. John Wiley and Sons, Inc., New York. 1960.

27. Martyn, Howe. *International Business*. The Free Press, New York. 1964.

28. Meister, I.W. *Managing the International Financial Function*. Business Policy Study #133. National Industrial Conference Board Inc., New York. 1970.

29. Prasad, S. Benjamin (Ed.). *Management in International Perspective*. Appleton-Century-Crofts, New York. 1967.

30. Pryor, Millard H., Jr. "Planning A Worldwide Business". *Harvard Business Review*. January-February, 1965. P. 130-9.

31. Robinson, Richard D. *International Business Policy*. Holt, Rinehart and Winston, Inc., New York. 1964.

32. Robinson, Richard D. *International Management*. Holt, Rinehart and Winston, Inc., New York, 1967.

33. Rolfe, Sidney E. and Walter Damm (Ed.). *The Multinational Corporation in the World Economy*. Praeger Publishers, Inc., New York, 1970.

34. Rose, Sanford. "Rewarding Strategies of Multinationalism." *Fortune*, LXXVIII, 4 (September 15, 1968), P. 104.

35. Rutenberg, David P. "Organizational Archtypes of a Multinational Company" *Management Science*. February, 1970. P. B-337;

36. Skinner, C. Wickham. "Management of International Production". *Harvard Business Review*. September-October 1964. P. 125-36.

37. Stieglitz, Harold. *Organizational Structures of International Companies*. National Industrial Conference Board. New York. 1965.

38. Theobald, Robert. *Profit Potential in the Developing Countries*. American Management Association. New York. 1962.

39. Vernon, Raymond. *Manager in the International Economy*. Prentice-Hall, Inc., Englewood-Cliffs, N.J. 1968.

40. Wilkins, Mira and Frank Ernest Hill. *American Business Abroad*. Wayne University Press, Detroit, Mich. 1966.

41. Tugendhat, Christopher, "Finding the Right Place for a New Plant", *The Multi-nationals*. Random House, New York, 1972.

APPENDIX

Abbreviations Used to Designate Foreign Currencies

Country	Currency	Abbreviation
AFGHANISTAN	Afghani	AF.
ALGERIA	Dinar	DIN.
ARGENTINA	Peso	P.
AUSTRALIA	Pound	A£
AUSTRIA	Schilling	S.
BAHAMA ISLANDS	Pound	B.£
BELGIUM	Franc	B.FR.
BERMUDA	Pound	B.£
BOLIVIA	Peso	P.
BRAZIL	Cruzeiro	CR.
BRITISH GUIANA	Dollar	B.W.I.$
BRITISH HONDURAS	Dollar	B.H.$
BURMA	Kyat	K.
BURUNDI	Franc	BFR.
CAMBODIA	Riel	R.
CAMEROON	Franc	C.F.A. FR.
CANADA	Dollar	C.$
CENTRAL AFRICAN REP.	Franc	C.F.A. FR.
CEYLON	Rupee	C.RS.
CHAD	Franc	C.F.A. FR.
CHILE	Escudo	ESC.
COLOMBIA	Peso	P.
CONGO (BRAZZAVILLE)	Franc	C.F.A. FR.
CONGO (LEOPOLDVILLE)	Franc	FR.
COSTA RICA	Colon	C.
CUBA	Peso	P.
CYPRUS	Pound	C£
CZECHOSLOVAKIA	Crown	KCS
DAHOMEY	Franc	C.F.A. FR.
DENMARK	Krone	KR.
DOMINICAN REPUBLIC	Peso	P.
ECUADOR	Sucre	S.
EGYPT (See UNITED ARAB REPUBLIC)		
EL SALVADOR	Colon	C.
ENGLAND (See UNITED KINGDOM)		
ETHIOPIA	Dollar	ETH.$
FINLAND	Markka	F.MKA.
FRANCE	Franc	F.

Country	Currency	Abbreviation
GABON	Franc	C.F.A. FR.
GERMANY (WEST)	Deutsche Mark	D.M.
GHANA	Pound	G£
GIBRALTAR	Pound	G£
GREECE	Drachma	DR.
GUATEMALA	Quetzal	Q.
GUINEA	Franc	G. FR.
HAITI	Gourde	GDE.
HONDURAS	Lempira	L.
HONG KONG	Dollar	HK$
HUNGARY	Forint	FT.
ICELAND	Krona	ICEL.KR.
INDIA	Rupee	R.
INDONESIA	Rupiah	R.
IRAN	Rial	RL.
IRAQ	Dinar	ID.
IRELAND (REPUBLIC)	Irish Pound	I£
ISRAEL	Pound	I£.
ITALY	Lira	LIT.
IVORY COAST	Franc	C.F.A. FR.
JAMAICA	Pound	J£
JAPAN	Yen	Y
JORDAN	Dinar	JD.
KENYA	Shilling	E.A.SH.
KOREA	Won	W.
KUWAIT	Dinar	DIN.
LAOS	Kip	K.
LEBANON	Pound	L£.
LIBERIA	U.S. Dollar	U.S.$
LIBYA	Pound	L£.
LUXEMBOURG	Franc	L.FC.
MACAO	Pataca	P.
MALAGASY REPUBLIC	Franc	MG. FR.
MALAYSIA	Dollar	MAL.$
MALI	Franc	M.FR.
MALTA	Pound	M£
MAURITANIA	Franc	C.P.A. FR.
MAURITIUS	Rupee	R.
MEXICO	Peso	P.
MOROCCO	Dirham	DIR.

Country	Currency	Abbreviation
NEPAL	Rupee	R.
NETHERLANDS	Guilder	GL. (F.)
NEW ZEALAND	Pound	NZ£
NICARAGUA	Cordoba	C.
NIGER	Franc	C.F.A. FR.
NIGERIA	Pound	WA£
NORWAY	Krone	KR.
PAKISTAN	Rupee	PAK.R.
PANAMA	Balboa	B.
PANAMA CANAL ZONE	U.S. Dollar	U.S.$
PARAGUAY	Guarani	G
PERU	Sol	S
PHILIPPINES	Peso	P.
POLAND	Zloty	ZL.
PORTUGAL	Escudo	ESC.
PUERTO RICO	U.S. Dollar	U.S.$
RHODESIA & NYASALAND	Pound	R£.
ROUMANIA	Leu	L.
RWANDA	Franc	R.FR.
SAUDI ARABIA	Riyal	RL.
SENEGAL	Franc	C.F.A. FR.
SIERRA LEONE	Pound	WA£
SOMALIA	Shilling	S.S.
SOUTH AFRICA	Rand	R.
SPAIN	Peseta	PTA.
SUDAN	Pound	S£
SURINAM	Guilder	S.FL.
SWEDEN	Krona	KR.
SWITZERLAND	Franc	S.FR.
SYRIAN ARAB REP.	Pound	S£
TAIWAN	Yuan	Y.
TANGANYIKA	Shilling	E.A.SH.
THAILAND	Baht	B.
TOGO	Franc	C.F.A. FR.
TRINIDAD & TOBAGO	Dollar	WI$
TUNISIA	Dinar	DIN.
TURKEY	Lira	TLT.
UGANDA	Shilling	EA.S.
UNION OF SOVIET SOCIALIST REPUBLICS	Rouble	R.
UNITED ARAB REPUBLIC	Pound	U.A.R.£

Country	Currency	Abbreviation
UNITED KINGDOM	Pound	£
UPPER VOLTA	Franc	C.F.A. FR.
URUGUAY	Peso	P.
VENEZUELA	Bolivar	B.
VIET-NAM (SOUTH)	Piastre	P.
VIRGIN ISLANDS	U.S. Dollar	U.S.$
YUGOSLAVIA	Dinar	DIN.

Foreign Firm and Corporation Terms

Abbreviations	Foreign	English Equivalents
	Abogado (Spanish)	Lawyer
A/B	Aktiebolaget (Swedish)	Joint Stock Company
A en P.	Asociacion en Participacion (Span.)	Association in Participation
A. G.	Aktiengesellschaft (German)	Joint Stock Company
A/S	Aktieselskabet (Danish)	Joint Stock Company
A/S	Aktieselskapet (Norwegian)	Joint Stock Company
Br.	Broderna (Swedish)	Brothers
Br.	Brodrene (Danish and Norwegian)	Brothers
	Bussan (Japanese)	Products
Ca.	Compagnia (Italian)	Company
Cia.	Companhia (Portuguese)	Company
Cia.	Compania (Spanish)	Company
Cie.	Compagnie (French)	Company
Com.	Comanditario (Spanish)	Partner (silent)
Com.	Comisionista (Spanish)	Commission Merchant
C. por A.	Compania por Acciones (Spanish)	Stock Company
	de (French, Spanish)	of
	di (Italian)	of
	do (Portuguese)	of
	e (Spanish, Portuguese)	and
	ehemals (German)	formerly
	et (French)	and
	Contador (Spanish)	Accountant
Etabs.	Etablissements (French)	Establishments
Eftf.	Efterfolger (Norwegian)	Successor
Eftr.	Eftertradare (Swedish)	Successor
	Frères (French)	Brothers
	Figlio, Figli (Italian)	Son, Sons
	Filho (Portuguese)	Son
	Fils (French)	Son, Sons
F-lli.	Fratelli (Italian)	Brothers
F-llo.	Fratello (Italian)	Brother
	Gerente (Spanish)	Manager
Ges.	Gesellschaft (German)	Company
G.m.b.H.	Gesellschaft mit beschränkter Haftung (German)	Limited Liability Company
G.K.	Gomei Kaisha (Japanese)	Unlimited Partnership
Gebr.	Gebrüder (German)	Brothers
Hers.	Heritiers (French)	Heirs
H/B	Handelsbolaget (Swedish)	Trading Company
H. mij.	Handelmaatschappij (Dutch)	Trading Company
Handelsges.	Handelsgesellschaft (German)	Trading Company
H.ver.	Handelsvereeniging (Dutch)	Commercial Association
Handels A/B	Handelsaktiebolaget (Swedish)	Commercial Corporation
Hno.	Hermano (Spanish)	Brother
Hnos.	Hermanos (Spanish)	Brothers
Hers.	Herdeiros (Portuguese)	Heirs

Abbreviations	Foreign	English Equivalents
Hereds.	Herederos (Spanish)	Heirs
Hnos. en Liq.	Hermanos en Liquidacion (Spanish)	Brothers in Liquidation
	Hijos (Spanish)	Sons
Inh.	Inhaber (German)	Proprietor
Ing.	Ingenieur (German)	Engineer
	Irmaos (Portuguese)	Brothers
	Jefe (Spanish)	Head of Department
K.G.	Kommanditgesellschaft (German)	Limited Silent Partnership
K.B.	Kommanditbolaget (Swedish)	Limited Silent Partnership
K.S.	Kommanditselskabet (Danish)	Limited Silent Partnership
K.K.	Kabushiki Kaisha (Japanese)	Joint Stock Company
K.G.K.	Kabushiki Goshi Kaisha (Japanese)	Joint Stock Limited Partnership
K.	Kaisha (Japanese)	Company
K.	Kompaniet (Danish)	Company
	Kokeisha (Japanese)	Successors
	Kyodai (Japanese)	Brothers
Ltd.	(English)	Limited
Ltda.	Limitada (Spanish)	Limited
Lda.	Limitada (Portuguese)	Limited
	Musuko (Japanese)	Sons
Mij.	Maatschappij (Dutch)	Company
	Maison (French)	House (or Store)
Nachf.	Nachfolger (German)	Successor
N/V	Naamlooze Vennootschap (Dutch)	Stock Company
	og (Norwegian)	and
O/Y	Osakeyhtio (Finnish)	Stock Company
Pty.	(English)	Proprietary
Pty. Ltd.	(English)	Proprietary Limited
Prop.	(English)	Proprietor (owner)
S.A. (Soc. Anon.)	Sociedad Anonima (Spanish)	Corporation
S.A.	Sociedade Anonima (Portuguese)	Corporation
S.A.	Societa Anonima (Italian)	Corporation
S.A.	Société Anonyme (French)	Corporation
S.Acc.	Società Accomandita (Italian)	Limited Partnership
S.A. de C.V.	Sociedad Anonima de Capital Variable (Spanish)	Stock Company of Variable Capital
S.A.R.L.	Société a Responsabilité Limitée (French)	Limited Liability Company
S. de R.L.	Sociedad de Responsabilidad Limitada (Spanish)	Partnership of Limited Liability
S. en C.	Sociedad en Comandita (Spanish)	Limited Silent Partnership
S. en C.	Sociedade en Commandita (Portuguese)	Limited Silent Partnership
S. en C.	Société en Commandite (French)	Limited Silent Partnership
S. en C. por A.	Sociedad en Comandita por Acciones (Spanish)	Limited Partnership by Shares
S. en N. C.	Sociedad en Nombre Colectivo (Spanish)	Collective Partnership
S. en N. C.	Société en Nom Colectif (French)	Joint Stock Company

Abbreviations	Foreign	English Equivalents
S. en P. de R.L.	Sociedad en Participacion de Responsabilidad Limitada (Spanish)	Firm in Participation with Limited Liability
	Shoyuken (Japanese)	Proprietorship
S. p. A.	Società per Azioni (Italian)	Stock Company
S. por A	Sociedad por Acciones (Spanish)	Stock Company
Soc.	Sociedad (Spanish)	Partnership or Company
Soc.	Sociedade (Portuguese)	Partnership or Company
Soc.	Société (French)	Partnership or Company
Sn.	Sohn (German)	Son
Sucs.	Sucesores (Spanish)	Successors
Sucs.	Sucessores (Portuguese)	Successors
Succs.	Successeurs (French)	Successors
Suc.	Sucursal (Spanish)	Branch
Test. de	Testamentaria de (Spanish)	Estate of
Ver.	Vereeniging (Dutch)	Association
Vda.	Viuda (Spanish)	Widow
V/h	Vorheen (Dutch)	formerly
Vva.	Viuva (Portuguese)	Widow
Vve.	Veuve (French)	Widow
Wwe.	Witwe (German)	Widow
	y (Spanish)	and
Zn.	Zoon (Dutch)	Son
Znen.	Zoonen (Dutch)	Sons